Ethical Leadership in Human Services:

A Multi-Dimensional Approach

Susan Schissler Manning

Boston ■ New York ■ San Francisco
Mexico City ■ Montreal ■ Toronto ■ London ■ Madrid ■ Munich ■ Paris
Hong Kong ■ Singapore ■ Tokyo ■ Cape Town ■ Sydney

Series Editor: *Patricia Quinlin*
Editor-in-Chief: *Karen Hanson*
Series Editorial Assistant: *Annemarie Kennedy*
Marketing Manager: *Taryn Wahlquist*
Composition Prepress Buyer: *Linda Cox*
Manufacturing Manager: *JoAnne Sweeney*
Editorial-Production Coordinator: *Paul Mihailidis*
Editorial-Production Service: *Modern Graphics, Inc.*
Electronic Composition: *Modern Graphics, Inc.*

For related titles and support materials, visit our online catalog at www.ablongman.com

Between the time Website information is gathered and then published, it is not unusual for some sites to have closed. Also, the transcription of URLs can result in unintended typographical errors. The publisher would appreciate notification where these errors occur so that they may be corrected in subsequent editions.

Library of Congress Cataloging-in-Publication Data

Manning, Susan Schissler.
    Ethical leadership in human services : a multi-dimensional approach / Susan Schissler Manning.—1st ed.
        p.   cm.
    Includes bibliographical references and index.
    ISBN: 0-205-33565-9
    1. Social work administration—Moral and ethical aspects.   2. Human services—Management—Moral end ethical aspects.   I. Title.
    HV41 .M277 2003
    174′.93613—dc21

                                                                                                2002026026

Printed in the United States of America

10   9   8   7   6   5   4   3   2   1   07   06   05   04   03   02

"Love is ever the beginning of knowledge, as fire is to light"
Thomas Carlyle

To my parents, who encouraged me to pursue
learning through the hardest of circumstances.

To my partner in life, Kelly Gaul, who inspired me to accomplish this work.

CONTENTS

3   Ethical Leadership Through Transformation   48

PREFACE

My interest in ethical leadership started through my own experiences in managing and administering programs in public mental health. Dilemmas that challenged my leadership happened on a daily basis, and there was little time or attention allocated to a conscious process of thinking about and discussing these dilemmas. My graduate program in social work had some content and emphasis on the ethics of clinical practice, but almost nothing on the ethics of leadership and administration. I decided to do a project on ethics in management and administration as part of my graduate study in the social planning and administration concentration. This project opened the door for me to a variety of materials on ethics and the necessary components of an ethical reasoning process for managers/administrators. I returned to doctoral work after years of administrative responsibility, and, again, ethics "reared its head" in the form of my research focus. Under the guidance of my professors, I began to formulate a research question that could explore the terrain of ethics for social workers in leadership positions in the mental health sector. The result was a qualitative dissertation: a grounded theory approach to capture the experience of social work leaders making ethical decisions. These experiences are the starting point for this book. It combines my own leadership experience; the results of my research on ethical decisionmaking for leaders; and the knowledge of social work, ethics, and business experts integrated into a model that I believe encompasses the essence of ethical leadership.

This is not a book about learning how to be a leader or how to administer programs. Instead, it is about the moral terrain of leadership: the values, theories, strategies, behaviors, and skills that provide a framework for ethical decisions, ethical behaviors, and ethical cultures in human service organizations. The model brought forward here is an attempt to capture the "essence" of ethics in leadership; it is an integrated view that connects the ethics of the leader to the architecture of the organization. Rather than approaching ethics in leadership from the perspective of specific ethical dilemmas with strategies and theories to resolve them, this model provides a comprehensive approach to the nature of ethical leading within the context of the organization. Any individual involved in leading, administering, and managing human service organizations, in both the public and private sector, can use this approach to develop strategies that increase the opportunities for ethical practices.

I would like to comment on what this book is, and is not. This book is a reflection of some of my own thinking and experience, grounded in the sociological paradigm of radical humanism, where I found myself as I worked on my dissertation. You will see the critical perspective coming through the critiques of bureaucracy and the abuse of power. My heart rests in an emancipatory project that I believe is essential to social work and part of the nature of ethics and morality. The critical perspective is not meant to deny the importance of bureaucracies in the delivery of human services. Instead, my intention is to improve and revitalize the moral and ethical functioning of such institutions.

This is not a "how-to" primer about ethics. The book does not provide specific or particular answers to administrative or managerial ethical dilemmas. There is not a right answer that is prescriptive for any ethical dilemma, which is, of course, the nature of a dilemma. Although the content should help to provide a context and some resources for solving ethical problems, the actual answers and decisions are left up to the reader or leader. What the content should do is provide a context for thinking about the nature of ethical dilemmas in leadership and organizations and some organizational tinkering that will help to create an ethical climate. This, in turn, will help prevent unethical practices. Although the daily ethical dilemmas of leadership are not preventable, there are ways to communicate messages about values and practices throughout the organization that are useful to everyone in thinking about ethical and unethical behavior.

Second, this is not solely a practice text for social work students learning about leadership in community systems and organizations, although, as a social worker, the professional ideals and values do ground this work. It is not meant to provide theories, strategies, and skills specific to leadership development beyond the transformational leadership theory discussed in Chapter 3. Instead the book is focused on a contextual, multidimensional view of ethics in leadership. Thus, it is meant to be useful to leaders involved in the administration of human services from a variety of professional disciplines. It should also be helpful to social work, managerial, and business students as they conceptualize their leadership approach.

Finally, this book is not presented in a value-neutral fashion in relation to the ethics of leadership. Particular values and theoretical points of view are offered as critical to ethical leadership. For example, social justice is considered to be a primary value. The underlying values of the transformational leadership paradigm are promoted in this book as being integral to ethical leading. Sharing power and empowerment and inclusiveness and participation are all presented as reinforcing the ethics of leadership.

Throughout the book, I have used examples and real-life scenarios brought forward from managers, administrators, executive directors, and social work discipline chiefs from my research on ethical decisions (Manning, 1990). I have also incorporated material from another study on the impacts of culture and gender on creating ethical policy and the ethics of collaboration (Manning, 1994). These stories bring the human experience to bear on the ethical dilemmas of leadership.

The book is organized according to the multidimensional framework discussed at the beginning of the chapter. The individual as an ethical leader is developed in Part I. Ethical resources and traditions are discussed in Part II. The nature of organizations, their cultures, and structures as ethical systems are presented in Part III. Please refer to the Part introductions for detailed description of those chapters.

ACKNOWLEDGMENTS

There are many people that have my most profound appreciation. I would like to start by addressing the social work leaders in mental health who participated in my research on ethics. Their willingness to participate and their openness about the intractable and painful dilemmas they encountered on a daily basis were an inspiration to me and to the results of the study. Interacting with this group of almost 50 individuals impressed upon me how very lucky I am to be a social worker and a colleague with leaders such as these.

I would like to express my appreciation for the role models in leadership that I have been blessed with. From supervisors in the field to faculty colleagues and administrators, I have learned much about leadership and ethics. Individuals such as Kay Gilchrist, my clinical supervisor in mental health; Dr. Jean East, a former social work administrator and current faculty colleague; and Dr. Enid Cox demonstrated the thoughtful, loving servant leadership that taught me and so many others about being ethical through their powerful role modeling. My dissertation chair and loyal colleague, Dr. Judy Wise, has been a part of this work from the beginning. Along with Dr. Cox and Dr. Wise, Dr. Ruth Parsons, Dr. Sue Henry, Dr. Pam Metz, Dr. Connie Calkin, and Dr. Linda Cobb-Reilly have demonstrated the courage to act on their convictions, when it mattered most. Administrators such as Dean Catherine Alter, Assistant Dean Linda Clark, and former Provost William Zaranka have modeled important leader characteristics. Deans Alter and Clark promotes feminist principles of participation, openness and inclusiveness. Dr. Zaranka demonstrated the risks that are necessary in order to stand firm for the principles that have enhanced the ethical culture of our university. Graduate students (masters and Ph.D.) have taught me more about ethics than they probably ever learned from me. Their willingness to take the hard road and their emotional investment in caring about doing the "right" thing have been an ongoing inspiration.

I have had amazing sources of support. My loving "T'wanda" friends provided unfailing belief in my ability to do this work and continuous support. My friends and family have not only tolerated my total preoccupation with the project, but have also celebrated the fact that I was doing it. My loving partner of 23 years never wavered in support.

I have had a lot of help. Pat Quinlin and Annemarie Kennedy from Allyn and Bacon, and Marty Tenney from Modern Graphics, have been responsive and creative, tolerating numerous emails and phone calls, always responding with kindness and patience. My friend and support, Neysa Folmer, was available for both emotional and technical support. It was Neysa who met me on a Saturday to send this monster off to the publisher. And, finally, thank you to my reviewers, Martha Raske, University of

Southern Indiana and Frederick G. Reamer, Rhode Island College, who so carefully read and critiqued early chapters provided me with helpful advice and critique that strengthened this final product. There are too many people to thank individually; this is only a beginning and many more people helped in direct and indirect ways. To you all, I say "Thank you."

PART ONE

The Moral Terrain of Human Service Leadership

Part I (Chapters 1 through 4) provides the foundation of leadership for *individuals* as ethical leaders and the moral terrain they tread. This section helps us think about the connection between ethics and leadership within the context of human services, where the impact of leadership is focused.

Chapter 1 discusses the essence and nature of ethical leadership. Professional leaders have a dual responsibility: the responsibility of service and a public duty to society. Practical ethics is presented as an approach that links theory and practice for professional leaders. A multidimensional framework is developed that conceptualizes leaders as developing ethical practice across individual, organizational, and societal systems.

Chapter 2 provides the contextual background to ethical leadership within human service organizations. Human service organizations have unique characteristics with implications for the ethical practices of leaders. The historical context of social work and business ethics, as well as the intersection between social work and business through privatization, creates an opportunity for a new conceptualization of the essence of ethics for leaders.

Chapter 3 provides an approach for ethical leadership practice that is theory based. An overview of two leadership paradigms—transactional and transformational theories—begins the chapter. Transformational theories have the capacity, through the dimensions of vision and morality, to provide a coherent framework for the integration of ethics into leadership. This leadership paradigm is discussed in relation to moral direction and responsibility, contribution to the public good, value-based practice, the motivation to act, and an action philosophy approach.

Chapter 4 provides a framework for conceptualizing leadership, ethics, and power. The role of power and authority in ethical decisions and dilemmas is explored. Because the use and abuse of power is at the heart of administrative and organizational ethics (Levy, 1982), this chapter discusses three dimensions of the manifestation of power that is wielded by leaders. Specific examples of the ethical use of power, and abuses of power are brought forward. The second part of the chapter develops the argument that leaders and constituents must be knowledgeable about expanding their scope of influence in order to impact ethical practices and policies through a conscious use of self. The attitudes and functions of leadership that add to increased influence are integrated with practical strategies.

1 The Essence of Ethical Leadership

THE FOCUS IN THIS CHAPTER IS ON THE FOLLOWING AREAS:

- The essence of leadership
- Dual responsibilities of professional social work
- Practical ethics
- Dimensions of ethical leadership

Ethical leadership has never been more important to human service organizations. The context of a rapidly changing society, with human service delivery increasingly located in the private sphere, has had a dramatic effect on the funding and provision of human services. Economic and social well-being of individuals, families, and communities—the public "good"—in part rests squarely on the capacities of the human service sector. However, the human service sector has taken a "back seat" to the economic sector, which has dominated the attention of society in recent years. Residual effects of economic dominance are reflected in the increasing consumerism and materialism of society. Cost-efficiency and revenue production are the buzzwords of service delivery. Traditional public and nonprofit services are now marketed as products to sell by agencies that have shareholders as their primary interest. Response to human need is fast becoming the lowest priority of a well-to-do society.

The emphasis on economic dominance affects the ability of the government to assist citizens in critical areas, such as education, employment, and health care, placing the system "seriously out of balance" (Nanus & Dobbs, 1999, p. 29). Ethical leadership in human services is an opportunity to commit to the social sector of society, adding balance to the system by increasing the social goods produced. The social goods produced through the human service sector strengthen individuals, families, organizations, and communities through the services provided in health and mental health care, education, social welfare, criminal justice, and many other fields of practice. The public good that is generated by a society, then, is inextricably connected to the human service delivery system.

Leadership ethics are a function of relationships with many constituencies. Leaders have responsibility for the good or harm that is produced to those who receive services, or those who are represented, as well as to the community and society (Levy, 1993). In addition, leaders in human services have an ethical obligation to improve the organization's contribution to society by providing the opportunity to move their organizations to a ". . . higher level of excellence, service, and benefit . . ." (Nanus & Dobbs, 1999). Leaders in organizations, then, are the hearts, pumping the "life blood" of values, philosophy, and commitment into the ethics of organizational life.

Leaders have an especially important role in providing heart to their organizations. Leaders in human services are surrounded by the dimensions of ethics in leadership on several levels. First, they must develop a critical self-awareness of their own values and the moral vision that guides their leadership. Leaders have a public responsibility to provide leadership with a moral purpose, leadership that contributes to the public good in society. Second, they must integrate these values and vision into a leadership approach, guided by theory that can accommodate this ethical dimension. Third, they must routinely resolve the ethical dilemmas of administration and management on a daily basis, with an ethical framework of decisionmaking. Fourth, ethical leaders must have the ability to shape their organization's culture and structure so that the architecture of the organization promotes ethical decisions and behaviors on the part of all employees. These dimensions are especially true for social work leaders who are in the forefront of the leadership in human services. Therefore, ethical leadership must be multidimensional.

Social Work and Ethical Leadership

The capacity of human service leaders to identify and pursue the public good through moral vision and ethical organizational practices should be social work's paramount concern for the 21st century. Capacity is more than knowledge, skills, and abilities. The motivation, courage, and willingness to address moral and ethical concerns must also be a part of every person's commitment to leadership.

Social workers have a major role in the leadership of human service organizations. The results of their leadership in social service institutions ". . . play a significant role in social change . . . the poor and disempowered . . . experience society first hand through the institutions designed to serve or subjugate them, depending on one's perspective" (Fisher & Karger, 1997, p. 151). Service or subjugation may be largely dependent on a leader's awareness of the ethical challenges embedded in the daily operations of service delivery and the willingness to confront them. And they must confront them every day. Rhodes (1986, p. 10) argues that "Almost every decision that a social worker makes, even a technical one, is a decision about ethics." At the institutional and service level, then, the ethics of leadership are instrumental.

Social Work Leadership

However, leadership has not received adequate attention in social work (Brilliant, 1986), and the ethics of leadership are not well developed. Sarri (1992, p. 40), in her essay about the conservative nature of the profession, argues that, due to social work's identification as a "woman's profession," the profession reflects women's status in general in society: "that of low power and subordination." Further, social work has been like a "house divided." There is ambivalence in the profession about the degree that social work should emphasize leadership and reform versus accommodation of political and economic interests. Finally, the bureaucratic structure of social welfare and human service organizations promotes "conformity and compliance" rather than "action and reform" (p. 41).

Leadership has not received the attention necessary to meet the contemporary challenges of social service. There are many examples of the fallout that results from social work's loss of a leading role in the shaping of human service reforms. Welfare reform has been commandeered by the political will and ideology of politicians competing for votes from a citizenry that does not understand the complexities of domestic violence, mental illness, and centuries of discrimination and racism. Managed health and mental health care have had some success at reducing costs, but only temporarily. Currently, costs are escalating again, and access to quality care, particularly for those who are most oppressed due to poverty, mental illness, and so forth is greatly reduced. In the meantime, for-profit managed care companies have benefited from the revenue for "managing care" that previously would have gone toward providing care. Something is wrong with this picture.

The Council on Social Work Education (1998) has identified leadership development as a core concern. Recommended areas for further attention include work on conceptualization of social work leadership, specific content on leadership in the curriculum, and focused leadership training of undergraduate and graduate students (Brilliant, 1986; Rank & Hutchison, 2000). The lack of emphasis on leadership has led to ". . . social work losing ground in the leadership of its own organizations" (Moran, Frans, & Gibson, 1995, p. 104).

A recent study of social work leaders' perceptions of leadership is relevant. Interviews with a random sample of 75 deans and directors from Council of Social Work Education (CSWE)-accredited programs and 75 executive directors and presidents of local chapters of National Association of Social Workers (NASW) resulted in five common elements that these leaders defined as critical to the concept of leadership (Rank & Hutchison, 2000). The elements included proaction, values and ethics, empowerment, vision, and communication. These elements are imperative to social work leadership because of the profession's mission, values, and knowledge base. The challenge for social work is to integrate these elements with a definition and theory of leadership that can provide guidance for ethical and moral issues.

The thesis for ethical leadership that is promoted through this book is congruent with the elements identified by the deans and directors. Transformational leadership (discussed in Chapter 3) incorporates values and ethics as one of the core elements of the paradigm. Further, the focus of leading is on connecting relationships, building community, and empowering constituents; thus, communication is the major activity of leaders. Finally, the nature of leadership in human services has to be visionary, with an emphasis on moving forward, that is, influencing others to develop and improve the resources and services available in a society with a widening gap between the wealthy and the poor. Visionary leadership rests on the moral courage of leaders to step forward and lead the human services sector toward actions that contribute to the public good. Robert Kennedy said,

> Few are willing to brave the disapproval of their fellows, the censure of their colleagues, the wrath of their society. Moral courage is a rarer commodity than bravery in battle or great intelligence. Yet it is the one essential, vital quality for those who seek to change a world that yields most painfully to change.

Never has moral courage been more necessary for professional leaders.

This book integrates the previous elements into a framework for ethical leadership. The essence of leadership in human services is conceptualized as ethics. Ethics are the core, the heart of leading and include private duties of service and public duties to the common good. Therefore, personal, professional, and practical ethics are integrated into a multidimensional perspective of ethical leadership in human service organizations. The concepts and principles of transformational leadership are integrated with ethical resources (ethical theories, principles, and philosophy) to provide a framework for leaders in human service organizations. This chapter is an introduction to the essence of ethical leadership. These themes are emphasized and developed further in subsequent chapters of the book. However, if social work leaders think about themselves as the heart, what can be understood as the essence of their moral mission?

Ethics as the Essence

The *essence* of something is powerful indeed. It is the thesis of this book that ethics must be the essence of leadership if leaders are to accomplish the moral mission of human service delivery systems (see Figure 1.1). Many different disciplines enrich this discussion about essence as an important element or entity. In qualitative research, "essence" is described as arriving at the *heart of the matter*; the researcher finds what is meaningful about *day-to-day experience* and promotes it through the research process. Ethical leaders bring forward the essence of ethics in organizations through the identification of central moral values and the development of ethical policies and practices essential to the purpose of the organization. The importance of moral behavior and decisions in the face-to-face interactions of the daily work of all members of the organization is accentuated. The essence of ethical leadership strives toward decisions that are ethical not by accident, but by intention.

Essence also means the "individual, real, or ultimate nature of a thing" (Webster's New Collegiate Dictionary, 1977, p. 391). The essence of human service organizations is the mission, which defines the purpose of the organization or the *moral constitution* for leaders and constituents. The mission provides the moral force behind the organization's function.

Ethics as:

The heart of the matter
Day-to-day experience of leadership
Identification and promotion of crucial values
Moral behavior and decisions

The ultimate nature of things
Purpose and mission of the organization
Moral constitution

The permanent fixture of organizational philosophy and practices
Ethical culture, policies, and structures
Ethics by intention

The utmost importance
Ethics are paramount.

A volatile substance with special qualities
Creates new energy
Unique power

FIGURE 1.1 Ethics as the Essence of Leadership

Essence is defined as something permanent as contrasted with an accidental element of being (Webster's New Collegiate Dictionary, 1977, p. 391). When ethics are the essence of the organization, they become a permanent fixture of organizational philosophy and practices. The organizational culture and structures are shaped to promote moral and ethical behavior in an intentional way, not as an afterthought or as an accident. Also, consider "*of the essence*," which means "of the utmost importance" (p. 391). Ethical leaders will describe the moral and ethical status of the organization as paramount.

In chemistry, essence is portrayed as an entity. For example, essence is a volatile substance, ". . . a constituent or derivative . . . possessing the special qualities . . . in concentrated form" (Webster's New Collegiate Dictionary, 1977, p. 391). The process of integrating ethics into organizational practices results in new energy for the system. When people create relationships that are based on working with ethical issues, power is created as well. Ethical and moral issues have a unique power in systems: the power to introduce and promote what ought to be done and the power to change the balance of good and evil.

The essence of ethics has a relationship to leadership, to all constituents in and related to the organization, and to the special responsibilities of professional leaders. First, ethics as the essence of leadership is examined.

The Essence of Ethics for Leaders

Leadership is not value neutral; it is not a mechanized set of tasks and techniques. Leadership conveys the essence of what human beings believe to be important and has the capacity to illuminate the best of who we can be and what we can accomplish. Levy (1988) noted in regard to the essence of ethics that expectations about a leader's ethics are different from other expectations of leadership. Ethics are distinct from other behavioral expectations due to the leader's ability to affect people and interests through decisions or omissions that can produce good or harm. He said the following:

> Emerson to the contrary notwithstanding, I suggest that the true test of civilization is not so much—as he said—"the kind of [person] man the country turns out," as the justice and fairness with which people in such strategic positions deal with others even when they don't have to (p. 23, inclusive language added).

The essence of leadership is ethics. A leader's ability to make a choice about good or harm is an essential argument of this book.

The special qualities of leadership are the visions, values and moral positions that individuals bring to the role that are capable of transforming the nature of work and the good (or harm) that are produced. Leaders must perceive a comprehensive moral and ethical point of their vision, as well as the organization's purpose. The point requires reflections about several questions:

- What is valued?
- What is important?
- What is the context?
- What is missing?
- What should be considered good or harmful?
- Who may be impacted?
- In what way?
- What is my obligation?
- To whom?
- What is the obligation of the organization?
- What is my professional obligation?
- What can be developed that promotes moral and ethical behavior?

The approach to this book is to provoke, and to promote, thinking (imagining, creating, questioning, and challenging) about these questions of ethical leadership. Incremental decision frameworks that provide a step-by-step approach to making decisions are helpful, but do not provide the breadth necessary to think beyond particular dilemmas. Because ethical leading is a vision, a role, an activity, and a day-to-day enactment of moral values, policies, and practices, a conceptual framework that can guide the leader is useful. This book is a kind of conceptual framework. However, ethics are not just the business and responsibility of leaders. All constituents must attend to, and feel responsible for, the policies and practices of an organization as well.

The Essence of Ethics Is for Everybody

Leaders have a profound responsibility for the ethics of their organizations and the ethics of their own decisions, but leaders are also like every other person. Employees, board members, consumers, and others also have this responsibility. Often, a person's reaction to discussions or topics that involve ethics is one of unfamiliarity; people have a sense that ethics are the concern of philosophers and intellectuals, best considered from "the ivory tower of academia." Ordinary people do not always perceive themselves as ethics experts. Sometimes, when professionals are unsure, the professional code of ethics becomes the resource for instruction about what to do in a difficult situation. However, codes of ethics can only provide guides and values. Ethics in everyday practice is a subject all can delve into successfully and can find useful in improving the moral and ethical dimensions of work. As Hannah Arendt (a noted Jewish philosopher) said, "Thinking about responsibility can no longer be left to 'specialists' as though [it], like higher mathematics, were the monopoly of a specialized discipline" (Arendt, 1978, p. 13). In this postmodern era of rapid change, with profound moral implications attached to those changes, leaders and constituents must embrace ethics together. This book is organized to provide any leader (legitimated or natural) and/or constituent with practical, theoretical, and philosophical strategies to develop ethical leadership. The underlying assumptions of the book are that all constituents have the capacity for moral leadership and that all constituents must commit to the moral responsibility for organizational practices. Further, the leader's moral and ethical role is to nurture and sustain the involvement of all constituents in the moral and ethical climate of the organization. The content of the book accentuates this responsibility, as well as strategies to do so.

The Essence of Ethics for Professional Leaders

Ethics, as the essence of leadership, is imperative for the professions, and professional leaders. Society today is highly influenced by the involvement of professionals. Even with this substantial involvement, perhaps as a result of it, there has been erosion of trust in professionals on the part of the public. Integrating ethics into leadership, as *the heart of the matter*, has the potential to help re-create the trust that is necessary for professional services.

All of the professions have acquired new power as specialized expertise and technology is required (Jennings, Callahan, & Wolf, 1987). An increase in power carries a related ethical responsibility. Jennings, Callahan, and Wolf argue that "Professional ethics should express the moral bond linking the professions, the individuals they serve, and the society as a whole (p. 3). Leaders in human service organizations are in a unique and critical role in relation to this responsibility. They are directly responsible for the provision of services and the related ethical obligations to clients, other agencies, and interest groups. However, they are also in a position, as Jennings,

Callahan, and Wolf argue, to enact the public duties of the professions: "the obligations and responsibilities owed in service to the public as a whole" (p. 3). Professional leadership must encompass not only the public duties of the profession, but the private duties as well.

The Dual Responsibility of Social Work: Private and Public Duties

The social work profession is in the unique position of having both private and public duties. Jennings (2001) refers to this position as having a "dual responsibility." Private duties arise from the professional mandate to serve the best interests of the client in private and public settings. Most of the private duties arise through the relationships between providers and consumers of service. The relationships are formed in the process of providing services. Human service organizations, by their nature, are based on relationships with consumers (see Chapter 2 for further discussion). For example, in public settings, case workers who serve clients in social welfare agencies, clinicians who provide therapeutic relationships with consumers in mental health agencies, and school social workers who develop relationships with children and families have private duties. Private duties also occur through relationships in private practice settings and private for-profit organizations. The professional obligations to the best interests of the client are not deterred or weakened by the nature of the setting. Administrators and managers in leadership positions also have private duties to clients through the ethical responsibility for advocacy for resources to meet client needs (NASW, 1996; Reamer, 1998). The advocacy for resources enhances the ability to the organization to provide the best possibility of meeting clients' needs. Client needs are also affected by the expertise of the provider. Thus, the administrator is also responsible for allocating and structuring the resources necessary for supervision and training of providers who are involved in direct services with clients (NASW, 1996; Reamer, 1998).

The public duties of professionals are related to the roles and responsibilities of contributing to the common good for society. For example, creating and maintaining service delivery systems through administrative and managerial roles; contributing to policy development and analysis in regard to social problems and solutions; strengthening community capacity through organizing, development, and advocacy are contributions to the common good. This dual role contributes to some unique issues related to ethics and leadership. The discussion that follows explores more specifically the dual responsibilities of social work.

Professional Ethics of Service

The moral authority of the social work profession provides the foundation for ethical leadership. The basis for the "grounding" of professional ethics is a professional mandate for an ethic of service. Professionals "profess" or "declare publicly" to serve persons who are seeking a particular good. Because this is a public promise ". . . once made the pledge belongs to the public" (Koehn, 1994, p. 64). The professionals' declaration to serve transforms their work from a career to a *calling*. Professionals place the best interests of the client over and above their personal self-interest or the interests of other stakeholders.

Professionals must be trustworthy in order to have moral authority. The trustworthiness of a professional is based on having the best interests of clients at heart, which translates into real action, not just rhetoric, on the behalf of clients. In order to be trustworthy, the professional must be competent (have the required knowledge, skill, expertise, and so forth) to provide the needed service or take the required action. Further, the service should be rendered according to the principles and guidelines put forward in the professional code of ethics. The ethical mandate, then, for social workers and other professions with private duties (for example, medicine, psychology, or nursing) is to be competent in their occupational duty, serve according to a professional code of ethics, and ensure that service delivered and agency practices are in the best interests of the consumers of service.

Public Duties of the Professions

Professions also have a public duty to society. Professionals act as the *public custodian*, nurturing and interpreting the basic values of society. Values, such as social justice, access to health care, civil liberties, fairness in the distribution of benefits and burdens, economic considerations, and so forth are examples of the moral issues that are promulgated or shaped through professional human services. Professionals translate these values into ". . . concrete institutional forms and modes of social practice" (Jennings, Callahan, & Wolf, 1987). The public duties of a profession are less developed in professional codes of ethics, and the private duties to clients continue to receive more emphasis in professional codes of ethics, education and scholarship about ethics.

The social work code of ethics does include standards in regard to ethical responsibilities to the broader society (NASW, 1996). The code is concerned with ". . . issues related to the general welfare of society, promoting public participation in shaping social policies and institutions, social workers' involvement in public emergencies, and social workers' involvement in social and political action" (Reamer, 1998, p. 247). The revised code is explicit about political action in regard to the improvement of social conditions to meet basic human needs and to promote social justice. It also accentuates the importance of maintaining the "fundamental commitment to serving those who are most at risk" (p. 254). To fulfill this obligation, social work leaders must understand the processes of oppression, injustice, and exploitation and challenge those processes within organizations and in the larger community.

The ethical is political.   Leaders in human services are required to take a political position about their basis for practice again and again. To not take a position is, in fact, a position: agreement with the status quo. Rhodes (1986, p. 14), in a critique of the previous code, notes that social work takes an "odd ethical stand." She argues that the code does acknowledge that ethical choices are made in the context of a larger political framework, but "remains silent" about what political or social or economic foundation should be the basis for practice.

Fisher and Karger (1997) do take a position about social work and the professions' position in relation to politics. They argue that the government has retreated from progressive social policy and social responsibility and that advancing the public good requires a stronger government because the ". . . state is the only institution that has the resources necessary to rebuild America's neglected social and public infrastructure" (p. 177). The public good, according to Fisher and Karger, "is incompatible with large disparities in wealth and power, nor can it coexist with discrimination of any kind. Public life is the arena for addressing and struggling over these inequities and inequalities, and the public sector is an important part of public life" (p. 178). In that vein, the public life can be impacted by leadership and constituents in organizations who "redesign institutions" and "rethink strategies" for changing them. A focus on increased interaction among diverse groups and increased participation of constituents at all levels helps to promote the identification of issues necessary for social change and enhances the capacities of people to engage and participate in political action and public life.

Jennings, Callahan, and Wolf (1987) argue that the rapid rate of change in institutional settings and arrangements, where most professionals practice, brings forward an acute need to clarify the ethical obligations of professionals in relation to public duties. Professionals in leadership positions convey messages about the profession's public duties through their actions and decisions in the public arena. The attention invested in examining the ethical obligations related to public duty is part of the responsibility of ethical leadership.

The duty to make the invisible visible.   Leaders in human service organizations have a duty to ". . . make the invisible visible, to show the underside of a system that otherwise seems to be functioning adequately" (Jennings, Callahan, & Wolf, 1987, p. 9). This duty to the public interest provides accurate information to policymakers, citizens, and other interested parties about the state of our social welfare and human service system. In the process, values of social justice, self-determination, and altruism are asserted into the public dialogue. This duty can only be enacted through effective relationships and ethical organizational structures. A leader's ability to create and maintain communication processes with direct service workers; consumers of services; and social, political, and economic representatives in the community becomes the highway for "making the invisible visible" to society. An example of making the invisible visible is a team leader who described his work as ongoing needs assessment. He tracks and documents the unmet service needs of mental health consumers. He reports the results periodically to upper level administrators, consumer advocates, and political figures, including board members for their use in planning, policymaking, and so forth. He provides the upper echelon with real life examples of the experience of consumers—that of deprivation as well as the successes that result from helpful service strategies. This theme—making the invisible visible—is a repeated theme in this book. Bringing forward moral and ethical issues for comment and dialogue, the activity of feedback, is a critical activity at all levels of leadership.

Clarity of moral vision. One of the trends in regard to public duties is what Jennings, Callahan, and Wolf (1987) refer to as the "professionalization of leadership" (p. 4). Leadership requires special expertise and technical skills in order to cope with the complex and multidimensional problems of organizations, but note the following:

> Professionalism should be more than technical expertise, and leadership ultimately requires more than a technical or instrumental perspective. Many of our society's most pressing problems are fundamentally moral problems. They raise questions about the ends and values our institutions should serve, and about the justifiable means to achieve those ends. Hence leadership requires clarity of moral vision as well as specialized expertise. In a society marked by the widespread professionalization of leadership, the professions must be attentive to their emerging public roles and responsibilities (p. 4).

Expertise, then, is not enough. Professional leaders have a moral responsibility to contribute to the public good through their expertise and technical knowledge. The public duties of a professional leader are tied to one's professional mission, the organizational mission, and the public roles and responsibilities. All have ethical implications.

Professional ethics has tended to focus on services to clients, with some attention to public policy and government. An additional perspective, "practical ethics," interjects the institutional context into ethics and leadership in human service organizations.

Practical Ethics

Practical ethics is an approach that has been developing over many years, initially at the Hastings Center and Kennedy Institute at Georgetown University in response to the complex issues in the field of bioethics. Practical ethics is also articulated by scholars from the Program in Ethics and the Professions at Harvard (Thompson, 1999). Practical ethics has three particular characteristics. It seeks to bridge theory and practice, has as its focus the institutional context, and asks political questions. First, practical ethics is a linking discipline. Although moral and political philosophy are essential to understanding professional and applied ethics, the traditional theories and principles are not enough to resolve complex ethical dilemmas. Also, moral reasoning requires additional elements for the practical resolution of ethical conflicts: the development of moral perception and moral character. Moral perception is ". . . the ability to recognize an ethical issue in a complex set of circumstances." Moral character is ". . . the disposition to live ethically in a coherent way over time" (Thompson, 1999, p. 1). Moral character and moral perception are discussed extensively in Chapters 5, 6, and 7.

Practical ethics draws on a variety of disciplines and forms of knowledge to shape a rich conceptualization of moral life. Practical ethics includes professional codes of ethics, but does so within the parameters of the broader social context of ethical conflicts. From this approach, there is a component of critique: examining the ways that codes of ethics reinforce "parochial and technical conceptions of professional life" (Thompson, 1999, p. 2). The goal of practical ethics is to uncover and promote the primary moral assumptions and values of a profession that are the foundation of its mission.

Second, practical ethics is directed toward the intermediate associations of society, the institutions that mediate between the relationships among individuals and the larger structures of society. This focus can attend to the organizational rules, policies, and practices that have ethical implications, for example, allocation of resources in agencies, rights of employees and clients, and so forth. Practical ethics pays attention to the "moral life" that resides within the structures of society, including the roles within institutions, and the relationship of those roles to the organizations in which they are situated. Subsequently, this approach is congruent with the ideas developed in Part III. People, their roles, and relationships reside within the bureaucratic structures of human services. The structures, culture, and climates of those institutions affect their moral life and moral agency. Ethical leadership, then, must be concerned with shaping ethical cultures and structures within the organization.

Finally, practical ethics has a political nature. There is a focus on the distribution of power and authority and the question "Who should decide?" in relation to particular ethical dilemmas. The use and abuse of power is a critical element in the ethics of leadership (Manning, 1990). The right decision and the right to make the decision confront leaders in relation to the differences and disagreements among constituents (employees, consumers, funders, and community citizens) in ethical conflicts (see Chapter 4). Leaders must evaluate their use of power, as well as the level of participation for other constituents in the organization or served by the organization.

The political nature of practical ethics also addresses the issue of accountability of the professions in relation to the public good. Thompson (1999) argues, "The pressing challenge for the future is to forge, in principle and in practice, a union of the traditional ideal of the autonomous profession (preserving the ethics of service) and the modern demand for accountability (acknowledging an ethics of responsibility)" (p. 4). This union is especially salient for leaders responsible for multiple constituencies and challenged by multidimensional ethical issues. They are professionals, working with other professional and occupational groups within the culture and structure of an organization, who are responsible for a moral vision that translates into concrete contributions to the public good. This responsibility requires an understanding and format for ethical complexity. Leaders, in order to be ethically responsible, must have a framework that captures multiple dimensions.

The Dimensions of Ethical Leadership

It is apparent from the preceding discussion that ethical leadership in human services is multidimensional. Leaders are responsible for integrating various dimensions of ethics and morality through their leadership. A multidimensional framework provides leaders with a flexible, dynamic approach to recognize and resolve the ethical dilemmas of leadership in human services, develop ethical cultures and ethical systems in organizations, and shape a moral vision and mission that contributes to the public good. Dimensions such as a) the personal and professional morality of the leader(s), b) with a theoretical approach to leadership—*transformational leadership*—that incorporates ethics, values, and morality, c) informed by ethical resources and models, d) practicing in ethical organizations, culture, structures and policies, with e) social responsibility to society are necessary. These five dimensions are discussed and integrated throughout Parts I, II, and III.

The following defined and described dimensions (Figure 1.2) are component parts of a larger whole and function similar to social systems theory, that is, the dimensions are distinct, separate elements and, at the same time, interrelate as part of

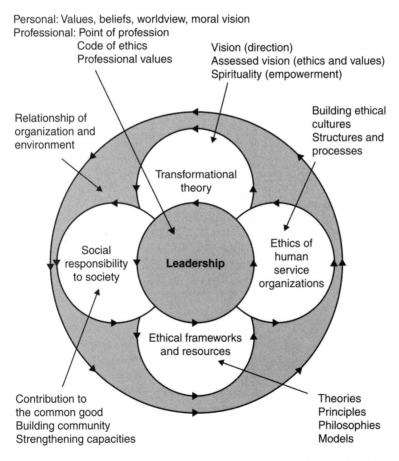

FIGURE 1.2 **Multidimensional Ethical Framework for Leadership**

the whole. The linkages are through the activities, behaviors, and moral vision of the leader and constituents. They operate through a dynamic process that is always in flux and change. A change in one dimension affects every other dimension. All of the dimensions intersect; thus, each dimension influences and is influenced by every other dimension. The patterns of interaction that develop between and among the various dimensions provide energy to sustain the ethical system.

Leadership is the core of the system. The leadership circle consists of the identified, formal leader(s) in an organization and the natural, informal leaders who develop and step forward in delegated or spontaneous ways. Even though leadership is situated in the center of the dimensions, opportunity exists for all constituents to shape and change the ethical and moral nature of the system through the informal nature of leadership by commenting, offering feedback, supporting or resisting particular practices, and so forth.

The whole—the multidimensional ethical system—is made up of its component parts. If one part does not receive adequate attention, an ethical void exists that affects the other dimensions. For example, leaders can be conscientious and ethical in their own practices, but, if the structures and processes of the organization contribute to an immoral or unethical culture, consumers of services, employees, and the public could be impacted negatively. For example, "Some organizations have a set of beliefs and/or way of doing things that can result in managers resorting to ethically dubious tactics simply to get the job done" (Toffler, 1986, p. 26). The culture of the organization negatively impacts behaviors. The social responsibility of the organization is then jeopardized. However, the thesis of this multidimensional approach is that ethical leadership can make a difference. It begins with the leader, the ethical starting point, the central dimension.

Leadership: The Ethical Starting Point

Leaders are individuals with their own *personal morality* and ethical starting points. They bring to the role the values and beliefs that make up their personal socialization and moral life. This *personal worldview* provides a lens for how they perceive moral and ethical issues. A leader's level of self-awareness in regard to personal morality has a profound influence on the moral and ethical considerations of that leadership role. A person's place in his/her own moral, life, and career development affects the reasoning process about ethical issues. Moral development and moral sensitivity make a difference in whether a moral or ethical issue is identified. Gender, age, socialization, and experience have an impact on awareness and the necessary skills to resolve ethical dilemmas (Dobrin, 1989; Gilligan, 1982; Manning, 1990). Also, how a person defines the leadership role (for example, manager or administrator) dictates choice of priorities, perception of influence, and use of time and energy in regard to moral issues (Toffler, 1986). Leaders must continually decide what role they will play, based on their own perceptions and the influence from others. However, as Ritchie (1988, p. 172) states in regard to leadership, ". . . *we* decide, and in that role decision we explicitly or implicitly define our ethical criteria."

Social work leaders and other professionals also have a professional starting point: the responsibility to incorporate professional values and purpose into their decision processes. The *"point of the profession"* must be actualized through the mission and activities of the organization (Green, 1987). A leader's decisions and actions reflect this. Professional values and the professional code of ethics, then, are relevant to the decision process. In addition, as part of ethical leading, a moral vision to guide leadership and organizational behavior is important. Leaders have a public responsibility to provide leadership with a moral purpose, or leadership that contributes to the public good in society. Therefore, a leadership paradigm is necessary that incorporates moral vision.

Transformational Leadership

The second dimension is a theoretical foundation for leadership. Theory informs practice and helps to explain what to do, why to do it, how to do it, and sometimes when to do it. Ethical leadership requires theory that incorporates ethics as a consideration to particular decisions, but, most important, as a fundamental element of the approach. The theory must have the potential to integrate personal and professional values, a moral direction, and the moral transformation of individuals and organizations. The major paradigms of leadership theories include transactional and transformational approaches. The transformational paradigm incorporates vision, ethics and values, and spirituality as critical components of leadership. Transformational theories support the transformation of followers into leaders and leaders into moral agents (Burns, 1978).

An equitable and effective distribution of power to constituents is important. Empowerment, as well as the ability to use power and influence toward enhancing good and removing harm, is important to ethical organizations. The commitment of constituents to the mission and moral vision is directly related to their participation in the decision processes. Empowerment and participation of constituents are core elements of transformational leadership theory. The theory can help to integrate moral and ethical considerations into the process of leadership. However, further moral and ethical resources are needed to cope with and resolve the complex ethical challenges of human service delivery.

Ethical Resources and Traditions for Decisionmaking

The third dimension is the use of ethical resources. Leaders in human services are challenged by the ethical dilemmas of administration and management on a daily basis. An ethical reasoning process for decisionmaking has to be useful for the routine and the extraordinary. The development of a reasoning process includes an understanding of the ethical resources available and how to apply them to actual decisions. Ethical theories, philosophies, and principles are resources that add depth to understanding the nature of a dilemma and the possible alternatives for a solution.

Leadership is comprised of working with the complexities of human behavior and interconnected organizational systems. The complexity and ambiguity of human service dilemmas require an understanding of the contextual issues that affect the reasoning process. The ability to use ethical resources, not as prescriptions or rules, but to shed light on the nature of the ethical issue, enhances the quality of the decision. Further, learning to understand the point of the matter, which is not always apparent on the surface, contributes to the reasoning process. Finally, developing awareness about what constitutes an ethical issue is critical to making decisions that are ethical by intention. Ethical decisions for leaders take place in organizations, which leads to the fourth dimension.

Building Ethical Organizations

This dimension is concerned with the ability and motivation of leaders to shape their organization's culture and structure, such that the *architecture* of the organization promotes ethical decisions and behaviors on the part of all employees. Leaders can transform the ethical nature of the workplace through communication processes, group norms and values, organizational culture, and the structural aspects of organization.

The culture of an organization promotes a sense of how to be and what is expected of employees, consumers of services, and others, or "the way we do things around here" (Deal, 1987). The culture sends the message to all employees about the shared values and ethical agreements of the agency. Some of the primary components and proponents of organizational culture include the mission, explicit policy, implicit policy, and the ethical climate (Manning, 1990).

The design or structure of an organization provides both internal and external opportunities and constraints for ethical decisions and behaviors. It is important for leaders to be knowledgeable about the development of structures and cultures that enhance ethical actions and an ethical organization. The nature of bureaucracy is such that isolation, fragmentation, and narrow distribution of information and authority are inherent. It is not uncommon for leaders and constituents to experience a separation from their own morality under the pressure of achieving the organizational ideal (Jackall, 1988; Ladd, 1970; Rhodes, 1986). Creating structures that promote individual responsibility, participation of all constituents, opportunities for ethical communication and action, and formal feedback loops for self-regulation of ethical issues are part of leadership. Ethical organizations, in turn, contribute to the good of society.

Social Responsibility of Human Service Organizations

The final dimension for ethical leadership in human services is promoting the social responsibility of the organization, the contribution to the common good of the community in which it is located. Leaders have responsibilities to many constituencies or stakeholders, including consumers of service, employees, board members, fiscal entities, community citizens, political and social groups, other agencies, and the human service sector of society. The organization has a responsibility beyond fulfilling its mission. Human service organizations have a great capacity to help build community through strengthening the connections of individuals, groups, and environmental systems. The organization has a primary culture shaping responsibility as well. The values that are enacted through the process of delivering services convey a message to society about the nature of social problems and resources connected to the agency's mission. Ethical leadership includes an attention to this responsibility to the public good.

A multidimensional approach to ethics in leadership goes beyond analyzing particular dilemmas or developing an ethical framework for decisions. This approach attempts to capture the essence of ethics in leadership, or leadership that has an ethical influence across all systems, where ethics are considered an integral part of every decision. Every individual in an organization, through ethical leadership, has both a responsibility and a contribution to make toward ethical leading. This is the essence of leadership; this is the "heart of the matter."

Conclusion

This chapter has provided an overview of the elements of ethical leadership. Ethics as the essence of leadership opened the chapter. Professional leaders have an ethical responsibility toward service as well as public responsibilities to society. The integration of practical ethics was presented as a conceptualization that provides a useful, relevant perspective to the ethics of leadership in organizations. A multidimensional framework for ethical leadership was presented as a needed comprehensive approach to ethical leadership. This framework embodies all of the topics included in the book; the dimensions described in this first chapter are developed more specifically throughout. Leadership, for purposes of this book, is specifically related to leadership of human service organizations. The next chapter introduces the reader to the terrain of human service organizations.

QUESTIONS AND APPLICATIONS

1. Conceptualize the "essence" of ethics in regard to your leadership:
   - How do ethics integrate into your day-to-day experience?
   - As a leader, what ethical premises would you want to represent as permanent fixtures of your leadership?
   - How would you use ethics as an "essence" to revitalize your organization?

2. Think about the private and public duties discussed in this chapter. Identify one or two examples of the duty to serve and delineate the barriers that negatively impact service to clients in your organization.

3. Think of an example of an "invisible" condition of your organization's service system that should be made public in order to improve social service delivery and/or social

policy. What relationships are currently developed or needed that would strengthen the opportunities to make this condition visible?

4. Think critically about the multidimensional approach to ethical leadership.
   ■ What areas are your strengths?
   ■ What areas need additional knowledge, skills, or understanding?
   ■ What is missing from the framework that would enhance the moral and ethical functions of leadership?

CHAPTER

2

Human Service Organizations: The Context for Ethical Leadership

THE FOCUS OF THIS CHAPTER IS ON THE FOLLOWING AREAS:

- Unique ethical nature of human services
- Characteristics of human service organizations
- History and nature of social work ethics
- Circumstances of ethics in human services
- History and nature of business ethics
- Intersection of social service and business ethics

Leadership of human service delivery systems brings forward many complex ethical challenges that are located in a particular context: the organization. The moral nature of human service organizations is multidimensional, with responsibilities to consumers, employees, and society. Perhaps the greatest ethical challenge is that human services have, as their primary purpose, *serving people*. Hasenfeld (1992, p. 3) refers to human service organizations as "an enigma." These organizations symbolize society's duties to attend to the well-being of citizens and to provide a safety net for those who are unable to take care of themselves. This view is contradicted by the distrust in society of professional care and the delivery of human services. There is a concern on the part of the public that such organizations are ". . . wasteful, fostering dependency, obtrusive and controlling" (Hasenfeld, 1992, p. 3). Therefore, leadership in human services is connected to the moral issues of affecting people in serious, life-changing ways and attending to public trust through the moral contract with society. An understanding of human service organizations within this context helps leaders to develop their moral vision for leadership.

The nature and history of social work and business ethics is an important developmental background for thinking about contemporary ethical leadership. The boundaries between business and social work are increasingly blurred in the delivery of human services. Privatization of human service agencies, as well as the integration of organizational theory and technology into social service organizations, has affected social work leadership and practice in a profound manner. Further, administration of human service organizations is based on the same or similar theories, technologies, and requirements as the administration of business and governmental organizations. The current changes in human service delivery systems require an understanding of the history and application of both social work and business ethics. This understanding provides readers with a "standing point": a position from which they can view the historical traditions in order to perceive necessary changes and future visions (Green, 1987). Leaders, with a perspective of history, can promote the needed moral and ethical directions for human service delivery systems.

In this section, characteristics of human service organizations and their contribution to society provide the setting or background, or the location for the ethical issues that challenge leaders in human services. Social work and business ethics from a historical perspective provide the developmental groundwork for ethical leadership today. The intersections of social work and business reveal differences, but also some common ground, such as moral and ethical responsibilities that are the same for both. Finally, an overview of the ethical circumstances of administrative ethics sets the scene for leadership in both public and private agencies.

The Unique Nature of Human Service Organizations

The entire life cycle for humans, from birth to death, is mediated by formal organizations that impact personal status and behavior. Human service organizations function to protect, maintain, and/or enhance the personal well-being of individuals through services that define, shape, or alter their personal characteristics and attributes (Hasenfeld, 1983). Human service organizations are distinguished from other bureaucracies in two ways. First, people are the raw material of the organization. Second, human service organizations are mandated to promote and protect the welfare of the people they serve.

Human beings turn to these organizations to meet their needs in areas that are critical to basic daily life, such as food, housing, employment, health and mental health care, social welfare, and so forth. Subsequently, their dependence on the organization is increased and the organization acquires power to shape their lives. People in leadership positions within the organization control the resources, while the client receiving services has little influence over the policy of the organization. The individual's loss of power vis-à-vis the human service organization is a fundamental characteristic of social service delivery systems (Coleman, 1973).

Characteristics of Human Service Organizations

Human service organizations have unique characteristics that produce ethical dilemmas that are both similar to, and different from, other business dilemmas (see Figure
2.1). A primary difference is that people are directly impacted by services that are
mandated through the mission of these organizations. In addition, human service organizations contribute to the culture of society in profound ways. Leaders, with an
ethical imperative to accomplish the mission of the organization, also have an ethical
responsibility to contribute to progressive ideals and a greater public good. This
unique set of characteristics has moral implications, particularly because the characteristics are directed toward changing people. The following sections describe these
characteristics (Hasenfeld, 1992; Hasenfeld & English, 1974).

Working with People Is Moral Work.   The consumers of services are people who
have moral values; this affects most of the organization's activities. Value conflicts are
a given, and this requires an awareness of conflicts on the part of providers and administrators. Service technologies must be morally justified because every activity related to the client has significant moral consequences. Every action taken in the
provision of service contains a moral judgment and statement about the client's social
worth. The labeling process that is inherent in most human services conveys a message about the worth of consumers to society. For example, labels that traditionally invoke stigma—mental illness or welfare recipient or homelessness—may convey
assumptions about a person's ability to contribute or capacity to live as an autonomous
person.
　　The underlying moral questions in regard to the delivery of services concerns
the civil and moral rights of people, or their autonomy and self-determination. The
manner in which clients are involved in service decisions, the consent process, and
client choice about the nature of interventions provided are all examples of moral issues about rights. Also, Hasenfeld argues that the allocation of resources including
"money, time, and expertise" reflect decisions about social worth (1992, p. 6). The
moral implications of the decisions and actions that take place in relation to service
delivery are usually implicit, ". . . embedded in the organizational routines they become part of the 'invisible hand' that controls workers' behaviors and actions"
(Hasenfeld, 1992, p. 6).

- Working with people is moral work.
- Human services is "gendered work."
- People are complicated; goals are problematic.
- Turbulent environments affect external support.
- Technologies are indeterminate.
- Core activities are through relationships.
- Transforming people is difficult to measure.

FIGURE 2.1   Characteristics of Human Service Organizations

Gender Is a Moral Issue in Human Services.   Hasenfeld (1992) posits that gender is an important issue for human service organizations. The workforce is primarily women, particularly in the direct service positions. In contrast, positions in administrative and authoritative roles are often predominately filled by men. There are two important implications as a result of this disparity (Hasenfeld, 1992, p. 7). First, women bring particular values to their work as providers, particularly values of "caregiving, empathy, nurturing, and cooperation" (Hasenfeld, 1992, p. 7). These values are in conflict with the norms of bureaucracy and traditional male values, which promote "competition, individualism, and instrumentalism" (Hasenfeld, 1992, p. 7). The conflict in values results in a restriction of women's capacities and strengths as well as a restriction of opportunities to pursue leadership positions. Further, women traditionally earn lower salaries than men and receive less rewards. Human services as a gendered workplace brings forward moral implications for leaders. Employee morale, opportunity for advancement, role modeling for female consumers of services, and fair hiring and promotion practices are just a few of the moral challenges leaders must confront in response to gender disparity.

People Are Complicated. Goals Are Problematic.   The goals of human service organizations are vague and problematic. It is much more difficult to agree about achieving desired welfare and well-being needs of people than to transform inanimate objects and to construct products. The identification of goals is a multidimensional process that includes the needs and desires of the client system, the available technology, the knowledge and skills of the direct service providers, and the resources of the organization. In addition, the success of the technology used to reach goals is dependent on clients' willingness and commitment to the change process. The *compliance* of consumers of services is controlled by the organization through tracking and matching of consumer to the most appropriate service. For example, the person with persistent mental illness may be admitted to a partial care track, even if currently working or functioning at a level that requires less intensive care. Second, compliance is achieved by "reinforcing socially sanctioned client roles" (Hasenfeld, 1992, pp. 16–17). Psychiatric consumers may be given little opportunity to participate in decisions regarding their treatment plans, or the program goals and choices for the unit as compared with an empowerment philosophy that provides full participation. The result of this kind of "institutionalization," even in community service delivery, is the iatrogenic effect of helping, or learned helplessness. The choices made are invariably moral choices.

Turbulent Environments Affect External Support.   The moral ambiguity on the part of society toward human services promotes a turbulent environment that surrounds the organization with many interest groups trying to achieve their aims through the organization (Hasenfeld, 1992, p. 10). The organizations' dependence on external funding sources increases dependence on, and sensitivity to, the environment and changes in the environment. Recent legislation, new rules and regulations from accrediting bodies, and revised professional standards all affect organizational survival. The organization is in a position of constantly justifying its legitimacy to fiscal authorities and, at the same time, must be responsive to the changing moral climate of professional and community groups and society. Mental health agencies, for example, must compete with private providers for state contracts that fund services and, in doing so, must meet particular theoretical and technological requirements. Also, the increasing consumer activism in mental health and social welfare systems impacts the program philosophies of institutions.

Indeterminate Technologies.   The technologies used within human service organizations do not provide complete knowledge about how to achieve desired outcomes. The people who are served are complex individuals with some common characteristics that are interrelated, but vary greatly in terms of their own unique characteristics. The knowledge about how people function and how to change them is partial and incomplete. As a result, many of the outcomes that the organization is expected to transform cannot be observed or measured adequately or accurately. Also, Hasenfeld (1992) argues that technology is directly connected to the institutional environment and the norms and values of society. Technologies gain legitimization as they are accepted in the larger institutional environment and promote popular norms and values. For example, the use of antidepressant medications has become an important method of treatment in the cost-saving and short-term treatment models promulgated by a managed health care environment and is quickly becoming a major for-profit strategy.

Core Activities Through Relationship.   The core activities consist of relationships between staff and clients. Thus, the nature and quality of these relations is a critical element in the success or failure of the organization accomplishing its mission. In order to receive help, clients must cooperate, and, as Hasenfeld (1992) argues, cooperation requires trust. Due to the primacy of staff-client relations and the role of professionals from a variety of disciplines who provide services, the direct service staff exercises considerable discretion in performing duties. They exercise more autonomy than in business or industrial organizations. The ability to exercise discretion on the part of providers "means that the clients become dependent on the goodwill of the workers, and thus are vulnerable to abuse" (Hasenfeld, 1992, p. 18). Further, there is an unequal distribution of power between staff and clients due to the staff's access to information about the client, their knowledge and expertise to help the client, and the control that staff can exert over access to services and resources. The dependency of the client on the organization and service staff, combined with unequal power distribution and the staff's use of discretion provide a fertile ground for moral and ethical dilemmas in the delivery of services.

Transformation of People Is Difficult to Measure.   Human service organizations have more difficulty with reliable and valid measures of effectiveness. This results in more resistance to change and innovation. The lack of feedback enables organizations to reify claims of success and reinforce the dominant service technologies. The lack of reliable measures decreases the capacity to innovate because there is not an accurate yardstick to compare performance to new developments in their particular field of service. Most important, moral choices about what is evaluated have moral implications. Hasenfeld (1992, p. 14) notes, "measuring reduction in morbidity without attention to the quality of life of those who survive is a moral choice." Measures of effectiveness emerge from "the moral systems embraced by the organization" (Hasenfeld, 1992, p. 14).

The previous characteristics result in organizations that stand in contrast to the typical bureaucratic organizations in business and industry. Human service organizations process people. They have the power to shape their lives, and this power is not reciprocal. There are important moral implications that arise about the consequences of service delivery to the service consumers, to employees, and to society.

Ethical Responsibility of Human Service Organizations

The ethical responsibility of the human service organization is grounded in several areas. The *commitment of the organization*, the *sanction of the community*, and the *nature of the service* provided is a commitment to society (Joseph, 1983). The mission mandates a public commitment to serve, and this commitment implies serious responsibilities. As discussed earlier in the section on relationship, the "vulnerability of the client seeking help" demands that organizations consider the nature and meaning of that vulnerability and respond accordingly (Joseph, 1983, p. 54). Also, the moral challenge to consumers' vulnerability is an obligation of "competence" that is prescribed to the organization, both professionally and administratively. Voluntary organizations (nonprofit) make further assertions. "It will serve all; it will not seek profit from the client's need; and, its self-interest is subservient to that of the community" (Joseph, 1983, p. 53). Human services are literally "in service" to consumers and the community. Therefore, for what they have been created to do in relation to ameliorating a human need, they must "commit themselves to do," and they "incur the responsibility to do it" (Levy, 1993, pp. 6–7). The ethics of the organization are functions, then, of this responsibility.

The sanction of the community is given with the trust that the agencies concerned will provide services that address the purposes for which the agency was created (Levy, 1993). Further, the *community trust* is dependent upon the integrity of the policies that are enunciated. Organizational documents such as the mission, values statement, policies and procedures, and code of ethics of the organization are contracts with the public and the public trust. The organization has ethical obligations to earn the public trust.

In addition, the voluntary and private sector of human services *provide society with social innovations* that move the service delivery system forward (Smith, 1988). The practical testing of new social ideas, and technological innovations help to build social capital. The private sector, according to Smith, is the "social risk capital of human society" (1988, p. 2) and is able to embrace errors and to attempt experiments that are based on a commitment to a value or idea that has the potential to improve the human condition.

In the process of creating innovations, agencies can become a *"forum to counter-vailing definitions of reality and morality"* (Smith, 1988). In this regard, human service organizations can challenge the existing notions about what is good and what ought to be done in society. Smith argues that "If these definitions of reality and morality are sufficiently compelling to people . . . groups grow into huge social movements and can change the course of history . . ."(1988, p. 3). Examples include the impact of small activist consumer organizations for the mentally ill that have grown into a national movement for consumer empowerment. Similarly, the Alliance for the Mentally Ill started with small associations of families and has become a national force.

Clearly, human service organizations in the voluntary and private sector have *moral roles as leaders*. Smith calls the voluntary sector the ". . . gadfly, dreamer, and moral leader in society" (1988, p. 3). Their participation, locally, nationally, and internationally, challenges the existing structures of human service delivery and creates new definitions of reality.

The people in organizations also have a moral commitment to *shape and support values that are congruent* in service delivery as well as the internal functions and relationships of the organization. Levy (1979, p. 280) describes it this way:

> Perhaps most fundamentally in the ethics of management . . . is the congruence which should be aspired to between the ethics associated with the service of the organization and the ethics of its internal organization. Each feeds on the other and symbolizes the uniqueness of such organizations. If social justice . . . is the watchword of social work, then it should be a matter of ethical course for justice to characterize all of the internal operations and relationships of the organization, and a matter of ethical course for each staff member to act accordingly, whatever his or her position in the administrative hierarchy.

This is the challenge for social work leaders in human services: to establish ethical organizations that promote critical values expressed through the behavior and decisions of all employees. This congruence of the values of service and organizational climate results in ethical service delivery that protects and enhances the well-being of vulnerable populations, reflects the agency's commitment to the community served, and strengthens the public trust. Guidance from the profession to help accomplish this is fragmented. The history of social work ethics provides some insight about what exists and what is yet to be developed by future leaders.

The History of Social Work Ethics in Organizations

Discussions about ethics in social work and the moral aspects of practice date back to the beginning of the profession. However, the nature of the concerns about ethics has changed in response to the maturation of the profession and historical and political developments (Reamer, 1980; 1998b). The Judeo-Christian tradition in Western societies has been a formative element in the development of the profession. Early social work was influenced by religious and moral values so that social work and religious morality were virtually inseparable. The humanitarian influence of 18th century philosophers and the liberalism of 19th century social thinkers helped to moderate the religious influence. Through time, social work became more concerned with a science-based, technologically oriented profession and became more secular in its value orientation. This required social work to eliminate religious bias from its basic assumptions (Yelaja, 1982).

The meaning of "moral" has changed in social work from an evaluation (and sometimes judgment) of the client's morality to a focus on practitioners and the moral mandate of the profession (Reamer, 1980). The first move away from the focus on the morality of the poor and destitute happened in relation to the settlement house movement and the progressive reform in the early 20th century (Reamer, 1995). Then, social problems related to basic human needs (health, housing, employment, and education) became the focus of social work. This macro perspective reflected ethical issues related to human service obligations. The 1960s again brought forward a public focus with emphasis on the issues of civil rights, justice, and institutional responsibility for good and harm.

Ethics in Leadership and Organizational Practice

The literature on ethics in social work leadership and organizational practice has been relatively recent (past 25 years) in relation to the history of the profession and sparse when compared to direct practice discussions and debate. Most of the literature on social work professional ethics has been located in the area of work with small size systems, such as individuals, couples, and families through direct or clinical practice. Levy (1979, 1982) articulated some of the first major discussions through publications on social work ethics in administration, bringing the profession current ethically with the developing indirect or macro focus of social work. Levy's scholarship led the way to the ethics of social work with larger size systems. Other articles and book chapters have focused on specific ethical issues and dilemmas of indirect practice, with increasing frequency (for example, Cohen, 1987; Gottfried, 1998; Gummer, 1984, 1999; Howe, 1980; Karger, 1981; Lewis, 1989; Northen, 1998; Patti, 1985; Reamer, 1987, 1988, 1993, 2001; Reisch & Taylor, 1983; Rhodes, 1985; Sarri, 1982; Strom-Gottfried, 1998).

There are differences of opinion about the inclusion of ethics in administrative practice, which traditionally has been informed by rational/legal theories of organization and management. Two phenomena have created this omission of moral anchoring in the theory and practice literature of administration and leadership: the tradition of American pragmatism and the nature of bureaucracy as a mechanism of order, rationality, and authority (Slavin, 1982). These phenomena have portrayed the organization as ethically neutral. The focus is on pursuing mission and objectives through a rational decisionmaking process (see Chapter 8).

Social work has been guided by a "value-free" science for the past half century, with related concerns for methods, effectiveness, and outcomes. Organizational and managerial theories imported into social work that are the basis of an administrative orientation reflect an objective, neutral position. From its history, social work finds it-self in a paradoxical position in regard to professional values. Science, some argue, is value free. In contrast, social work is a normative profession founded on religious and humanistic values. The tension that exists between a heritage of value tradition and a scientifically based professional status can create confusion and contradictions for leaders. They are confronted with a problem of duality in relation to ethical issues; they represent the values of professional social work, yet work within the rationality of a formal organizational structure with theories that are supposedly objective and value free (Manning, 1990).

Internal and External Self-Regulation

Self-regulation is essential to professional ethics and professional leadership. A pro-fessional ethic includes internal and external attributes of any set of rules, ideals, or guidelines for a field of practice (Newton, 1981). The internal aspect, a person's *con-science*, is the more serious and important because it has its roots in each individual practitioner of the profession. The *code of ethics*, the external aspect, is more visible, logically coherent, and enforceable. This aspect is linked to the professional organi-zation and is the product of a political process.

Neither aspect of the professional ethic, taken alone, is satisfactory. Pro-fessionals, as individuals, can be ill informed, uninformed, or misinformed. Also, they can be clouded by their own subjective and contradictory personal expression of feel-ings and values (see Chapter 5). On the other hand, the code of ethics can be a con-tradiction in terms, principles, and guidelines. In outward appearance, it is a set of guidelines to be applied to any situation. In actuality, it is hardly adequate for the in-finite number of unique situations that present ethical dilemmas. These two aspects, conscience and ethical code, work together with difficulty under the most stable con-ditions (Newton, 1981).

Professions must develop a code and attend to code revision as one of their high-est priorities because there is a direct link between the demand for autonomy by the profession and the willingness to take explicit collective responsibility for professional conduct. The code is a contract with the public to ensure the foundation for the pub-lic's trust. However, codes of ethics also contain contradictions and inconsistencies and are quickly outdated by changes in the profession and in society. Newton (1981, p. 46) argues this:

> It is the essence of conscience to resist prior decision of cases by rules, which is pre-cisely what a Code aims at doing. And when the practice which the ethics is supposed to guide is changing rapidly to meet changing conditions, putting tremendous strain on individual practitioners and organizations alike, the maintenance of a coherent ethic may be an all but impossible task, and the harrowing political task of code development must seem like an exercise in futility . . . Yet it must be done.

Social work and other professional administrators are in a difficult and somewhat con-fusing position in regard to the code of ethics and the issue of self-regulation. This is due to the lack of guidelines in current and past professional codes that specify the ethical obligations of administrators and organizations for which leaders in a variety of roles have primary responsibility.

For example, this lack of emphasis on ethics in leadership is reflected in the development of the social work code of ethics. The 1979 version demonstrated the imbalance between ethical content in direct practice and content for those engaged in indirect practice (for example, administration, management, community practice, and so forth). Only one section describes the social worker's responsibility to employers and to employing agencies, with a few references to standards relevant to leadership (for example, social work administration, collegial relationships, responsibility to clients, and responsibility to promote the general welfare) scattered throughout the code (NASW, 1979).

The newly revised version of the code (NASW, 1996) has a section on ethical responsibilities in practice settings that refers to supervision and consultation, administration, and other areas relevant to the ethical standards of indirect practice. There are also standards throughout the code that have some reference to indirect practice decisions. Although the new version of the code is improved for indirect practice, it has not yet developed the breadth and depth necessary to guide the myriad decisions in leadership that have ethical dimensions and implications. The commercialization and privatization of human services and the increasing preoccupation with profit and organizational survival accentuate many of the dilemmas of administration. These types of ethical dilemmas are not fully addressed in even the most revised code for social work.

A professional code of ethics that is designed to guide and govern the moral aspects of organizational practice must represent a consensus among both persons and institutions about preferred behaviors for particular organizational circumstances. A few principles of ethics in social work administration have been codified, but many have not yet been formulated to the point of testing for consensus (Levy, 1982). The internal aspect of self-regulation referred to earlier in this chapter, the experience, perspectives, and feelings of the leader(s), is in a dialectical relationship with the code. This process is the heart of the professional ethic as Newton (1981, p. 49) states:

> On this account, the point of . . . setting down a professional ethic in the form of a code, is the enterprise itself: the dialogue among professionals, on their personal professional commitment and the direction of the profession as a whole . . . mirrors the individual practitioner's internal dialogue of personal feeling and objective justification.

An ethical responsibility and activity of leadership, then, includes initiating dialogue with other leaders in a variety of positions. The dialogue that mirrors the experience of each administrator/manager becomes a medium of expression for the further development of the administrative and organizational guidelines of professional codes of ethics.

In this regard, the literature on ethical issues in administration and management is increasing (Reamer, 1998b). Discussions on the ethical aspects of supervision, consultation, ethics committees, and organizational ethics provide the opportunity to discuss and debate particular ethical issues in order to work toward codification and consensus. In the meantime, social work leaders in organizational and community practice are on their own with respect to the code of ethics, more than other social work practitioners, in determining the right course of action.

Codes of ethics are a useful resource to provide guidance if practitioners use them and are familiar with the content. Berliner (1989) posits that few NASW members have read or are familiar with the social work code of ethics and that ethics complaints are few and far between. Other authors point out the superficial treatment accorded ethical issues in social work texts (Rhodes, 1986). The textbooks on administrative practice sometimes include no content on ethics at all. This situation is vastly improved by the emphasis on values and ethics by the CSWE. Values and ethics are now becoming routine content in social work curriculum. However, experts agree that codes of ethics are not adequate, alone, to cope with complex issues and conflicting values. Ethical frameworks and decisionmaking systems must be combined with the code of ethics. A framework that provides for ethical reflection and analysis and that incorporates philosophical methods as well as ethical skills, is needed in social work for leaders in organizations (Joseph, 1983). The following discussions of some of the circumstances that produce ethical dilemmas in leadership demonstrate why ethical frameworks are required.

Circumstances that Produce Ethical Dilemmas in Human Services

There are countless circumstances that produce ethical dilemmas on a daily basis, precipitated by the nature and work of the profession in human service organiza-

I Dilemmas in Relation to the Nature of Social Work
  ▪ Enacting social work purpose and values
  ▪ Competing claims and duty to aid
  ▪ Negative versus posititive obligations
  ▪ Political ideology and social work
  ▪ Obligation to reform society
II Dilemmas in relation to the function of leaders
  ▪ The use and abuse of power
III Dilemmas of Organizational Design and Requirements
  ▪ Responsibility to funders versus consumers of service
  ▪ Dilemmas of bureaucratic design
  ▪ Organizational forces versus client need
IV Dilemmas about Resources
  ▪ Rationing of resources
  ▪ Cost containment and the profit motive

FIGURE 2.2   Circumstances of Ethics in Human Services

tions (see Figure 2.2). The following discussion highlights some general themes, but is not inclusive of all ethical issues. When possible, qualitative interview material from a study on the experiences of social work administrators and managers in making ethical decisions is integrated into the discussion to provide real-life examples (Manning, 1990). The following categories of ethical dilemmas include dilemmas in regard to the nature of social work, dilemmas related to the function of leaders, dilemmas in relation to the nature of organizational design and purpose, and dilemmas about resources.

Dilemmas in Relation to the Nature of Social Work

Social work leaders work in and for human service organizations that are mandated and supported by external bodies to achieve certain goals for society's well-being. The organization's substantive goals are to process and change people in socially approved ways. The purpose and values of social work create many dilemmas.

Enacting Social Work Purpose and Values.   Ethical decisions are at the core of service delivery; services must be delivered in a manner that is congruent with social work's mission and purpose. Social work values connect social work purpose to administration and leadership through the actions and decisions of leaders that reflect those values. Therefore, the ethics associated with the service of the organization and the ethics of the internal operation must be congruent (Gross, 1973; Levy, 1983; Patti, 1985). However, this is not always the case. In their critique of the social service workplace, Fisher and Karger (1997) propose that social work programs that were created to protect vulnerable populations are now experienced as oppressive to those populations. Further, social workers who are employed by social service agencies are repressed by the workplace conditions and policies of those agencies. In these situations, social work purpose and values are incongruent with the actions and policies of the organization. Social work leaders, then, are faced with the ethical challenge of aligning the values of the profession with the fundamental activities of service delivery and employee relationships.

Competing Claims and Duty to Aid.   The profession of social work has traditionally been based on the obligation to assist those in need. This is especially true for those who are least able to help themselves. Social work leaders have also argued that the care for those in need cannot be left totally to the efforts of private citizens and organizations; the government must assume some of the responsibility. Therefore, social work assumes a "*duty to aid*" (Reamer, 1982, p. 43). This duty is particularly difficult in a society where needs are escalating and resources are diminishing. Administrators in government agencies and private organizations are routinely making choices among the "competing claims of those in need." One example is the administrator's responsibility to a client's complaint against an agency employee. Issues such as sexual abuse by clinicians, wrongful treatment, and malpractice come to the attention of the administrator. The client's due-process rights and protection of employees and agency from unfair allegations can cause conflict. The administrator is in the position of facilitating the client's accusations for investigation, and, at the same time, protecting the agency from a lawsuit (Manning, 1990).

Negative versus Positive Obligations.   For social work, there is an ongoing conflict between *negative and positive obligations*, which is the delicate balance between respecting the autonomy of individuals and intervening to help change "intolerable living conditions, self-destructive or threatening behavior, and emotional misery" (Reamer, 1982, p. 44). Although the most obvious examples occur in direct practice, social work administrators are often responsible for social control functions for society and therefore are under considerable pressure to intervene in clients' lives for those reasons. For example, mental health administrators reported frequent requests from community citizens and leaders to hospitalize disruptive members who are infringing on the peace of the community, even though the person's mental status did not meet criteria for involuntary treatment (Manning, 1990). However, organizational survival depends on the goodwill of the community, adding pressure on the administrator to be responsive to community demands. In addition, administrators have an impact on subordinates' autonomy by imposing required conditions for employment (for example, personnel policies requiring drug treatment, mental health counseling, and so forth). At the same time, administrators are responsible for creating respect for the voluntary nature of employment as well as individual dignity and autonomy.

Political Ideology and Social Work.   The growth of the welfare state, according to Reamer (1982), represents another conflict of values. Freedom from government interference is often at odds with the security that is derived from government-sponsored programs and services. Social work administrators and policymakers are in positions that frequently confront them with these difficult choices between values. Political ideology and economic doctrine determine decisions concerning the role of government. However, because these decisions include judgments about "rights, duties, and obligations as they relate to human welfare," these decisions are ethical in principle (Reamer, 1982, p. 54). It is in this arena that Rhodes' (1985) argument that "the ethical is also political" is notable.

Obligation to Reform Society.   Social work as a profession has an ethical responsibility to the broader society that is delineated in the code of ethics. From local to global levels, social workers are expected to promote the ". . . development of people, their communities, and their environments" (NASW, 1996). This obligation is especially salient for social work leaders who are in the position of assessing the need for service, providing services, and evaluating the efficacy of services. The responsibility to inform policymakers about the implications and results of policy in relation to service delivery can create ethical conflicts, often in relation to job security and self-interest as one manager said:

> It would feel better if we were working on a level, too, for some longer range things and to be honest and to be able to say, "here's a thousand people in your area that are

not getting service. You just need to know that. They are out there, and half of them are ready to beat their kids, and the other half is ready to beat themselves. It's going to happen, and don't be surprised if there's a few suicides around . . . " But you can't do that. Your directors say, "Don't you be doing that. And don't you be pissing people off" (Manning, 1990, p. 193).

Managers and administrators have an ethical obligation to inform policymakers and decisionmakers to make the invisible visible, within the organization and the external environment, in regard to the moral effects of policy in order to reform and improve the general society.

Dilemmas in Relation to the Function of Leaders

There will be an extensive discussion in Chapter 4 about the nature of power and the relationship to ethical leadership. What follows is a brief introduction to power as part of leadership dilemmas.

The Use and Abuse of Power.   The ethical questions that concern social work reflect the status of the profession, made up of practitioners who have *the authority to intervene* in the lives of others (Reamer, 1982). The critical concept is that of authority. The authority to intervene in others' lives is greater for the social work executive than for other practitioners for they have power through their position in the hierarchy of the organization and through the function of relationships with others. They wield authority that can adversely affect subordinates, clients, board members, and other community representatives. In fact, Levy (1982, p. 61) states that the executive or administrator is vested with "virtually unlimited power" over many things and many people.

The organization executive is viewed as the ideal type where the ethics of the organization are embodied (Levy, 1982). This position of leadership is ambiguous in that both power and accountability are pervasive. Levy (1982) argues that whatever executives have the power and duty to do, they also have the opportunity to do or not do. Whether the opportunity is taken or not is at the base of ethical or unethical behavior. However, leaders in organizations also have an ethical duty to do their assigned responsibility for the organization. In this context, the leadership is responsible for carrying out the organizational purpose.

This organizational responsibility carries with it a constant pressure to ensure the agency's economic survival with limited resources. This "combination of power and pressure can be treacherous for subordinates" (Levy, 1979, p. 281). Resources are sometimes distributed according to political power, rather than program need. One manager stated, "The danger of getting into too much manipulation and political juggling in order to get what you want, is that you get caught up in the game and lose sight of the ethical foundation for why you're doing it. The more time you spend in 'political' activities, the more of a 'political creature' you become" (Manning, 1990). The ethical responsibility of executives requires that they be able to view the needs of individuals as well as the immediate requirements of the organization, and this is an ethical balancing act.

Dilemmas of Organizational Design and Requirements

Leaders work within organizations and are ultimately responsible for the success of the organization in accomplishing the mission. However, the nature of organizational design and the requirements for success, and even survival, can create dilemmas.

Responsibility to Funders versus Consumers of Service.   Ethical dilemmas result from conflicts between the needs and demands of those who provide financial resources to agencies and the needs of those receiving services. The survival of the organization is sometimes dependent on relationships and contracts with funding entities (for example, local, state, and federal government contracts; other human service entities such as criminal justice; foundations; and so forth) that have program expectations, service delivery requirements, and demands for the priority of clients served. For example, an agency may prioritize court-ordered referrals over voluntary admissions because court-ordered clients are ordered to pay for services, or the court has a contract for payment. The single mother with kids who has little or no ability to pay is placed on a waiting list. Nonprofit and public administrators voiced concerns about the poor, people of color, and the more difficult, recalcitrant clients having less opportunity for service (Manning, 1990). Human service leaders must be aware of opportunities and constraints in order to act as an expert or advocate of agencies or programs under their responsibility, rather than a functionary for those who provide the fiscal resources (Sarri, 1982).

The Ethical Dilemmas of Bureaucracy.   Other ethical issues are attached to the bureaucratic organization and organizational survival. The social work leader works within, and is sometimes responsible for, a bureaucracy. Organizational and social work theorists and ethicists (Jackall, 1988; Ladd, 1970; Rhodes, 1985) argue that *the bureaucratic form* poses some particular ethical problems for social workers (see Chapter 8). Decision processes that are promoted within the bureaucratic form of organization can undermine social workers' ordinary concepts of morality. Further, human service agencies in particular can undermine morality because of ". . . their contradictory nature; their *stated* goal is to help clients, yet their actual operation serves the interest of preserving the bureaucracy" (Rhodes, 1985, p. 134). One manager (Manning, 1990, p. 207) noted that "The same kind of rote exercises are done over and over . . . the system rewards stasis . . . it is caught up in self-perpetuation, rather than for the consumer . . . the involvement of the consumer is viewed as extremely threatening."

A leader's awareness of this conflict is necessary, or decisions will be made as if they do not have moral dimensions. The administrators are especially vulnerable because they are directly accountable for reaching organizational objectives, directing an efficient operation that is cost-effective, and maintaining the survival of the organization in the face of shrinking resources. All of these activities, in various ways, can subvert the goal of serving clients.

Organizational Forces versus Client Need.   *Organizational forces* sometimes determine the nature of the work by *institutional rules* rather than client need. The routinized procedures and selected theoretical models define a narrow range of client problems and prescribe limited means to resolve problems. Thus, "instead of providing care and 'empowerment,' they become a force for social control or for ineffective, palliative measures" (Rhodes, 1985, p. 133). Further, the nature of individuals with their own unique characteristics, with associated complex needs for services, is sacrificed for efficiency and profit. Social work managers described fostering dependency of clients by offering the "Cadillac model" of care to clients with Medicaid for reimbursement reasons, while uninsured clients did not have access to the same frequency or intensity of a treatment modality (Manning, 1990, p. 181). Administrators and managers have an ethical responsibility to remain sensitive to the potential shaping influence of programs and procedures and also to be attuned to the complexities and needs of people.

Administrators and managers are often confronted with the advances of science in the forms of new technologies that bring value-based decisions to the forefront. Christensen (1986, p. 72) argues that information technology is transformative in its potential. Because of this potential, leadership has the responsibility of "explicating the value dimensions of computer technology" (Christensen, 1986, p. 72). Decisions about the design, operation, use, and implementation of management information systems are value bound. Implications for clients and personnel in areas such as confidentiality, treatment decisions, cost-benefit analysis, and so forth have the potential for good and harm.

Dilemmas About Resources

Resources are essential to the survival of the organization and to the quality and range of the services provided, but resources also become the nexus of many ethical choices and dilemmas. Choices that restrict cost, ration services, and produce revenue ultimately have ethical dimensions to be considered and usually reflect a dilemma in regard to those choices.

Rationing of Resources.   In this era of diminishing resources, an ongoing ethical dilemma is the *distribution of limited resources and services* (Reamer, 1982). Resources can include money, time, services, positions of employment, personnel, and so forth. The recipients of those resources can range from individual clients to entire agencies or programs. The criteria that are developed and used to decide who will benefit, and who will not, reflect different distribution values and different principles of distributive justice. As leaders distribute the resources of a particular social policy, they also must be attentive to the morality of the goals and the procedures used to implement that policy. For example, new technologies in health care combined with increased demands for access to those technologies bring forward difficult questions about criteria to follow in the allocation of these resources (Reamer, 1985). Distribution based on need versus ability to pay or triage strategies versus "first-come, first-served" or demographic variables such as age to justify distribution are all examples of decisions that administrators in health care are faced with daily.

Program retrenchment and layoffs are also related to the distribution of scarce resources. Ethical guidelines are needed to guide the leadership of organizations when faced with decisions about retrenchment (Reisch & Taylor, 1983). There is a great risk that the most disadvantaged and least powerful clients and/or employees will be further disadvantaged when retrenchment occurs. The conflicting values of loyalty to agency and professional responsibility to employees and clients are paramount in these situations (Reisch & Taylor, 1983).

The nature of the *process* of retrenchment and reduction in force also contains ethical implications. One manager described it this way:

> The part I struggle with is that under the RIF [reduction in force] format, the supervisor, me, gets told on Thursday what supervisees have to come in on Friday to get chopped, and they are to be gone that day . . . I personally believe that that's unethical . . . not because its severe, but because its not balanced . . . We would not tolerate any employee doing that to us (Manning, 1990, p. 190).

Administrators also discussed the ethics of hiring people to fill permanent positions knowing a layoff could occur at any time.

Cost-Containment and the Profit Motive. Cost-containment appears to have assumed the quality of a primary value in human service administration (Joseph, 1983). This emphasis, combined with a focus on efficiency, has profound implications for policies concerning service to clients. Cost-containment and profit were identified by social work managers and administrators as the basis for the most frequent and difficult dilemmas (Manning, 1990). Decisions about intervention become determined by the economic status of the client, rather than clinical justifications. A middle manager described an agency policy (not written) whereby families on medicaid were seen first on an individual basis and then as a family in order to "bill top fee" and make up a budget deficit. She stated, "That decision came from a financial base, and it eats at me . . . I feel like we are ripping off ourselves by ripping off the government" (Manning, 1990, p. 180). Short-term models of treatment are chosen for efficiency rather than efficacy; intake and termination procedures are developed with funders in mind, sometimes at the risk of lower quality service to clients. Weil (1983, p. 44) posits that the increasing preoccupation with organizational survival intensifies the possibility of ". . . sacrificing program goals, program effectiveness, and vulnerable populations . . . ."

The competition with for-profit organizations in the provision of human services brings forward a different set of ethical issues: the conflict between the service ideal and the profit motive (Joseph, 1983). A client's "ability to pay" has become a decisive factor in admission criteria. Nonprofit managers in the previous study (Manning, 1990) described limiting services to lower economic groups because the agency had to generate income from those with ability to pay and those with insurance. One manager describe it as "the prostitute theory . . . I want the money first" (Manning, 1990, p. 180). The "profit mission," embedded in the capitalist economy, is the counterpart of cost-containment. Although the free market should ensure competency and accountability, the issues of payment and profit have developed a two-tiered system of care, with different levels of quality and intensity, according to economic status.

Managers in for-profit agencies experience pressure to create programs to generate revenue, rather than as a response to demonstrated need. The phrases "Is it a moneymaker?" and "Does it attract clients?" create an atmosphere that mental health is a product rather than a service (Manning, 1990, p. 182). One manager described it as "Now we've got such an incredible number competing for the market share that the drive is to capture the most market share you can and to create or drive demand . . . and, that's a bizarre concept for social workers" (Manning, 1990, p. 182). Joseph (1983) argues that these issues of cost-containment and competition with the profit sector for agency survival raise two fundamental ethical concerns: the ethical responsibility of the organization and the question about how a decisionmaking model for organizations interfaces with an ethical decisionmaking model.

Social work leaders and the organizations they represent have a *social responsibility* as their main objective. The ethical criteria imposed by social responsibility are somewhat different from the criteria for business. A brief history of business ethics accentuates some of the differences.

Business Ethics

Although social work ethics have been around for a century, ethics in business have existed since the Sumerians, nearly 6,000 years ago (Solomon, 1993) or since the beginning of business (De George, 1987). *Business ethics*, however, have only been around a very short time. The field of business ethics only began to develop after the 1960s. For most of those 6,000 years, the issue of using trade to make a profit was considered a lack of virtue. It wasn't until the 17th century that the attitude toward profit-making changed. The change came about as a result of urbanization, more centralized societies, the evolution of consumerism, and the growth and advancement of technology and industry with the necessary new social structures.

Initially ethics in business were dominated by the socialists, as a strategy against the "amorality of business thinking" (Solomon, 1993, p. 356). Business thinking was viewed as a threat of the free market to traditional values and private interests eroding the control of government over the public good. There was also primary activity in the theological and religious sectors (De George, 1987). In the 1870s, the social encyclicals of the popes brought forward questions about just wages and the morality of capitalism. These writings were the foundation for Catholic social ethics, with concerns for morality in business as well as other areas. Issues such as the ". . . rights of workers to decent conditions of employment and a living wage; for moral values as opposed to materialistic ones; and for improving the lot of the poor" were raised (De George, 1987, p. 201). These moral issues are still viable for human service organizations today.

However, business ethics in contemporary society are viewed differently. Ethics in business are directed toward understanding the underlying values of business decisions and identifying the ideals of business. For example, the current focus on profit, from an ethical perspective, would be viewed within the context of social responsibility and productivity.

The Profit Motive

The ideal of profit within a context of social responsibility rests on the altruistic motives of corporate executives. Altruism has been challenged in recent years by the spread of "economic imperialism," the pervasive pattern of economic calculations and interest incorporated into domains, such as education, health care, and other human service institutions once regarded as noneconomic (Kanungo & Mendoca, 1996). As an example, students seeking an education in institutions of higher learning no longer consider the search for truth as their primary motivation. Instead, the consideration of salary potential takes precedence. Hospitals, drug manufacturers, and health care providers market health care products and services like cosmetics or furniture, as something to buy rather than something that is part of business's social responsibility with intrinsic value to the well-being of human beings. A recent editorial in the *Denver Post* (O'Brien, 2001, p. 9) provides example. Pharmaceutical firms have been named as defendants in an antitrust suit for practices that included paying generic manufacturers to "... refrain from introducing lower-cost pharmaceuticals" at a time when prices for medications are "soaring." Drug manufacturers also extend their ability to control patent monopolies by tactics that include multiple patents for dosage, color, or form on the same drug. As the editorial points out, these tactics "victimize" older citizens and those with chronic illnesses who routinely take prescription drugs.

The nature of business is broader than economic interests, which is "the myth of the profit motive" (Solomon, 1993, p. 357). The pursuit of profits and the limited focus on the "rights of the stockholders" is a limited and narrow version of the nature of business as, "... an end in itself." Instead, for purposes of business ethics, it is important to assess the richness of motives and activities that are directed toward profits that encourage hard work, build better organizations, and "serve society better." Kanungo and Mendoca (1996, p. 3) echo this view. They note, "Although no one would deny that business must be profitable, the sole preoccupation with profit to the exclusion or neglect of other considerations is no longer acceptable."

Competition

Another myth is the degree to which businesses are competitive. Palmer (1996, p. 200) discusses competitiveness as one of the "monsters" that produce unethical behavior. Ascribing to the "battleground mentality" with language that promotes competition (for example, "wins," "the enemy," and so forth) can be counterproductive. Divisiveness can develop from competition within an organization, such that different units and departments attempt to undercut each other at the expense of the organization.

Although competition is critical to the survival of an organization, Solomon (1993, p. 358) argues that "... Business life is first of all fundamentally cooperative." Shared interests, agreed upon norms of behavior and the location of businesses within a community contribute to the necessity of co-operation as well as competition. Corporate culture as a metaphor captures the social nature of business. It "recognizes the place of people in the organization as the fundamental structure of business life. It openly embraces the idea of ethics. It recognizes that shared values hold a culture together" (Solomon, 1993, p. 358). Further, a corporate culture is inseparable from the larger cultures of community and society. This confronts the tendency to isolate business and business values from the rest of society. As Solomon notes, "Breaking down this sense of isolation is the first task of business ethics" (1993, p. 359).

Social Responsibility

The argument that managers in a corporation have only fiduciary responsibility to the stockholders is fast becoming outdated (Jennings, Callahan, & Wolf, 1987). These ethicists note "stockholders on the average have far less of a stake in the firm than employees, managers, customers, suppliers, and even the community . . ." where the business is located (Jennings, Callahan, & Wolf, 1987, p. 17). Solomon supports this notion and promotes the ideal of social responsibility to "stakeholders" (1993, p. 360). This group is defined as, ". . . All of those who are affected and have legitimate expectations and rights regarding the actions of the company, and these include the employees, the consumers and the suppliers as well as the surrounding community and the society at large." Thus, the social responsibility of a business is part of a primary concern to serve all that are affected by its activities within the free market economy.

The purpose of business is to serve the public through providing needed and desirable products and services. However, business must protect the public from harm that could result from unsafe products, and the activities and processes necessary for the production of goods and services. The ethical dilemmas for business related to public service are related to the quality and safety of products and services, threats to the environment, and harmful or deceptive advertising strategies (Solomon, 1993).

Responsibility to Employees

Working conditions, roles, and responsibilities of employees bring forward ethical issues in business. Subsistence wages, lack of appropriate space, and demeaning work environments cause conflicts between the "commodity" model of labor and employee rights. Employee loyalty to the corporation is impacted by the previous conditions. In addition, conflict between corporate values and personal values develops when employees are expected to meet demands they ascertain are unethical or immoral. The person identified as a "whistleblower" is often a result of this circumstance. There are contemporary examples in the recent disclosures about ENRON, WorldCom, and other corporate scandals where employees have come forward about unethical practices.

Corporate Ethics

The problems of corporate ethics are centered on three aspects: ". . . the development of the executive as a moral person; the influence of organization as a moral environment; and the actions needed to map a high road to economic and ethical performance—and to mount guardrails to keep corporate wayfarers on track" (Andrews, 1989, p. 99). These aspects encompass the focus on leadership; on the structures and processes of the organization; and the values, principles, and guidelines necessary to promote ethical behavior in corporations and in human service organizations. Given the privatization of the public sector, leaders must be prepared to manage and administer human services in for-profit, not-for-profit, and public agencies. What are the commonalties and differences in relation to ethical issues for professional leaders such as social workers and business leaders?

The Intersection of Social Services and Business Ethics

The line between public social service agencies and for-profit businesses is no longer distinct. Privatization of the human service sector has changed the nature of the service delivery system. The luxury of professionally administered nonprofit and public agencies, with a public mandate to provide human services that emphasize quality, a comprehensive continuum of care, and full access to services for vulnerable populations, is rapidly disappearing. Traditional social service providers compete with for-profit corporations to address human services needs. A new paradigm for the human service delivery system is now a reality.

Privatization is the process of transferring government systems and roles to private business (Fisher & Karger, 1997). In the process a, ". . . reorientation of political, social, economic, and cultural institutions to corporate needs, values, goals, and leaders," occurs (Fisher & Karger, 1997, p. 11). Four critical elements accompany this change in policy, according to Fisher and Karger (1997):

1. Economic issues such as cost-savings, cost-effectiveness, or profit become the first priority.
2. Private businesses become the preference for the allocation of social choices, rather than public policy.
3. Public institutions are viewed as supplemental to the private market, and must integrate the private sector as participants in a major way.
4. Public or not-for-profit programs adopt and model themselves after the methods of for-profit, private businesses.

These elements have the potential to alter the mission of social work fundamentally in the provision of services, if not addressed as moral issues by human service leaders. The intersection of public and nonprofit social service delivery and private, for-profit business provides for both commonalties and differences in relation to ethics. The following discussion highlights the issues that are of interest in relation to the ethics of public and private human service delivery. Ethical responsibilities that are common to all of the previous organizational types include *social responsibility*, *operational efficiency*, and the *moral obligations of work*. The ethical responsibilities that are different between private, for-profit and voluntary, nonprofit and public organizations include *values*, *organizational bases of power*, and the *role of the board of directors*.

Social Responsibility

Both private and public organizations have a social responsibility to the community. Public and nonprofit agencies have a mandate to serve the community. Public agencies provide programs and services that meet the criteria of mandated standards (through legislation and policy), according to the stated mission or purpose for the agency's existence. Nonprofit agencies have as their primary purpose to ". . . maximize the social goods they produce for both society and the people who participate in them. Social goods are the end, the fundamental purpose or mission, for which nonprofit organizations exist and the basis of their legitimacy" (Nanus & Dobbs, 1999, p. 38). Such agencies have a great capacity to contribute to the public good through expansion of services, creating entrepreneurial public/private partnerships, and discovering and developing services for new, unaddressed social needs.

Private organizations, according to Drucker (1968, p. 461), also have a responsibility to society:

> What is most important is that management realize that it must consider the impact of every business policy and business action upon society. It has to consider whether the action is likely to promote the public good, to advance the basic beliefs of our society, to contribute to its stability, strength and harmony.

The "new theory" of corporate responsibility for the public good challenges the right to make a profit as a relative right, subservient to at least a "moral minimum" that regulates everyone's activity in society (Jennings, Callahan, & Wolf, 1987). Corporations must now take on their duties of citizenship and routinely evaluate the potential contributions and harms to society. In recognition of this responsibility, private, for-profit businesses have begun to emphasize the importance of organizational codes of ethics, value statements, and the ethical actions of their leaders.

Social responsibility is also promoted through agency practices and technology. Human service organizations, both public and private are "moral entrepreneurs," in that they are in a position of influencing social policy and the institutional environment through the practices used in the delivery of services (Hasenfeld, 1992, p. 11). Public perceptions about the nature and capacities of consumers are affected by the moral categorization of clients. For example, mental health clinics that adopt an empowerment model enacted through partnership with clients promote messages to the community about client competency and at the same time combat stigma about mental illness.

Operational Efficiency

Private businesses have to perform in response to market pressure to secure their profitability. Strategies include improving the quantity and quality of services and reducing costs. Public-sector leaders are more likely to prioritize fairness and inclusiveness in their operations in order to allow for the fullest democratic participation of the public (Petrick & Quinn, 1997). Nonprofit and for-profit social service agencies are increasingly caught up in cost-containment policies that have ". . . Assumed the quality of a primary value" (Joseph, 1983). Policy that rests on the value of cost-containment has a substantial influence on service delivery. For example, intake and termination policies can have a dramatic effect on access to services. The choice of practice models based on the value of cost-efficiency affects practice decisions in relation to effectiveness versus expediency (for example, short-term models of care may be applied universally though they are effective with only particular populations with particular problems). Programs are reduced or sometimes dissolved altogether to ensure the fiscal survival of the agency. In addition, when downsizing does occur, adequate preparation of clients and employees is not always provided, adding to the ethical quagmire (Reisch & Taylor, 1983).

Moral Obligations of Work

Both social work and business leaders are responsible for the ethical challenges that are inherent in relationships with employees who work in the organization. The policies and procedures of the organization, hiring process, supervisory arrangements, termination policies, salary classification systems, promotion opportunities, and use of power through relationships with constituents are examples of areas that create potential ethical dilemmas in relationships with employees. Ethical responsibilities related to fairness, justice, and trust develop within these areas. As one manager said, "Anything that messes with someone else's life is an ethical dilemma . . ." (Manning, 1990, p. 189).

There is a difference, however, for public and nonprofit organizations. Dilemmas that occur in relation to the good of the employee versus the good of the agency or versus the good of the client cause frequent ethical conflicts for human service leaders that are different from business leaders, who work with products. Managers feel a responsibility to protect their staff, and for the most part, only the best interests of the client supersede that priority (Manning, 1990). An upper administrator stated "The most difficult is firing someone who's not mean or vicious—just incompetent . . . Who am I working for, staff or clients? . . . Answer . . . clients" (Manning, 1990, p. 189).

Treating employees respectfully is part of an ethical relationship. A frequent dilemma of people in leadership is whether to empower staff through informing and including them in decisions versus protecting or excluding them from disruptive information. The added conflict is the protection of the organization from staff reaction to potentially disruptive information and the feedback that can occur from that (Manning, 1990).

The occupational ethics of administrators in business and human services have a commonality: that they do their job right based on an understanding of organizational processes and theories and are successful in achieving the goals and purposes of the organization (Levy, 1982). However, Levy argues that, "It is not only what works that commands their attention, but also what they agree they owe to others by way of occupational duty" (Levy, 1982, p. 21). Occupational ethics requires an emphasis on the ethical obligations inherent in a leader's relationship with employees.

The following areas are more divergent in focus, priority, or strategy. The next discussions demonstrate some of the differences between types of organizations.

Values

The values that organizations ascribe to are reflected through the administrative and managerial actions and decisions that make up the operations of the system. An important distinction for social services is that these organizations have particular values associated with the nature of the services provided. The values associated with the service, empowerment, for example, should then be congruent with all of the "internal operations and relationships of the organization" (Levy, 1979, p. 280). Every administrator's actions, ideally, are guided by those core values.

Further, social work leaders are also guided by the values of the profession. The code of ethics identifies several core values that should guide the practice of social work in any practice capacity. Those values include *service, social justice, dignity* and *worth of the person,* the *importance of human relationships, integrity,* and *competence* (NASW, 1996). Finally, the public or nonprofit leader is responsible for the diverse values of the community that are articulated through a personal and democratic process. These values become lost when values are reduced to economic considerations only (Petrick & Quinn, 1997).

Private, for-profit businesses, on the other hand, have as their primary goal to *maximize market value.* This may include increasing shareholders investment value, expanding market share, producing profits, and providing products and services for those with the resources to invest and purchase (Petrick & Quinn, 1997). The actions and decisions of these leaders are influenced by the value of optimizing market share. This "reductionist economic value system" (Petrick & Quinn, 1997, p. 16) reflects an underlying assumption that labor, products/services, and shares of stock can all be interpreted through concrete economic values as Petrick & Quinn (1997, p. 16) note, ". . . Everything and everyone has a price."

The contradiction between social work and business values is one of the main contradictions of contemporary society and social work ethics, according to Alexander (1985). This contradiction is most apparent through the privatization of human service organizations. Alexander (1985, p. 6) labels it the "accountability contradiction": the corruption of administrative technology in human services by demanding the application of business management values in the provision of services for social needs. There is the ongoing danger of giving in to the "lure of efficiency" without understanding the ultimate outcome, which is the activation of hidden value premises of the market that are activated through the application of such technology.

Organizational Sources of Power

Leaders in both social work and business have a responsibility to multiple constituencies: consumers of services; employees; community representatives; and other economic, political, and social entities. However, business leaders base their source of power on meeting the *economic wants and needs of the buying public*. If they are providing what community citizens want, they are meeting their responsibilities. However, the "wants" of those who are unable to participate in the buying public because of poverty or other disadvantages are not necessarily met due to restricted participation.

The source of power for public leaders is based on citizen participation through the ability to vote their preferences, even if they lack buying power (Petrick and Quinn, 1997). In addition, public agencies are accountable to taxpayers for the services produced. The source of power for a nonprofit agency rests in the agreement with the community that is served, reflected through the mission and directed through community representatives on the board of directors. For example, the representatives on the board of a mental health center may include consumers of mental health services, consumer advocates (for example, Alliance for the Mentally Ill), as well as other community citizens. Involvement in this level of decision capacity provides opportunities to shape the service delivery system.

Organizational Sources of Governance

For-profit boards of directors are different from nonprofit boards. Both kinds of boards provide control, service, and strategy for the organization. For-profit boards have as a primary responsibility the alignment of "the interests of management with those of shareholders" (Brower & Shrader, 2000, p. 148). For-profit boards sometimes have demands that are in conflict, such as making the greatest profits for shareholders and at the same time being a good community citizen, or producing the highest quality product at a competitive price diverts their responsibility to employees. These conflictual demands are sometimes used to justify immoral or unethical decisions and actions (Klein, 1991). In addition, there is "significant financial compensation" for directors to serve on a for-profit board, which complicates the motivation to make the most "selfless" decision about ethical issues (Brower & Shrader, 2000). Finally, information about the operations of a for-profit business are typically more unavailable to public scrutiny.

Nonprofit board members are volunteers and are not paid for their time. They usually are motivated to give service because of altruistic reasons, for example, giving back to the community, helping a disadvantaged population, or helping an agency that has helped them before (Brower & Shrader, 2000). In addition, the mission of the organization is usually connected to service of some sort to the community or to a particular clientele. The lack of a money-making motive makes it easier to fulfill the obligation of protecting the best interests of all stakeholders (Brower & Shrader, 2000, p. 147). Operating funds for the organization they direct are raised through charitable donations and community fund-raisers, which heightens the "sense of accountability" to represent the agency honestly and to be concerned for the best interests of all stakeholders: community, employees, and consumers (Brower & Shrader, 2000, p. 148).

Duties of the Profession.   Social work (or other professional) leaders/administrators are also accountable for the ethics of their profession, or what Levy (1982, p. 22) refers to as ". . . the hazards of dual identity." The professional administrators must not only be accountable for administrative ethics, but also for the expectations of their profession, and, as mentioned in the discussion about dilemmas, the ethics of administration and the ethics of a profession can, at times, be in conflict.

The mission in the social work code of ethics emphasizes the "historic and enduring commitment to enhancing well-being and helping meet the basic needs of all people with particular attention to the needs and empowerment of people who are vulnerable, oppressed and living in poverty" (Reamer, 1998, p. 494). It is this commitment to all people, particularly those who are vulnerable and oppressed, that makes the ethical requirements for human services leaders different from that of business.

Conclusion

The focus of discussion in this chapter is the context where leaders in human services make ethical decisions. The unique nature and characteristics of human service organizations provide the environment for the ethical nature of the decisions that are made there. The circumstances that produce some of the most intractable dilemmas provide another part of the context of human services: the interrelationship between the leader, the organization, and the environmental and moral influences that are ongoing. History gives us a perspective of the development of ethics in social work and in business and provides the foundation for the direction that both social work and business leaders must initiate as part of the leadership role. A comparison of some of the central ethical themes tells the story that there is no place to hide from ethics. Leaders in nonprofit and public organizations will experience many of the same ethical dilemmas as leaders in private for-profit businesses. A discussion of the intersection of social work and business is provided because of the increasing combination of private, for-profit, private nonprofit, and public agencies delivering human services. The issues that are similar and different can be informative in considering the duty of leadership in every human service organization. Leaders can anticipate working in any of these. The theoretical models they choose will inform their role within these organizations. The next chapter provides an overview of such leadership theories and the relationship to ethical leadership.

QUESTIONS AND APPLICATIONS

1. Consider the unique characteristics of human service organizations from the perspective of structurally negative effects of human services posited by McKnight, 1989.
   - In what ways does our organization emphasize the deficiencies of consumers?
   - In what ways does your organization reduce either the cash income or market choices of consumers?
   - In what ways does the delivery of services decrease participation of clients in community life?
   - In what ways does your organization's participation in an organizational environment (as part of an aggregate of human service organizations) increase the dependency of consumers on services rather than the community? Or neutralize the positive effects of individual programs because of the proliferation of human services?

2. Consider the most recent version of the Social Work Code of Ethics (see Appendix C). What are one or two principles that should be developed and codified for organizational and community practitioners that are not currently in the code? What is the nature of the ethical issue or duty you have chosen? How does the contemporary literature address this issue(s)?

3. What is a current example in your agency of one or more of the circumstances that produce dilemmas discussed earlier in the chapter? How has this dilemma affected your leadership?

4. How have privatization and an increased pressure for revenue generation impacted you as an ethical leader?

5. How should leadership of a for-profit organization balance the responsibility of increasing return to the shareholders and also meeting the social responsibilities of the organization? What are the current tensions in regard to profit in your organization? What should be changed?

3 Ethical Leadership Through Transformation

- The need for ethical leadership
- Definitions of leadership
- Two leadership paradigms: transactional and transformational
- The moral dimensions of leadership
- The moral responsibilities of leadership
- Characteristics/attributes for ethical leadership

Leadership is in the literature spotlight in business and in the public professions. As we move into the new millennium, there is an emphasis on the need for leadership and the complexities of developing effective moral leadership. In our postmodern society, chaos and corruption prevail. Organizations are created while others go out of business. Programs that are effective and necessary are eliminated, while profit-making programs that serve those who have the least need find a solid market share. Social policy initiatives that have great promise fail. Leaders, even with "good intentions, and moral convictions, even with technical competence," do not always achieve success (Dobel, 1998, p. 74). From a realist perspective, it is argued that leaders cannot afford ethics in this world of increasing responsibilities, political and economic intimidation, and competitive interests. However, an alternative view would argue that leaders should follow the requirements of ethics. Improvement in ethical decision-making can reduce costs associated with unethical workplace conduct, can prevent the erosion of integrity, and can contribute to increased profitability and a better organizational culture (Petrick & Quinn, 1997). Further, ethical leadership leads to the development of quality human services, empowered consumers and community citizens, and committed employees.

Leadership is a somewhat amorphous concept that is often inclusive of many different types of roles: administrative, managerial, political, and activist, among others. Most of the roles connected to leadership have a degree of authority or power that is attached to leading. It is the use, and/or the abuse, of that power and authority that adds an inherent ethical implication to leadership (discussed extensively in Chapter 4). The ethical aspects of leadership are more than power holding and power wielding; also important to the leader are the motives, aspirations, and higher needs of constituents that are necessary to engage the full person in meaningful contributions to self, organization, and community.

Two major paradigms of leadership theory are discussed in the literature, transactional and transformational, each with related assumptions, values, and philosophies. The transformational paradigm offers a congruence with the previous elements of social work leadership (discussed in Chapter 1) and offers the promise of moral and ethical leadership, or leadership that ". . . Can produce social change that will satisfy followers' authentic needs" (Burns, 1978, p. 4). Transformational leadership will be the lens for all the subsequent chapters. The concepts, values, and assumptions that are discussed here will reappear throughout this book, in relationship with the critical responsibilities of leadership.

Definitions of Leadership

Leadership has been defined in the leadership literature in many ways, based on many different theories that have evolved over several decades. Further, as leadership theory has become more pronounced, a blurring of the terms—leadership and management—has occurred. Sometimes one is used in place of the other. The concept of leadership has evolved from the "functional task" focus of management to a "transforming personal" focus. Ritchie (1988, p. 171) states, "I regard management as taking care of things—money, inventory, equipment, production processes—while I define a leader as one who develops people. Things are managed; people are led."

Burns (1978) comments that more than 130 definitions are found in one study on leadership alone. Two contemporary definitions capture the essence of ethical leadership based on the emphasis of relationship and use of power between leader(s) and constituents. First, Gardner (1990, p. 1) defines leadership as ". . . The process of persuasion or example by which an individual or team induces a group to pursue objectives held by the leader or shared by the leader and constituents." Persuasion implies the use of argument, or reasoning, to achieve commitment to the purpose or objectives. A reasoning process has implicit within its definition the possibility of logic, such as sharing of the facts, discussing the purpose, relating the issue to a contextual background, and identifying potential negatives and benefits of the objectives. Persuasion also implies the dialogue necessary for "voice," the *speaking and listening* referred to in the discussion about vision later in this chapter. Leaders who persuade are acknowledging constituents' *choice* to pursue objectives, or a more equal distribution of power. The use of "example" provides for leaders as role models, demonstrating important values and behaviors by "walking their talk." Ethical standards and values are more easily learned through a leader creating the opportunity for reflection and analysis, as well as modeling the desired values and behaviors (Joseph, 1991).

The second definition, a social work definition of leadership, includes the elements necessary for social work in the new millennium: "Social work leadership is the communication of vision, guided by the NASW Code of Ethics, to create proactive processes that empower individuals, families, groups, organizations, and communities" (Rank & Hutchison, 2000, p. 14). This definition accentuates the elements necessary for social change from a social work perspective, including an ability to anticipate, communicate and shape future directions; an ethical distribution and use of power; and the importance of collective goals. The social work definition of leadership is congruent with a transformational theory of leadership. However, for the sake of comparison, and to help readers make distinctions about the leadership theories they have learned, a brief discussion of both transactional and transformational leadership paradigms follows.

Leadership Paradigms

There are extensive amounts of literature on leadership theories, models, and characteristics. The following discussion does not provide detail about specific theories, but instead describes two paradigms of leadership that can be compared and contrasted in relation to moral and ethical issues of leadership. The two paradigms encompass many theories and models. The point is to bring forward the important underlying values and assumptions of each paradigm. Readers must evaluate how these paradigms fit with their own leadership approach and the integration of ethics into that approach (see Table 3.1).

The transformational paradigm is presented as a leadership paradigm that holds great potential for incorporating values and ethics into the daily process of leading. However, first the transactional paradigm will be discussed. This paradigm contains some of the early, landmark theories of leadership and is still prevalent in organizations today.

Transactional Leadership Theory

Transactional theories are "*means-oriented*" theories (Burns, 1978). The focus of the theory is on the transaction, or the "means" to arrive at a particular goal or objective within an organization. A transactional mode of leadership is ". . . The reciprocal process of mobilizing, by persons with certain motives and values, various economic, political, and other resources, in a context of competition and conflict, in order to realize goals independently or mutually held by both leaders and followers" (Burns, 1978, p. 425). Transactional leaders are focused on creating a bargain for individual interests who eventually go their separate ways, rather than the mutual effort of people who are interested in collective interests and have a common purpose.

The leader engages others (employees, agencies, or consumers) through *an exchange* of valued things—salary, rewards, perks, material resources, such as space or fixtures, furniture, status, promotional opportunities, incentives, and so forth—for

TABLE 3.1 Comparison of Transactional and Transformational Theories

	Transactional	Transformational
	Means oriented based on exchange	*Ends oriented based on transformational collective purposes through relationships*
Assumptions	Employees motivated by safety, security, and belonging	Employees motivated by growth, potential, self-actualization, moral purposes, ability to move to better selves
Appeal	Appeals to employee self-interest	Appeals to higher ideas and moral values
Values	Honesty, fairness, responsibility, honoring of commitments and reciprocity	End values of liberty, justice, equality, peace, and humanitarianism
Goals	Meets the individual goals of leaders and followers	Meets collective purposes and goals
Leadership	Discrete acts and behaviors	Visioning, relationship, communication of moral purpose, and critical values
Problemsolving	Found in leader	Focused on leaders and constituents; mutual responsibility
Distribution of power	"Power-over"—using rewards conceived and legitimate bases	"Power-with"—using expert, referent and inspirational bases
Influence	Unidirectional—leader to follower	Multidimensional—distributed among all in work environment

accomplishment of tasks, responsibilities, or duties. The objective of the exchange or transaction is to get compliance (for example, from employees) to accomplish the objective through their particular job responsibilities and tasks. Each person recognizes the differences in the level of power and the attitudes of the other. Each has an individual purpose that is related to the other's by virtue of both purposes being advanced through the bargaining process. However, beyond this, the bargainers do not have an enduring purpose that binds the relationship.

An underlying assumption of this paradigm is that employees are motivated by *safety*, *security*, and *belonging*. The transaction appeals to employee self-interest (for example, pay and status is exchanged for work effort). The organization supplies the necessary environment and reward system in exchange for the employee's labor. The values relevant to an exchange are *honesty*, *fairness*, *responsibility*, *honoring of commitments*, and *reciprocity*, or what Burns (1978) refers to as "modal values." These are the values of "means" and ensure that transactional leading will work. This paradigm can contribute to human purpose by meeting the individual goals of leaders and followers (such as basic survival needs) that may then contribute to achieving goals that are higher in value (such as aesthetic needs).

This paradigm can also appeal to fear, greed, hatred, and jealousy. These emotions are initiated through the individualistic and competitive assumptions of transactions. Transactions are made on the basis of self-interest and organizational interest. Reward systems such as incentives and "merit bonuses" can promote a sense of competition; employees work against each other for the limited rewards, rather than with each other for a common goal.

The functions of leadership within this paradigm take place through *discrete acts and behaviors*. The tasks, activities, and daily decisions become the stage for leading. Problemsolving in the organization is focused on the leader, rather than on the group. There is an overemphasis on power in this paradigm; leaders use reward, coercive, and legitimate bases of power to "perpetuate the status quo" (Petrick & Quinn, 1997, p. 219). Often total power or coercive power is associated with the leader. The leader exerts an authoritarian style of power—*power-over*—in relation to constituents. Often this power is vested through the authority assigned to the particular position of the leader in the organization. The use of influence is mostly one way from the leader to the constituent. Examples of transactional theories include trait theory, behavioral theories (for example, Blake and Mouton (1964), task and relationship; Hershey and Blanchard (1977), initiating structure and consideration), situational theories (Robert House (1971), path-goal theory; Fielder (1978), contingency theory), Weber's theory of bureaucracy (1947; 1978), and the decisionmaking theories of Herbert Simon (1976) and Vroom Yetton (1964) among many others. The characteristics and strategies of transactional theories are missing the dimensions of direction and ethics that are represented through a transformational approach.

Transformational Leadership Theory

Transformational leadership (Burns, 1978; Gardner, 1990) is a theory about ends rather than means. Transformational theories add the dimensions of *direction* (vision/purpose), *ethics/morality*, and *spirituality*. Transformational leadership has the capacity to ". . . shape and alter and elevate the motives and values and goals of followers through the vital *teaching* role of leadership" (Burns, 1978, p. 425). An important underlying assumption of transforming leadership is that people can be united in the pursuit of higher goals. Realizing the goals results in significant change that represents the combined interests of leaders and constituents (Burns, 1978). Thus, a transformational definition of leadership provides for social change, implies a value for shared interests, and strives for a higher level of moral and ethical behavior within the organization. Important benefits result from this kind of leadership. The shared interests and collective vision support the decision process of the organization. Thus, ". . . the major decisions that move . . . organizations toward the greater good are those that create a new reality for both their clients and for the community they serve" (Nanus & Dobbs, 1999, p. 141). Employees, or constituents, also benefit from this new reality through the process of their work.

Transformational leadership focuses on engaging people through *relationship*; leaders and constituents, through the pursuit of goals, raise each other to higher levels of motivation and morality. This engagement is directed toward *achieving a partic-*

ular end or purpose, but the process of working toward the purpose also has the potential to achieve individual ends as well. This characteristic provides an *emancipatory* nature to leadership whereby there is the potential to change the status quo of individuals, the organization, and the community. The influence process occurs between individuals and also has an institutional level process, that is, mobilizing power to change social systems and reform institutions. On the institutional level, leaders are involved in shaping, expressing, and mediating conflict among groups of people, within and external to the organization.

This approach dismantles the traditional hierarchy. The focus is on the *empowerment* of people to generate meaning in their work, and through their work to find meaning in their lives. Leadership is a *process* rather than a series of discrete acts. It is a ". . . stream of evolving interrelationships in which leaders are continuously evoking motivational responses from followers and modifying their [the leader's] behavior as they meet responsiveness or resistance, in a ceaseless process of flow and counterflow" (Burns, 1978, p. 440). In this process of relationship, power and influence are mutual and reciprocal; it is "*power-with*" rather than "power-over." Leaders use expert and referent power to implement change. The leader promotes the development of self-efficacy and internalized shared values by constituents. The result is cooperative networks of empowered constituents that have an investment in moving the organization forward (Petrick & Quinn, 1997).

Transforming leadership can be used by anyone in the organization, in any type or level of position. Thus, all employees, consumers of service, and others have the potential to lead in addition to the formalized leadership. People can influence their peers, supervisors, or supervisees through the relational component that follows the formal and informal lines of communication. Transforming leadership occurs in the day-to-day acts of ordinary people, but is not an ordinary or common way of being. Influence is exercised from a base of inspiration, rather than influence based on legitimated authority, respect for rules, and the traditions of the bureaucracy.

Leaders appeal to higher ideas and moral values. There is the assumption that we can move from our everyday selves to better selves. The values relevant to transformation are what Burns (1978) refers to as "end-values." They include *liberty, justice, equality, peace*, and *humanitarianism*. These values appeal to a *collective* purpose: the common good. The collective, rather than individual focus, generates commitment to the purpose. As Burns (1978, p. 426) notes, "Leaders and followers are engaged in a common enterprise; they are dependent on each other, their fortunes rise and fall together, they share the results of planned change together."

Finally, transforming leadership has impact at the institutional level, according to Burns (1978). Here leading is concerned with shaping, expressing, and mediating conflict through organizational culture and empowerment. Organizational values are defined and integrated into ethical cultures. Power is mobilized to change systems and reform the institution. Leadership at the institutional level has the potential to create a higher level of morality at all levels of the organization, as a result of everyone's influence.

Transformational approaches include charismatic, servant, visionary, and feminist approaches, among others. Transformational theorists include Burns, John

Gardner, Bert Nanus, Warren Bennis, Houzes and Posner, Tichy and Devanna, Marshall Sashkin, Sally Helgesen, Margaret Wheatley, and many others. The assumptions, values, and concepts discussed by these theorists are congruent with the elements identified as necessary for social work leadership in the new millennium.

The Moral Dimensions of Transformational Leadership

Transformational leadership provides a coherent framework for the elements of the social work definition of leadership mentioned earlier: vision, ethics, proactive processes, and empowerment. All of these elements are considered relevant and necessary to transformational leadership. These elements are discussed in relation to the dimensions of transformational leadership. The dimensions that follow include the dimensions of *direction*, *assessed vision*, *proactive processes*, and *empowerment*.

The Direction Dimension of Leadership— Vision and Voice

Think of a vision as a road map for something desired for the future. Vision for an organization provides the ability to portray some definite possibility that has not yet been achieved (Green, 1987). The vision "invites entrance" into the future through the committed efforts of leaders and constituents. A vision is congruent with the organizational mission; working toward accomplishing a vision is taking a step closer to the mission. The vision provides leaders and constituents with a purpose to work toward: a preferred future. The vision becomes a tool to incorporate the moral and social responsibility of the leader, constituents, and the organization. The moral ends that people commit to achieving become a valued and meaningful purpose for work. The personal commitment and ownership in the organization's vision transforms the experience of work from a job to a calling.

Wheatley and Kellner-Rogers (1998) build on the importance of purpose in a discussion about community. The clarity about the purpose changes the nature of relationships.

> This type of community does not ask people to forfeit their freedom as a condition of belonging. It avoids the magnetic pull of proscribing behaviors and beliefs, it avoids becoming doctrinaire and dictatorial, it stays focused on what its members are trying to create together, and diversity flourishes within it. Belonging together is defined by a shared sense of purpose, not by shared beliefs about specific behaviors (Wheatley & Kellner-Rogers, 1998, p. 15).

This kind of community in an organization is founded on a passion to achieve a moral purpose and celebrates all of the unique contributions that unite people in accomplishing the vision.

Vision as Fields of Energy

Vision can be thought of as a destination, but Wheatley (1999) suggests vision is more conceptually powerful when considered as a metaphor of "fields." Fields of energy enable leaders to convey ideas and values; fields provide ". . . conceptual controls . . . it is the *ideas of business* that are controlling, not some manager with authority" (Wheatley, 1999, p. 57). Leaders can use the field metaphor to express and model meaning, seeking in the process a deeper level of morality and integrity through words and acts. The metaphor of a radio beacon tower transmitting information throughout the organization ". . . stating, clarifying, reflecting, modeling, filling all of the spaces with the messages we care about" (Wheatley, 1999, p. 57) is a helpful illustration of fields. However, transmission of ideas cannot be a one-way process.

Physicist Evelyn Fox Keller argues that metaphors of vision reflect the traditional western notions of science (Helgesen, 1990, p. 223). The metaphors of "illumination," "to see the light," a "clear view," and so forth convey an abstract perspective that is one-dimensional. That is, seeing is a one-way process that does not acknowledge the relationship component of leading. Helgesen (1990) introduces the idea of "voice" as necessary to relationship and interconnectedness with others. Voice, as a metaphor of speaking and listening, brings in the contextual issues related to the complexity of human beings. Speaking and listening are basic elements of interaction. "What is heard always influences what is said" (Helgesen, 1990, p. 223). Therefore, although vision can define the ends or purposes of an organization, it is voice that is "the means for getting it across . . . through voice, value for connectedness is nurtured" (Helgesen, 1990, p. 223). The vision conveyed by leaders, then, can be conveyed through fields of ideas *and* provide for feedback and involvement of others through voice by *speaking* and *listening* (see Figure 3.1).

Assessed Vision—The Moral and Ethical Dimension of Leadership

Leadership from a transformational perspective is not value neutral. Instead, ethical considerations are intrinsic to the role and responsibility of the leader. Professional leaders have a contract with the public to successfully fulfill the mission of the organization according to the values and principles of their profession. For example, social work leaders must be able to envision and then enact the purpose and values of social work as intrinsic to their work. Professionals, to make sense of everyday practice, must understand the *point of the profession* (Green, 1987).

The Point of the Profession

Assessed vision includes the point of a profession the ethical mandates that are embedded in the profession's values and mission. Professions that have ethical problems are reflecting a problem in conceptualizing the point of the profession. In fact, Green argues that the term, "professional ethics," is an oxymoron. The redundancy of the

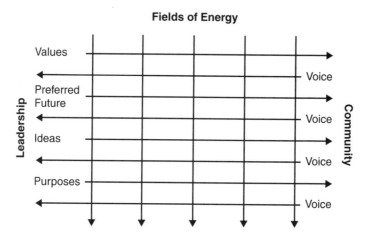

FIGURE 3.1   Vision Through Fields of Energy

phrase reflects a commitment to the "fallacy of displacement," a failure to see or understand the point of the profession. Professional education is focused on teaching the theories and skills of practice. However, the *point* of the skill(s) or application of a particular theory is sometimes not emphasized. For example, future managers and administrators are often taught the skills of budgeting and planning, but not *the point* of budgeting and planning, which is a principal means of making values concrete and distributing goods in an ethical manner.

To be a member of a profession implies a kind of practice that is not incidental, but essentially a moral enterprise. The norms and values of a profession must be derived from the moral purpose. Green (1987, p. 181) states ". . . (a profession) is always practiced in response to some fundamental human need or social good whose advancement is already a moral aim." The NASW Code of Ethics (1996, p. 1) puts forward the social work profession's moral aim in the form of a preamble that explicates the mission of social work:

> The primary mission of the social work profession is to enhance human well-being and help meet the basic human needs of all people, with particular attention to the needs and empowerment of people who are vulnerable, oppressed, and living in poverty. A historic and defining feature of social work is the profession's focus on individual well-being in a social context and the well-being of society. Fundamental to social work is attention to the environmental forces that create, contribute to, and address problems in living.
>
> Social workers promote social justice and social change with and on behalf of clients [individuals, families, groups, organizations, and communities]. Social workers are sensitive to cultural and ethnic diversity and strive to end discrimination, oppression, poverty, and other forms of social injustice . . . Social workers seek to enhance the capacity of people to address their own needs. Social workers also seek to promote the responsiveness of organizations, communities, and other social institutions to individuals' needs and social problems (see Appendix C).

The previous mission is rooted in six core values that provide the foundation for the purpose of social work:

- Service
- Social justice
- Dignity and worth of the person
- Importance of human relationships
- Integrity
- Competence

The mission of the profession, combined with the previous values provides a moral framework for leadership in social service organizations. Leaders must conceptualize the *point* of their practice and draw from the mission and values of social work to develop and enact the moral dimension of their work. The visioning process and the metaphor of voice are part of the process of transmitting that conceptualization. However, the process of adhering to the mission and values of a profession is not as simple as it seems. Practice takes place within a social environment that has a profound effect on leadership and that effect is reciprocal.

Proactive Processes of Ethical Leadership

Transformational leadership offers an approach that is centered on relationships with constituents. Membership in the organization as *community* becomes central to facilitating the moral development of individuals and the organization. In addition, the *processes of interaction* between leaders and constituents contain ethical implications. Leadership is always carried on within a community of some kind, and the leader is a member of that community. For leaders of human services, there are multiple communities (employees, consumers, and citizens) of membership. Memberships are a form of attachment that change over time. Some are temporary, and some are more durable. Membership in a community provides the context for creating a *conscience of community* (Green, 1987) and an *ethics of intimacy* (Toulmin, 1981).

Conscience of Community.   The ethics of organizations cannot be the responsibility of leaders by themselves. People from all levels and roles must take responsibility for ethical issues. People in the organizational community can develop "a way of thinking about organizations, leadership, and membership which respects and supports ethical relationships" (Ritchie, 1988, p. 181). The conscience of an organizational community starts with the *attachment* of membership. This attachment is always forged by social norms, which help us to determine the limits and constraints on behavior and to develop judgment about what is right or wrong and good or bad (Green, 1987). Social norms help individuals as *members* critically evaluate the behavior and processes of the community and themselves. Thus, social norms that develop as results of membership are critical to what Green calls "the conscience of membership." Leaders and constituents participate in creating, evaluating, and shaping the social norms of the organization toward increasingly more ethical behaviors, decisions, and policies (see Chapters 9 and 10 on organizational culture).

Ethics of Intimacy.   The work of leaders in creating community within the organization helps to facilitate moral relationships that can be based on *discretion*, rather than dictated by rules. Toulmin (1981) argues that there is a sharp difference between the *ethics of relationships with intimates* or associates and the ethics of strangers. Ethical dilemmas with people who are less known or out of our circle of intimates prompt a return to general ethical principles for guidance. Ethical issues with associates allow for reasonableness or responsiveness rather than the imposition of uniformity or equality. He describes a view posited by Tolstoy of the moral universe as "Only as far as a person can walk . . . by taking the train, a moral agent leaves the sphere of truly moral actions for a world of strangers" (Toulmin, 1981, p. 34). Working in a community of intimates provides for allowances for personalities, situations, and preferences; there is the potential for the use of discretion and judgment in ethical choices. Relationships between strangers require respect for moral and ethical rules, rather than discretion, in order to ensure equity and trust.

The leader's focus on developing community through the relationships of the organization provides an opportunity for the development of ethical cultures. In this developmental process, members are educated and informed about the nature of moral and ethical behaviors and decisions, which increases their moral development and the ethical climate of the organization. Further, leaders and constituents can model the balancing of conflicting values and situational characteristics through the use of judgment and discretion. The resulting empowerment of members and ethical impact on the organization reinforce the nature of community.

The postindustrial model of leadership developed by Rost (1991, 1993) builds on transformational leadership and emphasizes the *partnership* between leaders and followers. The focus of this approach rests on the choices of the community in pursuit of the common good. Rost argues that leaders must be attuned to ethical decisions, policies, and programs, but must also have an *ethical process* in doing so. An ethical process would include the following criteria. First, the influence that is exerted with constituents should be based on persuasion, not coercion, and should flow in both directions. The element of choice should be a part of participation, that is, people must be able to choose to participate. Finally, goals are created jointly through open discussion, with the opportunity for disagreement and debate. Rost (1991, p. 161) offers an ethical standard of the process of leadership as ". . . ethical if the people in the relationship (the leaders and followers) freely agree that the intended changes fairly reflect their mutual purposes." This standard represents an implied value of empowerment for leaders as a process and as an outcome for the organizational community.

Empowerment

Empowerment as a concept has been elucidated and applied in almost every field from business to mental health and from social work to community psychology. Torre

(1985, p. 180) defines empowerment as "... a process through which people become strong enough to participate within, share control of, and influence events and institutions affecting their lives ... ." A philosophy of empowerment on the part of leadership can enhance the competence and contributions of employees and service consumers. More important, empowerment as a part of leadership has ethical implications.

The transformational influence process as noted in the section on proactive processes involves relationships among and between people. Most religious traditions support the ideal of love your neighbor (Kanungo & Mendoca, 1996). Love in this sense is the affirmation of other people and the ability to give the gift of the self. This love, through giving, is also self-affirming. Leaders affirm others through *promoting the growth and development* of constituents, and through creating working conditions and cultures that promote empowerment. Further, the nature of work contains an ethical imperative. Work is not just a way to support oneself and one's family. Work is ...

> "... an essential means of self-development and the development of society—its science, technology, and culture. It is a free, conscious act of a human being and, as a consequence, work acquires its value from the dignity of the human being as a person. Work—its content and context—should, therefore, promote rather than damage the dignity of the human being (Kanungo & Mendoca, 1996, p. 70).

Transactional leadership may view work as a social exchange commodity, with the employer holding the right to treat employees as instruments of production or service. However, from an ethical perspective, the organization must treat employees as autonomous persons working for themselves, which is consistent with the dignity of human beings (Kanungo & Mendoca, 1996, p. 70).

Empowerment represents a psychological sense of oneself and a developmental process (Gutierrez, Parsons, & Cox, 1998). The process of empowerment integrates a sense of greater self-efficacy and competence, interpersonal and coping skills, and a capacity and willingness to act on individual or shared problems in the work environment.

Empowerment is both a relational and a motivational construct (Conger & Kanungo, 1988). From a business perspective, the relational view of empowerment is directly related to the delegation, or *sharing*, of formal authority in the organization. Transformational leadership incorporates *sharing power* as a core assumption for the leadership process, but empowerment is more than delegating authority and decisionmaking opportunities to constituents. Empowerment can only happen through full *participation and self-determination*. The techniques of delegating power are not enough. The psychological mechanisms that underlie empowerment are not included in this approach (Kanungo & Mendoca, 1996).

Thinking about empowerment as a motivational construct allows leaders to promote the benefits to employees and consumers of service of a sense of *self-efficacy*, or a perception that they can adequately cope with the demands of their work environment. In addition, individuals are motivated to be self-determining, that is, to have the self-efficacy to cope with the demands of the workplace and to experience the control and influence that is possible through choice. The leader's role is to create the conditions necessary to enable and enhance employees' and consumers' opportunities for self-efficacy and self-determination through the structures and processes of the organization (see Chapters 9, 10, and 11).

Empowerment will flow from the values and norms of the organizational culture if the values and norms are congruent with empowerment. Values such as self-determination, collaboration instead of competition, excellence in performance, nondiscrimination, and participation all are consistent with the empowerment of constituents. The most powerful mechanism for leaders to use in empowering constituents is their own *consciousness*, an awareness of the differences in the distribution of power and a heightened understanding of the processes necessary to promote empowerment. The leader's responsibility to shape an organization that is empowering has moral implications. The following discussion highlights some other moral responsibilities for leaders.

The Moral Responsibilities of Leadership

Leaders have responsibilities as a result of their actions. Leaders make decisions and take actions that result in change. Leadership, whether from formal authority or from charismatic or spontaneous actions at any level or role, makes a difference in the lives of others in relation to benefits and harm. The moral responsibilities discussed in the following sections (see Figure 3.2) are congruent with a transformational approach to leadership. These discussions provide a perspective for leaders about the broad ethical responsibilities of leadership.

Responsibility to Constituents

Gardner (1990) in his examination of leadership today argues that there is a moral dimension of leadership that is related to the responsibility to constituents. He said, "We believe, with Immanuel Kant, that individuals should be treated as ends in themselves, not as a means to the leader's end, not as objects to be manipulated" (Gardner, 1990, p. 73). The responsibility to constituents is characterized by the objectives of a leader in four areas: the release of human possibilities, shared purposes of individuals and group, regeneration of values, and encouragement of individual initiative and responsibility.

The Release of Human Possibilities.   The *release of human possibilities*, according to Gardner (1990), is directly connected to the fulfillment of possibilities. The release of human possibilities is the greatest asset to society and one of the most important and fundamental of leadership goals. Human beings bring with them a myriad of unsuspected strengths and capacities, undiscovered gifts, and infinite talent and energy to

Responsibility to constituents
- Release of human possibilities
- Shared purposes of individuals and groups
- Regeneration of values
- Encouragement of individual initiative and responsibility

Sacrifice
- Dancing with pain and injury
- Gravity of duty above self-interest

Voices of conscience
- Moral imagination and memory
- Member of organizational community
- Nurture voices of conscience through culture and structure
- Critical imagination

Craft and competence
- Required expertise, training, and abilities to lead
- Attention to competence of others

Proactive processes of leadership
- Organization as community
- Process of interaction
- Conscience of community
- Ethics of intimacy
- Ethical process

Empowerment
- Love your neighbor
- Promote growth and development
- Share authority
- Participation and self-determination of constituents
- Consciousness of conditions to promote empowerment

FIGURE 3.2 Moral Responsibility of Leadership

invest in the enactment of a meaningful purpose. Often, individuals have been stymied by a lack of opportunity or challenge or their capacities have been hidden by earlier defeats. Gardner (1990, p. 74) argues this:

> It is a matter of self-interest for every society to remove obstacles to human growth and performance. The battles we wage against physical and mental illness, prejudice, ignorance and poverty are not just exercises in compassion. They are battles for the release of human talent and energy.

This objective conveys an attitude on the part of leaders to promote and enhance personal growth, development, and learning on the part of constituents: employees, consumers of service, and community citizens.

Shared Purposes of Individuals and Groups.   The *shared purposes of individuals and groups* are also the moral responsibility of leaders. People become fully who they are in relationship with others. Even as individuals discover hidden talents and are motivated to use them, there is the necessity of belonging and finding support within a group. As Wheatley and Kellner-Rogers (1999, p. 62) note, "Ethics is how we behave when we decide we belong together." Individuals who involve themselves in a group, through the nature of their work, have an investment in the nature of the group. The leader has an important responsibility to nurture the individual and group relationships and the ethical nature of those relationships. In order to develop ethical behaviors among people, agreements have to be made between people. As Wheatley and Kellner-Rogers say, ". . . Behaviors are rooted in our agreements" (1999, p. 63). The implicit and explicit norms and values—the agreements—that develop in an organization's culture are the embodiment of this moral responsibility (discussed further in Chapters 9 and 10).

Regeneration of Values.   The *regeneration of values* is a result of the ". . . mys-terious community-building impulse of the species" (Gardner, 1990, p. 78). Human beings have been in the process of creating and re-creating value systems over time. These value systems are made up of norms and standards, myths, legends, shared symbols, and shared assumptions. Many of these values, norms, and standards become a function of law or culture, which helps to channel human talent and energy toward a common good, rather than toward evil purposes. Gardner argues that the power of ideas in human conduct is basic, ". . . to keep alive values that are not so easy to embed in laws . . ." (1990, p. 77). Leaders are responsible for promoting values, such as moral responsibility, care for others, celebration of differentness, mutual respect, honor, and integrity. These are the values that are critical to multiculturalism, empowerment, and community building. In turn, leaders must also make room for dissent; they must provide for the process of value generation through ". . . the scene of conflict . . . ," such that dissensus and dialogue lead to consensus and agreement (Gardner, 1990, p. 77).

Value regeneration also is important in regard to the organization's contribution to public philosophies (Jennings, Callahan, & Wolf, 1987). Leaders and organizations participate in the public sphere, and the values and actions of leaders and organizations become part of the moral discourse of society. Professional values become a part of the public debate and contribute to the necessary process of a society determining its character. In particular, human service leaders help to shape the culture in regard to how society thinks about social problems and what are necessary solutions. As Jennings, Callahan, and Wolf, 1987, p. 10) noted in an article on the public duties of the professions, ". . . today's moral aspirations may become tomorrow's expectations, and society's demands." Frederick Reamer, a well-known social work ethicist, responded in the same article that there was a decline in the profession's advocacy of public welfare issues in favor of an emphasis on professionalism, licensure, and insurance coverage. Reamer (1987, p. 15) recommends a renewal of the promotion of the public good by social work, "Both the public and private sectors must reawaken their commitment to the concept of [public] welfare, viewed in its most noble form." This is a regeneration of values.

Individual Initiative and Responsibility.   Constituents must take *individual initiative and responsibility* in order to participate in the creation of ethical purposes, work cultures, and services to clients. Through this dimension, leaders can "bring alive" the interest and willingness of constituents to share the leadership task. Leaders' motivation and ability to nurture active involvement of others provide for a stimulating work environment and the development of constituents' sense of responsibility for the goals and mission of the organization. This moral dimension is directly related to the distribution of power in an organization, and the level of participation that is possible for constituents (see discussions in Chapters 4, 8, and 11).

Active constituents—those who are involved in the decision processes and feel responsibility for the results of decisions—help to prevent an abuse of power in the organization. Secrecy is reduced, while the burden of difficult ethical dilemmas is shared. Also, when people are informed of relevant information and participate in the decision, they are invested in the results. Active constituents are the safety valve for unethical practices. Through participation they can give feedback and feel the responsibility to do so. Gardner (1990, p. 79) argues the following:

> Unrelenting autocracy down the chain of command undermines initiative. It says by implication that your responsibility is not to identify problems beyond those implicit in your orders, not to think about solutions . . . The disclaimer in the Navy used to be, 'it didn't happen on my watch.' Followers who are passively awaiting orders have lost much of their capacity to be of help.

Leaders, according to Gardner (1990), improve the vitality of the organization through inviting participation and initiative. Delegation of authority and responsibility, valuing individual uniqueness and capacity, and respecting constituents through consulting and listening are just a few of the mechanisms that nurture initiative.

The development of individual initiative contributes to the empowerment of all constituents, employees and consumers of service. Participation in decisions, taking action, providing critical feedback, and contributing to the well-being of the organization and public good are factors that support a process of empowerment (Gutirrez, Parsons, & Cox, 1998). Further, human service organizations are often a haven for the disenfranchised and powerless. Leaders who facilitate constituents to conceive of themselves as actors rather than victims provide an opportunity for them to be change agents in their communities (Nanus & Dobbs, 1999).

Attributes and Characteristics for Ethical Leadership

The arrival of charismatic leaders on the heels of the great man theory promotes the myth that there are particular characteristics a person must be born with or develop in order to lead. Ethical leadership does not require a particular personality, gender, or bent; it does require that a person be willing to sacrifice, act as the voice of conscience, and have the craft and competence to do the job.

Sacrifice

The leader's willingness and ability to sacrifice provides the most clear and evident moral voice to constituents. Facing and resolving ethical dilemmas from the position of leadership is often painful and uncomfortable. Ritchie (1988, p. 181) uses the metaphor of the dancer who ". . . always dances with pain, and usually with injury . . . the burden of resolving a variety of paradoxical demands and choosing defensible strategies will always be painful if one is really sensitive to the ethical considerations in organizational life." Leaders who hold responsibility for complex issues and mul-tiple constituencies have to manage with pain and sometimes injury.

Leaders are frequently challenged by dilemmas that position duty or obligation against their own self-interest. It is in this conflict that the "gravity of duty" is most prominent (Green, 1987). Leaders must grapple with the question, "Under what conditions would I find it imperative to resign, rather than participate in an unethical practice or situation?" In a study on the ethical decisions of social work administrators and managers (Manning, 1990), participants discussed the bottom line as the place where they would give up their position over the ethical quandary in question. One administrator, in response to decisions about placement of clients on the basis of funding instead of need, said, "I sort of got my high horse up and said, 'hey, if you're going to make my decisions for me, then I can't work here'" (Manning, 1990, p. 269). This leader reported a positive response to her willingness to sacrifice her own employment. Her superiors acquiesced and respected her ethical judgment. A nursing professor, in her address to graduating master's students, reminds them, "there is no shame in being fired or resigning for ethical reasons" (Gregg, 1985). The role modeling that results from sacrifice in the name of duty is a powerful indicator of the moral message being communicated throughout the organization. The leader articulates and represents the moral responsibility that must be taken, even in the face of potential personal and financial loss.

Voice of Conscience

The work of the leader in communicating a moral vision is located in a developmental process for the organization and constituents. Green (1987) discusses the importance of *social memory*. Social memory is made up of *moral imagination* and *memory*. The interdependence of the two composes the voices of conscience for the organization. Memory is critical to moral leadership because leadership is rooted in the history of the organization. Change results from examining the traditions, expressing dissatisfaction with the traditions, and creating new traditions. Therefore, critique of "what is" or "what has been" is always an important factor in change. However, it is difficult to criticize the current state of affairs without standing somewhere (see Figure 3.3). The voice of conscience must be as a member of the organizational community, not as an outsider. Therefore, although the critical observer, the voice for moral change, may speak out against the "... lived life of the community, they still speak always from within it" (Green, 1987). The leader or constituents who want to initiate moral leadership must be viewed as an insider. Thus, it is especially important to keep close ties with all constituents and with the work of the organization. Distance creates an outsider status that reduces the power to critique and lead.

The leader's moral responsibility is to nurture, through relationships, organizational culture and structures. The culture and architecture hold the potential of the organization to develop the voices of conscience. The work of Hannah Arendt (1963, 1978), a Jewish zionist political philosopher, and Paul Tillich (1952), a Lutheran theologian and philosopher are useful here. Arendt argues the importance of thinking in order to combat the banality of evil. She argues that the banality of evil is a result of moral thoughtlessness; we simply do not think about our specific actions in terms of the moral consequences. She developed an orientation that includes three concepts: 1) the importance of developing a habit of independent thinking and judgment, 2) the

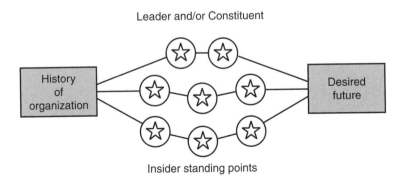

FIGURE 3.3 Voice of Conscience

need to understand and resist individual and organizational phenomena that is evil, and 3) the importance of acting civically, as a citizen with others. The task of leaders and constituents is to be thinkers for the organization. Each must not only judge how to act, but also persuade each other on the best moral course of action. Arendt (1978) argues that thinking is an end in itself, not just for the rational knowledge that results, but for the meaning that can be inferred about the moral nature of the situation. As leaders and constituents think and shape each other, the moral functioning of everyone is *transformed*.

Tillich (1952) adds to this conceptualization by adding the dimension of courage. The courage to be authentic to oneself is the ability to follow one's own reason and to stand up to irrational authority, whether it is a superior or the authority of a group. There is a danger that, in order to be a part of the larger group, there can be a loss of self, but we also have to have the courage to be a part of the larger community (Tillich, 1952). Participation in the group is part of how the self is affirmed. Thus, the threat of exclusion from the group, because of expressing the voice of conscience, can impair both the leaders' and constituents' expression of conscience.

The development of opportunities for voices of conscience rests, then, on the ability of individuals to resist the organization's pressure to act or be immoral. It also rests on the ability of constituents and leaders to act as "institution citizen," that is, the ability to be in loyal opposition to the organization for moral purposes (Arendt, 1963). Loyal opposition is acting in the best interests of the organization from the individual's moral point of view, which helps to promote the visualizing of a moral future. In turn, the vision of a moral future requires *critical imagination*.

Critical imagination is the ability to see beyond the present into the future (Green, 1987). In the earlier discussion about vision, the future is presented as a preferred future. The criticism of the present allows both leaders and constituents to consider new beginnings of an ethical and moral nature that invite all in the organizational community to participate in creating a better moral culture and purpose.

Craft and Competence

Ethical leaders are also competent leaders. It is readily apparent from clinical practice that it is unethical to practice outside of a person's *expertise*, *training*, and *abilities*. The same can be said for the skills and expertise needed for leadership in organizations. Green (1987, p. 182) notes that the ethics of leadership are not fundamentally drawn from technical competence, but ethical leadership: ". . . cannot be exercised without it . . . Only in the modern world do we think excellence in such practical matters as planning, motivating, and managing budgets are not moral demands." The ancient Greek philosophers agreed with this contemporary idea; they taught that a moral life is a life of skill. Leaders, then, who are also administrators and managers, have a variety of complex skills and specialized knowledge that are necessary to be moral leaders.

There are two consequences to the mistaken assumption that inept people are not immoral (Green, 1987). First, if we believe that technical knowledge and expertise are not moral demands, competence is easy to ignore as a requirement of ethical leadership. Conversely, when management and technical skill are the only important considerations, leadership is viewed as having little to do with ethics. It is easy to see that moral competence requires both technical knowledge and expertise and ethical knowledge and expertise. Leaders must acquire both as an intentional building of competence and craft.

Attention to *the competence of others* is also part of a leader's commitment to craft. It is necessary to develop a "conscience of craft" that sets the expectation for excellence in the work of others (Green, 1987). This is especially important in human services because the activities take place through relationships with others and have profound impacts on the recipient of services. The leader consciously communicates an unwillingness to accept inept or incompetent performance from constituents in the organization. The work with constituents through the relationships and interactions of the organizational community influences leaders and constituents to develop a consciousness of craft in the organization.

Conclusion

This chapter introduced the reader to the need for ethical leadership, particularly in human service organizations. Leadership was defined, and a social work definition of leadership was presented as a lens for the book that is congruent with the transformational leadership paradigm. Two paradigms of leadership—transactional and transformational—were discussed. Transformational leadership was recommended as the approach most congruent with the moral and ethical imperatives of leadership and with social work. The moral dimensions of leadership—direction, ethics, proactive processes, and empowerment—were brought forward for consideration. A conceptual framework for leadership should include more than particular theories. The moral responsibilities of leadership were examined, as well as several important characteristics that are necessary to be a moral leader.

The transformational approach is a framework to guide the leadership of individuals. This approach emphasizes empowerment and participation of constituents. However, not all leaders share power, but power is at the heart of ethical and unethical actions and behaviors, particularly for people in leadership positions. The next chapter takes a look at the use and abuse of power in leadership.

QUESTIONS AND APPLICATIONS

1. Conceptualize your own leadership approach. How do the transactional and transformational paradigms apply to your leadership? In what way are morality and ethics embedded in your leadership approach?

- What would you add?
- What would you change?

2. Think about moral vision and the moral responsibilities of leadership. Develop a moral vision for your leadership and your work. How are the mission and values of social work (or your profession) enacted through your vision?

3. Assess your actions and attributes as a leader from the perspectives of sacrifice, craft and competence, and as a voice of conscience for others. What attributes should be strengthened?

4 Ethical Decisions: The Use and Abuse of Power

THE FOCUS IN THIS CHAPTER IS ON THE FOLLOWING AREAS:

- The nature of power for ethical leadership
- The manifestations of power
  - Through obtaining the privilege of role and position
  - Through mobilizing bias
  - Through constructing meaning
- Perceptions of leaders' and constituents' power
- Powerlessness and the cycle of alienation
- Moral, professional, and social consequences of powerlessness
- Power to use for ethical action

Formal leaders, by the nature of their position, have access to and wield a tremendous amount of power. We can think of leadership as inextricably connected to power. As Brady (1990, p. 2) notes, "Managers are powerful, and, where there is power, there is potential for good and evil." Thus, the manner is which leaders use power is the essence of the ethics of leadership. The potential for achieving a greater good or for causing harm to the multiple constituencies of leaders rests on the use or abuse of power.

Power is a complex construct. It is ambiguous, not always observable, difficult to measure, and dynamic in its representation and enactment. Within American society, there is a great deal of ambivalence about power; power ". . . is America's last dirty word" (Johnson, 2001, p. 65). Powerful people are admired and sometimes resented and/or despised, but almost always in the public interest. In addition, there is reluctance on the part of both leaders and constituents to acknowledge power and the way that power is wielded. This can be particularly true for those in the "helping" professions, such as social work, psychology, nursing, and so forth. Some professions, social work for example, take pride in a partnership approach with consumers, employees, and communities. Equality and empowerment are valued and even prescribed. However, leaders who are unaware of, or reluctant to acknowledge, the level and impact of their power are vulnerable to the harm that can result from corruption or ignorance. Leaders must develop a consciousness, as well as conscientiousness, about their power and its impact on others in order to be ethical leaders.

The potential to harm or to benefit others rests in the leader's awareness, use, and/or abuse of power. How power is used, or abused, is observable through decisions that are made and policies that are formulated by people in leadership positions. There are wrong decisions that are the result of power being misused through negligence, bias, or ignorance. There are also incorrect decisions that promote the leaders' own interests or that harm or benefit others; these are all decisions about ethics (Brady, 1990).

The ability to influence positively, then, is a key factor in the manifestation of power. In order to develop an ethical framework that is effective in the workplace, leaders must learn how to use their own power in morally transformative ways. To do so requires an understanding of the nature of power in the workplace. This chapter will delineate the role of power in ethical decisions, that is, how power is wielded to harm and to help. A model of decisionmaking that incorporates power as an ethical influence and the importance of leader discretion provide a perspective about the positive use of power.

The Nature of Power in Leadership

Power is the ability to influence others toward the goals or outcomes that an individual desires, or requires, for the organization or for the individual. Power is vested in positions of authority (*legitimate power*), but is also available through other means. The power associated with a role or position gives the person with the power the right to exert power that is appropriate to job performance and organizational policy. The social bases of power include *coercive power*, *reward power*, *expert power*, and *referent power* (French & Raven, 1959).

Coercive power uses punishment, restriction, or penalties to influence or coerce people to do something. The range of coercion is a continuum from physical force to subtle, unspoken threats or admonishments. Demotions, loss of budget, loss of job security, reprimands, and so forth are examples of coercion. *Reward* power relies on providing something of value to others to induce performance. Rewards can be something material, such as salary increases, a larger office, new furniture, educational leave, and so forth or something intangible such as validation, acknowledgement, mentoring, delegation of authority, and so forth.

Expert power is not connected to position or role, but emanates from the individual at any level of the organization. The knowledge, skills, and characteristics of the individual are valued by others and result in that person being viewed as powerful because of what he or she can provide. *Referent* power can also be drawn on without access to particular position or role. Referent power relies on qualities of a person that other people admire and to which they feel attracted. Charisma, dynamism, honor, integrity, and reputation are examples of characteristics that may generate referent power.

All of the social bases of power can lead to misuse and ultimate harm. Leaders with legitimate power who act as if they do not have it will eventually use it, which is a surprise to the employees who thought they were partners in all decisions. Natural leaders who have developed a great deal of referent and expert power have a dramatic impact on decisions by a team or unit. A denial of their impact results in participation without responsibility for the outcome. Both examples cause poor morale, confusion, and conflict in the organization and ultimately have an effect on the quality of services to consumers.

But first, how does power enter into the ethics of leadership?

The Manifestations of Power

Power is an interactive variable that exists through relationships between leaders and constituents within and across organizational boundaries. The ethical issues and dilemmas that occur for leaders almost always include the variable of power. Handler's (1992) analysis of the manifestations of power in relation to clients and organizations is helpful and will be used here to explain this complex dynamic in regard to all constituents. There are three dimensions of power (Lukes, 1974). First is the one-dimensional approach that describes a person with influence getting people to do what they would not ordinarily do. This is similar to how we conceptualize the typical hierarchical arrangements of authority in organizations and the decisionmaking process. From this one-dimensional view, "quiescence," or the inactivity of subordinates (or clients), is not because *they are constrained* by power, but *by their own characteristics*. Their lack of participation or inaction is seen as their being apathetic, ineffective, or alienated.

The two-dimensional view of power brings forward a second face. The mobilization of bias is the leader's use of structures and processes in the organization as a determining influence for decisions, actions, and policies. Beyond the decision processes are the structure and activity that ". . . operates to exclude participants and issues altogether; that is, power not only involves who gets what, when, and how, but also who gets left out and how" (Handler, 1992, p. 278). This view highlights the barriers to giving feedback and to expressing complaints or concerns. In this dimension, constituents are silenced by lack of opportunity to voice concerns and by the structures and strategies used by leaders to restrict access to decisionmaking. These processes result in a *mobilization of bias*.

The third view explains the absence of participation by constituents by analyzing the *manipulated consensus*. Here, the leaders exercise power by ". . . influencing, shaping, or determining his [the constituent] very wants" (Handler, 1992, p. 279). This third dimension presents power as influenced by the social construction of meaning by both leaders and constituents. Constituents willingly acquiesce to their own subjugation. The processes in organizations that control information and socialization are critical to how constituents perceive what is communicated through the organization and the ethical or unethical nature of it. Also, how constituents perceive their own personal power, "... the psychological adaptations of the oppressed to escape the subjective sense of powerlessness" (Handler, 1992, p. 280), is also critical. From this view, we collude in our own exploitation and are so trapped in roles, we do not see ourselves as unfree (Lukes, 1974).

These three dimensions are integrated with the following factors that increase the ethical risks of abuse of power by leadership (see Figure 4.1). First, the executive or upper administrator in an organization is vested with "virtually unlimited power" over many things and many people (Levy, 1982, p. 61). Second, the structure and process of organizations, particularly bureaucracies, distributes power primarily to the managerial elite (Hasenfeld, 1983). Third, the perception of constituents frequently is that they lack the power to follow their own moral conscience.

The First Dimension: Power that Resides in Position

The factors in the following sections demonstrate the ethical dimensions of the power that is associated with leadership roles and positions in the organizational hierarchy. The power that resides in a particular role or position is related to the legitimate

Power of the Privileged: Role and Position

Includes power to:
- Affect lives and well-being of people
- Promote self-interest
- Distribute resources
- Design and implement rules and policies
- Use latitude and discretion
- Be privileged

Power Through the Mobilization of Bias

Includes power through:
- Organization rules, policies, and regulations
- Organizational structure and processes
- Control of decision processes
- Access to and control of information

Power Through the Construction of Meaning

Includes power through:
- Perceptions of leaders' power
  - The halo effect
  - Loss of moral conscience
  - Moral thoughtlessness
- Constituents perception of personal power
  - Powerlessness and alienation
  - Cycle of alienation
- Moral, professional, and social consequences of powerlessness

FIGURE 4.1   The Dimensions of Power for Leaders

authority assigned to that role or position. The power itself is neutral; it is the use or abuse of the power by the person that results in ethical or unethical actions.

Power to Affect the Lives and Well-Being of People. Leaders in administrative and managerial positions have *the power to affect the lives and well-being of people* under their authority in good or harmful ways (Brady, 1990). The effects can be material, such as personnel decisions that increase salary, rewards, and promotions, or the opposite, including disciplinary actions, demotions, or unwanted transfers. The effects can also be more related to psychological well-being and job satisfaction, such as policies and decisions that affect employee morale. In the first instance, several people may be interested in, and qualified for, a promotion. In addition to the direct effect on individuals, the process that is used—the policies that are followed—in making a choice has ethical implications.

Organizational issues, policies, and decisions that affect employee morale, negatively or positively, have the potential to benefit or harm others. The strategies used by leaders to resolve employee conflicts also are an example of wielding power. For example, the administrator who acts after hearing only one side of the story and applies coercion or punishment to an employee is using power in ways that can harm. In contrast, the resolution of conflict through a fair, interactive process of all involved provides an ethical means to improve employee relations and establishes fairness as a value in the organization. Also, decisions about what persons should make up a work unit or project team—decisions about personalities—are not only concerned with the social gratification of work life, but can spell the difference between success and failure of a team.

The Power to Promote Self-Interests. People in positions in upper levels of the hierarchy have the power to decide about issues that can *promote their own interests*, rather than the interests of the consumers of service, employees, and the organization. Leaders that take credit for other employees' contributions and creativity are one example. Jackall (1988, p. 21) found that credit flows up through the hierarchical structure. Further, ". . . authority provides a license to steal ideas, even in front of those who originated them." In another representation of self-interest, Enz (1988) found that top managers ascribed more power to the departments that they judged held more similar values to their own. The ethical implications are many. Managers may foster the political power of those departments that communicate similar values. The pressure to see things the same way as top management can subvert other values that may be important to the organization. Feedback that contradicts managerial values may be stifled, which restricts organizational learning and the opportunity to evaluate the efficacy of particular values.

Those in highest positions are insulated from the pressures of managerial work at the middle levels and protect themselves from the impact of policies and decisions through the "privilege of authority." Jackall (1988, p. 20) in his landmark study of corporate managers found that "It is characteristic of this authority system [the bureaucracy] that details are pushed down and credit is pulled up." Further, protecting themselves from too much knowledge about the messy details of organizational functioning keep administrators from being confronted with the burden of guilty knowledge. This protection of self also paves the way for blame time and the tendency to "kill the messenger" if they are bringing bad news.

Another way to avoid the responsibility for choices and decisions is to blame the role or position. There is a temptation for leaders to believe that their power resides in the position, not in themselves (Brummer, 1985). Thus, it is easy to excuse their decisions and the impact of decisions because such a choice was required by the position. Brummer (1985, p. 87) in describing the phenomenology of decisionmaking argued that personal values are never removed from occupational or corporate decisions: "One always puts a moral stamp on a decision—by default if no other way."

The Power to Distribute Resources.   People in higher levels of the hierarchy wield *power through distributing resources* in the organization (Brady, 1990). Resources that are scarce become a medium for wielding power when individuals or units are dependent on those resources (Morgan, 1997). There must be dependence on the part of individuals, units, departments, and so forth before resources can be used as a control strategy. Morgan (1997) notes that some of the "Machiavellian" among leaders increase their own power through creating a dependence of others on themselves through the control of critical resources. Discretionary funds are resources that provide the ability to control others. Beyond the budget for current operations, discretionary funds provide the opportunity to use uncommitted resources for new initiatives or as a slush fund to influence individuals or units. The budget becomes symbolic of a leader's ability to influence the organization. As an example, one manager reported (Manning, 1990, p. 229) the following:

> It got to the point where if you fought what they were doing, then your group suffered by not getting the resources, because then you were not their favorite group . . . like one year I got half of everyone else's operating budget . . . oh yeah, it was an out and out punishment.

This manager experienced administrative abuse of power in response to his overt disagreements with a policy issue.

Decisions about resources are made at every level. Decisions about the control of, and access to, revenue, technology, capital expenditures, personnel, space, furniture, and so forth all require ethical judgments about the use of resources. Access to the personal time of leaders provides stakeholders with the ability to influence. Thus, time is a resource that gets distributed. Administrators make decisions about how, with whom, and when to spend *time* with community citizens, board members, consumers, and employees. Who is given access and who is excluded become questions of ethics. Decisions about charitable contributions—to what organization and at what allocation level—require judgments about the distribution of resources.

Whenever resources are distributed, the issue of fairness becomes important, but decisions about resources are complex. Fairness does not always mean equal because special considerations of individuals and organizational survival may be evident. For example, someone with a physical disability may require new furniture, even though that person is new to the organization and when other employees with more seniority have been waiting for furniture as well.

Power to Design and Implement Policy.   Executives, administrators, and managers have the power to *design and implement rules and policies* (Brady, 1990). The ethical quality of rules and policies rests on who has participated in developing them. Leaders have the power to appoint those who will be integrally involved or to determine the mechanisms to use in the development of critical policies for the organization. Further, the leader's relationship to the rules of an organization is not "mechanical." Rather, people with higher positions in the hierarchy use discretion in response to rules, for example, to wave a particular rule for a particular person or to change rules. Policies, such as tardiness, use of sick leave, dress codes, and so forth, can be applied differently to different individuals, according to the discretion of the administrator or manager.

Executives, because of their role in the organization, have a great amount of *latitude* in their decisionmaking capacity (Brummer, 1985, p. 85). At the level of macro policy formation, there is the potential for significant social and economic policy impact. Higher level administrators have the ultimate responsibility for the *gravity* of policymaking that affects many people, both inside and outside the organization. The power to develop policy can force moral and ethical dilemmas upon subordinates, what Brummer (1985, p. 86) calls "the web of wrongdoing." The web is the result of "progressively anesthetizing the conscience of subordinates."

Status as a "superior" to others in a "subordinate" status provides leaders with more flexibility to ". . . infuse their own right and wrong into . . . policies" (Brummer, 1985, p. 86). The latitude for subordinates is not as great. Middle managers often find themselves faced with the choice of cooperating or challenging a policy that seems unethical because they lack the opportunity to exert their own discretion. The effect is a limited ability to search for innovative ways to respond to the demands of conscience.

Power of Privilege.   The *power of privilege* is always associated with people in high positions. Therefore, "Leaders almost always enjoy greater privileges than followers do. The greater the power of leaders, generally the greater are the rewards they receive" (Johnson, 2001, p. 14). A recent newspaper article noted that, even in the face of an economic downturn with subsequent downsizing of personnel in large corporations, the Chief Executive Officers (CEOs) of those corporations were being compensated in unprecedented amounts. For example, in 2000, the salary and bonuses for CEOs jumped by 18 percent as compared to the average of 3 percent for the average worker (Longworth, 2001).

There is a connection between power and privilege. Leaders are vulnerable to the abuse of both power and privilege, and abuse of one often leads to abuse of the other. Ethical issues always reside at the intersection of power and privilege. Boards of directors and CEOs have to determine the appropriate reward for increased risk and responsibility of top-level executives and administrators. Questions about the distribution of rewards to those in power and to those who have the least power and privilege must be considered in relation to the needs of followers, consumers of service, and organizational well-being. The participants who have responsibility for these decision processes will make the difference in ethical or unethical distributions of privilege. How participants are appointed, and in what capacity, brings forward the power that is distributed through the structure and process of an organization.

The Second Face: Power Associated with Structure and Process

The structures and processes of any organization become the vehicles to use and abuse power. Issues not made public, decisions not made, agendas controlled, and critiques suppressed are ways to wield and shape influence over others. This dimension of the manifestation of power is associated with the policies, structures, and activities that create barriers to the expression of concerns and challenges about ethical practices by constituents. This second dimension adds the mobilization of bias, which, in covert ways, builds a culture that minimizes feedback to agency practices. Challenges "... are suffocated before they are voiced, or kept covert; or killed before they gain access to the relevant decision-making arena; or failing all of these things, maimed or destroyed in the decision-implementing stage of the policy process (Handler, 1992, p. 279). It is in this dimension that the organizational culture, made up of values and beliefs, traditions, rules, procedures, and rituals, is developed to benefit some groups in the organization to the detriment of other groups (for example, administrative elite versus direct service staff or consumers of service). The following examples in processes and structures provide opportunities to analyze where and how bias is mobilized.

Organizational Rules, Policies, and Regulations. *Organizational rules, policies, and regulations* are traditionally viewed as rational instruments that are intended to aid in task performance (Morgan, 1997). However, Morgan (1977, p. 175) argues that they are best understood as "... the products and reflections of struggle for political control." Excessive rules and regulations can be developed in a bureaucracy to avoid accountability for liability or malpractice lawsuits. If the employee follows the rules, even if nonsensical or in some situations unethical, the agency feels protected from liability. Policies that are developed to protect the agency rather than to enhance services to clients impede the spirit of doing the right thing. For example, agencies develop informed consent policies and procedures to meet the letter of the law and to protect the agency from liability. However, the process and document may be complex in language, time consuming to read, and lacking in the human assistance necessary to ensure understanding. If clients do not have a clear understanding of what is being disclosed, they are unable to give true consent (Manning & Gaul, 1997). Thus, the bias of valuing client autonomy is mobilized even though authentic autonomy is missing. Clients and employees are influenced by this bias, such that it may be difficult to challenge or question.

Risk management policies rest on documentary processes whereby documentation in the client record, employee personnel file, and/or human resources department provide evidence for the institution's defense against malpractice or negligence (Townsend, 1998). Risk management is to help protect the safety of those receiving services and to reduce liability of the organization. However, the process is managed through individual cases rather than collaborative discussion, which could lead to collective action. The risk management process can discourage the challenges that arise through collaboration and discussion in relation to existing agency and/or professional practices. The bias that is mobilized is the *perception* of safety based on documentation of incidents rather than a broader conceptualization of the meaning of the incidents and the connection to work life. A current example is the controversy over using restraints with emotionally disturbed children, adolescents, and adults. The activities of restraint as a therapeutic measure are well documented because of the requirements of legislation. However, collaborative discussion is necessary to evaluate the therapeutic efficacy in the use of restraints in an agency. A policy process in the organization that requires feedback and review based on collaboration provides opportunities to correct or prevent unethical practices, rather than the mobilization of bias, that is, this practice is safe because of the documentation.

Organizational Structure and Design.

Organizational structure and design shapes the distribution of power through centralization and decentralization. The degree of autonomy and independence or interdependence that particular departments or units possess is engineered through the architecture of the design. The size and status of a department, unit, or program sometimes indicates power. Competition for positions and for priority in program services by leaders creates a climate of divisiveness that works against the agency mission, quality of service delivery, and employee morale. The divide-and-rule strategy is enacted through organizational structure decisions that connote abuses of power (Morgan, 1997).

People often resist changes through reorganization that would result in higher quality service delivery or more efficient and accessible services because the change could mean a loss in power or status. Managers and administrators cling to old job descriptions that are outdated. Employees may use job descriptions to resist new performance expectations or changes in job design.

Control of Decision Processes.

The *control of decision processes* is also a strategy that leaders use to wield power (Morgan, 1997). The endless string of meetings that accomplish little or the hidden agendas for closed meetings that don't allow participation in decision outcomes are examples of processes that wield power. Morgan discusses three strategies that leaders use to control the decision processes in an organization: *premises*, *processes*, and *issues and objectives*. These strategies are neutral. It is the use or abuse of the strategies that define the ethical dilemma for leaders.

The *premises* of decisions are how the leadership approaches a particular decision. A leader's avoidance of particular hot topics that challenge current practices is an example. Social control strategies are used. The premises of decisions are a social construction that conveys how organizational employees or groups will perceive an issue. For example, managers described minimizing the impact of something they considered unethical because they did not have a choice about implementing it (Manning,

1990, p. 271). One manager's strategy was "... to minimize the extent of how unethical it was, so when it actually went to the team, it somehow got dressed up more and looked better." Vocabulary, structures of communication, attitudes, and beliefs all exert influence on how others will think about the ethical meaning of the problem or issue. What is ultimately communicated through the process are messages that convey "who we are" and "the way we do things around here."

The *processes* of decisionmaking are the activities—open or closed or obvious or secret—that culminates in particular decisions being made. The hierarchy of an organization categorizes the power particular groups hold in the organization by limiting participation in decision processes (Townsend, 1998). Ethical questions that leaders must confront about decision processes include the following:

- How should the decision be made?
- Who should be involved?
- Who will be impacted by the decision?
- Are they represented in the decision process?
- When should the decision be made?

The process of creating an agenda for a meeting, who controls what is added to the agenda, and when are items carried over (and over) are all examples of processes that can be used to empower or to abuse power.

Issues and objectives for decisionmaking can be influenced by preparation, infusion of information and knowledge, reports, and critical discussion. Decisionmakers think about an issue and decide based on the level of information that is shared about the issue. Opportunities to influence the outcome of a decision, constructively or destructively, are based on the eloquence, command of the facts, and passionate commitment of the individuals who speak to the issue. Facts can be distorted and fragmented. Decisions can be made prior to asking for input or discussion. The leader's commitment to an honest decision process is part of the ethical responsibility of leadership.

Access to and Control of Information.   *Access to and control of information* is also a source of power for leaders with the potential for abuse. Just as information and knowledge is one of the primary components necessary for empowerment, a lack of access to information and knowledge creates differences in the distribution of power among employees. Leaders, by nature of their position in the hierarchy, have access to more information and to the decision processes of the organization. Leaders have the ability to access personnel information; can participate in problem solving, policymaking, and planning strategies; and are integrally involved with board members, key managers, and political figures in the community. The depth and breadth of knowledge and information that leaders are exposed to requires an ethical responsibility to use the information toward good rather than harm.

Johnson (2001) refers to "the shadow of deceit" as one of the ethical pitfalls of access to information on the part of leaders. He describes several of the activities that lead to deceit. Leaders must grapple with whether to release information and to what parties. They are often faced with the temptation to lie or distort the facts in order to protect themselves. Frequently, top-level management find themselves placing a spin on a public relations issue in order to protect the agency or individuals within the agency. Deceptive practices can include a lack of disclosure about knowledge that a leader holds or withholding information that others need. Leaders are also deceptive when they use available information for their own personal benefit rather than for the good of the organization. Leaders may be deceptive through release of information practices, for example, violating the privacy of others, releasing information to the wrong people, or preventing constituents from releasing information that others have a legitimate right to know (Johnson, 2001). Deceptive practices destroy trust with employees, consumers, and community.

Leaders are responsible for *protecting the privacy* of their employees as well as the privacy of the consumers seeking services. A recent incident at the Air Force Academy in Colorado brings this responsibility home (Denver Post, 2001). A list of cadets with a variety of academic, mental health, and substance abuse problems, as well as cadets with honor code violations, was released to every cadet in the academy inadvertently. The military leadership that was responsible sent a follow-up memo requiring all cadets to ignore the information. However, after the fact is too late; the damage to many individuals' reputation and invasion of privacy had been accomplished.

Manipulated Consensus: Power Through the Construction of Meaning

The third dimension of the manifestation of power is enacted through what Paulo Freire (1970) calls a "culture of silence." The culture of silence develops through the nonparticipation of constituents in critical decision processes. In this dimension, constituents participate in their own subjugation. Participation and consciousness are mutual and reciprocal. As constituents participate less in the policies and practices of an organization, they have less consciousness about the moral issues embedded in policy and practices. Constituents are more likely, then, to reflect the voices of the leaders, rather than bringing forward feedback and challenges to unethical practices and policies. According to Handler (1992), as constituents become echoes of those in leadership positions, the culture of silence develops further and lends legitimacy to those in power. Further, if constituents do speak up about an issue, they are vulnerable to manipulation (Handler, 1992). An important dynamic in this process is the perception of the leaders' power and constituents' perception of their own power.

Perception of Leaders' Power. Constituents' *perception of leaders' power* is an important determinant in their moral behavior. Leaders are perceived by others as having varying levels of power. Sometimes a leader's power is inadvertent; others view the leader as having more power or the potential of power than the leader would perceive as reality. Also, constituents' assessment of their own power changes based on complex factors—self-esteem, role in the organization, relationship with leaders and peers, years of experience, opportunities to use power, the outcome of those opportunities, and so forth—that are dynamic and change with time. When the perception of power attached to leaders (particularly those who are in a superior position) inhibits action in relation to moral issues, there are two major effects. First, constituents experience erosion of their own moral conscience. Second, distorted perceptions of the power of others affect the constituents' awareness of, and ability to give feedback about, ethical and unethical issues and practices. Although constituents may perceive themselves as powerless, their action or inaction has a "... considerable impact upon the lives and choices of other people" (Brummer, 1985, p. 87).

John Nance (2001), a retired military officer who teaches about leadership, talks about the *halo effect* of leadership. Followers put a halo on the head of leaders. If there is a problem, followers may assume they are wrong rather than viewing the leader as wrong. The halo effect prevents followers from giving feedback in critical situations. He gives as an example the new copilot who was afraid to say something when he detected something wrong with the way the pilot (a very experienced senior officer) was flying the plane (he appeared to be asleep). It turned out that the pilot was dead. He let the dead pilot fly the plane in, rather than comment on his concerns and discover that the captain was incapacitated. Three people died as a result.

The Manifestation of Powerlessness

The landmark research study known as the Milgram Experiment provided some telling results about followers' perception of *authority* and the effect on *moral conscience* (Milgram, 1974). Volunteers were told that they were going to participate in a study about others' ability to learn. They were placed near what appeared to be a generator that had switches labeled from 15 volts to 450 volts. They could view the "learner," who was sitting in a chair with electrodes on his or her wrists, through a window. The volunteer was to apply a shock ordered by the researcher (a person they perceived to be in authority) when the learner made a mistake with memorization. Though the participants became uncomfortable with the orders and the subsequent discomfort on the part of the learners, they continued when instructed to do so. Even when the learners exhibited what appeared to be serious pain and fainted from the shocks, more than two-thirds of the participants administered the most severe level of shocks when ordered to do so. The results demonstrated that most people, when ordered to do something by someone in authority, will obey, even when it violates their own conscience.

The individual attributes of the participants were not related to sadistic tendencies. People simply perceived that the person giving the orders was a legitimate authority and that increased their tendency to obey. The results from these experiments demonstrate how the Holocaust and the war crimes of the Nazis, as well as other groups who have committed genocide, are possible. Further research has demonstrated the same outcome: "Most people will obey external authority over the dictates of conscience" (Markula Center for Applied Ethics, 2000, p. 2).

Experts on moral thoughtlessness provide further insight into this phenomenon. Hannah Arendt (1963) has studied *moral thoughtlessness* through examining what happened in the Holocaust. Adolph Eichmann was the ultimate example of "moral thoughtlessness under severe organizational pressure" (Neilson, 1984, p. 186). Two factors about moral thoughtlessness are highlighted. First, Eichmann worked in an organizational environment that required immediate obedience to orders without referring to personal conscience. Second, Eichmann was emotionally distanced from the reality that ensued as a result of his orders: the extermination of millions of people. Arendt (1963, p. 287) concluded that Eichmann was not stupid, but thoughtless. "[He was] ignorant of everything that was not directly, technically, and bureaucratically connected with his job."

Constituents' Perceptions of Powerlessness

When constituents perceive that they are powerless and are unable to address or question unethical practices, a process of distancing from their personal moral conscience results. This distancing has profound implications for the person and for the organization (see Figure 4.2). As individuals are required to do things that are ethically questionable, they are drawn into the "web of wrongdoing," which affects their moral character and sensitivity. As constituents participate less in the decisions that have moral and ethical implications, ". . . moral sensitivities become progressively dulled" (Brummer, 1985, p. 86). Further, as subordinates relinquish autonomy to those with more real or perceived power, they experience a subtle loss of control over their own life. The loss of their personal morality affects their sense of personal integrity and further dulls the senses and awareness of unethical behavior in the future; an experience of alienation from themselves and the organization occurs. This process results in a peculiar reciprocity whereby both organizations and employees lose the ability to self-regulate (Brummer, 1985) (see Figure 4.2).

Powerlessness and Alienation

Managers and administrators who feel unable to act on their personal and professional moral conscience experience *alienation* (Manning, 1990). They describe a pervasive sense of compromise, that is, a separation from their internal values that is necessary to maintain personal integrity. In Manning's (1990) study about ethical decisionmaking, managers and administrators reported that separation from personal moral conscience resulted in significant effects on their emotional and physical health. The characteristics of alienation included feeling *powerless*, *overwhelmed*, and *resigned* (see Figure 4.3).

Powerlessness

Powerlessness occurs when managers or constituents experience little or no ability to influence decisions that compromise their personal morality. One person said (Manning, 1990, p. 277) this:

> The only conflict, because you knew when things got presented it was not open to discussion . . . was the constant one of how much of this am I willing to tolerate before I finally resolve that it's not worth it. Most of us knew that there's no sense trying to

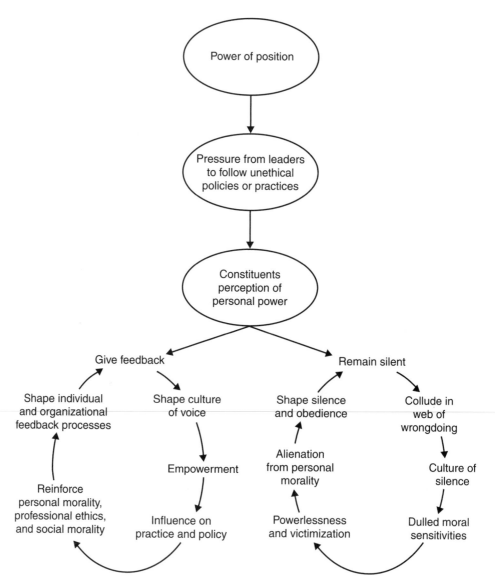

FIGURE 4.2   Cycles of Power and Powerlessness

bump it up either . . . because up sometimes looks like down, so that wasn't going to do any good.

The experience of powerlessness forces a restriction on possibilities, alternatives, or even sources of support. Managers find themselves unable to conceive of any way to influence ethical or unethical practices.

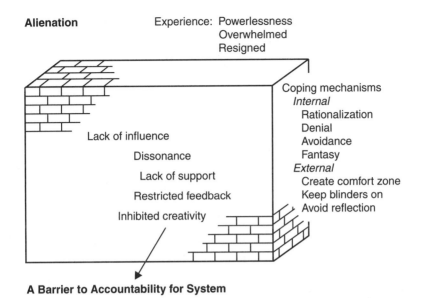

Alienation   Experience: Powerlessness
                                    Overwhelmed
                                    Resigned

Coping mechanisms
Internal
   Rationalization
   Denial
   Avoidance
   Fantasy
External
   Create comfort zone
   Keep blinders on
   Avoid reflection

Lack of influence

Dissonance

Lack of support

Restricted feedback

Inhibited creativity

A Barrier to Accountability for System

FIGURE 4.3   **Characteristics of Alienation**

Overwhelmed

The feeling of being *overwhelmed* by situations that are morally dissonant is somewhat different. One manager said (Manning, 1990,t p. 277), "I'm carrying this big, heavy platter and I can pretty much carry it . . . but it's like the more stuff they pile on it . . . eventually it's just going to get to the point where I won't be able to sustain the weight of it anymore, and when that comes, I'm going to pitch it." The everyday duties and responsibilities with ethical implications begin to feel like a burden that is not possible to carry.

Resignation

Resignation was another characteristic of alienation. Resignation in response to moral and ethical issues in an organization is particularly disturbing because the person becomes resigned to unethical practices, their own and others', within the organization. A manager said (Manning, 1990, p. 277), "I'm just resigned about it, I ignore it . . . just focus on teaching . . . don't want to fight anymore and that's part of the problem . . . it takes time and energy."

Alienation

Alienation, in the previous study (Manning, 1990), was correlated with managers who experienced *dissonance* within the organization in three ways. First, there was a sense of having the responsibility for something without the necessary control to be responsible.

> . . . Having control over nothing, but having responsibility for everything, and always feeling like, "If only I had done this, and maybe . . . ," but knowing inside that really I don't have any control over that, other than to provide ethical care to people . . . and then the resources to provide ethical care are taken away . . . so there's a big piece of disparity there (Manning, 1990, p. 278).

Second, the incongruity between personal and organizational values affected administrators and managers. Jackall's (1988, p. 6) landmark study on corporate managers and morality found that bureaucratic work caused people to "bracket" their moral values that they adhere to outside the workplace and to conform to the organization form. He quotes a vice president as saying "What is right in the corporation is what the guy above you wants. That's what morality is in the corporation."

Finally, managers in human service organizations found that the accountability for standards that are unrealistic promoted dissonance and provoked ethical quandaries. Staff ratios, patient census standards, and performance evaluations based on units of service were cited as examples of standards that managers felt they had little control of. One manager explained (Manning, 1990, p. 278) it this way: ". . . Like the regional office will develop your census goals for the year in relationship to what they need to cover their expenses. Not in relationship to anything that has to do with like, how many people in your neighborhood will come to your bar and grill. It's more like, 'we need you to have 38 this year.'" Similar to this example, the standards did not always relate to the best interests of consumers or to the needs of the community.

Coping with Alienation

Managers and administrators who feel alienated use particular coping mechanisms. The coping mechanisms have implications for the consciousness that is necessary to notice ethical or unethical practices and then to give feedback. Several administrators and managers identified *rationalization* as one way to cope with unethical practices they felt powerless to change. They found themselves devising reasons for why a practice or policy could be justified. For example, "no one was really hurt by it" (Manning, 1990, p. 280).

Other managers described *"keeping the blinders on"* against anything that is dissonant. Keeping the blinders on becomes a way to avoid any potential awareness or confrontations about unethical practices. If you don't see it, don't hear it, and don't respond to it, you can avoid the responsibility for it. One manager (Manning, 1990, p. 280) described it as "Bring it down to the world and the parts I have control over . . . find projects to work on . . . wait it out, it will pass." Another example was (Manning, 1990, p. 281) "I don't dig down into why I'm doing it." A middle manager (Manning, 1990, p. 281) described avoiding meetings when she knows she will be confronted with ethical issues that "I will not be able to live with." She would also avoid people who might bring up unethical issues. I ". . . avoid getting drawn into it . . . don't say anything." Avoiding the ethical and moral issues that are dissonant with a leader's personal and professional morality only further reduces the leader's or constituent's ability to self-regulate and to assist the organization in self-regulation.

The Cycle of Alienation

After constituents (subordinates, other managers, or administrators) feel alienated from their own morality, they experience feeling victimized, intimidated, and apprehensive of future situations (Manning, 1990). Even though the threat of job loss keeps them in what feels like an untenable situation, they are constantly evaluating "How much can you lower your own ethics based on personal needs of your own?" The experience is a catch-22 because, although employees can stay in their position, they experience a loss in the meaning of their work. The loss of meaning affects motivation, morale, and loyalty. Employees' performance is reduced, and their contribution to the workplace is minimized. Some managers (Manning, 1990, p. 282) simply distanced from it altogether. Others reported a "constant state of conflict," "feeling crazy," and "feeling embarrassed and ashamed" (Manning, 1990, p. 282).

The cycle of alienation (see Figure 4.4) occurs as ethical quandaries force individuals to experience a separation of their actions from their personal and professional morality. A sense of powerlessness ensues. The discomfort described previously leads to coping mechanisms of denial and avoidance. Denial and avoidance promote a decline in motivation to take action against unethical practices, which, in turn, leads to an increased sense of powerlessness and alienation. The opportunities for support and feedback and for shared ownership with others are avoided because collaboration would further confront the conflict the person experiences. Thus, isolation and withdrawal act as a buffer to those realizations, but increase a sense of aloneness with the dilemma. One middle manager (Manning, 1990, p. 283) described his alienation poignantly:

> It's sort of like my Grandmother told me once. She lives along a four lane highway, and there's no traffic lights and older people live all along this in retirement homes. And what they do is, the traffic is so high and there's no lights and when you have to make a left hand turn into traffic . . . the old people would get so frustrated about just sitting there and waiting and waiting and never being able to cross it, eventually they just closed their eyes and gun it. It's almost like road kill, you know, they'd sweep them out every once in a while. And I think, one of these days they're going to get me, you know, when that happens they'll just sweep me out.

This manager did not feel there were any opportunities for ethical action or the possibility of changing what he was experiencing as a manager in a for-profit human service agency. The day-to-day decisions about ethics made by administrators, managers, and other employees do have an impact beyond the moral integrity of the individual. These decisions have a cumulative effect with profound moral, social, and professional implications.

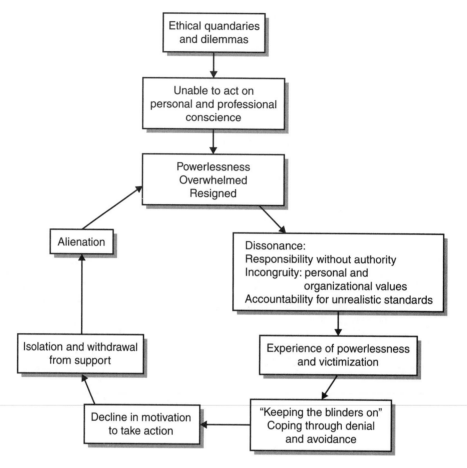

FIGURE 4.4   Cycle of Alienation

Moral, Professional, and Social Consequences of Powerlessness

The power of the individual to influence moral, professional, and social processes is profound. Similarly, an individual's perception of powerlessness to influence has multiple consequences. As mentioned earlier in the discussion on the cycle of alienation (p. 146), the *moral consequence* to the person in the form of dulled moral character, and loss of moral integrity is considerable. The personal policy of relinquishing control to higher authorities erodes a person's ability to act ethically. Further, as each individual experiences a loss of moral integrity, this furthers the possibility of the "banality of evil." People become more and more focused on the tasks and performance of the bureaucracy and less atune to the moral aspects of those tasks and performance. A discussion of some of the multiple consequences follows.

Self-Regulation of Individuals and the Organization

The self-regulation of the employees and the organization depends on the self-correcting facet of employees (Brummer, 1985; Manning, 1990). Employees who are caught up in the web of wrongdoing and who feel powerless to challenge or give feedback about unethical policies and practices also impact the moral well-being of the organization, the community, and their profession (Brummer, 1985). It is an interesting paradox that the employee who feels powerless and remains silenced about unethical practices is in fact enacting a choice about those practices; thus, the powerless exerts some form of power. Brummer (1985, p. 86) argues that ". . . Every decision to abide by or ignore the demands of conscience is a choice and, as such, involves the initiation of a policy or precedent of choice by the subordinate." There is a great deal of power in inaction. The failure to act contributes to a culture of inaction and silence about moral issues, such as influencing others in the organization to also remain silent. The day-to-day decisions model for others either an atmosphere of self-correction or one of obedience. The culture of inaction that occurs contributes to an atmosphere of obedience that prevents future actions or challenges on the part of constituents.

Violations of Professional Behavior

The unethical policies and practices of an organization can also be violations of *professional behavior*. The self-regulating mechanisms of the professions have a beneficial effect for human service agencies through each individual's conscience and the professional code. Professional codes help shape agency practices, particularly in regard to quality of care and primacy of care to consumers. Also, relationships with colleagues and loyalty to the agency are promoted through most codes of ethics. As professionals participate in unethical practices, they are ignoring their code of ethics. The self-correcting process that codes reinforce is dulled or eliminated.

A code of ethics reflects consensus among persons and institutions about what reflects appropriate ethical behaviors (as discussed in Chapter 2). As obedience and inaction promote a dulled sensitivity to moral issues, further development of the professional code about organizational practices is impacted negatively. Individuals who are transgressing the guidelines in place will have little interest in pursuing future ethical guidelines. When professional codes are no longer adequate to regulate the ethical behaviors of professionals in organizations, regulations from government and other entities are bound to follow. An example is the legislation that has developed in response to ethical abuses in the managed health and mental health care systems. Managed care organizations have been slow to regulate their own practices, and government has had to provide controls. We see the same trend in corporate practices. As corporations falter financially due to hidden and questionable accounting practices, there is a necessity for stronger governmental regulations.

Social Cost

Finally, the *social cost* is connected to the impact of organizational policies or practices on those most effected: individuals and society. A negative, harmful, or destructive consequence to people, communities, environments, and society cannot be averted if those who are aware of the impact do not take action, for example, by giving feedback. This is especially important for human service agencies because their product is providing service to human beings. The process and results of service delivery affect the well-being of human beings and communities. Professionals, as discussed in Chapter 1, have a responsibility to make the invisible visible. Feedback from individuals in human service agencies helps to inform the community about areas of human services that are not functioning adequately. In addition, the social costs of inaction and silence affect the culture of communities. Every decision and action communicates a message to society about what is valued, and indirectly, what society values (Manning, 1997).

Clearly, powerlessness on the part of constituents can have critical detrimental effects. The failure to challenge organizational practices that are unethical and harmful not only allows those practices to continue, but also restricts the quality and range of choice of those directly harmed. Brummer (1985, p. 87) paraphrases Edmund Burke: "All that is required for evil to win out is for good people to do nothing about it." Ethical leadership must include ways for managers, administrators, and constituents to be empowered to act and to give feedback.

The Power to Take Ethical Action

The power to act ethically resides in leaders at all levels of the organization. The role or position of an individual does provide a legitimate level of authority (discussed in the section about the first dimension of power). However, leadership is not only relegated to the higher administrative positions of an organization. Leaders occupy managerial and supervisory roles as well as direct service positions. The ability to influence ethical practices and to confront unethical ones requires skills of influence that go beyond legitimate authority. The results of a study on ethical decisions by human services leaders (Manning, 1990) revealed that managers and administrators viewed their ability to influence as crucial to the ability to make ethical decisions. The leader's ability to decide ethically was directly related to wielding power, either through conscious use of self or the legitimated power associated with the role or position. The positive use of power by leaders created resources, confronted unethical practices, helped to develop ethical climate and culture, and reinforced accountability of individuals and of the organization. Leaders' abuse of power restricted feedback, reinforced systems that inhibited creativity and problem finding, and promoted barriers to accountability systems. Examples from the research will be quoted throughout this section.

Power as an attribute for ethical leadership is discussed first as using the power that resides in the *position*. However, power for ethical leadership can also be developed through the use of influence that is derived in other ways, such as through *attitudes* and through particular *functions* that are available to all leaders (see Figure 4.5).

Power from Legitimate Authority

An executive director described (Manning, 1990, p. 260) his power in this way: "The power on top is a lot more than the power on the bottom . . . I have the power to in-

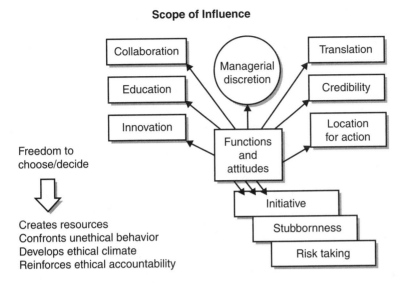

FIGURE 4.5   Power To Act Ethically

flict my ethical beliefs on 148 people." An upper level administrator said, "I don't know if this level is unique, but people listen a lot to what I say at this level" (Manning, 1990, p. 260). The power that rests in the position a leader holds has several sources, including duty, relationships with others, and the position in the administrative hierarchy (Levy, 1982).

All eyes are on the CEOs; employees, consumers, and community citizens observe their ability to accomplish the agency's mission. The chief executive has paramount responsibility, *a duty*, to achieve the organization's purpose; this is a contract with the public and with the community. The human service organization's quality of service delivery depends on a professional staff who must be knowledgeable and skilled. The executive sets the tone, climate, and character for the agency and the staff to accomplish their mission.

Administrators and CEOs may excuse decisions and policies at this level because their decisions are required by the position or role. However, this is an avoidance of the accountability for the personal values that are embedded in such decisions. The executive or administrative policymaker has the ability to "put his or her moral stamp on a decision, by default if in no other way (Brummer, 1985, p. 87). Leaders in positions at the upper levels of the hierarchy have the opportunity to put a moral stamp on the entire organization. Whatever values they promote and integrate into policy can influence the ethical climate and culture of the organization, as well as external entities. One administrator noted (Manning, 1990, p. 261), "I think the scope of influence, for me, has been . . . there's a far greater possibility to reach, to affect, to influence people in the community, other agencies in the community, within your own field, outside of your field, the legislators."

Leaders have roles in a variety of levels in an organization, for example, executive director, upper administrator, middle manager, and supervisor to name just a few. The higher people are in the hierarchy of the agency means the more they have access to the legitimate power of the position and accountability for agency function.

Managers described two kinds of power associated with the role: legitimate power of the position and power developed through use of self. Legitimate power was not viewed as having considerable weight in relation to power at higher levels. Use of self appeared to be an important way to develop influence, but managers experienced influence differently, according to their perception of their own power. One said, "I don't have the power and authority in a middle manager position to make real change happen . . . I can only influence and facilitate." In contrast, others experienced a different sense of power. "I like the role of empowering people to develop ethics and values that are needed as professionals," and "I'm pretty good at getting people fired up to take on a challenge" (Manning, 1990, p. 245).

Middle managers also experienced a sense of isolation in their position. They noted that they lack contact with peers for support and reality checks, either because of time constraints or because of organizational structures that prohibited many interactions with other managers. One (Manning, 1990, p. 244) said middle management is ". . . the gray area of management . . . clinicians and administrators are more black and white." The gray area of leadership—middle management and supervisory roles—requires more than the power that rests in a hierarchical position. Leaders at this level must use the power attached to who they are and how they negotiate their organizational terrain. Attitudes of influence and some particular behaviors that develop influence are ways to increase their scope of influence toward ethical practices and policies.

The Power Attached to Attitude

Attitudes are "a mental position" toward something, or "a feeling of emotion about a state or fact" (Webster, 1977, p. 73). There is something about the way managers view the decision or situation that affects their approach and ability to influence (Manning, 1990). Three attributes from Manning (1990) are paramount: *initiative*, *stubbornness*, and *risk taking*.

Initiative.   Leaders that would take the *initiative* and had a proactive attitude when faced with ethical dilemmas felt influential in relation to those dilemmas. They had a mindset that was positive about the outcome. For example (Manning, 1990, p. 263), "I always assume there is a solution . . . if you never explore the possibilities, you never come up with alternatives . . . creativity and stubbornness are important . . . most problems are solvable." Managers described structuring meetings with a problem-finding agenda by requesting and encouraging constituents to bring up ethical issues and challenges to the organization. Leaders who took initiative would anticipate ethical concerns ahead of time and then ". . . feed information to administration ahead of time . . . the more information that people have, the better to plan around it"

(Manning, 1990, p. 263). This kind of initiative prevented a reactive approach when ethical challenges were raised in response to new plans and projects.

Stubbornness.   Managers and administrators described attitudes of *stubbornness*, or a persistence and tenacity that helped them pursue the right thing in decisions and solutions. The stubbornness was especially directed toward keeping ethical issues on the agenda with higher administrators and executive directors. Leaders described the visibility of an ethical issue as important: first to bring to the attention of superiors and then to keep attention focused on the issue. One manager said (Manning, 1990, p. 264), "Keep it on the agenda, and don't take NO for an answer." Another described stubbornness somewhat differently: ". . . through supporting my position in an intelligent way . . . so that's what I went ahead and did and I didn't give up . . . and it worked" (Manning, 1990, p. 264). The willingness to be persistent and stubborn in bringing ethical issues forward and finding various ways to keep the issues salient proved to help increase influence. This attitude helps confront the tactics and strategies described in the section on mobilization of bias.

Risk Takers.   Managers who described themselves as *risk takers* experienced the ability to influence the resolution of ethical dilemmas. However, most also acknowledged that risk—going beyond the expected—included the willingness to accept the associated responsibility for the results. Leaders must be willing to take risks when doing the right thing demands it, even in the face of reprimand. Friedman argues that values must be the lens "through which pass the facts that become your judgments, and to stick to those values in the face of opposition, can be risky" (1990, p. 113). Being willing to risk means going against the odds. The outcome is not always predictable. However, when a leader has an attitude of facing risky ethical situations, there is an increased possibility the ethical issues will be addressed.

Power Attached to Function

Leaders have the opportunity to create influence through their actions, functions, and behaviors. These functions are especially helpful to middle managers and supervisors, who have less legitimate or positional authority, but are in the position of influencing policy and practices in an organization. The following functions were identified and described by managers and administrators as strategies that increase influence beyond the power associated with a role or position. The functions of *collaboration*, *education*, *innovation*, *translation*, and *managerial discretion* are discussed.

Collaboration.   The goals of *collaboration* are to increase the resources, options, and support available to a leader when confronted with an ethical dilemma (for example, scarce resources). Managers who collaborate make personal and political relationships a priority because of the influence that is derived from them. Collaboration was discussed by many managers as a form of politics at the middle manager level as ". . . the nature of the middle position" (Manning, 1990, p. 265). Collaborative activities took place within and outside of the organization. Two elements of collaboration that were helpful in enhancing influence were *personal relationships* and *shared ownership* of the ethical dilemma.

Developing relationships is the key to collaboration. One administrator (Manning, 1990, p. 265), when asked to identify the key thing to succeeding in several different agencies working together, said "... it was personal relationships." Because relationships are the foundation in collaboration, managers reinforced the importance of including everyone who would be impacted by the ethical dilemma. Further, relationship building provides support and is reciprocal. For example, "Relationship building is politics ... you scratch my back, I'll scratch yours ... reciprocal relationships" (Manning, 1990, p. 266).

Collaboration offers the opportunity of shared ownership. Therefore, managers must have willingness to compromise, to give and take, and to arrive at a mutual solution. One manager (Manning, 1990, p. 265) noted: "always include everyone who will be impacted ... not give up ownership, but share ownership ... you cannot be wimpy, whiny, offensive, or get into power trips when you ask someone to stretch what they are doing." Shared ownership offers increased autonomy and self-determination of all involved through participation in the problem-solving process. For example, involving consumers who are impacted by rationing decisions increases their investment in the decision.

The importance of shared ownership for leaders who face multiple ethical dilemmas cannot be overstated. Shared ownership of ethical quandaries relieves stress and the pressure of feeling all of the responsibility for an organization's ethical problems; it makes a "social work problem into a systems problem" (Manning, 1990, p. 267). One high-level leader (Manning, 1990, p. 267) described the strategy of bringing ethical issues to the attention of everyone on the unit and increasing the responsibility and the investment in the issue "... from one person to twenty." Further, shared ownership provides multiple voices and perspectives, which improve the quality of the reasoning process about the ethical issue. As ethical dilemmas are assessed in relation to the moral and value issues they represent, colleagues and consumers think about the dilemma differently.

Collaboration, then, increases influence in the following ways:

- Increasing resources and options
- Decreasing the sense of isolation of the manager
- Communicating a sense of unity and commonality
- Increasing investment in the decision and/or solution by more people
- Emphasizing a systems approach
- Transforming informational items to ethical issues
- Enhancing the ethical reasoning process through multiple perspectives

An important element of the collaborative process is education.

Education. The function of *education* is centered on informing others about the ethical nature of policies and practices. Educating is influencing others by giving them information that may change their perspective about the issue. It is empowering to the manager because it asserts an opinion, value, or perspective directly. Administrators and managers described educating as teaching, and as informing without alienating. One administrator (Manning, 1990, p. 268) also described advocacy for the agency as a component of informing: "I provide documentation of the potential ramifications to top administration . . . I want to make sure they are informed."

The power of education is that it makes ethical issues and dilemmas overt, rather than covert. Informing and educating others, at all levels, about the implications of decisions and policies increases the accountability of the organization and individuals to decide in a rational way. As one person (Manning, 1990, p. 268) put it, "be conscious of making the choice, don't slide in one direction or the other just to go along."

A component of education is *ammunition*. When additional influence is needed, many managers bring in the ammunition (their own term). Ammunition is the use of something else that has more legitimized authority or that can add weight to the leader's point of view. One manager (Manning, 1990, pp. 268–269) said "you can bring in the hard line [data], and you can bring in the soft line [rationale], but that's not good enough because the bottom line is politics . . . so bring in the outside regulations (for example, Joint Commission on Accreditation of Hospitals [JCAH], Medicaid), or use what other hospitals are doing." The ammunition of what other agencies are doing was a common theme; this ammunition helped to support standards of care, develop ethical policy, and demonstrate examples of the problem.

Another strategy was to bring in data about what other agencies are doing to support standards of care, develop ethical policy, and provide examples of the issue. The use of a consultant, someone from outside the organization or unit who can make it a bigger issue, was also part of ammunition. Sometimes individuals who are viewed as being in high-status positions are brought forward as ammunition. Several managers and administrators (Manning, 1990, p. 269) mentioned, for example, "refer it to the doctor."

The final example of ammunition is the use of the bottom line. The bottom line is the realization by leaders that they can give up the job over the ethical issue in question. When an employee reaches the bottom line, the superior is confronted with choosing between the loss of that person or compromising on the issue. Education, then, can increase influence in the following ways:

- Informing others about the ethical nature of policies and practices
- Influencing others through information
- Asserting opinions, values, and perspectives directly
- Teaching about ethical issues
- Making ethical dilemmas overt
- Using ammunition to support ethical concerns

However, sometimes collaboration and education are not enough. The scarcity of resources sometimes requires actions that are more creative.

Creativity and Innovation. The ability to *create and innovate* when faced with ethical dilemmas that emanate from shortages and that seem to lack concrete solutions (for example, scarcity of resources) helps to expand the options and possibilities of leaders to act ethically. Innovation is a function of influence whereby leaders direct their energy and power into the development of nontraditional ideas and solutions. Managers and administrators (Manning, 1990, p. 270) have described innovation in different ways. "There's a wonderful aliveness in . . . not the power as much as, when I say power, I hate that word in a way because it brings in so many negative things, but I mean power to create . . . and I love that. I'm surely not in it for the money." "The scarce resources have forced a better job of community alternatives . . . and developed some ingenious ways to help people."

The key to innovation and creativity is a system that can tolerate it or, better yet, provide support for leaders to develop innovative and creative ideas. As one manager noted (Manning, 1990, pp. 270–271), "Creativity to create a win-win situation is difficult to do in a rigid agency . . . there has to be latitude for creativity . . . flexibility in order to make good decisions. Otherwise it becomes a double-bind . . . decide what the agency wants you to decide, or what the client and staff together decide." Leaders, by participating with staff, consumers, community members, and so forth, can create alternatives and make decisions about difficult ethical dilemmas, particularly if the agency does not stand in the way.

Creativity and innovation can increase influence in the following ways:

- Create new resources
- Create alternatives that increase choice
- Create energy and interest in innovative solutions

Translation and Interpretation.   Leaders in middle manager and supervisory roles often are in a position to *translate and interpret* between two or more other layers in the hierarchy. Subsequently, the leader translates the information and decisions from upper administration down to the direct service staff and translates the input and reaction from the staff back up the hierarchical ladder. The information may be changed, reinterpreted, distorted, or reported in a different language in the process as a strategy of influence. These strategies can be used to be more ethical or to reduce the impact of participating in unethical policies and strategies. Leaders must make distinctions in the use of translation and interpretation in order to influence decisions toward the ethical and to avoid colluding in policies that are unethical.

The translation provides managers with some influence over the way the message affects them, and the translation influences the effect on the staff who carry out the imperative. One manager (Manning, 1990, p. 272) described that role as the middle man, ". . . and that is playing the middle. You're in the middle then cause you're trying to translate that maybe borderline ethical stuff into something you can live with . . . and still implement the agenda." In this example, a manager is dealing with unethical issues by changing the way they look, and protecting himself or herself and staff from the moral impact of the practice.

In contrast, leaders can use translation toward moral good, either for themselves and/or the organization. One manager did not take ownership of messages from upper administration with which he did not agree. His peer said that (Manning, 1990, p. 272), "he was very open . . . If his supervisor gave him a directive and he didn't like it, he would do it, but he would tell his team, 'I think this is nonsense, I think it may be unethical of them, but we've got to do it because this is the directive.' And he left. He just quit . . . left the agency." Two things occurred in this transaction that were important ethically. First, the questionable policy or practice was identified as such. The manager interpreted what was presented by administration as unacceptable. Even if not faced directly by the manager, this opened the door to others confronting or questioning it. Second, this manager left the agency because of the dissonance between his moral integrity and the expectations of superiors. Although this did not relieve the ethical problems at the agency, it did send a strong message of choice to subordinates and peers.

The presentation of information by leaders also can make a difference in increasing influence. Leaders have an opportunity to make an impact on the way that others in the organization or community think about an ethical issue. One leader (Manning, 1990, p. 272) related that "I try to figure out how to say things to upper administration in a way that can be heard . . . I'm more emotional . . . I'm constantly working on how to say it." An executive director (Manning, 1990, p. 273) uses the presentation of information and choices about language to influence policymakers. She discussed that ". . . packaging things in different words that will be heard . . . 'early intervention' instead of 'prevention' to fit with the growing trend, and to talk about needs in terms that will relate to criteria for funding." The leaders' ability to communicate, to demonstrate passion about an issue, and to think strategically about the presentation of information can enhance their influence to effect ethical policies and practices with all constituencies.

Translation and interpretation can increase influence in the following ways:

- Identify ethical issues overtly
- Delineate ethical choices to constituents
- Present information strategically
- Use language that resonates with responders
- Communicate and demonstrate passion about the ethical issue

Discretion and Independent Judgment. A leader's use of *discretion and independent judgment* is a major factor in empowerment and influence. Hasenfeld (1992, p. 276) defines discretion as ". . . involving the existence of choice, as contrasted with decisions dictated by rules." Discretion is using the leeway available in the organization and the manager's sense of judgment about the right course of action. Thus, the leader must use a conscious use of self to create influence where none is experienced through situational or organizational factors. One manager (Manning, 1990, p. 273) described discretion as ". . . a way to circumvent the system and still be within budget and policy." Leaders employ discretion to decide about what battles to fight, what information to share or withhold, how to interpret policy, and when to go against or around policy because of moral reasons. For instance, one manager (Manning, 1990, p. 273) related using discretion to determine when to interpret or mandate unpopular decisions from above and ". . . when to take a stand."

The activity of interpreting policy and rules can be done with discretion. Leaders can work in the client's, employees', or organization's best interest when rules, regulations, or policy do not serve the moral aspects of a particular situation. For example, a manager (Manning, 1990, p. 274) uses his own letterhead to write letters of reference for employees when the agency policy prohibited letters of reference because of liability. "That's the only way I've gotten around that. But my basic rule of thumb is that if the organizational expectation for the employee is any different than the other way around, then it's unethical." Another example is a team leader of an emergency/crisis evaluation unit that gave a homeless client a ride to a motel even though agency policy prohibited taking clients in personal vehicles. This leader evaluated the risks of a vulnerable client (that he had known for several years) not making it to the arranged housing versus the risk of the organization being harmed. In his judgment, going around the policy *in this situation* was the right thing to do.

Toulmin (1981) argues against tyrannical absolutism and advocates for the use of discretion as a reassertion of ethical objectivity. The demand for equality of treatment through the administration of social services has resulted in a preponderance of principles and rules that impede and obstruct the use of individual discretion. Toulmin reminds us that equity does not require "uniformity or equality"; rather, what is needed is the ability to apply general rules or policies to individual situations in a reasonable and sensitive way. Toulmin (1981, p. 34) says the following:

> Moral wisdom is exercised not by those who stick by a single principle come what may, absolutely and without exception, but rather by those who understand that, in the long run, no principle—however absolute—can avoid running up against another equally absolute principle; and by those who have the experience and discrimination needed to balance conflicting considerations in the most humane way.

The importance of leaders maintaining a consciousness about choice is critical to learning to exercise influence. Rules, procedures, and policies are rampant in bureaucracies and can dictate rigid responses to complex human situations. Choices and discretion also abound as opportunities to increase the options and influence available to resolve ethical dilemmas.

Discretion and independent judgment can increase influence in the following ways:

- Expanding choice through use of leeway available in organizations
- Relying on practice wisdom to support independent judgment
- Applying general rules and policies in reasonable and sensitive ways
- Maintaining a consciousness about choice

Narrow the Boundaries.   The scope of influence is sometimes increased for managers when they *narrow the boundaries of location* where decisions must be made. Narrowing the boundaries results in exercising more control (Manning, 1990).

Leaders can assess where in the system they have more influence and then focus the decision process in those situations in which they have more control. For example, one manager described the following:

> So I have sort of tried to make it a smaller community. Because I think to try to stay a part of that larger community has been for me very self-defeating . . . in terms of incentive . . . and motivation on the job, and clinicians feeling that they have, in fact, some say about how the program develops and how it looks.

The ability to focus on the ethical issues of a smaller unit provides leaders and constituents with a sense of moral self-determination. As in the domino effect, the resulting ethical decisions have an impact on the larger system.

The Cycle of Influence

Influence also has its own cycle (see Figure 4.6). The scope of influence, enacted through attitudes, functions, discretion, and location, is enhanced through conscious use of self. In turn, the increased sense of influence affects the leader's confidence, which increases the use of discretion and independent judgment. As leaders are more actively involved in shaping ethical decisions and impacting the moral climate of the organization, a sense of energy and renewal is initiated. The freedom to speak out and

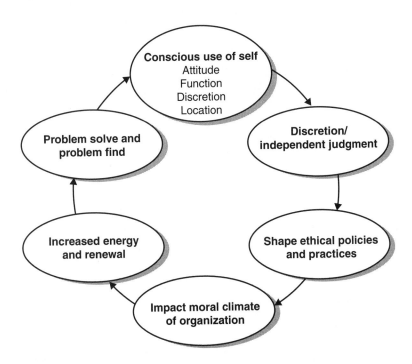

FIGURE 4.6   Cycle of Influence

to give input, or to shape and influence ethical decisions, creates a sense of hope and renewed energy to problem solve and problem find. The ability to influence the agendas of the organization, to bring ethical issues to the attention of the necessary decisionmakers, and to provide feedback about unethical practices is a critical part of empowerment for leaders. Just as these activities empower leaders, so can they empower constituents by supporting them in the same activities. This will be discussed further in Chapters 9, 10, and 11.

The level in the organizational hierarchy does make a difference in the experience of power and the use of discretion (Manning, 1990). Upper administrators are more likely to use discretion about policy. Younger and less experienced managers at lower levels are more likely to turn to policy and procedure for guidance. Leaders who use discretion actively reported that they experience themselves as more powerful and having a broader range of movement and action.

The use of collaboration is empowering through sharing ownership with others; the use of discretion is empowering through taking ownership independently. Influence, then, is expansionistic and future oriented. In contrast, alienation causes a narrowing of perspective and restricted awareness of alternatives; the focus is myopic and trapped in the past or present, without hope for the future.

Conclusion

This chapter has introduced the reader to the dynamic processes of power and the relationship of power to ethical actions and decisions. A leader's understanding of the power that comes with the role and the power that is developed through attitudes and functions can facilitate the influence necessary to resolve ethical dilemmas and to enhance ethical cultures. The *freedom to choose* is the essence of ethical leadership and ethical action. Leaders and constituents who are restricted from acting on their moral conscience find themselves alienated from their own moral integrity. Further, their alienation reduces their contribution to the self-regulation of the organization.

The ability and/or willingness to abuse power is at the core of unethical policies and practices. An awareness of the manifestation of power in all the different dimensions provides the leader with the *consciousness* and *conscientiousness* needed to avoid the abuse of power. In addition, leaders can empower constituents more effectively by recognizing the interactive quality of perceptions, position, and powerlessness. As constituents experience the freedom to choose, to give feedback, to question, and to problem find, the ethical climate of the organization is enhanced. The next chapter places leaders in their own starting point: the personal, professional, and moral places that have developed through personal and professional socialization.

QUESTIONS AND APPLICATIONS

1. Consider the three dimensions of manifesting power for leaders: power in the position, power through structure and process, and power through the construction of meaning.

- Identify and discuss an example of your own use of power (or that of a superior) in relation to each of those dimensions.
- In what way was there an abuse of power?
- How could the power be used in an ethical manner in each of your examples?

2. Describe a situation where you felt alienated in your work. What values were being restricted or oppressed. What kept you from speaking out or taking action? What would have changed the cycle of alienation that was occurring?

3. Identify an ethical challenge for leadership in your agency. How would you use positive influence—through role and position, through your own attitudes, or through particular functions (for example, collaboration or translation)—to help solve or positively impact the ethical issue?

PART TWO

Ethical Resources:
Traditions and Tools
for Ethical Leadership

Chapter 5 moves from leadership and power to the starting point of leaders as moral agents. Leaders have individual and unique starting points, personal perspectives about ethics and morality that affect their approach to ethical decisions. Within these starting points are personal and professional values that have influence on ethical leading. The role of moral development and professional socialization contributes to a leader's perspective about ethical and moral issues in the organization. Moral sensitivity and moral identity are identified as critical to ethical leadership. This chapter discusses leaders' internal guides and attitudes that affect sensitivity to the moral issues and choices about decisions. Role identity is discussed in relation to the leaders' perception about their scope of influence to affect ethical issues. The chapter closes with a discussion about personal reflection and awareness; it emphasizes the importance of leader's consciousness of their personal starting points.

Chapters 6 and 7 provide the discussion about ethical resources that can be drawn on by leaders to help with ethical analysis, ethical reasoning, and the resolution of ethical dilemmas. These chapters are organized according to a framework of moral citizenship: awareness, feeling, thinking, and action. Chapter 6 opens with a discussion of the language of ethics and the nature of dilemmas. Contextual issues (for example, ambiguity and complexity of ethical dilemmas) and different examples of philosophical approaches to ethics (for example, caring and justice orientations) help broaden our thinking about an ethical-reasoning process. Awareness and feeling are discussed as the first two components of moral citizenship. Chapter 6 discusses moral theories of caring (Feminist, Afrocentric, and Ghandian) and considers these theories in regard to a leader's responsibility to relationship and community.

Chapter 7 provides a discussion of thinking and action. Ethical resources, such as theories (for example, deontological, teleological, and so forth), principles, and philosophical paradigms (for example, justice, rights based, and so forth) provide time-honored traditions that help to broaden the decisionmaker's perspective and to apply a reasoning process to ethical dilemmas. The final emphasis of the chapter is on taking effective action. Moral citizenship is directed toward consciousness and activities that promote ethical decisions, behaviors, and practices by intention (Manning, 1990). A framework of questions to guide the analysis of moral and ethical dilemmas and to provoke new ways to consider the nature of dilemmas ends the chapter.

The individual leader, based on the previous four chapters, is prepared, conceptually, to think about and take action through ethical leadership within a human service organization.

CHAPTER

5

Starting Points: Where a Leader Begins with Ethics

THE FOCUS IN THIS CHAPTER IS ON THE FOLLOWING AREAS:

- Understanding your starting points
- Understanding what stage you are in: moral, life, and career development
- Understanding what hat you wear: role identity and scope of influence
- Understanding internal guides and individual justifiers for ethics
- Understanding attitudes and approaches: opportunity or constraint
- Knowing yourself through reflection and self-awareness

Leaders experience ethical dilemmas, as well as approach and resolve them, from different and unique perspectives. Individual perspectives and moral judgment are formed through a variety of developmental stages, life experiences, and socialization processes. The learning that accumulates from the exposure to significant others (for example, parents, family, peers, teachers, religious leaders, and so forth), combined with the life experiences in childhood, adolescence, and adulthood, integrates with professional and occupational socialization that develops over a lifetime. This amalgam of life and work experience results in a particular approach or world view, or a lens through which ethical issues and dilemmas are viewed. This lens could be thought of as a *starting point* (Manning, 1990).

Starting points affect leaders in several ways: their awareness of ethical issues, their willingness to take action, the ability and motivation to use judgment and discretion, and, ultimately, the kinds of decisions made or actions taken to resolve the dilemma. Starting points are influenced by a person's developmental stage: emotionally, psychologically, and in regard to moral judgment and identification. In addition, individual personality factors and characteristics, the underlying rationale that leaders use to inform themselves, personal and professional socialization and values, and a leader's individual approach to an ethical issue all have an impact on the process and resolution of ethical problems. Starting points also include the role or position that provides the leader with influence and spheres of responsibility. The attitudinal and structural factors that help in defining what is ethical or unethical are elements that influence ethical decisions.

Starting points, then, have a profound effect on a leader's perception, understanding, and resolution of ethical and moral issues. Thus, the ability to develop self-awareness skills through reflection, deliberation, and dialogue with others is essential for ethical leadership. This chapter explores the individual and idiosyncratic characteristics the leader brings to the process of ethical decisionmaking, with some discussion about the resulting implications. Again, the voices of administrators and managers bring real-life examples to the discussion (Manning, 1990).

What Stage Are You In?

The starting point of ethical leadership includes developmental factors that influence the breadth and depth of ethical reasoning and awareness. Development affects how leaders approach and think about an ethical dilemma in a number of ways: moral and ethical development, life stage development, and career development. Perspectives on ethical issues are influenced by prior socialization and developmental stages as well as the situational factors, such as work roles, professional context, and organizational culture (Holland & Kilpatrick, 1991).

Moral Judgment: Thinking and the Ability to See the Moral Problem

Leaders face ethical challenges with varying abilities to use moral judgment. Moral judgments reflect efforts to establish some sort of order from the chaos of social experience (Gilligan, 1981). Moral judgment, according to Kohlberg and Elfenbein (1975, p. 634)

> . . . is not simply logical reasoning applied to moral problems. In the first place, moral judgment involves role-taking, taking the point of view of others conceived as *subjects* and coordinating those points of view, whereas logic involves only coordinating points of view with respect to objects. Secondly, moral judgement, unlike logical reasoning, rests upon principles of justice or fairness.

Therefore, the level of moral judgment of a leader reflects one's ability to identify with the experience, feelings, opinions, values, and meanings of those involved in an ethical dilemma and to care about promoting fairness as part of the resolution.

Moral judgments are the result of cognitive structures that are brought to bear on experience as well as the experiences themselves. It is this interaction of thought and experience that results in the moral development of individuals. Lawrence

Kohlberg and Jean Piaget are two well-known cognitive theorists that have promoted intellectual growth, or stages of moral judgment, as the key to understanding moral development (Damon, 1999).

Stages of Moral Judgment

Kohlberg (1981) developed six stages of moral judgment that are organized into three levels of moral reasoning (see Figure 5.1, Levels I, II, and III). The six stages reflect an individual's conception of justice. Each stage represents a higher level reorganization of the moral concepts of preceding stages, allowing for a more complex and differentiated understanding of the moral issues involved. The higher stages of moral judgment, then, would predict a more just solution to moral dilemmas. Each stage also reflected an increased capacity to ". . . take the point of view of the other—an expanded perspective conducive to a fairer resolution of the dilemma" (Gilligan, 1981, p. 142). These stages are useful for describing and understanding intellectual growth. However, the model does not explain an individual's actual behavior. Also, Kohlberg's research was located in a particular period of time and with respondents who were located in a particular place in their own development (adolescent boys). In general, Kohlberg and Piaget found that moral judgment begins for younger children with moral beliefs oriented toward power and authority. Over time and several stages of development, there is a growing realization that social norms and expectations are made by people. Therefore, it is possible to renegotiate social rules. Further, an understanding of the reciprocity of relationships provides the foundation for fairness, rather than obedience to a higher level of authority.

Logic of Justification

I. **Preconventional Level–Emphasis on Self-interest**
    Stage 1: Fear of punishment/importance of approval
    Stage 2: Beginning autonomy/justice and fairness reached through reciprocity and exchange

II. **Conventional Level–Social approval and relationships**
    Stage 3: Importance of approval of the group
    Stage 4: Meeting standards, rules, and laws of society to preserve social order

III. **Postconventional–Abstract ideals transcend societal morality**
    Stage 5: Equality and reciprocity through personal conscience and social contract
    Stage 6: Universal rights/individual functions autonomously and impartially

Logic of Responsibility

IV. **Contextual Relativism and Ethical Responsibility**
    ■ *From moral to ethical environment*
    ■ *From formal to existential*
    ■ *From self-interest to relationship of self and other*

V. **Problem Finding**
    ■ *Focus on questions rather than solutions*
    ■ *Meaning making–same issues from different and broader perspectives*
    ■ *Others as ends rather than means*
    ■ *Contextual understanding of differences*

FIGURE 5.1 Stages of Moral Development

The first level of Kohlberg's model is the preconventional level, which reflects an emphasis on an individual's self-interest, rather than judging what is right or wrong according to the standards of society. Fear of punishment from people in authority is the main reason that a person will follow the rules. The second stage of this level moves the person to consider some emerging autonomy and the realization that justice can be thought of as fairness and can be achieved through reciprocity or exchange. Level II is called the conventional level and the focus is on social approval and considering both individual needs and those of the group. The basic criteria for determining what is right or wrong are relationships with others and the social norms and rules of society. Stage 3 is focused on the precedence of the group's perspectives about moral issues and a concern for gaining approval from others. In Stage 4, the relational perspective is extended to society, that is, meeting the standards and laws of society in order to preserve the social order.

The third level is the postconventional level, which is directed toward abstract ideals and transcends the limits of the morality of society. Here an individual may be concerned with equality and reciprocity through their own conscience and their understanding of a social contract with others. At the highest stage, these principles become the foundation for universal rights. At the postconventional level, an individual does not necessarily reject the legitimacy of rules for society, but thinks critically about them and critiques their relevance and usefulness in regard to moral issues. The postconventional individual has a capacity "for reflection, logical reasoning, responsibility, and an inner source of morality and justice" (Bommer et al., 1987, p. 273).

At this highest stage, Gilligan (1981, p. 143) points out the following:

> The Golden Rule is now understood in its fullest implication as Kant's categorical imperative—to act on that maxim which you can at the same time will to be a universal law. . . . Moral judgment, freed from both individual and societal constraints and anchored instead in principles of justice, becomes autonomous in its function and universal in its impartial application.

Leaders with a postconventional level of moral judgment exhibit independent judgment and a sense of ethical responsibility for the collective, whether it be the organization, community, and/or society, in personal and professional life. These stages are part of a paradigm that places moral judgment in the logic of justification and choice through a justice orientation. Other experts have added dimensions that extend our understanding of moral judgment toward a developmental continuum that includes responsibility and consequences as part of ethical decisionmaking.

Moving from Moral to Ethical Responsibility

A shift from the logic of justification and choice to a focus on responsibility and the consequences of actions provides a broader perspective in moral judgment and a step toward ethical reasoning. Perry's (1968) work added a new stage: contextual relativism. Contextual relativism brings forward a consideration of the complex, multidimensional, and individual aspects of moral and ethical problems and requires the ability to develop an awareness of multiplicity. Multiplicity means there is a diversity of opinion and values that are ". . . recognized as legitimate in situations where right answers are not yet known" (Perry, 1981, p. 79). The search for the right answer comes to an end with the realization that a right answer cannot be found outside of the context in which the question is asked. This level of development requires letting go of prescriptions and absolutes. Instead, the decisionmaker must consider all the differences and diversities in a particular situation or dilemma, rather than applying an objective moral truth across situations. The requirements of contextual relativism make the decisionmakers both more accountable and more free in their choices.

Problem Finding.   Part of ethical responsibility is *problem finding*. Arlin (1975) concentrated on the development of a higher cognitive stage that is focused on the ability to ask questions, rather than find solutions. Arlin viewed *problem finding* as a different stage of cognitive development and separate from the problem-solving focus of Kohlberg's moral stages of development. Problem finding is the ability to raise higher order questions about the implications and transformation of particular situations and systems necessary for creative intelligence. Adults have the capacity for this level of thinking due to the creative capacity of adult intelligence. Leaders with the capacity to problem find are able to identify potential ethical quandaries and scenarios proactively, and to project potential impacts of decisions into future possibilities. This translates into decisions, practices, and policies that can prevent possible harm to others and/or the environment. Problem finding is congruent with the double loop learning strategies discussed in Chapter 4.

Justice and Care.   The shift to ethical responsibility in a complex, multidimensional world moves the decisionmaker from the self-centered interest of justification to an emphasis on the relationship between self and other, which are issues of intimacy (Gilligan, 1981). Through this shift, there is a rediscovery of the moral problem: the recognition of the interdependence of human beings who are in contact with each other's lives. The moral issues of intimacy require relating to others as ends rather than means and an ability to shift perspectives based on a ". . . contextual understanding of actual differences in points of view . . ."(Gilligan, 1981, p. 156). Gilligan's later work, *In a Different Voice* (1982), developed a mode of reasoning based on care, responsibility, and relationship that builds on this work (see Chapter 6).

A moral orientation based on a care perspective "draws attention to problems of detachment or abandonment and holds up an ideal of attention and response to need" (Gilligan & Attanucci, 1988, p. 73). In contrast, a justice perspective attends to issues of inequality and oppression, informed by the ideals of reciprocity and equal respect (Gilligan & Attanucci, 1988). These two moral orientations capture different concerns: not treating others unfairly and not ignoring someone in need. These orientations are not mutually exclusive. In fact, "from a developmental standpoint, inequality and attachment are universal human experiences"(Gilligan & Attanucci, 1988, p. 73). The ethics of care, or responsibility mode of reasoning, views moral choice through a web of complex relationships that have both interdependence and diversity (Rhodes,

1985). The reasoning process is based on feelings of compassion and concerns in regard to the consequences of a decision on the lives of people involved, rather than the
logic of justification based on abstract principles. The "particular needs [of people]
take precedence over considerations of fairness" (Rhodes, 1985, p. 102).

Research on the orientations of justice and care demonstrated that concerns
about both are represented in how people think about real-life dilemmas (Gilligan &
Attanucci, 1988). However, individuals tend to focus on one set of concerns while the
other is only minimally represented. In addition, the authors found that there was an
association between moral orientation and gender. Both men and women use both
orientations, but ". . . the Care Focus dilemmas are more likely to be presented by
women and Justice Focus dilemmas by men." It is important to note that both perspectives are reflective of mature moral reasoning. However, the tension between
these perspectives provides a lens to deepen understanding of moral and ethical
dilemmas (Gilligan & Attanucci, 1988, p. 82):

> . . . Detachment, which is the mark of mature moral judgment in the justice perspec-
> tive, becomes *the* moral problem in the care perspective–the failure to attend to need.
> Conversely, attention to the particular needs and circumstances of individuals, the
> mark of mature moral judgment in the care perspective, becomes *the* moral problem in
> the justice perspective–failure to treat others fairly, as equals.

Social work leaders and other professionals in human service delivery agencies have to
attend to ethical issues of justice and need routinely. If leaders approach dilemmas
from a particular orientation, it can promote a tendency to lose sight of the other in
arriving at a decision. Awareness of that tendency can promote a richer, more complex process of analyzing dilemmas that is inclusive of the ideals of both.

The Helix of Ethical Growth.   The stages of moral judgment, contextual relativism, problem finding, and moral orientation relate to a metaphor that strengthens
moral judgment: the helix. Perry (1981, p. 97) offers a model for growth in moral
judgment as ". . . neither the straight line nor the circle, but a helix, perhaps with an
expanding radius to show that when we face the 'same' old issues we do so from a different and broader perspective" (see Figure 5.2). The notion of a spiral, circling
upward with an ever-broadening radius, projects the possibility of building on experience, considering new viewpoints with the awareness of multiplicity, and having an in-
finite trajectory of learning that informs the reasoning process of individual leaders.
The metaphor of the helix points to the helpfulness of education that enhances a capacity to shift perspectives toward the experience of other's lives. It also embodies the
importance of the discovery of ignorance as a foundation to question what was for-
merly taken for granted. Finally, problem-finding behavior and the motivation to
problem find through questions about moral and ethical issues provides momentum
for a broadening, upward spiral.

The capacity for moral response depends on an individual's motivation to address the moral problem, regardless of a leader's stage of moral judgment. Thinking
about moral problems is not the same thing as acting on them. Leaders must want

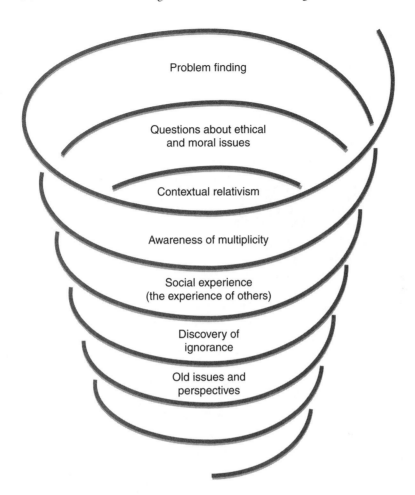

FIGURE 5.2 The Helix of Growth in Moral Judgment

to do something about the moral problem, which leads us to a discussion about moral identity.

Moral Identity: The Motivation to Do "The Right Thing"

Living a moral life, at work and at home, is a complicated phenomenon. Theorists have attempted to explain moral behavior for many decades. The previous theories that stress social influence and experience and intellectual development provide some understanding of moral behavior. However, Damon (1999, p. 75) argues that none of these theories are sufficient to capture the "essential dimensions of moral life: character and commitment." No matter what theoretical explanation is given for the development of values and beliefs that guide moral life, it is the moral behavior that follows the belief that brings forward the critical question: "What makes them live up to their ideals or not?"

This question is critical for leaders, who may ascribe to particular beliefs, such as "Administrators *should* treat employees fairly." However, Damon (1999) posits that the important salutation is one of personal ownership and commitment. "I *want* to treat employees fairly." This commitment is one of *moral identity*. When people use moral principles to define themselves and to understand why they will take a particular course of action, they are demonstrating their moral identity. This distinction between what should be done and what a person wants to do is crucial to understanding the variety of moral behavior. People may share many ideals, but the difference is "the resolve to act on those ideals" (Damon, 1999, p. 76).

In that regard, Anne Colby (1994) studied people who were viewed as the ideal of moral behavior, which were those well known for charity and civil rights work. She determined that the levels of moral reasoning (for example, Kohlberg's levels of moral development) for these leaders were similar to everyone else. However, there was a high level of integration between their self-identity and moral concerns. People whose self-definition includes moral goals are more aware of moral issues in day-to-day life and feel some responsibility for those moral issues. This is in contrast to people who are aware of moral problems, but who view the moral issues as someone else's problem. For them, their own inaction does not challenge their self-definition. For example, a manager described his reactive view of ethical development (Manning, 1990, p. 249):

> I went out to manage the world I live in, in a way that is comfortable . . . Ethical development would require me to be in a position where I'm uncomfortable—for me to make another step in ego development—and I'm not looking to put myself in an uncomfortable position. But life brings those along invariably, and I'll grow from that . . . Like I say, I'm not going out looking for the boogie man to scare me and I won't do that. But . . . when the boogie man comes, I'll learn.

This view reflects a lack of moral vision and goals. Instead, his perspective of moral issues is dependent upon what the job offers up and the situations that force a response.

The development of a moral identity, then, is connected with the moral and ethical dimensions of transformational leadership discussed in Chapter 3. The leader must articulate, and identify with, a moral vision. The moral vision is then integrated with the organizational mission and the purpose of the social work profession. Moral identity develops over time and emanates from a person's life and career development.

Life Stage Development and Personal Factors

The stages in development through which people have transitioned, and their experience through life, provide a foundation and varying levels of preparation for ethical leadership. Life experience—what we have been through—prepares leaders through a heightened awareness of ethical issues and broadened range of responses from past experiences. Learning theories, based on research about behavioral norms and values, conclude that moral behavior is context-bound, varying according to the situation and independent of beliefs. Therefore, age and stage of development are part of the foundation for ethical action.

Gender

Gender has an influence on leaders' starting points as well. As discussed earlier in this chapter, the moral orientation that informs an individual's response to moral dilemmas has some relationship to gender. Women are more likely to use a care orientation, whereas men tend to be oriented by justice or a rights orientation (Gilligan & Attanucci, 1988). A study that reviewed the literature on women's cognitive development, with interviews of more than 500 women, supported Gilligan's (1982) research. They found that women's morality is more focused on caring, rather than an impersonal, abstract reasoning process (Belenky, Clinchy, Goldberger, & Tarule, 1986). A study on ethical judgments of male and female social workers (Dobrin, 1989) measured ethical judgment scores based on Rest's Defining Issues Test (1979), a standard instrument in the measurement of moral development. Dobrin (1989) found that the Defining Issues Test (DIT) scores differed significantly in favor of the females, contrary to the hypothesis of the study. Male social workers in private practice and in sectarian settings (for example, administrators) scored significantly lower than females. Dobrin (1989, p. 454) concluded that the findings may indicate that "... males in sectarian settings are highly committed to ideological or religious positions, because their adherence to religious ideology seems to override ethical judgments." He also posited that the administrative role might place concerns about adhering to agency policy on male administrators to the detriment of ethical judgments. Dobrin noted that "The relatively low scores of males in sectarian agencies also needs attention. It appears that ideology and authority may supersede principled ethical judgments" (Dobrin, 1989, p. 454). This research supported the argument that abstract reasoning and caring are not incompatible for men or women.

Gender can also have an effect on the behavior of leaders in their organizational role, as well as an effect on the organization. A female manager (Manning, 1990, p. 249) felt that her gender affected the way she approached an ethical dilemma, particularly if she is trying to persuade upper administration. She stated, "As a woman I must be perceived as non-emotional, not angry or hysterical . . . it makes a difference in how seriously your concerns will be addressed." If women perceive that they must present a different orientation, one that is more logical or abstract, the organization may miss out on the perspectives that an orientation of care can bring. This orientation may be particularly needed in organizations that have an administrative hierarchy that is mostly male.

The presence of gender can also influence the culture of an organization in regard to ethical issues. A male manager (Manning, 1990, p. 249) noted that "the influence of women in a traditionally male system had made the system more humane." In contrast, systems that are primarily female may lack the different contributions to organizational culture that men might bring. Leaders who perceive the contributions of gender differences in regard to ethical culture will use those contributions toward developing a higher level of moral reasoning in the organization.

Career Development

A leader's work experience and position on a career ladder may affect perspective about ethical decisions. Observations from a particular study (Manning, 1990) revealed these themes. Younger leaders, often in supervisory or midmanagement roles, often have less experience than senior leaders. They may feel more powerless and inadequate to cope with powerful organizational cultures. They had less awareness about options and resources, and this seemed connected to a narrower conceptualization of the ethical issue(s), alternatives, and potential consequences. In this study, some younger managers chose to leave the system rather than stay and feel immobilized. One person related (Manning, 1990, p. 250), "Do we participate in these systems that we can't have [an] impact on, or get out of it?" However, younger leaders felt more enthusiasm, energy, and intensity about the moral and ethical issues that they identified or with which they were confronted.

Leaders with more organizational experience have more background and knowledge to manipulate the administrative and political arena, so they feel that they have more ability to influence decisions (Manning, 1990). Work experience adds to more comfort and familiarity with the use of professional judgment and discretion, which provides more freedom to make choices. More experienced leaders, then, have more ability to take action in response to implicit and explicit policies that may be unethical. They have had many previous experiences, in many different situations, and did not have to reinvent the wheel to determine an ethical response. An older, more experienced administrator noted that her frustration was partially developmental; she'd been there 20 years. Now she's learned (Manning, 1990, p. 250) ". . . to pare it down . . . at some point arrive at how much of the action you're going to mark off . . . how much of the pie can I get my hands into, and then impact that sphere." The wisdom that develops with experience is evident in this response. Her understanding of narrowing the boundaries in order to have an impact is an example. However, some described themselves as burned out and detached. This psychological state dulled their sensitivity to ethical issues, thus affecting awareness, and prevented a full commitment to the resolution of ethical and moral issues.

People in leadership positions that are less experienced can use consultation and collaboration with others to provide the support and reflection needed to grapple with complex ethical issues. Those who are more confident, but less motivated and more burned out, can look for the interested, motivated, and caring energy of the newly promoted, or new-to-the-organization individuals to help stimulate ethical sensitivity and concern. The benefits and deficits of experience are but one aspect of the work environment that has an effect on the leader's approach to ethics. An important dimension is the role or position the person occupies.

What Hat Are You Wearing?

The role or position a leader occupies, and how the individual leader perceives that role or position, makes a difference in decisionmaking. The leader's identification with the role dictates the priorities chosen; the scope of influence perceived and wielded; and choices about where, and how, a leader spends time and energy in relation to ethical issues. The structural factors of position in the hierarchy give the leader role definition and the authority to make decisions at particular levels (as discussed in Chapter 4).

The following sections describe administrative and middle manager roles, as described by individuals in those roles (Manning, 1990, pp. 240–245).

The Role of Administrator

Administrators described the role as ". . . directly connected to the political arena" (Manning, 1990, p. 240). The political and legal climate, as well as the requirements of funders, shaped the administrators' decisions. The major ethical dilemmas they identified were the dilemmas surrounding multiple constituencies: survival of the organization versus well-being of employees, quality of service to consumers, and community demands. One director said, "Who am I? . . . I have a belief in facilitating the client getting heard, and I'm looking for technical ways to disqualify their claim [against the agency] at the same time" (Manning, 1990, p. 242).

The decision functions are primarily definitional and visionary, drawing from the multiple perspectives of the community, the employees, and the consumers of service. Therefore, they define who is the client based on these changing circumstances. They also define the ethical positions for the organization. Thus, where they draw the line between acting political and defining the ethical was a major topic for this group. Upper administrators experience considerable power and scope of influence. One administrator noted (Manning, 1990, p. 241), "How I am and what I do goes all the way down the line . . . and affects managers, supervisors, and clinicians and how they deal with others . . . whether I want it to or not."

Administrators noted that this level of responsibility for an organization is a lonely position. However, top-level administrators are more protected from the emotional implications of the decisions they make, and/or they are less open about sharing them. One administrator expressed (Manning, 1990, p. 242) what seemed to be the tone of the rest, "It comes with the territory."

Middle Managers and Supervisors

Middle managers are the middle of the sandwich. Middle managers, as a group, described the role as "conflictual," "difficult," and "intense" (Manning, 1990, p. 242). The middle manager is a person torn between the professional staff and their clients, as well as the managerial responsibilities for agency survival. One manager said, "The

role is unique because of the position in the system . . . hands on, client specific decisions and set policy for direct service provision at the same time." Accountability to
both levels—administrative and direct service—requires an ability to perceive both
points of view. This dual perspective was the basis for a general level of ambivalence
and ambiguousness that managers experienced about ethical decisions on a regular
basis. "It was a lot more conflicted being a manager, rather than a clinician . . . [I]
could block out the administrative realities as a clinician" (Manning,1990, p. 243).

Middle managers influence the ethic and are responsible for carrying it out.
They experience the ethical dilemmas from both directions: implementing policy and
decisions from above and initiating the decisions to line staff. They are the ones who
deal with the emotional reactions to decisions, acting as a buffer for upper administration. Middle managers described their roles as "the bad messenger" and "the
hatchet person." There was concern about whether line staff would kill the messenger. This experience was shared across organizations. One manager said, "We're
viewed as unethical because every decision is going to be unfavorable to someone"
(Manning, 1990, p. 243).

The managerial level is also responsible to multiple constituencies—consumers,
supervisees, administration, and the community—". . . all with their own agendas"
(Manning, 1990, p. 243). For example, middle managers are responsible to convey the
ethical views of staff to upper administration, selling the team's perspective to administration. One said, "If they don't hear it, then it's my responsibility and I feel I haven't
presented well or something's lacking" (Manning, 1990, p. 243).

However, the ethical dilemmas they experienced as most conflictual are those of
resource distribution. One manager noted, "We are responsible for optimal patient
care and reasonable allocation of diminishing resources . . . so we're talking compromise, which brings on ethics" (Manning, 1990, p. 244).

Upper administrators and executive directors, then, define the ethic for the organization and strongly influence the success or failure of an ethical climate. Leaders
at this level have the power and authority at hand and must choose how to use it ethically. Middle management also influences the ethic, but has considerably more responsibility for carrying out the policies and practices decided upon at a higher level.
Thus, leaders at this level primarily use translation, interpretation, collaboration, and
discretion as functions of influence (see Chapter 4).

Identity and Ethical Influence.   Role identity appears to have an impact on a
leader's perception of influence in the organization. An interesting phenomenon occurs in relation to leaders' perception of their role and the degree of influence they
believe can be wielded. Middle managers at similar levels in similar agencies identified with their role (and the resulting influence) in different ways (Manning, 1990).
Managers who identified with the responsibility and authority of higher levels in the
organization, for example, an administrative role, also experienced a higher level of influence. Managers who identified with a clinician or direct service role experienced
more ambivalence about their ability to influence unethical practices and policies.
Leaders' identification with levels of authority also were demonstrated in a study by
Holland and Kilpatrick (1990). They found that a dimension about internalized and

externalized authority was also linked to organizational role. This dimension was the "locus of authority for ethical judgments" (Holland & Kilpatrick, 1990, p. 141). Respondents located their authority along a continuum that varied from internalized, individual responsibility for decisions to reliance on external authority, often through compliance with policy, laws, and higher administrative decisions.

Interestingly, social workers at the direct service level were more apt to exert internalized authority than supervisors, who tended toward compliance with external authority and institutional policy. Supervisors may be more vulnerable to negative consequences if they go against agency policy or prerogative, and clinicians may have a strong motivation to do what is right for their clients. Perception is a dynamic process that has an impact on behavior. The old adages, "People only have as much power as you are willing to give them," and "You have as much power as you are willing to use," appear to have some merit as they apply to the perceptions of leaders. Leaders who perceive themselves as having the responsibility and the authority to take action about ethical issues are more likely to do so than those who view the authority as external to themselves.

Role Identity and Ethical Sensitivity.

In addition, role identity affects what ethical issues leaders pay attention to or feel compelled to address (Manning, 1990). Middle level leaders and supervisors are more conflicted about the ethical implications of policies that affect clinical or service issues and employee well-being because they are closer to the impact of those issues on supervisees and consumers of services. Administrators and directors are more attuned to the political and legal climate and the ethical dilemmas that emanate from those arenas. They are less affected by ethical practices and policies in regard to the day-to-day delivery of services and are less aware of that impact, unless there are potential legal, political, or community ramifications. The discussion in Chapter 6 on *awareness* demonstrates that what we pay attention to ultimately is what we take action about.

The availability of *choice* also makes a difference in what captures a person's attention. Choice is a central concern for leaders who are faced with a dilemma that is initiated by a superior (Toffler, 1986). Our socialization to authority, with childhood associations of punishment if we do not obey, affects the *feeling* about freedom to choose. Toffler (1986, p. 31) says the following:

> . . . We should distinguish situations in which there really is little or no choice for the manager, because organizational sanctions are severe and/or the claims of other stakeholders are strong, from those in which there is the opportunity to choose an action, but where the manager thinks that he has no power to do so.

Choices are always a possibility, but the consequences of not following orders can be severe (for example, loss of job, losing consideration for promotion, demotion, and so forth). A moral person, because of the responsibility for others (family, consumers, peers, and supervisees) may decide to obey, realizing the choice means risking the well-being of family or others. That position is different from thinking there isn't a choice at all, including the possibility of questioning and challenging the directive.

Choice requires an internal mechanism that prompts a response. The internal guides that motivate responses are useful to consider.

The Internal Guide: Individual Justifications for Ethics

Leaders respond to more than ethical reasoning processes, rules, laws, and policies. Each individual has internal guides or justifiers that provide some intrinsic rationale for the ethical decisions they make. It is helpful to develop consciousness and clarity about the internal justifiers that inform decisions so that the justifiers can be evaluated for relevance, appropriateness, and usefulness. For example, social work leaders identified the internal justifiers of the best interests of the client, personal belief system, and what would be virtuous behavior (Manning, 1990).

The Client Comes First

Professional social work leaders identified the primary values or purposes of the profession as providing important guidance in dilemmas. When ethical quandaries occur, professional principles are helpful. In the social work profession, attention to the interests and needs of the client is an ethical guideline that is primary in the code of ethics as well as the professional socialization process. Many leaders identified this rationale as the basis of what they believed was the right way to decide. Several examples reflect the importance of this rationale (Manning, 1990, p. 251): "The quality of service to clients is the justification for everything that goes on." Also, "The value of what's best for the client comes first, then the agency, then the staff . . . and the value of what's best for the client is more important than erring with administration." In this last example, the leader used this rationale to prioritize the demands and needs of competing stakeholders. In an another example, this justifier provides the rationale for administrative support to supervisees for decisions or actions that may be questioned by others in the organization. She said (Manning, 1990, p. 252), "As long as an employee acts in the client's best interests, I will support them regardless of the flack." The internal justifier of client well-being is useful in reducing conflict about what to decide, adding clarity to the decision process.

Be True to Yourself

Consistency with what an individual leader believes also constitutes an important rationale for decisions. Such statements (Manning, 1990, p. 252) as "I make decisions consistent with my ethical, professional, and moral beliefs" and "Being true to myself and to my ethical and moral decisions about service delivery" demonstrate how leaders describe the importance of consistency between their personal and professional beliefs and their actions. The process of becoming aware of the beliefs that guide behavior is important. Awareness is connected to an action that demonstrates some meaning for the leader. An upper administrator (p. 252) captures this by saying ". . . Know who I am and what I am about and conduct myself accordingly."

The consistency with personal and professional beliefs becomes a function of directed behavior that can extend beyond particular decisions. Through *conscious use of self*, leaders can not only use a framework for daily decisions, but also follow a vision. Vision gives direction about future that is part of their starting point and guides their decisions by ". . . knowing who you are and what changes you're trying to make . . ." (p. 253). The clarity in regard to a professional, ethical vision acts as a guide to decisions and behaviors. In contrast, a lack of clarity can lead to fragmentation and confusion for both leaders and constituents.

Professional Values and Purpose.   Professional values and purpose also inform leaders about being true to themselves by bringing forward the essence of their professional purpose. Clarity about purpose helps to sort out the competing demands and to evaluate the potential harms and benefits. One manager described it this way (Manning, 1990, p. 253): "Social workers have a social conscience, we look out for underserved populations." Another manager related to the social work mission of focusing on the well-being of individuals in the social context of their environment to help sort out the complexity of a particular dilemma. He said, "social workers think context . . . the whole system and how all the pieces interact . . . in terms of values and ethics it helps" (Manning, 1990, p. 253).

Professional values are the source of professional responsibility and accountability (Linzer, 1999). A leader's decisions and actions will be assessed by others in relation to the profession's expectations of what values ought to be promoted. Further, the professional values that are internalized also are enacted through the purpose and function of the human service organization and the related goals.

Personal Values and Beliefs.   A person's sense of being true to oneself greatly rests on the integrity of personal values and beliefs. However, personal values and beliefs are formed in childhood through a process of socialization that is profound in its lack of consciousness. The cognitive abilities of children from preschool age through latency age are limited to concrete operations. Young children lack the ability to think critically about the content and information they are absorbing; they are unable to evaluate the meaning or implications of the values, beliefs, practices, traditions, and norms of those who come in contact with them on a daily basis. In addition, socialization happens through relationship with those who are most important to their own survival, such as parents, extended family, teachers, religious leaders, neighbors, and so forth. Thus, personal values and beliefs in childhood develop without insight. Only as adolescents and adults is it possible to begin the process of understanding the nature and meaning of beliefs and values and the impact on moral and ethical behavior. Further, socialization continues through professional education, again from important people who have a particular "authority over"; professors, mentors, supervisors, and so forth have the ability to influence the career paths and successes of students in significant ways. The ability to evaluate the values that are communicated and internalized through this intense socialization process is often difficult.

Leaders can draw on personal values that reinforce professional and ethical behavior. In fact, Levy (1982, p. 68) argues that the ethics of social work administration ". . . amounts to value-oriented prescriptions of executive conduct . . . ," which rely on the executive having a clear sense of complicated moral issues, a capacity for responsibility, and competence as a moral requirement. However, personal values are sometimes in conflict with others' values (employees, consumers, board members, and community citizens) and with professional values. In these situations, leaders must be able to make a distinction between giving their personal values preference or providing their values as representative of other positions or possibilities that can be considered, free of coercion or threat of punishment. Linzer (1999, p. 24) captures this by stating the following:

> Practitioners must be true to themselves . . . they come with their personal and professional values, knowledge, and skills. They are not value-free, nor must they leave their personal values at home. They represent their personal values in the kinds of questions they ask and the comments they make. . . . Only when the practitioner insists that the client [or other constituencies in the dilemma, e.g., employee, supervisee, consumer of service, citizen, etc.] conform to the practitioner's personal values are professional norms violated and the actions unethical.

Being true to oneself is only compromised by a lack of insight about the promotion of personal values and beliefs. Therefore, a habit of formal reflection about personal values is necessary.

Religious and Spiritual Values.   Even though social work and many other professions are secular in nature, leaders within the professions may bring *religious and spiritual values* and training to their perception of ethical dilemmas. One administrator stated (Manning, 1990, p. 253), "I was brought up Catholic . . . seventeen years of my life in Catholic schools, and I do believe in a lot of the Judeo-Christian ethics . . . I've kind of thrown out the ones I think are ridiculous, but I kept a lot of them." There is debate within the profession about the place of religious ideology, even though the roots of the profession were formed in a Judeo-Christian heritage (Holland, 1989). Over time a secular identification has developed that is based on a technical and theoretical conceptualization. This is especially evident in the content of administrative and managerial practice texts, theories, and techniques. Holland (1989, p. 37) would argue that, rather than recreate the past, ". . . we need to identify the spirit that motivated . . . and find ways to translate and apply that spirit to our present condition . . . give present meaning to the values of love, justice, and community that gave birth to our profession."

The use of religious values does not mean that the leader or other constituents imposes religious views on the other. Rather, expressed values such as mutual responsibility, doing good for others, and justice toward one another are expressed through caring behavior (Holland, 1989). For example, a manager (Manning, 1990, p. 253) in mental health described religious upbringing as one of the strongest shapers of her leadership approach: ". . . being responsible, looking out for other people . . . not control other people . . . and being aware of how power infringes on other people."

Conflicts between personal and professional values in relation to an ethical dilemma are common, particularly in regard to values in which there is a deep commitment. Examples include religious, spiritual, feminist, and cultural values and beliefs. As mentioned earlier in the discussion or personal values and beliefs, the strategy of identifying personal values overtly, as a potential alternative or consideration in the dilemma, rather than as a bias to which other parties must conform, provides a synthesis of personal and professional values (Levy, 1976; Linzer, 1999).

The Bottom Line. Finally, an important rationale that leaders bring to ethical issues that informs them about what they will or will not do is *the bottom line*. The bottom line is the invisible and unspoken boundary. It is the line in the sand before personal integrity is jeopardized by unethical conduct or decisions. For some leaders, the bottom line is specific to particular principles. For example, "when it comes to life and death, I will not under any circumstances make resources the reason I make a decision" (Manning, 1990, p. 254). For this leader, protecting life was paramount over cost and availability of resources. General conditions that are promoted or missing in an organization can become part of a bottom line. One person said (Manning, 1990, p. 254), "I couldn't work in an agency where flexibility is not available to act ethically." Personal tolerance is a marker that some leaders use to determine their bottom line. One person described, "there is a bottom line ethically for what we will tolerate . . . a certain cut off point . . . so proceed with that . . . you can hold your head up thinking you did what you could" (Manning, 1990, p. 254). Personal tolerance is determined by an internal, intuitive feeling of what is possible or not possible and then acting on the feeling by resisting or refusing.

Attitudes: A Leader's Approach to Ethical Dilemmas

The starting point of a leader includes the attitudes that become somewhat characteristic to personality and worldview. In addition, a leader's perception of what is an ethical dilemma is the first step in taking action about it. Both awareness and perception are a social construction that can affect the outcome.

What Is Ethical?

The first step in analyzing an ethical issue is the determination that it is an ethical issue. To decide that a dilemma is an ethical dilemma provides the leader with the opportunity to be ethical by intention, rather than by accident or to be conscious of unethical behavior and/or decisions, rather than unconsciously, even with the best intentions. Hannah Arendt's discovery that "the moral problem is a problem of thought" is central to understanding moral judgment (Gilligan, 1981, p. 140). Morality is a social construction based on human thinking, rather than an objective experience. Our constructions of what is moral or immoral are embedded in what is contextually relative to our understanding and the ability to think about consequences, the experiences and impacts on the other, and our ethical responsibilities.

Ethical sensitivity is an important characteristic in identifying ethical issues. It is the ". . . capacity to value the relative importance of the ethical dimensions or features of a situation" (Petrick & Quinn, 1997, p. 91). If a leader has the ability to exert ethical sensitivity, they will not only see the ethical implications of an issue, but will appreciate the importance of the ethical implications. To do so requires an awareness of the socialization that takes place in management, administrative, and social work education that promotes a focus on the technical and an avoidance of value conflicts. Petrick and Quinn note that moral sensitivity is similar to insight; there is an appreciation of the moral issues embedded in a situation. To have insight about moral considerations does not imply support, or even agreement, with particular policies. For example, leaders may or may not agree with some aspects of sexual harassment policies (for example, anonymity of the accuser). However, a person's moral sensitivity provides insight about the moral issues that are the basis of such policies.

The experience of managers and administrators demonstrates that there is a lack of consensus about the nature of ethics, particularly in organizational settings (Manning, 1990). A range of definitions from "everything is ethical" to "nothing is ethical" have been brought forward. For example, "there is an ethical implication in almost everything . . . you can't deal with people without having ethics involved," and "every decision is an ethical decision" (Manning, 1990, p. 255). At the other end of the continuum, a manager noted, "I don't usually feel like I'm making ethical decisions as a manager . . . Because I'm making decisions that seem to me to be more in the line of the reality principle" (pp. 255–256). Many managers and administrators see administrative decisions as the value-neutral activity of carrying out organizational tasks to meet goals. They simply do not perceive the decisions or tasks as having moral implications.

Other factors also influence how leaders perceive and define what is ethical. *Language* that is used to identify and describe what is being discussed affects perception. Sometimes the term "ethical" is not often used in discussions in the organization. A middle manager stated, "We don't talk about 'ethical dilemmas' . . . we process it in terms of a clinical framework or an administrative framework" (Manning, 1990, p. 256). When ethical issues are framed only as clinical or service issues or as technical administrative topics, important factors of ethical analysis and reasoning (for example, risks, benefits, harms, principles, and so forth) are left out of the discussion.

An ability to see *the bigger picture*, beyond the immediate and specific daily activities, in order to grasp the larger ethical issues can also cloud the nature of ethics. One manager noted (Manning, 1990, p. 256), "It is difficult to empathize with clinical issues and have a greater picture at the same time." In contrast, some administrators have described difficulties separating the greater picture from specific and individual situations that may or may not be ethical in nature. For example, vulnerable populations, such as children, people with serious mental illness, or the elderly, may be viewed as in need of protection because of their status. Therefore, any issues surrounding their care and protection were viewed as automatically ethical in nature.

The greater picture, in that instance, has a *parental* view that may not be ethical.

The *time* that is made available for leaders and constituents to discuss and define the ethical has an impact on what is determined to be an ethical issue. Managers, administrators, and supervisors who are so overwhelmed with the tasks of the organization that they are unable to step back and reflect about the nature of the decisions they are making are unlikely to define many situations as having an ethical element. *Resources* also have a definitional influence on decisionmakers. One person (Manning, 1990, p. 256) said, "you know your ethical decisions have to be shaped by what your options are . . . It appears to me that oftentimes we're making a decision between horrible and more horrible." The restricted availability of options (for example, revenue, access to hospital beds, referral sources, client openings, and so forth) that can produce alternatives may create conditions for leaders where ethical issues are not defined as such due to resignation and an unwillingness to see themselves as participating in unethical actions.

Opportunity or Constraint

Starting points for individuals also include the attitudes that are characteristic of a leader's approach to quandaries and dilemmas. Attitudes have an effect on the influence that can be brought to bear on the situation. Attitudes about the nature of the work also affect the internal sense of satisfaction that can be gained from leadership roles and responsibilities. *Opportunity* and *constraint* are two different attitudes, lenses that refract a different outcome because of the difference in perspective. In addition, the *context* or environment of the organization or setting makes a difference in the leader's starting point.

Opportunities. The ability to view adversity and conflict as a challenge to overcome can affect leaders' problem-solving and problem-finding behaviors. Some leaders described a sense of excitement about their part in solving problems and viewed those problems as integral to the role of leadership (Manning, 1990). The attitude of opportunity allows ethical challenges to become a source of interest, inspiration, and challenge. For example, one administrator related (Manning, 1990, p. 257), "I love a good mystery . . . I really love the investigative part of something . . . come to me with a mystery." Another (Manning, 1990, p. 257) said, "I thrive on conflict . . . when the fur gets flying, I get excited . . . time to go to work." This manager found that conflict provided the opportunity to dialogue and debate differences about values and practices. The discussions that resulted brought forward ethical issues and provided resolution, as well as identified other potential moral issues for consideration.

The lack of adequate resources for human service agencies is a constant condition and one that is at the basis of many ethical dilemmas. *Attitudes about scarcity* make a difference in relation to choice. One manager (Manning, 1990, p. 257) noted that scarcity could be viewed as "The money is there, it is just not being accessed, or, the money is not there, there are finite resources for too many needs." These two perspectives frame different possibilities. The optimistic view that resources are available, but not accessed, provides for creative strategies to develop access within the agency or from outside the agency. The more pessimistic view immediately restricts the options of the leader and narrows the analysis of possible alternatives. This view is indicative of a lens of constraint.

Constraints. The social construction of moral judgment is particularly powerful when ethical and moral dilemmas are viewed as constraints. Leaders who immediately feel constrained by ethical quandaries often begin to feel alienated, as discussed in Chapter 4. Leaders who viewed ethical dilemmas as constraints were also those who appeared to feel the most powerless in their organizations (Manning, 1990). This was especially true in the for-profit agencies, although not with every leader. These individuals experienced organizational values and activities as incongruent with their own values and beliefs. They developed ways to protect themselves from the incongruent values by avoiding the resulting ethical dilemmas. Denial and avoidance of meetings to control the possibility of being confronted with ethical problems were two common strategies. Rather than feel challenged by dilemmas, these leaders experienced defeat from the magnitude of the dilemmas, even before a process of problem solving could be initiated. Leaders who identified with the lens of constraint did not feel an internal sense of control about the situation. For example, one manager (Manning, 1990, p. 281) said this:

> I go into my disassociated position of, "I don't want to hear this" . . . It's painful for me to keep hearing about things that I can't change. And that probably goes right up the line. That's the reason that [her superior] can't hear from us, our complaints, is that she feels in the position where she can't change.

In this situation, both the manager and her administrator felt a lack of control over ethical quandaries, which reinforced the lens of constraint.

Personality characteristics, such as an individual's perception of locus of control, do have an effect on moral motivation. Locus of control refers to the degree one relies on oneself (internal) versus others (external) for reinforcement. People who have higher internal locus of control are more likely to be located in the postconventional level of moral reasoning (Maqsud, 1980). Their ability to rely on their own moral judgment provides for more freedom in assessing moral situations and less of a perception of restriction. Further, as discussed earlier, in Chapter 4 in relation to use of discretion, the perception of choice makes a difference in a leader feeling constrained. When managers ". . . take a superior's directive as a 'must do' without considering that they can question, challenge, or creatively carry out (do it in a way that feels 'right' to them) such orders" (Toffler, 1986, p. 32), they feel constrained. The lenses of opportunity and constraint are more than just the individual view; the context of the organization also has an effect.

Context. The context or environment of the organization affects the perception of individuals as they are challenged by dilemmas. Organizations that have developed a climate of creativity and innovation inspire and motivate leaders and workers to overcome the obstacles of restricted resources. A middle manager with experience in several human service agencies described it as follows (Manning, 1990, p. 258): "I've seen through the changes how creative people can be and how exciting it is to take on the challenge. It's not like [previous agency] where . . . people were overwhelmed and burned out and they're being asked to do more. But I came into a palace and some of the servants are gone, is what it feels like now." The metaphor of the palace, even without the same level of staffing, captures a spirit that is different from previous work environments. The climate promotes a willingness to commit effort toward ethical challenges.

The meaning of the mission and the values and principles that are sacrificed in the name of profit or cost-containment affect the perceptions of leaders. Individuals who have worked primarily in public or not-for-profit agencies may have difficulty with the change in philosophy in for-profit agencies. One manager (Manning, 1990, p. 259) who switched from a public to a for-profit noted, ". . . In the public sector you expected hypocrisies . . . and you could serve your idealism because you could say, we're really serving people who don't have any place to go, and it was meaningful. Now the scale is so incredibly bigger [of hypocrisy] . . . it really affects my narcissistic idealism." The ethical challenge in an era of privatization and emphasis on resources will be to develop ethical climates such that leaders and constituents perceive options and opportunities to perform ethically.

Individual Decisionmaking Styles

Leaders are people who bring to the activity of decisionmaking particular characteristics and styles that shape the decision process. Personal backgrounds affect perspectives about authority, relationships, and diversity. The experience and structure of discipline in the family in which a person grows up, the nature of family relationships, and degree of exposure and involvement with people who are different (for example, ethnicity, class, sexual orientation, religion, physical abilities, and so forth) make a difference in an individual's decision style (Toffler, 1986). Further, there is a body of literature within developmental psychology that supports the notion that family and peer groups have a large influence on moral development, with this development continuing into adulthood (Bandura, 1971, 1977). Therefore, choices about ethical and moral issues are socially influenced through multiple sources. The notion of "we are who we surround ourselves with" appears to be salient to individual characteristics in ethical decisions.

Research about individualized patterns of responses for social workers resulted in patterns of responding to dilemmas along three value dimensions (Holland & Kilpatrick, 1991). One dimension was a continuum that placed the emphasis on the goal or end result or on the means or process of the decision. This dimension describes the decisionmaker as more likely either to pay attention to standards, methods, or procedures to decide (deontological approach discussed in Chapter 7) *or* to focus on the outcome and the achievement of positive results (teleological approach discussed in Chapter 7), that is, the *ends* versus the *means* approach to finding the right answer.

The second dimension was an *interpersonal* orientation that described a range from autonomy and independence to mutuality and community. On this dimension, the leader may be more interested in fostering the individual *autonomy of stakeholders* and to avoid interfering in others' lives. The contrasting position would be to focus on nurturing and *building community* and the collective through the ethical and moral quandaries of leadership.

Finally, a dimension of *locus of authority* from *internalized to externalized* affected the person's ability to self-direct or tend toward compliance to others' authority. One end of this dimension emphasizes individual responsibility for choices and actions. Leaders who ascribe to this end of the dimension may have more ability to exercise discretion. The opposite position would be a reliance on agency policy, societal norms, laws, and external authority. The ability to rely on oneself and to use discretion in the face of complexity appears to be useful in the resolution of ethical dilemmas.

The ability to locate oneself in these dimensions is an important step toward self-awareness. Self-awareness in regard to one's moral development and identity, personal characteristics, approach to dilemmas, values and beliefs, and decision style is important in evaluating the effects of the personal on the professional and the ethical. Here, the *personal* is *political*; what the leader brings to the moral and ethical issues of leadership, as an individual, will influence the outcome of decision and behavior.

Reflection and Self-Awareness

The leader's unique individual characteristics, moral judgment, levels of life stage and career development, approaches and attitudes, and values have a clear effect on the decision process. Therefore, a heightened consciousness and self-awareness is important in relation to ethics. The hidden, embedded, and unconscious motivations, beliefs, and perspectives within one's personal life history must be made conscious in order to make decisions that are ethical by intention. Potential harms that occur due to unconscious processes can only be avoided through a deliberate effort of reflection and self-awareness.

The motivation to develop insight about hidden individual processes also promotes the potential use of values, characteristics, and traditions as strengths in the ethical analysis process. Each leader brings a unique self to the reasoning process. There is a greater possibility of using the unique discoveries of human experience in the process of responding to ethical challenges if individual perspectives have been uncovered and made overt; only what is known can be directed in useful ways.

Mattison (2000) has developed a sequence that integrates reflection and self-awareness into the decisionmaking process (Figure 5.3). This cycle of reflection can be a useful tool for assessing the idiosyncratic characteristics that individuals bring to the process. A series of questions developed by Mattison (2000, pp. 209–210), with some additions and modifications for this discussion, can facilitate insight about patterns of responding and individualized approaches to ethical decisionmaking.

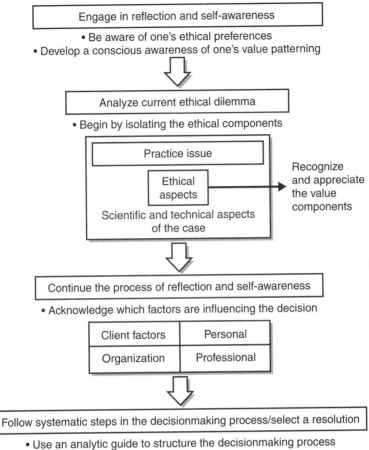

FIGURE 5.3 Cycle of Reflection

Source: Mattison, M. (2000). Ethical decision making: The person in the process. *Social Work, 45*(3), 201–212. Copyright 2000, National Association of Social Workers, Inc.

1. To what extent did personal values or philosophies influence the choice of action? What are the values and philosophies that influence you?
2. To what extent does professional socialization affect your ethical and political stance on the issue? In what way? What professional socialization may be harmful in resolving the issue?

3. To what extent did legal obligations [or liability] influence the decision?
4. Would you act outside of legal obligations if doing so would serve the stakeholder's best interests? Why? Why not?
5. To what extent did adhering to agency policy influence the decision?
6. If agency policy conflicted with other obligations, would you act outside of agency policy? Why? Why not?
7. To what extent did your role in the agency influence your choices?
8. In a conflict between self-determination and paternalism, which value do you judge to be more essential? Why?
9. In a conflict between the autonomy of the individual and the good of the collective, which value do you judge to be more essential? Why?
10. In selecting a choice of action, do you lean toward evaluating possible costs and benefits to the stakeholder or adherence to laws and policies as more important?
11. What aspects of your personal morality affect potential choices?
12. What individual justifications influence your analysis of the dilemma?
13. In what way does your place in moral, life, and career development affect your approach to the decision?
14. What level of moral judgment are you enacting through your assessment of the issue?

The cycle of reflection, consultation, and discussion with others and a continual emphasis on developing self-awareness and consciousness are important to the ethical reasoning process. A heightened awareness of personal starting points and standing points promotes the ability to use individual strengths and characteristics intentionally and to avoid the imposition of bias and personal preference without awareness.

Conclusion

This chapter discusses the centrality of the individual decisionmaker and the unique characteristics, attitudes, and values that each individual brings to the ethical reasoning process. Leaders have their own developmental process, as do constituents, that includes a particular place in moral, life, and career development. This location impacts the depth and breadth of perspective about moral issues, as well as awareness of potential alternatives. Individual leaders have their own paradigm of internal justifications and attitudes that inform their approach to moral and ethical issues. A conscious process of reflection and awareness in regard to personal and professional values and perspectives is necessary for moral and ethical reasoning. Leaders' ability to assess the locations, justifications, and approaches of their own and constituents' response to moral and ethical quandaries is the first step in building an ethical organization. Finally, the development of a moral identity that provides moral vision and commitment is an essential component of ethical leadership. The following two chapters provide an overview of an ethical framework—moral citizenship—that organizes a variety of philosophical and ethical theories to guide in considering ethical challenges.

QUESTIONS AND APPLICATIONS

1. Reflect on your starting points. Assess your own moral, life, and career development. What is the impact on your ability to be an ethical leader? What are your goals for further moral development? Where do you place yourself on the helix of moral growth?

2. Develop a statement of moral identity. What are the principles you commit to through your leadership? What are examples in your personal and professional life that reflect that commitment? How does your moral identity integrate with your moral vision?

3. Identify and discuss the internal guides that help you with ethical and moral challenges.

4. Assess your level of ethical sensitivity. What are your ethical blind spots? Ask for feedback from others about what they observe about your ethical sensitivity.

6 Ethical Resources: Traditions and Tools to Develop Ethical Awareness and Feeling

THE FOCUS IN THIS CHAPTER IS ON THE FOLLOWING AREAS:

- Values, morality, ethics, and dilemmas
- The role of values in ethical dilemmas
- Ambiguity, complexity, and feedback
- Moral citizenship–a framework for action
- Moral citizenship: awareness
- Moral citizenship: feeling

People in a leadership role work with moral and ethical issues, dilemmas, and decisions on a daily basis. The responsibilities associated with the ability to make a difference and bring about changes that otherwise may not occur have ethical implications (Dobel, 1998). In addition, the nature of the leadership position, endowed with legitimate and political authority and power, is often at the crux of many ethical dilemmas for leaders (as discussed in Chapter 4). Subsequently, leadership and ethics are intertwined. Administrators, managers, and other leaders are usually well meaning in their efforts to think about and resolve ethical dilemmas. However, good intentions are not enough. Decisions and behaviors must be based on an ethical reasoning process that directs the leader to be *ethical by intention* because of the potential good and harm that can result. Also, leaders set the tone for the moral and ethical culture of the organization through their activities and decisions, modeling values that are replicated at all levels of an organization. Leaders, then, have the opportunity to raise the moral and ethical climate of the organization through the way they approach and resolve ethical dilemmas and the moral quandaries of the organization.

This chapter identifies and discusses tools and traditions that help to discern, care about, and understand ethical dilemmas. These will be organized through a framework of moral citizenship, including awareness, feeling, thinking, and action (Manning, 1997). Awareness and feeling will be discussed in this chapter, followed by thinking and action in Chapter 7. The tools and traditions presented in these two chapters are an amalgam of traditional ethical theories and principles, with the addition of Eastern and contemporary approaches. Thinking about and choosing from different philosophical perspectives strengthens the leader's ability to analyze complex ethical situations and dilemmas and increases potential alternatives.

The goal of these two chapters is to broaden the thinking and analysis skills of leaders and to provide depth to the ethical-reasoning process. In all aspects, the importance of developing an awareness of the ambiguity of ethical issues, as well as understanding the complexity of situations that are reflective of human nature and the relationship between and among human beings is emphasized. A decisionmaking model is provided at the end of Chapter 7 to add guidance to thinking about ethical dilemmas. However, the approach in this segment is not to offer prescriptions or steps to follow. Instead, leaders are encouraged to integrate the thinking of ethicists, philosophers, and other leaders into their own analysis and to develop the approach that best fits the particular situation.

First, a discussion of some of the common terms helps to provide a foundation for understanding the tools and traditions and the application to real-life situations.

The Language of Ethics

Understanding the nature of ethics in leadership starts with basic definitions and the meanings of important terms; it will be useful for readers to share a common perspective with the author for the purposes of developing a common framework. The following definitions, with discussion, of *morality*, *values*, *ethics*, and *dilemmas* are the beginning of constructing an ethical model for leadership.

Morality: Personal, Social, and Institutional

The topic of contemporary ethics is concerned with questions about what is morally right. Thus, ethics is considered the moral branch of philosophy, that is, "the study of human conduct and values" (Webster, 1977, p. 748). Morality is uniquely social as an enterprise. It exists before the individual (who is inducted into it), and individuals become more or less participants in it. As an institution, morality integrates with other institutions, such as science, law, art, and religion. The primary question of morality is "How may or should we decide or determine what is morally right for a certain agent (oneself, a group, or society) to do, or what that agent morally ought to do in a certain situation" (Frankena, 1982, p. 12). Therefore, morality is concerned with, more or less, the "**what**," that is, what do individuals do or think in a situation based on the principles of right or wrong in behavior.

Morality is multidimensional: at the level of society, smaller collectives, and the individual. The societal level of morality aims for the rational self-guidance or self-determination in its members. Morality becomes a social system of regulation that acts as an instrument of society as a whole for the guidance of individuals and smaller groups. Forms of judgment (that have a certain moral quality, obligation, or responsibility), rules, principles, ideals and virtues (that can be expressed in more general judgments), and sanctions (and other sources of motivation, for example, praising and blaming) are all factors that are developed and promoted through society (Frankena, 1982). These factors identify the paramount concerns of citizens, as well as parameters for acceptable actions and behaviors.

Each individual also has a personal code of morality that is made up of values, beliefs, and practices that have developed through life and experience. The institutions mentioned previously influence individuals in the process of developing a personal code. In turn, individuals have an influence on the morality of society through their actions, decisions, and behaviors. For example, the act of voting—expressing a choice—on topics that have moral implications influences society's resolution of the moral questions. There is reciprocity, then, between the individual leader's personal morality (influenced by personal values and society) and the leader's influence on the moral code of society through the process and results of the leader's decisions. For example, when the leadership of for-profit hospitals reduce staffing to a bare minimum to increase profit margins for shareholders and quality of patient care is affected, the value of profit is promoted over the value of quality health care to society. Values, then, have a primary place in moral and ethical reasoning.

Values

Values are primary components of an ethical reasoning process. Personal, professional, organizational, and societal values can and do inform the decisionmaker in the course of reasoning about a dilemma or quandary. In addition, the values of other individuals or groups (for example, consumers of service, employees, colleagues, and other agencies) impact on the reasoning process. Values can be thought of as "what is considered good and desirable" (Bartlett, 1970, p. 63). Values are meant to serve as guides or criteria for selecting appropriate behaviors in a particular situation. Values are critical to ethics in that it is ". . . the application of values to human relationships and transactions" that make up the practice of ethics (Levy, 1993, p. 1).

Usually, values occur at a high level of generality while behaviors are more specific. However, when values remain generalized, they are often not helpful in determining specific behaviors or in providing guidance for behavior (Lowenthal, 1982). In addition, values and behavior are not always congruent; a person's actions may not reflect what would be expressed verbally as a value. Perlman (1976, p. 381) reinforced the importance of acting on values by concluding that "a value has small worth, except as it is moved, or is moveable, from believing into doing, from verbal affirmation into action." Values, then, are only helpful for guidance if they do result in some kind of action. Taking action is dependent on the courage, resolve, and commitment of the decisionmaker. When action is taken, the values that underlie the action should be explicit and open to comment.

Rhodes (1986, p. 84) argues that values are usually discussed in a misleading way as if social work practice is "politically and ethically neutral." Instead, she states, "The choice is not whether or when you bring values into [social work practice]; my point is that you cannot help bringing them in. . . . The choice then, is: what values, what ethical and political points of view, should you present. . . . ?" Values, according to Rhodes (1986), are presented through language, which has moral dimensions and sometimes disguises the underlying moral and political judgments; "Need, for example, suggests a deficiency within the client, rather than a right or condition to be met" (Rhodes, 1986, p. 87). Through professional socialization, ". . . our language becomes our thinking . . . ," resulting in the invisibility of the ethical and political dimensions. For instance, it is not uncommon in administrative discussions to refer to cost-efficiency and revenue streams almost unconsciously, as if these terms did not reflect major ethical dilemmas and quandaries in regard to access to service, quality of service, and attention to existing community need. Thus, the supposed value-neutral or nonpolitical stance is most dangerous because it conceals underlying assumptions and values that cannot be examined or challenged.

Values, then, are a key element in an ethical reasoning process. Values are "ethics in action" (Levy, 1976). Personal, group (for example, religious), societal, professional, and organizational values have an impact on decisions. Values are often unspoken and sometimes unconscious, although the impact is still significant. A conscious identification of the values of the decisionmaker, as well as the values of those who will be impacted by the decision, is important to the decision process.

A *process of reflection* (see Chapter 5), then, is important to leaders as they sort out the various components of a dilemma, including their own values and beliefs that are informing the way they perceive the nature of the dilemma and possible alternative solutions. Ethical analysis should include recognition of the ethical and political assumptions that are conveyed through the values of practice theories, language, and technology, with the intent to make them overt. A practical and effective way to make ethical and political assumptions explicit, as well as heightening awareness of embedded values, is to engage in dialogue with others.

Ethics and Applied Ethics

Ethics is the reflection of anyone who tries to determine what they really value and arrive at the right answer based on an ethical-reasoning process. Ethics provides the **why**, justifying a position from a moral point of view: the theory, logic, and reasoning process that brings individuals to what they think or do and results in an action, decision, or policy. For example, values or a personal moral code inform people about what they desire or believe is good (for example, personal privacy). Ethics can justify *why* privacy would be the right thing in a particular situation (based on principles of autonomy, justice, and so forth) and what ethical policies and guides could be enacted to protect privacy (for example, confidentiality and informed consent).

The term "ethics" comes from the Greek root "ethos," which means custom, usage, or habit. Few of us realize the extent to which custom relieves us of the necessity for thinking through our moral problems. However, custom does not clearly indicate what we *should* do in many situations. Where custom does speak, its direction is often disputed; human beings, then, inherit many unsolved problems and a community with diverse opinions (Leys, 1941). This is especially true for individuals in leadership positions who are constantly faced with ethical dilemmas that arise from the tensions among and between multiple constituencies. Ethics, and other disciplines that provide analysis and critique, are ways that reasonable men and women have proceeded to re-examine and revise policies and practices that have moral connotations.

There are many definitions of ethics, but two are particularly helpful for the purposes of this discussion for ethical leadership. First, Rachels (1980, p. 33) proposes the following:

> Ethics provides answers about what we ought to do, given that we are the kind of creatures we are, caring about the things we will care about, when we are as reasonable as we can be, living in the sort of circumstances in which we live.

This definition acknowledges the complexity and diversity of human beings, the situational aspects of ethical and moral quandaries, and the diversity of people and issues that motivate the emotional concern or attachment, the *appetite* necessary to prompt an ethical-reasoning process. Finally, the word "reasonable" provides emphasis on *thinking*, for example, the use of a variety of methods to establish the facts, consider them in the light of ethical theory, and develop a logic or justification for the right answer.

A nursing educator (Uustal, 1992), defines ethics as "the study of what is ideal in a rotten situation." This definition acknowledges that ethical dilemmas are never pleasant; in fact, dilemmas are usually difficult and often emotionally painful. The resolution of a dilemma is often less than ideal and usually has profound ramifications on those effected. However, with all of what is encompassed in a rotten situation, still there is the emphasis on finding the ideal, on doing what is right, and on committing to a rational process of discovering what "ought" to be decided.

Applied ethics seek the answers to practical questions about how to act, or what anyone does in asking what is right, good, or obligatory (Frankena, 1982). To *apply* (from the Latin *applicare*) means to "bring into contact, to lay upon, to lean against" (Kass, 1990, p. 9). Applied ethics move professional leaders from ethical theorizing and intellectual, abstract exercises to real-life integration of ethics in their practice. Theory is brought to bear *through* the leader as a moral agent, so applying theory is dependent upon the leader's motives to exert a moral will, the willingness to *lean against* a situation with a "moral shoulder." Applied ethics can be thought of as "ethics as theory with application" or "ethics as practice with reflection" (Kass, 1990, p. 10). This chapter is written from the perspective of the latter. The leader, through the experience and responsibilities of practice, reflects on the moral and ethical issues that are brought forward and uses a reasoning process (theory) to resolve them.

Aristotle argued that "thought, to be effective, must be inseparable from appetite;" what we think about things and what we feel about them must be congruent in order to be a true source of action (Kass, 1990, p. 9). Thinking and feeling cannot be integrated through the application of rational doctrines, principles, or rules without emotion or passion. Instead, our feelings educate us through practice and habit.

Although our emotions may be initially irrational, it is possible to use reason and to refine emotions through the process of deliberation and reflection. Applied ethics, for purposes of this book, then, starts with ethics as practice. The leader uses emotions and passions, as well as intellect, to identify, think about, and resolve ethical issues. Leaders can make a practical moral difference by doing what they do for moral reasons and then reflecting and theorizing on the ethical nature of what they do, which further informs their moral disposition as it is developed through practice. A good deal of leadership practice is involved with the resolution of dilemmas through the decision process.

Ethical Dilemmas: The Gruesome Twosome

The term, "dilemma," is a derivative of two Greek roots: *di*, which means *double*, and *lemma*, which means *proposition*. A dilemma is a predicament that seems to defy a satisfactory solution; we must choose between two options of near or equal value (Loewenthal, 1982). Leaders often have to make choices between two or more possible goods or two or more possible harms. The ultimate dilemma, then, is good versus good, or evil versus evil, rather than good versus evil, which, of course, is not a dilemma. For example, in this era of downsizing and emphasis on efficiency, many administrators and managers are faced with decisions involving reduction in force. The dilemma forces choices between dissolving different units or teams, choosing between individual positions, or reducing the budgets of all service programs. The potential results include loss of services to consumers, loss of economic livelihood of employees, and reduced quality of care, which are all potential evils. Dilemmas about the distribution of goods are equally difficult. Increased revenue to an agency may precipitate choices about creating new programs to meet community needs not currently served or increasing existing budgets to improve the quality, scope, and breadth of existing services and needs. The determination of who should benefit is a dilemma. Whether a choice is about who should benefit or who will be harmed, "A difficult problem becomes a dilemma when we are quite sure that we will be making a big mistake regardless of whatever path we choose" (Fleck-Henderson, 1991, p. 187).

The dilemmas that confront professional leaders may result from options that are not well defined or from solutions that create additional problems and harm for employees, consumers of services, community citizens, and society. Both usually result from an inadequate information-gathering and reasoning process. The multidimensional nature of dilemmas requires a thoughtful, time-consuming process of understanding the facts, identifying relevant values, applying ethical theories and ideas, and considering all of the ramifications, short term and long term. Shortcuts, although sometimes necessary, do not provide the opportunity for a reasoning process to occur.

Keith-Lucas (1977) describes some of the obvious dilemmas in human service professions as the tension between the following:

- The obligation to reform social structure and the obligation to help people cope with the social structure in which they find themselves—the immediate versus the future or changing the person or changing the environment

- The good of the individual and the good of the group or community
- The consumers' right to freedom of choice and what is perceived as good for them
- Responsibility to the consumers of service and responsibility for those who pay for it
- Equity (treating everyone evenhandedly) and fulfilling individual needs
- The scientific process and the humanistic process

Social work leaders in administrative and management positions (Manning, 1990) identified several major areas that resulted in ethical dilemmas: dilemmas about resources, dilemmas regarding conflicting duties to multiple constituencies, dilemmas regarding relationships with employees, dilemmas about service issues with consumers, and dilemmas regarding the obligation to reform society. Each category contained a myriad of particular ethical duties that placed fiscal, political, clinical, supervisory, and administrative responsibilities in conflict. Some examples from the first three categories are discussed as representative of the kinds of dilemmas that leaders face on a daily basis.

Dilemmas About Resources. The category about resources generated the most dilemmas and contained many different tensions related to scarcity of resources and cost-containment, agency survival and revenue generation, and quality of care and the profit motive. Dilemmas about resources centered on the theme that money drives clinical or service decisions, rather than the reverse. First, a scarcity of resources or an inadequate funding base produces a primary emphasis on cost-containment. Second, the profit motive becomes a major factor in clinical decisions as organizations pursue fiscal survival (not-for-profit) or corporate profit (for-profit). Third, the issues of revenue generation, cost-containment, and agency survival are a critical part of the administrator's role and responsibility.

Managers described dilemmas that placed *funding issues in conflict with quality clinical care and access to care.* The economic status of the client became a determining factor in relation to access to treatment. One manager (Manning, 1990, p. 180), concerned about excluding those with less income in favor of clients with higher ability to pay for services, described it as "... the prostitute theory, I want the money first." In contrast, some clients were provided services not needed in order to increase revenue. Families with Medicaid were provided individual sessions for each family member and then family sessions as well, in order to make up a budget deficit. The manager (Manning, 1990, p. 180) stated, "That decision came from a financial base, and it eats at me ... I feel like we are ripping of ourselves by ripping off the government."

Inequities among and between groups in relation to *access to service* because of funding reasons were also discussed. Contracts with financial resources, such as the court system, determined clinical decisions, such as length of stay. Clients who were ordered into treatment and had to pay for it took precedence over the single mother with kids who had little ability to pay for services. As one manager stated (Manning, 1990, p. 181), "what are we going to do about poor people?"

Fostering dependency of clients through recommendations of longer length of stay for insurance purposes was brought forward. The client with good insurance received the "cadillac model of care" while those without insurance did not have access to the intensity or length of stay that was needed. In addition, managers described creating demand for service (for census reasons and to generate revenue), rather than in response to demonstrated need in the community. "Is it a moneymaker?" was a common theme.

The *administrative objectives*, and the *strategies* used to meet the objectives, created dilemmas in relation to staffing and fairness to employees as well as clients. Census quotas promoted pressure to admit patients and also determined the ratio of employed staff. As the census went down, so did the number of employees. Reductions in force, use of contract rather than permanent staff, and high staff turnover were some of the effects of census-driven decisions. All of these strategies have an effect on quality of care for patients and fairness and job security for employees.

The effect of resource-driven decisions on administrators and managers was an increased focus on developing and maintaining political power and being political. This was defined as "securing your position through generating revenue, political relationships, selling yourself, etc. versus being a social worker" (Manning, 1990, p. 183). One manager noted (Manning, 1990, p. 183),

> The danger of getting into too much manipulation and political juggling in order to get what you want, is that you get caught up in the game and lose sight of the ethical foundation for why you're doing it. The more time you spend in 'political' activities, the more of a 'political creature' you become.

The moral price for the unethical resolution of resource dilemmas was high.

Multiple Constituencies.   The ethical dilemmas surrounding responsibility to multiple constituencies are especially concerning to upper administrators. These are the *dilemmas of conflicting loyalties and responsibilities* to employees, consumers, community citizens and leaders, and fiscal agents of the organization. Executive directors and upper administrators expressed concern about deciding who gets priority when there are conflicting loyalties, duties, and obligations. Directors are often confronted with dilemmas about the rights of consumers in regard to concerns and complaints against the organization. The upper administrator often becomes the evaluator and decision-maker at the highest level. Issues such as malpractice allegations, wrongful treatment, discriminatory policies, and so forth come to their attention. The leader is faced with protecting the consumer's due process rights and protecting the employee and agency from inappropriate or unfair allegations. The dual responsibilities of facilitating an investigation of the allegations and protecting the organization from a lawsuit are in conflict.

Political pressure from community leaders to exert inappropriate or illegal social control of consumers was also identified as a dilemma. Frequently, community leaders were in a position to support or jeopardize funding for the agency. Administrators are also responsible for protecting consumer populations that are not served through their particular agency. Leaders work in the community with volunteer boards and collaborate with other agencies. They are frequently confronted with information about potential harm to consumers, which conflicts with respecting the autonomy of the other agency and protecting a mutually beneficial relationship.

Managers and administrators often experience conflict between advocating for a consumer or employee at the *risk of their own job security*. Many related feeling that they compromise values in order to protect the security and benefits of their position. Similarly, they had conflicting feelings about using resources on perks, such as equipment, furniture, conferences and meetings, when, at the same time, there were staff shortages and a lack of resources for consumer and program needs.

Multidisciplinary settings produce dilemmas related to differences in values and ethical codes among different professional groups. Only one decision can be made, and the interests and values of all have to be considered in order to maintain good working relationships. In for-profit hospitals, where physicians admit patients, managers described decisions that are sometimes made to facilitate the convenience of the doctor rather than to benefit patient care.

Relationships with Employees.

Dilemmas involving relationships with employees were particularly concerning to middle managers because of their role in implementing personnel policy and hiring, firing, and supervising staff. Firing employees was particularly troublesome for obvious reasons. Leaders feel a responsibility to protect their staff, and, for the most part, only the best interest of the clients superseded that priority. Firing someone often creates havoc with the person's team or department; incompetence or inadequate performance is not always highly visible. Further, when an employee is fired or resigns due to poor performance, leaders were faced with dilemmas concerning confidentiality of the employee's personnel record versus potential harm to future clients.

Reduction in Force (RIF) was a frequent dilemma that was also connected to hiring policies. Managers described filling permanent positions while knowing that a RIF could take place at any time. The procedure for RIF was also ethically problematic to managers (Manning, 1990, p. 190):

> The part I struggle with is that under the RIF format, the supervisor, me, gets told on Thursday what supervisees have to come in on Friday to get chopped, and they are to be gone that day ... Gone that day. And I personally believe that that's unethical ... not because its severe, but because it's not balanced ... We would not tolerate any employee doing that to us.

Performance measures were dilemmas because of subjectivity of the supervisor and also due to measurable performance standards for service that were not controllable by the employee. The organizational requirement for a certain level of direct services to ensure adequate funding often put employees at risk for substandard performance when they could not control the flow or length of involvement of consumers. This dilemma was complicated further by the pressure of the manager's performance evaluation, which was based on whether her employees met the standards. Both the manager's and the employees' job security was based on something neither could control.

Treating people respectfully was discussed as a dilemma in relation to the degree of openness of communication. The empowerment of staff through information and including them in the decision process was often in conflict with protecting them (and the agency) from potentially disruptive information. The distribution of benefits to employees, such as staff development funds, time off, vacation scheduling, and so forth brought forward ethical issues of fairness and equity.

These tensions cannot be resolved through prescriptions or principles. The attempt to rationalize solutions merely supports a professional need to find comforting illusions or conceals blindness to the facts (Keith-Lucas, 1977). Similarly, emphasizing only one side of the tension reduces understanding of the complexity of dilemmas by simplifying them. The information that is available from both sides of the dilemma provides for a comprehensive understanding of the dilemma and the potential consequences of the choice that is made. As in the dialectic, each side of the tension provides for what is valuable in the opposing point of view. By examining all sides, the complexity of the situation can be understood.

Ambiguity, Complexity, Context, and Other Quirks of Ethics

The nature of ethics—resolving quandaries that affect the well-being of people, animals, the environment, and our planet through relationship, responsibility, and duty—produces situations and dilemmas that are ambiguous and complex. Resolving dilemmas requires an ability to apply a reasoning process to situations that involve human beings in multidimensional roles, requirements, and experiences. The ability to sort out the individual and unique aspects of a situation and to understand the ethical implications—the potential goods and harms that flow from particular solutions—helps to make the right decisions.

In order to move to ethical wisdom, we must first abandon the idea that our convictions are accurate and/or right. We have to acknowledge that there are no safe understandings or certain knowledge. Prescriptive rules, laws, policies, and regulations can add guidance and be reassuring, but they do not provide the reasoning process necessary to resolve situations that develop from conflicting values, goods, and harms. Moral and ethical dilemmas are ambiguous; they can be understood in many different ways. Thus, Hannah Arendt (1978) has argued that the capacity for moral response is dependent on the ability to recognize and then to discern the moral problem (discussed in Chapter 5). By sifting through various understandings of the moral meaning of a situation, the moral and ethical issues become clearer. A leader's ability to attend to the relevant contextual factors in a situation, which is the recognition of the social construction of situations, rather than perceiving the issues as unidimensional or as an objective reality, allows moral judgment to be transformed (Gilligan, 1981). This transformation "... points ... to the realization that since actions have consequence, and commitment of one sort or another is embedded in the very fabric of life, responsibility is in the end unavoidable" (Gilligan, 1981, p. 140). The realization of ethical responsibility is the starting point for ethical understanding and the first step in moral citizenship.

Moral Citizenship

Moral citizenship is a framework to organize the multiple elements of an ethical-reasoning process (Manning, 1997). The framework is structured on awareness, feeling, thinking, and action (see Figure 6.1). Moral citizenship is based on premises developed by Arendt (1963). Leaders, as moral citizens, must be able to think independently and to use independent judgment. They must be able to resist individual, organizational, and professional phenomena that are morally harmful. Finally, they will engage in dialogue about complex ethical issues and request and offer feedback, rather than avoid dilemmas and/or the perspectives and understandings from others (Manning, 1997).

Moral citizenship is transformational; leaders who are moral citizens have the capacity to change organizational and community structures that are oppressive to structures that are more congruent with ethics and social work purpose. The skills of transformation include social consciousness and social conscience (Manning, 1997). Social consciousness is to know: to seek knowledge about the moral nature of situations and to make a point of finding out what is missing and necessary. Consciousness also includes awareness and the commitment to consciously heighten awareness so moral situations are discerned. Finally, consciousness requires action, or acting as a moral citizen (Arendt, 1963). Consciousness focuses on the practical aspects of using awareness, thinking, feeling, and action to incorporate ethics into leadership.

Moral Citizenship

- To think independently and to use independent judgment
- To resist individual, organizational, and professional phenomena that are morally harmful
- To engage in dialogue and request feedback about ethical issues

Framework

- Awarenes—The ability to discern a moral problem
- Feeling—Caring about the moral problem, understanding the meaning, and being motivated to act
- Thinking—The ability to apply a reasoning process to the moral problem
- Acting—Taking action based on the awareness, feeling, and thinking and then reflecting on the action and evaluating the consequences

FIGURE 6.1 Moral Citizenship

For example, leaders have the opportunity and the obligation to make the invisible visible by bringing forward the underside of human service delivery systems: alerting the public to moral imperatives about service so that consideration and discussion can take place in the public arena. This process provides the opportunity for change and transformation of human service organizations and institutions (Jennings, Callahan, & Wolf, 1987). The leader's transformational practice, then, influences the ethics of colleagues, employees, consumers, community citizens, and other institutions.

Leaders also use their social conscience, which is the moral function and duty of promoting what is right or good in culture, not their personal interpretation of right or good, but through the lens of social work purpose (Towle, 1969). Every decision and action communicates a message to society about what social workers value and, indirectly, what society values. Thus, leaders in human service organizations have a moral responsibility for the power that they have to shape cultures (Jennings, Callahan, & Wolf, 1987). Consciousness and conscience are facilitated by ethical traditions and reasoning.

Traditions and Tools for Social Work

The ethical traditions and tools that are organized within a moral citizenship framework (Chapters 6 and 7) should be thought of as possibilities to stimulate moral sensitivity and moral imagination as well as ethical reasoning. Ethical theories and principles, from classical as well as from more contemporary philosophers, are presented as food for thought. However, Western ethical theories and principles provide an approach for leaders in social work and other human service professionals that is limited (Abramson, 1996; Allen, 1993; Imre, 1989; Rhodes, 1986). Abramson (1996, p. 2) offers this important criticism:

> . . . the fact that it [the principle's approach] has been considered to be timeless and universally applicable by its proponents when it is really culture-based and has failed to attend to differences associated with gender, race, ethnicity and class . . . it is too abstract, rational, and theoretical and thus often far from emotion and lived human experience; that it is too individualistic and does not make space for care, relationships and community; and that it is too secular and neglects the religious and spiritual dimensions of life.

This critique challenges social work leaders to develop an ethical approach that incorporates social work's purpose and values.

The consideration of what theory to transfer from other disciplines, such as philosophy, when social work has a unique definition of what the work itself means is difficult (Imre, 1989). Social work practice—clinical, community, and organizational—brings forward different moral problems that are unique to the profession. Leadership in a human service industry means that moral issues that arise often leave little time for reflection. Immediate decisions are required within a specific context, and the decisions have "serious consequences for all concerned (Imre, 1989, p. 20). Therefore, ethical theory and philosophy are a part of the social work approach, but also an emphasis on reflection, self-understanding, and criticism is needed (Imre, 1989). Taking into account the previous arguments, feminist, Afrocentric, and Ghandian ethical ideals that are consonant with the values of social work—relationship, community, and the quality of life of human beings—are integrated into the framework of moral citizenship.

Ethical traditions for social work and other professional leaders, then, must include a variety of perspectives that are a good fit for the work of the profession, for the experience of leaders and practitioners, and to further the professional ideal. The ethical traditions brought forward in Chapters 6 and 7 are to inform leaders so that ethical leadership becomes "habitual practice" that flows from "heart and mind," or practice that reflects the leader's self-expression and manifests the essence of one's personal and professional self (Kass, 1990, p. 10). Awareness, feeling, thinking, and action are the framework for these intentions.

Awareness: The Ability to See

The first step of moral consciousness is awareness. We must be aware that there is a need for action to take place. We must see the possibility of an ethical dilemma and then be able to comment; the issue must be brought forward for consideration. Hannah Arendt (1963), a political philosopher who has examined ethical decisions and behaviors of the Holocaust, argues that an awareness of individual and organizational phenomena that is evil is the first step toward understanding and resisting; a person must be able to *discern* the moral problem.

All ethical reasoning begins with the leaders' *perception* of their environment. Perception is not passive or neutral; it is active and structured from personal and social concerns (Goodpaster, 1983). A morally responsible leader will look for and take seriously as much information as possible to discern the moral issues. In contrast, Goodpaster (1983, p. 8) describes an example of a lack of moral perception:

> Someone who ran across a crowded park oblivious to the presence of others, stepping on adults and children as if they were part of the landscape would clearly exhibit a lack of moral perception. Such a person might 'see' those in his or her environment, but would respond to that information in much the same way as to rocks or logs, i.e., as potential hazards on a running course, not as human beings.

Moral perception, then, depends on the ability to recognize moral issues that require attention and the leader's perspectives about the way in which moral issues are managed.

Moral and ethical dilemmas can be perceived from both objective and subjective frames of reference (Fleck-Henderson, 1991). The subjective sense of a dilemma is precipitated by decisions that are experienced as difficult or the discomfort a person feels when something does not seem right. The subjective discomfort may be in relation to the leader's experience, the organization or setting, and/or activities and behaviors taking place. An objective dilemma is one where there are obvious conflicts of interest, obligations, or claims; the moral dilemma exists in the situation and stands out clearly.

Obstacles to Awareness

Subtle and covert obstacles can blind awareness in organizations and can impede the ability to see (see Figure 6.2). Petrick and Quinn (1997, p. 89) describe leaders who have difficulty seeing ethical issues as having "moral attention deficit disorder." Characteristics of that disorder include the following:

> . . . Inattention to ethical situations (e.g., they do not observe, listen to, or concentrate on ethical conflicts and are easily distracted by the flow of business activity); impulsive urge to be decisive (e.g., they act without prior reflection and are prone to rationalize after acting, rather than reason to a conclusion before acting); and hyperactive need to perform (e.g., rather than dwell in the stillness of ethical awareness or listen to their moral feelings, they rush about with restless energy and feel pressure to keep busy at work.

These characteristics are personal to the behavior of the leader. However, there are other obstacles that affect one's ability to see. *Contextual*, *behavioral*, and *psychological obstacles* can impede the ability to comprehend potential ethical concerns.

Contextual Obstacles. Curtain (2000) argues that conflicts of interest—the funder's, the client's, the provider's, or the organization's—are exacerbated by the strategies adopted by organizations to save money and/or make a profit. For example, managed care organizations have an emphasis on cost-containment and profit, often attained through cutbacks, layoffs, and so forth. This has introduced the element of *fear* to leaders and constituents. People fear loss of position, income, status, and autonomy. Fear affects what is seen, what is identified as an ethical issue, and also what choices are made in ethical dilemmas.

- Moral attention deficit disorder (MADD)
- Contextual
  Intellectual, moral, and cultural climate
  Organizational climate
  Technological and legalistic nature of society
- Behavioral
- Psychological
  Leader illusions: Favorability, optimism, control
  "us versus them"
- Focus on extreme examples

FIGURE 6.2   Obstacles to Awareness

A manager (Manning, 1990, p. 281) who experienced fear about her job security stated that she deliberately avoids meetings, or sets them up a long time apart, when she knows she will be confronted with ethical issues that ". . . I will not be able to live with. . . ." She also reiterated avoiding the people who tend to confront her with those kinds of issues: ". . . have to avoid getting drawn into it . . . don't say anything." This manager deliberately structured her work life so that her awareness of unethical practices would not be provoked.

The *"intellectual, moral, and cultural climate* in which practice occurs" affects awareness of ethical issues in leadership. For example, the climate in relation to health care has changed. Health care has become a marketplace. Services are products, marketed to the highest bidder, changing the fundamental relationship of care providers and receivers. External fiscal agents now have undue influence on leadership; their requirements affect the discernment of potential moral problems. Marketing services for profit to the highest bidder rather than attending to need, promotes a blindness that inhibits seeing the underlying moral and ethical issues. The reliance on external agents for the revenue to survive as an agency has an effect on defining who the agency views as the client: the payor of the service or the consumer of the service.

The decision about *who is the customer* impacts the awareness of ethical issues. Funders request highly structured formats with particular requirements through the contract with the agency. Length and type of services are dictated. For example, an administrator was confronted by a clinician about the corporate contract controlling the technology used to deliver clinical services (Manning, 1990, p. 203). He said, ". . . on the grounds of ethics, you can't legislate a clinical decision." The administrator's awareness about the clinical repercussions was compromised by the climate created by financial survival.

The *organizational climate* also affects the level of awareness of ethical or unethical behavior (Longenecker, 1985). Leaders work within organizational systems that *encourage, discourage, or ignore the ethical factors* in decisions. Further, the managerial processes necessary to any business, religious institution, human service organization or government affect the ethical quality of decisions. For example, the development of organizational priorities—mission, goals, and objectives—have an impact. Longenecker (1985, p. 66) states, ". . . managers are responsible for articulating in some way the fundamental purposes or priorities of an organization. They develop an understanding of why an organization exists and the values which are important to its existence." Thus, the ethical dilemmas of leadership are buried, invisible, in the priorities that are given special attention, shaping the ethical nature of the organization sight unseen.

The *technological and legalistic* nature of society and business can desensitize leaders to ethical issues. The increasing reliance on policy and procedure, guidelines, standards, and regulations removes the obligation to think about what is being conveyed; the underlying effect of such policies goes unnoticed (Kass, 1990). For example, policies and procedures of disclosure and informed consent are followed pedantically to meet the letter of the law and avoid liability, rather than examining the ethical spirit— the issues of adequate disclosure, voluntariness, and comprehension—necessary to ethical application (Manning & Gaul, 1997).

Behavioral Obstacles.   *Subtle behavioral influences* also impact awareness and decisionmaking (Curtain, 2000). Leaders and constituents have all the *human characteristics* that make people *vulnerable to influence.* The desire to be accepted as part of the team can promote a professional blindness to potential ethical quandaries. The unspoken norms about being a team player can be difficult to challenge, especially for new members. As a person gains seniority and history with an organization, socialization to the organizational culture may cause blindness to unethical practices; one becomes a part of promoting "the way things are around here." The seduction of financial incentives acts on a person similar to fear about the loss of job security. A leader may find it difficult to jeopardize the potential of material perks and rewards through giving unsolicited feedback about ethical concerns.

Finally, *pressure to conform to organizational expectations* can cloud awareness. Employee/consumer ratios, census standards, performance evaluation standards, budget deficits, goals and objectives, and many other concrete examples of organizational expectations often take precedence over the awareness and examination of underlying ethical issues. Decisionmaking that is based on efficiency may simplify the moral issues reflected in decisions, losing the complexity of moral issues. The leader whose "cognitive pattern" is to decide automatically on behalf of the organization is an example (Petrick & Quinn, 1997, p. 90). Directors and upper administrators are vulnerable to the *political influences* that impact their success. The expectations of external funders influence leaders, particularly in times of scarce resources (Manning, 1990). As one leader stated, ". . . You don't want to bite the hand that feeds you" (Manning, 1990, p. 202).

Psychological Obstacles.   The *psychology* of leaders' *theories about themselves* can impede the moral view. Research has identified three *illusions* that leaders may hold about themselves that distort the reality of their worldview (Messick & Bazerman, 1996). First is the illusion of *favorability.* Here a person has an "unrealistically positive view of the self . . . more honest, ethical, capable, intelligent, courteous, insightful, and fair than others" (Messick & Bazerman, 1996, p. 18). The need to see oneself in a favorable way causes the person to filter and edit information to control how they see themselves in order to retain a positive image of themselves. Necessarily, the awareness of ethical issues that confront the favorable image becomes flawed also. The illusion of *optimism* also is an unrealistic view. This view promotes a belief that they are less susceptible than others to risks, thus distorting an accurate risk assessment and providing for potential exposure of themselves and the agency to ethical hazards. Finally, the illusion of *control* exaggerates the perception that the leader can control random events and is immune to common risks. These illusions can also result in ". . . a kind of organizational ethnocentrism" (Messick & Bazerman, 1996, p. 18), an illusion that the organization contributes more to society or is less harmful to society than other organizations. These kinds of illusions create barriers to awareness and the opportunity for moral and ethical improvement.

The *us versus them* mentality acts as a buffer against seeing and knowing the experience of vulnerable populations and groups (Friedman, 1989). Thus, ethical dilemmas and responsibilities in relation to those populations are hidden. For example, the medically indigent are not a group that most professional caregivers can identify as similar to themselves. "They are somebody else's problem . . . medical indigence does not happen to us; it happens to 'them'" (Friedman, 1989, p. 207). Curtain uses the analogy of the "torturer's horse" from Auden's poem who ". . . scratches its innocent behind on a tree" while the uninsured poor suffer. The us versus them mentality also becomes a form of bigotry, stereotyping, and ethnocentrism that hides subtle discrimination and dulls moral sensitivity. *Ethnocentrism* frames "the other" as different from ourselves and exaggerates the difference. Further, the difference is not just descriptively different, but evaluatively biased; their difference tends to be viewed as a negative difference (Messick & Bazerman, 1996). *Us versus them* is especially dangerous in relation to awareness or lack of awareness of ethical and moral issues because people are often unaware of their influence.

Ethical awareness and analysis often is focused on the extreme examples while the *ethics of everyday practice is ignored* (Kass, 1990). Fraud, whistle-blowing about large-scale organizational practices, financial mismanagement, and so forth are all important to consider, but the ordinary human encounters, the "occasion for the practice (and cultivation) of virtue and respect, and . . . for the exercise of responsibility and trust . . . ," are frequently not seen as ethical issues (Kass, 1990, p. 7).

Awareness and the Role of Feedback

A review of the obstacles to awareness demonstrates that the ability to ask for and give *feedback* and *to comment* on potential ethical issues to consider is critical to heightening awareness for leaders and constituents. The opportunity for reflection and consultation with others changes the way we perceive an ethical dilemma and provides new options and resources to consider in resolving dilemmas. Discussions with colleagues, supervisors, consultants, and so forth promote a more ethical-reasoning process than deciding in isolation. Research indicates that, if people reflect on a moral issue prior to dealing with it, they are more likely to follow their own conscience than respond to authority and do what they believe is wrong (Sherman, 2000). Therefore, feedback and reflection about the practices of individuals and organizations leads to moral action (Manning, 1990). When we observe or are affected by unethical practices and do not, or are unable, to comment, we are participating in that practice. To be aware and to comment, we must care about the moral and ethical aspects of situations.

Feeling: An Informed Heart

Caring is necessary to motivate ourselves to make the invisible visible and to consider moral and ethical quandaries. Caring is fluid, flowing from personal feelings and professional practice perspectives and experiences. Leaders who act as moral citizens must involve their emotions as a motivation to act. To know something intellectually does not create the impetus to do something about it. Leaders know that there are a disproportionate number of men in the upper administrative levels of the organization. They know that particular policies may create barriers for consumers to access services. They know that prejudice and stereotypes are affecting the performance and experience of a diverse work group. However, leaders must *care* about what they know in order to take action about it (Rachels, 1980).

Reflection and deliberation change what is cared about and provide the motivation to act. Reflection helps to understand the meaning of knowledge. For example, reading about the death of Matthew Shephard, the young, gay man in Wyoming, provides a certain level of information. However, hearing his mother discuss the loss of her son, sharing her personal story of pain and heartbreak, followed by reflection with others about the nature of that death—the relationship to homophobia, violence, and hate—promotes an emotional reaction to knowing. Camus, in *Reflections on a Guillotine*, provides another example of the difference between knowing and the meaning of what we know. He said, "We tolerate the death penalty because we think of it in euphemistic terms . . . the individual paid his debt to society . . . rather than attending to the sound of the head falling into the basket."

Capacity for Empathy

The Dalai Lama considers the regard for one another's feelings at a human level—the capacity for empathy—as one of the most important parts of ethical action (His Holiness The Dalai Lama, 1999). The sensitivity to others' experience is a powerful part of understanding the meaning of that experience. In Tibetan, this is called, "*shen dug ngal wa la mi so pa*," or translated it means "the inability to bear the sight of another's suffering" (His Holiness The Dalai Lama, 1999, p. 64). The ability to enter into someone else's pain is an important characteristic that is necessary to be motivated to take ethical action. The capacity for empathy becomes the source of *nying je*, generally translated as "compassion," although it means much more in terms of ideas that connote ". . . love, affection, kindness, gentleness, generosity of spirit, and warmheartedness . . . also used as a term of both sympathy and of endearment" (His Holiness, The Dalai Lama, 1999, p. 73).

Nying je is part of the category of emotions that includes a cognitive element, or reason. It is a combination of empathy and reason. The cognitive element helps to counteract the potential for randomness of feeling. Instead, *nying je* can be developed through sustained reflection, rehearsal, and practice so that we can connect further with others. The ability to connect with others increases the potential of caring about ethical issues. The Dalai Lama (1999, p. 74) notes that "the more we develop compassion, the more genuinely ethical our conduct will be."

Capacity for Indignation

In addition to empathy and connection with others, the ability to feel *indignation*— ". . . appropriate anger aroused by something unjust, mean, intolerable, or unworthy"—is helpful to awareness (Petrick & Quinn, 1997, p. 93). A leader's ability to express "a sense of outrage" in reaction to exploitation, harmful and destructive actions, and betrayals in the workplace is important to precipitate changes in the unethical conditions. Indignation creates energy and promotes the courage necessary to move forward with an identified unethical practice.

Caring and a Cause

A person's emotions help to counter the serious danger of viewing ethics as only rational problem solving (Kass, 1990). Ethical decisions that rest only on the rational do not . . .

> . . . fill the human void created by technological thinking, nor does it supply the fully human response to the need to act. Rather, rationalistic ethics becomes merely a countervailing technique, the ethicist another technical expert like the ophthalmologist or the cardiologist, in danger of being a specialist without vision and a moralist without heart (Kass, 1990, p. 7).

The natural inclination to care requires a particular moral disposition that is developed through practice. The leader's experience with "the that" leads to understanding "the why" (Kass, 1990). Thus, caring emanates from practice.

Caring and the idea of *a cause* are integrally connected. Leaders can revitalize their professions through revisiting the idea of cause. Charlotte Towle (1969, p. 278) argued that we must have a cause ". . . to care, to be concerned, to feel committed to carry, not just an informed head, but an 'informed heart.'" Mechanistic theories, strategies, and tactics of administration and management can block out the purpose that flows from the meaning of a cause. In addition, the focus on professionalization, fears of encroachment on professional territory, and preoccupation with technology can obstruct the true meaning and purpose of professional leading (Manning, 1990). Commitment to a cause provides a powerful emotional attachment to moral and ethical issues. Integrating the leader's moral vision with professional purpose and values provides a particularly potent focus or cause to follow for moral direction.

Leaders will find the real action in practicing ethics as the integration of their own emotions and passions, their character and habits, with behavior that reinforces who they are as people. Negotiating the many moral challenges of human beings in interaction with a service delivery system requires leaders who use their emotions, their ability to care, and their vision of a cause (Kass, 1990, pp. 9–10). In addition to the emotions and caring of the individual leader, there are moral theories that reflect a caring perspective in regard to ethical situations.

Moral Theory that Reflects Caring: Feminist, Afrocentric, and Ghandian

The development of moral theory for social work should start from the ". . . position that the primary underlying good in social work is caring" (Imre, 1989, p. 18). Social work (and other helping professions) needs moral theories that are relevant and useful to the purpose and challenges of practice. The ethic of care developed by Gilligan (1982) and others is a theory that is a good fit for social work values and purpose. The ethic of care provides a perspective that is contextual; responsibilities are found within a context, usually the context of special relationships. The ethic of care, then, is directed toward the interdependence of human beings. Thus, the importance of relationship is emphasized in the analysis of ethical quandaries. Rather than focusing on abstract principles and rules (as per classical ethical theories), a caring approach asks the moral question "what does a caring approach require in this situation?" (Imre, 1989, p. 22). The ethics of care begins with a focus on the people involved in the situation and an assessment of their needs and involvement with one another. There is a realization of the responsibility of the decisionmaker for the consequences and impacts on others, implicit in the decision process.

A Feminist Ethic of Care: Moral Sentiments and Relationship

An ethics of care is extended beyond the psychological explanation argued by Gilligan (1982) through the addition of a feminist ethical perspective that includes the political context, institutional and structural barriers, and issues of wealth and power that are inextricably linked to social work practice and ethics (Gould, 1988). The feminist orientation combines the ethic of responsibility with moral rights and the importance of moral sentiments. Justice becomes the "abstract form that caring takes when responsibility is not defined simply in private terms, but also is perceived in relation to societal commitments" (Gould, 1988, p. 414). Rights, from this perspective, are not defined in an individualistic model. Instead, rights and responsibilities are viewed through the collective, or what enhances the concept of a caring community. The feminist ethic connects the individual client (or employee, constituent, or citizen) and what is considered to be goods on their behalf to the institutional, organizational, and governmental responsibilities to promote those goods (Gould, 1988).

The feminist ethic also promotes action against oppression of any form (Abramson, 1996). Social and structural conditions that cause oppression and issues of race, class, and gender are examined beyond the particular experiences of the individual. For example, a complaint by a female about workplace discrimination would extend beyond the individual's situation to an examination of the organization's cultures, policies, and structures that may need to be changed in regard to gender oppression.

An Afrocentric Ethic of Care: Community, Spirituality, and Experience

An Afrocentric approach to ethics brings forward traditional African values and assumptions, as well as Black Feminist perspectives, and integrates them into moral sensitivity and response (Abramson, 1996). This approach considers the values of the community to which an individual or group belongs when analyzing dilemmas that affect the community's members. The importance of spirituality and its role in understanding and resolving moral and ethical quandaries is emphasized. Finally, the importance of each person's experience is acknowledged as valuable information in the decision process.

Ethical actions are not seen as separate from the group or community; the action is viewed as significant to all and all must be taken into account in an assessment of potential impacts, both benefits and harms. The decisionmakers would rely heavily on personal experience, their own as well as the experience of others who are affected, and would include as many factors as possible. Self-knowledge is valued as the basis for ethical practice, and dialogue with others is critical in accessing experiential and other forms of knowledge from those involved in the situation. Finally, the ethic of caring is also prominent. This ethic is based on appreciating the dignity and uniqueness of people and their ability to express themselves. Emotion is viewed as appropriate to share in the discussions about the ethical issue, and the leader's capacity for empathy with those involved is critical, communicated both verbally and nonverbally.

A Ghandian Ethic of Care: Social Justice and Service

The Ghandian approach to ethics is complementary to social work leadership in that the Ghandian methods integrate both service and social action, direct and indirect practice through ethical theory that has two primary foci, service and justice (Walz & Ritchie, 2000). The philosophical beliefs that provide the foundation for Ghandian ethical principles are congruent with the beliefs of feminist and Afrocentric ethics. They include ". . . cooperation over competition, interdependence over rugged individualism, compassion for others over pursuit of self-interest, and social justice over individual achievement" (Walz & Ritchie, 2000, p. 215). Walz and Ritchie (2000) delineate some of the concepts of Ghandian thought (in the following discussion) that are useful to an ethic of care when addressing leadership issues.

The *unity of all things* and the *harmonic nature of the universe* are concepts that place human beings as part of the universe, but not at its center. Conflict and competition are viewed as aberrations to an ordinarily harmonic system. The world, from this perspective, must be viewed as holistic, without a center or particular boundaries. Rather, ". . . all life is equal and to be respected; no part is greater than the whole. Each individual has an investment in maintaining and serving others because mankind is one" (Walz & Ritchie, 2000, p. 216). This Ghandian concept would fit with the adage, "What you do to others, you also do to yourself" (Walz & Ritchie, 2000). The ethic of a harmonic universe stresses the importance of broadening ethical responsibility beyond the organization to the environment. The processes of an organization have an effect on the external environment from an ecological perspective (for example, waste, pollution, use of resources, recyclable materials, and so forth), but also have an effect on the lives of people (consumers, employees, and community citizens). Policies and practices that support sustainable and just lifestyles for people are also a part of respecting the organization's role in maintaining a harmonic environment. Policies such as family leave, domestic partnership, and equal employment opportunity are examples.

Ahimsa means nonviolence or nonharming, similar to the principle of nonmaleficence (see Chapter 7). This concept promotes "right-mindedness and right actions" (Walz & Ritchie, 2000, p. 216) in regard to others, or finding the truth through the moral positions that we take. Through *ahimsa* the importance of relationship with others is the foundation of all connections in life. Walz and Ritchie (2000, p. 216) state that *ahimsa* requires that "love of all is the absolute ethical position toward which one strives." Love, in this sense, is similar to the principle of *agape*, which means

". . . spontaneous self-giving love expressed freely without calculation of cost or gain to the giver or merit on the part of the receiver" (Merriam-Webster, 1993, p. 39).

This concept promotes constructive, helpful, and nonexploitative relationships with others. As leaders work with employees, peers, and consumers, the quality of their relationships should include the characteristics of honesty and truthfulness rather than exploitation, deception, and manipulation of others for personal or organizational gain. In addition, the Ghandian approach to achieving social change can only be by truthful means. In contrast to a utilitarian approach, the means to an end cannot be compromised in order to reach that end, even if the end result is a good thing (see discussion of teleological and deontological theory in Chapter 7).

Ahimsa expresses the dual mandate of service and social justice. Giving to others is transformational in that the givers become the receivers as a result of their giving. Through serving others, people develop more depth and character and grow in their capacity to experience compassion. Attached to service is the pursuit of justice. Each individual has the ethical responsibility to confront injustice. Thus, at the individual relationship, organizational, and global level, the leader must initiate, and participate in, social action and activism to correct injustices.

The focus of correcting injustice and serving others is *sarvodaya*, or the welfare of all. *Sarvodaya* is an imperative to assist first those who are most needy. Leaders must develop awareness about vulnerable populations within their constituent groups—employees and consumers—and then assess practices, policies, and resource allocation in relation to those groups. *Sarvodaya* provides the moral justification for rationing of organizational resources (for example, programs, budget allocations, and other organizational benefits).

Another principle important to ethical leadership is *swadeshi*, the ethical responsibility to the "immediate local environment and community" (Walz & Ritchie, 2000, p. 218). Here the focus is on keeping organizations and the technology used in organizations at a scale that is humanized and more accessible to the people involved. Service to others and social action described previously should have a quality of immediacy such that the expression at the local level leads to a ripple effect that promotes change at larger levels. The dangers of large bureaucracies that are mechanized and impersonal are confronted through honoring *swadeshi*. Leaders can consider organizational design tools, such as decentralization and contemporary organizational models that promote flattened hierarchies and increased communication networks, as a way to keep the organization more personal and accessible (see Chapter 11). Further, the intimate nature of smaller units allow for innovative projects and the opportunity to demonstrate unique ethical practices and processes that can be replicated at larger levels. As Walz & Ritchie argue, *swadeshi* is the essence of the well-known phrase, "think globally, act locally" (2000, p. 219).

Conclusion

The nature of applied ethics is to integrate the emotions and the mind of a leader in a process of discerning, understanding, and resolving moral and ethical issues in leadership practice. The leader's ability to perceive and become aware of ethical issues is the critical first step as an ethical leader. Obstacles that can affect awareness are complex; psychological and behavioral obstacles interrelate with contextual obstacles. Thus, an important component of awareness is the leaders' knowledge about the obstacles that may confuse or deceive their perceptions of a situation or the obstacles that may conceal ethical issues.

Leaders who use their emotions as part of the experience of understanding moral and ethical quandaries will have a better sense of the meaning of the moral/ethical issue to the participants effected. Understanding the meaning of what is known increases the possibility of caring about it; moral action is then more likely to occur. Leaders can seek out reflection and deliberation through consultation with colleagues, supervisors, and consultants, as well as conversations with family and friends. In this process, leaders can identify their emotions further and understand more deeply the meaning of the moral/ethical issue. The process of deliberation provides an opportunity to refine emotions and to determine what factual information is needed to undertake a reasoning process (see Chapter 7).

Moral theory that embodies caring includes contributions from feminist, Afrocentric, and Ghandian thought, among many others. These theories emphasize the contextual elements of dilemmas and focus on the moral rights of the collective, rather than an individualistic view. An emphasis on valuing personal experience as knowledge and an appreciation of the uniqueness of individuals are precepts to a caring approach. Theories of caring expand the analysis of dilemmas to include the ethical responsibility to community and the environment and are founded on having helpful, constructive relationships with others. There is also a special consideration of the needs of the most vulnerable populations.

The analysis of ethical dilemmas from a caring approach provides the emphasis on relationship, meaning, and the good of the group. Theorists from the Western classical traditions in Chapter 7 support an emphasis on thinking, the contributions of the mind, and a rational process of reasoning.

QUESTIONS AND APPLICATIONS

1. Consider the obstacles to awareness discussed in this chapter. Identify and discuss with others at least one example of a contextual, behavioral, and psychological obstacle you have encountered that impedes the identification of ethical issues.

2. Conceptualize your professional cause or purpose as a leader. What is it you hope to accomplish over your lifetime as a professional and as a social worker? What are the emotional attachments to the moral and ethical issues of leadership that are necessary to accomplish your purpose? Write a letter to a close friend dated 20 years in the future and tell that person what you have accomplished in relation to your cause.

3. Consider the following ethical dilemma that was discussed earlier in this chapter:

   Under the reduction in force (RIF) format, the supervisor, me, gets told on Thursday what supervisees have to come in on Friday to get chopped, and they are to be gone that day. . . . I personally believe that that's unethical . . . not because it's severe, but because it's not balanced . . . We would not tolerate any employee doing that to us.

- What personal and professional values are connected to this dilemma?
- Analyze the dilemma from the perspectives of feminist, Afrocentric, and Ghandian moral principles. How does each inform you about the elements of the dilemma that could promote good or harm?
- How would each perspective lead to particular leadership actions and decisions about this dilemma?

7 Ethical Resources: Traditions and Tools to Develop Ethical Wisdom and Action

THE FOCUS IN THIS CHAPTER IS ON THE FOLLOWING AREAS:

- Moral citizenship: thinking
- Moral citizenship: action
- A decision framework

The previous chapter presented and discussed moral citizenship from the perspective of awareness and feeling in regard to ethical issues. Caring and enacting a cause were discussed as important elements of moral citizenship. Theories and ideals that emphasize aspects of caring in moral citizenship were presented. This chapter turns to the elements of thinking and action. As noted in the discussion about the nature of ethics, a reasoning process is necessary to arrive at an ethical solution. The element of thinking provides some ethical perspectives that can enhance the way we evaluate and analyze ethical situations. The element of action provides a discussion about the necessity of movement, of doing something as a result of the thinking process. A decision model that provides questions to consider completes this chapter.

Thinking: Rationality and Respect

Applied ethics is an approach to determine the right course of action, or what we morally ought to do in a particular situation, *all things considered*. Therefore, thinking about the situation is necessary. One would presume that thinking is easy; after all, thinking is part of daily life. However, there is a danger of not thinking about moral issues (Arendt, 1963). Let us return to Arendt's research on moral thoughtlessness focused on the actions of individuals during the Holocaust. Adolph Eichmann, a Nazi administrator who was responsible for the attempted extermination of the Jews during World War II, was identified as the ideal type of moral thoughtlessness. Eichmann was the ultimate administrator; his major concern was his organizational performance. He was also under severe organizational pressure to enact the wishes of Hitler. Two significant points about thinking are reflected through his actions (Nielson, 1984). First, the organizational environment required Eichmann to obey orders, rather than to pay attention to his personal moral conscience. Second, he was separated from the consequences of his orders and the orders he was following: the extermination of millions of people. Arendt (1963, p. 287) concluded that Eichmann was a "thoughtless" and "banal" man who . . .

> To put the matter colloquially, never realized what he was doing. . . . He was not stupid. It was sheer thoughtlessness—something by no means identical with stupidity. . . . [He was] ignorant of everything that was not directly, technically, and bureaucratically connected with his job.

The nature of the bureaucratic form of organization (discussed in Chapter 8), as in Eichmann's case, is just one factor that can have a major impact on leaders' thinking about moral issues. Many internal and external factors can impede thinking, too. Nevertheless, the ability to think about responsibility and consequences is a necessary part of an ethical decision process.

The discussion on thinking as a part of moral citizenship begins with two components of thinking: rationality and respect (see Figure 7.1). Rationality and respect are followed by material that is helpful in an ethical-reasoning process, the premises of decisions. An overview of some ethical theories and principles are offered to organize some of the important ideas and ideals to consider as part of a reasoning process.

Rationality

Two aspects related to thinking ethically—*rationality and respect*—are necessary for the morally responsible decisionmaker (Goodpaster, 1983). *Rationality* is a requirement to make the best ethical decisions; the best decision—the right course of action—is supported by the best reasons (Rachels, 1980). A rationale is an explanation based on a reasoning process, a justification that provides the logic, facts, premises, and supporting information that leads to a particular conclusion. Therefore, rationality pays ". . . careful attention to ends and means, alternatives and consequences, risks and opportunities . . ." (Goodpaster, 1983, p. 7). The facts in ethical and moral dilemmas are complex and multifaceted. The reasoning process helps to establish the facts, to determine what facts are necessary to a particular context or situation, and to apply the relevant ethical premises of the decision to the facts. All of these factors result in a particular moral conclusion. Rationality is self-directed; the leader is motivated to seek

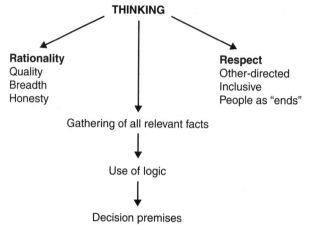

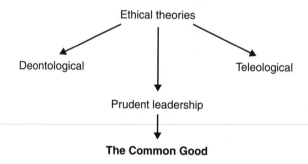

FIGURE 7.1   Thinking as a Reasoning Process

out all of the important and relevant information. Thus, the leader is ethical by intention (Goodpaster, 1983).

Leaders can improve the rationality of their thinking about ethical decisions by considering three criteria: *quality*, *breadth*, and *honesty* (Messick & Bazerman, 1996).

Quality.   *Quality* decisions help to avoid ethical mistakes. The quality of decisions are improved by making sure that all of the consequences of potential actions are considered and that accurate assessments of risks are assigned to each alternative solution. Further, Messick and Bazerman (1996, p. 20) argue for the general principle that personal flaws and biases are more apt to influence decisionmaking ". . . when decisions are intuitive, impulsive, or subjective rather than concrete, systematic, and objective." For example, developing quantitative measures for performance evaluation criteria eliminates the opportunity for subjective, possibly stereotypical, biases that influence the decisionmaker. In addition, systematic procedures of evaluation provide a process that is viewed by constituents as more fair and objective than impulsive or subjective decisions. Quality decisions are based on ". . . data rather than hunches . . . the best guide comes from close attention to the real world . . . not from memory and intuition" (Messick & Bazerman, 1996, p. 20). This implies a commitment to accurate record keeping and benchmarks that help to monitor the objective measurement of project and/or people performance.

Breadth.   The second criterion is *breadth*, an analysis of the full extent of consequences that decisions or policies may produce. The structures a leader uses for analysis can promote openness about the decision process. First, an ethical audit of any decision must include an assessment of all potential stakeholders and the outcomes for all stakeholders. Two possible strategies help to accomplish this. First, open up the decision process by inviting involvement or input from interested or impacted individuals or groups. Another option is to account for the differences that certain stakeholders have in access to information by making a point of including representatives of particular stakeholder groups as a part of the decisionmaking team. Messick and Bazerman (p. 21) recommend "broad consultation" that is based on an "active search to enlist all affected parties into the decision process . . . Openness itself is often a signal to potential opponents that nothing is being hidden and there is nothing to fear." An active effort to involve all interested stakeholders is part of recognizing the organization's role in the larger community; thus, the impact of decisions on the community must be assessed and addressed.

Finally, a leader's awareness and analysis of the future impact of policies and decisions is imperative. The American Indian philosophy that a decision should be evaluated based on the potential impact seven generations from the present is especially salient. An organization's use of resources or the postponement of financial responsibility places an unethical burden on subsequent generations. Decisions about recycling, paper versus Internet communications, renewable resource and transportation incentives, and so forth are small examples of social responsibility for the organization that go beyond the present.

Honesty.   The third criterion is *honesty*. Honesty with others does not imply that all information must be divulged. Messick and Bazerman (1996) acknowledge that some information is confidential or could impede the success of the organization. However, conscience can be a helpful guide to the ethical quality of projects and decisions. Conscience is the litmus test for whether a decision is ethical. "If an idea cannot stand the light of day or the scrutiny of public opinion, then it is probably a bad idea" (Messick & Bazerman, 1996, p. 21). In addition, rather than relying on one's own reaction to what is ethical, ". . . we should ask whether the people with the most to lose would accept the reasons for our actions. If not, we are probably on thin ice" (Messick & Bazerman, 1996, p. 21). Part of thinking, then, is an honest evaluation of the veracity and openness of any decision process about ethical issues. Along with examination of their own reasoning process, decisionmakers must also be concerned with the other.

Respect

Respect is other directed. Respect includes a consideration of the viewpoints and values of other people (Goodpaster, 1983). Leaders must be able to see beyond their own self-interest, values, subjective opinions and so forth. Immanuel Kant argued that people, especially those who may be affected parties, should be treated as *ends* and not as *means*. Treating others as "ends" provides a "self-imposed constraint" on rationality. As decisionmakers, it is important to realize that moral purposes are only valuable because they reside in a humanity that is shared by people who are likely to be affected by those purposes (Goodpaster, 1983).

Respect is especially salient when people who are different from the decisionmakers are involved in, or affected by, the decisions. For example, individuals and groups with different ethnic or racial background; religious beliefs; sexual orientation and identification; and cultural values, norms, and beliefs may not have their values and perspectives reflected in the reasoning process (Manning, 1997). The process of deciding is intimately connected to the personal, professional, and societal values that have been part of a leader's socialization; in turn, the values of diverse individuals and groups that are affected should also be included.

These two components—the self-directed component of rationality and the other-directed component of respect—combine to provide a spirit that is the foundation of moral responsibility (Goodpaster, 1983). Rationality also includes meaningful propositions or premises that help to inform the decisionmaker about the nature of ethical situations and dilemmas.

Decision Premises

Ethical and moral philosophy have been evolving since thousands of years before the time of the Greeks and Western civilization. All of the ancient civilizations and most religions have contributed to universal and culturally particular ideals. Some of the early Western writing about ethics is found in the works of Socrates, Protagoras, Plato, Aristotle, and other Greek philosophers. Their ideas about moral and ethical behavior are relevant today. The depth and breadth of their contributions are beyond what could be presented in this book. However, the following provide some examples about philosophical thought and how such ideas and ideals can inform leaders about ethics.

Socrates promoted the method of the dialectic, arguments and counterarguments to add breadth and depth to the understanding of moral knowledge. He argued that, "the only wisdom consists in knowing you know nothing" and that "people do not do evil voluntarily if they know (understand) the good" (Freeman, 2000, p. 39). His thinking reinforces the importance of seeing all sides of an issue and understanding the moral and ethical significance of each side. Also, part of leadership is supporting education for constituents about ethics and how to reason about good and evil, which, in turn, will promote more ethical behavior.

Protagoras put forth one of the first statements of moral relativism, saying that man is the measure of all things (reality is not the same for everyone). Moral relativism promotes the argument that moral standards are always relative; there are different moral standards because of culture, differences in government and society, and differences through time and history. An awareness of contextual relativism helps pursue the respect discussed earlier, taking into account the experience of the other.

Plato identified the importance of social justice as an imperative for life with one another in community. From Plato's early works, the concept of justice has been developed to include personal rights, the common good, and development and maintenance of principles and rules that provide for society's existence. Leadership in organizations is constantly confronted with dilemmas of justice for consumers, employees, and other constituents. An organization can promote policies and practices that further development of the organizational community as a community that treats each other in a just manner.

Aristotle provided the earliest effort (*Nicomachean Ethics*) (1987) to develop a systematic approach to ethics and the underlying principles. He started with questions about "What is the good life?" and provided early arguments about the nature of virtue. Virtue, for Aristotle, was about the ". . . excellence of a thing . . . and the effective performance of its proper function" (Freeman, 2000, p. 88). Aristotle was interested in ". . . giving meaning to human action . . ." and to the evaluation of that action from an ethical point of view (Freeman, 2000, p. 88). This idea is particularly important for professional leaders; virtuous leaders would be effective in fulfilling the roles and responsibilities of their position and would promote a moral climate for all constituents and the organization.

Aristotle defined virtue as being a good person. He further developed this definition by arguing that, to be a good person and to flourish, one must be able to reason well. In thinking about the development of character, he originated the doctrine of "lying in a mean." That is to say that a person should avoid in one's character the "extremes of excess and of deficiency, both of which hinder performance" (Freeman, 2000, p. 88). For example, the person with self-confidence is lying at the mean, with arrogance being excess and subservience a deficit. Aristotle began the inquiry about virtue, but it has continued to develop as an ethical model ever since. The ethics of virtue focus on the development of virtuous characteristics and traits of people in order to act ethically.

Virtue Ethics

These ethical models rest on certain ideals, or virtues, toward which we should strive and that allow for the full development of our humanity. A virtue is ". . . a disposition to act, desire, and feel that involves the exercise of judgment and that leads to a recognizable human excellence, an instance of human flourishing" (Freeman, 2000, p. 91). The point of acquiring virtues is not further guidance. It is not to tell us what to do, but to ensure that we will do the right thing willingly, based on the development and manifestation of attitudes, dispositions, or character traits. A person must "be this" rather than "do this," but "being" involves "trying to do" (Frankena, 1973). There is a distinction between doing what is good and being a good person. The *motivation* to do good, rather than choosing a right or correct behavior based on rules or principles, is what is important. For example, a "moral atrocity" is committed "when one acts rightly, but with bad motivations" (Freeman, 2000, p. 89).

Plato and other Greek philosophers developed four cardinal virtues:

- Wisdom
- Courage
- Temperance
- Justice

One cannot be derived from another and all other moral virtues can be derived from these four, or can be shown to be forms of them. Other derivatives of these virtues include honesty, compassion, generosity, fidelity, integrity, fairness, self-control, and prudence.

Leadership ethics are strengthened by virtue-based ethics because the focus is on the responsibility of the person. Dobel (1998) argues that, without this focus, the exercise of power reduces to what Havel called the "innocent power" of the individual actor who becomes an ". . . innocent tool of an 'innocent' anonymous power, legitimized by science, cybernetics, ideology, law, abstraction and objectivity—that is, by everything except personal responsibility to human beings as persons and neighbors" (Havel, 1986, pp. 136–158). Virtue ethics promotes the moral responsibility of the leader for actions taken and not taken.

The *principle of virtue* states that what is ethical is what develops moral virtues in us and our communities. Virtues are developed through learning and practice. "Just as the ability to run a marathon develops through much training and practice, so too does our capacity to be fair, to be courageous, or to be compassionate" (Markula Center for Applied Ethics, Ethics & Virtue, 2000). In time, virtues become habits. After they are acquired, they become a characteristic of that person. These character traits are developed within the communities where we grow up and to which we belong. Because an individual's character traits are not developed in isolation, important institutions and groups, such as family, school, church, and other private and public associations influence the virtuous traits that are valued by that community. The values and traits that are encouraged and the community role models that are celebrated affect the kinds of traits that are developed. Similarly, the individuals who reside there shape the values and traits of community (and organization).

Hence, community is at the heart of the virtue approach (Markula Center for Applied Ethics, Ethics & Virtue, 2000). The reciprocity of influence between individuals and the community fits for organizations as a community as well. As discussed in Chapter 3, transformational leadership has the capacity to support the development of virtuous traits among constituents, and constituents have the ability to influence the moral culture of the organization. The moral life, then, according to virtue ethics, is a process of trying to determine the kind of people we should be and contributing to the development of character within our communities (and within our organizations).

Virtue ethics, because they are community specific, have a disadvantage in that they can become ethnocentric, which becomes a position from which to exercise intolerance (Kitchener, 1996). Kitchener (1996, p. 4) states, "It is my own suspicion that as many acts of intolerance have been committed in the name of virtue as in the name of principle—from the burning of women as witches in Salem to the murder of abortion physicians in Florida." Virtue ethics, then, for the individual leader, organization, or community must be balanced with ethical principles and theories, as a way to evaluate "... both virtues and the actions committed in the name of virtue ..." (Kitchener, 1996, p. 5). Virtuous character combined with ethical principles and theories provide a wider range of understanding the nature of ethical issues and the balance necessary for deciding what we ought to do.

Ethical Principles

Principles help to bridge the subjective gulf of individual experience reflected through virtues. Frankena (1973) argued that "... principles without traits are impotent and traits without principles are blind" (Freeman, 2000, p. 93). Therefore, virtues and principles are complementary. Virtues help promote the right motivation, and principles provide concrete direction and guidance. Moral principles focus primarily on people's actions and doings. We apply them by asking what these ideas and principles require of us in response to particular dilemmas or circumstances.

Ross (1930) developed prima facie obligations that he argued were self-evident. These principles inform about what one should do if there are no other overriding moral considerations:

- Obligation of fidelity to keep promises and to tell the truth
- Obligation to make reparation to people for any injury we wrongfully caused
- Obligation to render services in return for any services rendered to us
- Obligation to assist and not to prevent distribution of happiness (goods, wealth, and resources) in accordance with merit
- Obligation to do whatever good we can for others to made their condition better
- Obligation to improve ourselves of virtue and intelligence
- Obligation not to injure others

These prima facie obligations are encompassed by the ethical principles of nonmaleficence, beneficence, fidelity, autonomy, and justice.

Nonmaleficence and beneficence are the principles that prescribe actions of preventing harm and doing good. Frankena (1973) sees beneficence and nonmaleficence as the same principle with a four-part hierarchy: a) do not inflict harm, b) prevent harm, c) remove harm, and d) do good. The hierarchy helps to prioritize behavior, and each one takes precedent over the next. Therefore, doing good is the highest priority. Further, refraining from harm is passive, whereas doing good implies a positive action. Thus, these two principles are at the heart of risk/benefit analysis and professional duty. The process of assessing and disclosing risks and benefits includes an assessment of potential harms that could result, as well as the benefits that may be produced, from a particular decision or action.

Beneficence, or the obligation to do good, is the professional duty to promote good for others. Beneficence can become "a slippery slope" in relation to the question "in whose best interests" (Freeman, 2000, p. 24). Leaders may consider particular actions to be in the best interests of their constituents (employees, clients, or community members) when the constituents have a different perspective or have not been consulted as to their perspective. *Parentalism*, more traditionally called *paternalism*, is the professional decision to act in a constituent's (client's) best interest, based on professional expertise and knowledge and against the autonomy or will of the constituent.

Fidelity is the principle that is important to constituents' trust in a leader. Fidelity has to do with faithfulness and a careful observance of duty as a professional (Freeman, 2000). Constituents must be able to trust that the leader will follow through on the performance of obligations. Also, professional leaders must be willing to devote themselves to the service of others and work toward a vision of a higher good.

Autonomy directs us to consider the self-determination of others (Manning & Gaul, 1997). This principle directs decisionmakers to honor each individual's right to autonomous actions and choices, which are not constrained by others. People can be autonomous only if they are self-governing. A person's autonomous choice does not necessarily ensure freedom from harm, or even good judgment. However, the nature of autonomy is that the person is still free to choose as long as the individual is a competent adult. In addition, authenticity is a part of autonomy. Individuals make life and work choices based on what is fitting to their experience, values, beliefs, and characteristics as people. Respecting authenticity requires an ability to consider people individually, that is, who they are as unique persons, rather than lumped into a group or collective.

The issue of autonomy is a frequent challenge for leaders in human services, either in relation to employees or to the autonomy of clients. The use of authority and power over others can impede or prohibit the autonomy of constituents. Employees may have unique characteristics and traditions that are jeopardized by work requirements or expectations. Also, organizational policies and procedures that affect consumers of service and employees, such as informed consent, confidentiality, and the right to refuse treatment, invoke the principle of autonomy and require an understanding of what is necessary to respect autonomy.

Justice. *Justice* has been a consistent ideal in Western civilization since the fundamental principle of justice was defined by Aristotle more than 2,000 years ago (Markula, Justice & Fairness, 2000). Aristotle said that "equals should be treated equally and unequals unequally." In contemporary terms, the principle means that "individuals should be treated the same, unless they differ in ways that are relevant to the situation in which they are involved" (Markula, Justice & Fairness, 2000, p. 2). For example, if two employees have the same job description and do the same work, and there are not relevant differences in the work they are doing, then, in justice, they should receive the same salary. When someone is paid more because of gender (for example, male) or ethnicity (for example, caucasian), there is an injustice—discrimination—because gender and race are not relevant to the work that is performed.

Criteria have been developed that provide a justification for treating people differently, but still justly (Markula, Justice & Fairness, 2000). *Need-based* criteria, championed by Karl Marx, make it possible to give benefits to the poor, those who have a greater *need*, which would not be made available to those who are more affluent. Social welfare benefits are an example of need-based justice. Criteria based on *equality* would mean that each person has an equal share of a benefit, for example, Medicare, or the same amount of annual leave in an organization. The person who arrives first at the company party has the best choice of the food, and the first in line for theatre tickets gets the best seats. Employees who do not perform well are given disciplinary actions that are not distributed to others. Both of these groups have met the criteria of *desert*, or justice according to *individual effort*. It is generally recognized as fair to reward those who have contributed more, for example, to a particular project or through numerous volunteer hours to help with various projects that support the agency mission. Those people are rewarded with particular resources (for example, monetary, recognition, and so forth) based on their *contributions or merits*.

Social or distributive justice is concerned with fairness; the fairness of how benefits and burdens, good and evil, are distributed. The institutions of society are responsible to make sure resources and burdens are distributed in ways that are fair and just. An underlying assumption is that justice is related to scarcity; there would not be a need for fairness if there were an unlimited amount of benefits accessible by all. Leaders and constituents in organizations are involved in issues of justice in many ways. For example, equitable employment policies (for example, hiring, promotion, performance reviews, and merit increases) ensure fairness in the distribution of benefits available through the organization. Policies, such as grievance, affirmative action, equal employment opportunity, sexual harassment, and so forth, also help to promote fairness in the distribution of benefits and burdens and to provide for due process within the organization. Decisions about the distribution and allocation of resources, often through budget processes, are always concerned with justice issues. Policies about access to services, consumer ability to afford services, and distribution of facilities where services are provided all contain issues relevant to equity and fairness.

Social justice also includes a *social contract* between people. John Rawls (1971) contribution was the concept that "people have the right to make agreements with one another and these agreements are binding on them" whether the agreements are formal (as in a written contract) or informal (as in a promise) (Freeman, 2000, p. 56). The social contract between people is the key to the concept of justice. Thomas Hobbes (1996) conceptualization of the golden rule (Do unto others that which you would have done to you) extends the idea of a social contract. This agreement among people outlines the mutual obligations and expectations. Applying social contracts between people with the golden rule provides an agreement among people that can be entered into willingly, chosen as a moral obligation through mutual consent and agreement, rather than being imposed by society. This approach requires ". . . the ability to see that one cannot pursue one's own self-interests without taking into consideration the interests of everyone else" (Freeman, 2000, p. 57). Leaders have to consider the impact of their decisions on all of the other constituents of the organization. In addition, establishing the social contract as a foundation for organizational culture helps to promote critical thinking about the nature of mutual obligations among and between all constituents.

Rawls (1971) further developed the idea of a social contract through an imaginary device that individuals can use to uncover moral principles. He suggested imagining a group of rational individuals, a legislative body so to speak, to determine principles to live by that would govern themselves in the future; they would take the the original position. Further, the principles could only be morally justified if agreed to by a group that did not know any of the particular characteristics they would possess in this future society, for example, gender, race, economic status, social position, and so forth. Thus, they were endowed with a veil of ignorance. He argued that first the group would agree to equality, that is, freedom for everyone. "Secondly, they would protect themselves in case they turned out to be the least advantaged in the society. In doing so they would agree . . . to the principle that allows for differences but also directs society to improve the circumstances of the less advantaged" (Freeman, 2000, p. 58). The original position and the veil of ignorance are metaphors that can be useful in creating ethical organizations. Leaders and constituents can create new ways to think about justice and fairness in the organization by considering the impact of practices and policies on all stakeholders.

Principles provide guidelines for thinking about ethical issues and dilemmas. They introduce particular moral premises into ethical situations and dilemmas. They help delineate the particular moral threats in situations. However, principles do not provide a theoretical approach, or how to consider and analyze the nature of a dilemma and the right resolution or answer.

Ethical Theories

Consider the following activity and think about your own reaction to the situation.

Activity: Imagine that you are on a spelunking expedition. You have entered a cave and traveled deeper into the caverns for several hours. The group has entered a small room with only one entrance, the one used to enter the cavern. The entire group except for the leader has entered. As the leader crawls through the entrance, a cave-in occurs. The way out is blocked by her body, which is covered with tons of rubble. She is alive, determined by a pulse in her wrist, which is sticking out of the rubble. It isn't possible to assess the degree of injury (for example, broken neck, internal injuries, and so forth) and moving her may cause more serious injury or death. Time passes, and no help has arrived. Further, the air in the small room is getting stale, and there is less oxygen to breathe. Would you remove her body, by any means possible, and, in the process, sacrifice her life in order to exit the cavern? Would you decide not to do anything to cause further injury or possibly death? What is the rationale for both responses? Integrate the reasons with the means versus the ends arguments that support the following theories (Abrams, 1989).

Two primary ethical theories have evolved that have as their primary focus two different ways to arrive at doing the right thing. The means used to achieve a particular good is one approach. A focus on what good can be produced, or what harm can be reduced—the end result—is another way to justify what is right. In the previous story, a decision based on *deontological theory* would be focused on the means, or duty. Individuals who approach the dilemma based on their motivation to use moral rules and principles to arrive at a decision would treat the leader, who is blocking the way out, as an end, not as a means to an end (escape). The duty to prevent harm to the leader would require that the group refrain from causing this person further injury or death, even at the risk of losing other lives. In contrast, *teleological theory* would require a calculation of what would provide the best end result. If the object was to save lives, the leader's life could be sacrificed in order to save the group, the greatest good for the greatest number. The following discussion provides further distinction between these ethical theories.

Deontological: Our Duty to Act Rightly.   The word deontological is derived from the Greek root, "deontos," which means "of the obligatory." This approach is based on the philosophy that actions are inherently right or wrong, apart from any consequences to which they might lead (Frankena, 1973). Ethical rules can be formulated and hold under all circumstances because they are inherently right. Further, a person that is motivated by duty is motivated by something beyond their own self-interest, that of universal law. A universal law is something all people ought to live up to whether they want to or not. The motivation, or good will, to act is the respect for obligations that one would be willing to have everyone else act on as well, thus a universal law. Deontologists profess that the means, or certain duties, principles, and rules, must be adhered to in all circumstances, regardless of the end result.

Immanuel Kant made deontological concepts central in an ethical system; morality is accomplished, at least in part, through the consistency and application of rules, principles, and duty. He developed categorical imperatives, unconditional demands that were morally necessary and obligatory under all circumstances.

Two categorical imperatives developed by Kant are useful in many ethical dilemmas: a) Act as if the maxim of your action by your will would become a universal law, and b) Act as to treat humanity, whether in your own person or in that of any other, always as an end and never as a means (Kant, 1963). The first imperative requires that principles for ethical action be universal without contradiction. The principle should apply across any situation or dilemma. In addition, the universal directives for action should not conflict by willing one thing for one's self and another thing for others (that is, do unto others as you would have them do unto you). The second imperative argues that people are ends in themselves and should never be treated as means to an end. One is obligated to act only in ways that respect the human dignity and moral rights of all persons. The end justifies the means would never be a justifiable argument for ethical action, according to this imperative.

Teleological: The Greatest Good.   Teleological is derived from the Greek root, "teleios," which means, "brought to its end or purpose." This is the classic utilitarian approach. The founder of modern utilitarianism was Jeremy Bentham. John Stuart Mill further developed this approach. Their policy was to seek "the greatest good for the greatest number." Teleologists justify ethical decisions in terms of the consequences of the decision or the ends achieved. A given course of action should not be chosen only because it is inherently good, but because it leads to desired results. The Principle of Utility states that the moral ends to be sought in all we do is the greatest possible balance of good over evil in the world as a whole. The morally right course of action would be the one ". . . that produces the greatest balance of benefits over harms for everyone affected . . . . utilitarianism does not care whether the benefits are produced by lies, manipulation, or coercion" (Markula, Calculating Consequences, 2000).

The judgment of what constitutes the greatest good is based on a unitary criteria that is used to evaluate the greatest good or the least harm based on that criteria (for example, economic criteria, such as cost-effectiveness, or assigning value to a personal preference, such as quality of life). The decisionmaker(s) identify various courses of action or choices and then determine all of the possible benefits or harms that would result from each course of action, according to the criteria chosen. Finally, the course of action is chosen according to what provides the greatest benefits after costs have been taken into account. The implication of the teleological approach is that, whatever the good and bad are, they are capable of being measured and balanced against each other in some quantitative or objective fashion.

There are some problems in applying the utilitarian approach (Markula, Calculating Consequences, 2000). First, in order to consider the consequences of a particular action to determine whether it is right, you must have knowledge, or access to knowledge, about all of the possible consequences. It is also necessary to attach some sort of value to the benefits and harms that could result. Not all benefits and costs are measurable, for example, the quality of life or the value of human dignity. Further, it is difficult to compare values such as cost-efficiency and cost-effectiveness with the value of life or human expression or aesthetic goods. The most serious difficulty with a utilitarian approach is that it does not include a consideration of justice and fairness. The focus on the end result can justify immoral practices because they result in a positive gain for an organization or for a society. The strength of this approach is that it requires concentration on the results of a decision, both immediate and more distant consequences. Utilitarianism also asks the decisionmaker to be impartial in calculating the interests of all stakeholders involved. Thus, self-interest of the decisionmaker cannot be satisfied over the interests of others.

Prudent Leadership

The means and the ends each add a different lens about ethical issues, but linking them is crucial to "prudent leadership" (Dobel, 1998, p. 78). Linking the means and ends in relation to leadership has several dimensions. First, Dobel argues for "finding the right means to attain an end." Reflect back to Chapter 4, in regard to power, and think about the many forms of influence available to leaders, from persuasion to coercion. The means a leader uses will affect the quality of relationships between the leader and constituents as well as the politics that are set into motion by the action. Second, leaders must evaluate the means and resources used, as well as postponed opportunities, in relationship to the end that is being sought. Are the means necessary proportionate to the resulting good, or is there a disproportionate amount of resources expended in order to arrive at a questionable good result? Third, the means that are used can have a profound effect on the success of the end result. When leaders use questionable tactics or abuse authority and power to achieve a particular end, employees, citizens, and consumers may sabotage or undercut the result because of resentment and anger, ". . . the moral residuals of excessive and immoral methods to attain goals" (Dobel, 1998, p. 78). The use of coercion ". . . looms as the most dangerous means . . ." in relation to legitimacy of an achievement (Dobel, 1998, p. 78). The more leaders use coercion to attain a goal, the less likely it will be that the goal will be viewed as legitimate or will endure over time.

A Rights Approach

A rights approach to thinking about ethics promotes the philosophy that human beings have certain moral rights, for example, rights to life, liberty, happiness, and well-being; freedom from pain and suffering; and so forth (Fox, 1997). When we ascribe those rights to others as well as ourselves, we are acknowledging the existence of a moral community. A moral community is innately social, as was discussed earlier. The social community is based on interaction of human beings where there is a mutual understanding and recognition of the autonomy and "personhood" of others (Fox, 1997, p. 129). Membership in a moral community requires that each person commits to guarantee other human beings the opportunity for autonomous action, self-determination and expression, and an equal opportunity to actualize their fullest potential, things that a person would also wish for oneself. Therefore, the rights approach acknowledges the fundamental right of each person to be respected and to be perceived as a free and equal person that is capable of making his or her own decisions. The principle states, "An action or policy is morally right only if those persons affected by the decision are not used merely as instruments for advancing some goal, but are fully informed and treated only as they have freely and knowingly consented to be treated" (Markula, 2000, Rights Approach, p. 2).

The rights approach is congruent with transformational leadership theory. The recognition of each constituents' self-determination and right to self-actualize is similar to the principles of empowerment. The emphasis on disclosure of information and consent processes promotes participation and inclusiveness in resolving ethical dilemmas and issues. The focus on mutual responsibility and commitment to respect the autonomy of others provides for developing a higher level of morality within the organizational culture; the organization is transformed to moral community. The rights approach turns our attention to the moral responsibility of relationships with others. Another approach also recognizes the good of the whole.

The Common Good

In recent years, the news media has consistently reported an increasing preoccupation with self-interest and individualism and an eroding concern for the common good of society. Policy issues range from economic concerns (the widening gap between the poor and the wealthy) to health care (rising costs and decreasing access for those uninsured), with increasing appeals to return to a vision of the common good. The common good "... consists primarily of having the social systems, institutions, and environments on which we all depend work in a manner that benefits all people" (Markula, 2000, The Common Good, p. 1). Issues that become part of the common good include health care, safety and security, a protected natural environment, and a healthy economic system. The principle states, "What is ethical is what advances the common good" (Markula, 2000, The Common Good, p. 2).

The common good requires cooperation from many people, because each individual's own good is interconnected with the good of the whole. When too few concern themselves with the good of the whole, it is much more difficult to develop and maintain the institutions that benefit all. Obstacles to working toward the common good are many in a pluralistic society. For example, it is difficult to agree on what should be valued or promoted as the common good with a multitude of voices with different opinions. Where there is agreement, such as affordable health care, there may be differences in the value attached as compared to other goods that are desired, for example, a strong military for security, strengthened education system, and so forth. These factors interfere with a sustained effort to promote a particular common good. In addition, some people do more of their share of sacrifice than others to achieve a particular common good, based on personal motivation and commitment. Finally, the American tradition of individualism and the focus on individual rights can act as a barrier to sacrifice personal goals for the sake of the common good (Markula, 2000, The Common Good).

Social work leaders are bound to a commitment to the common good by virtue of the purpose of social work. A commitment to vulnerable populations and meeting their basic human needs has long been associated with the social work profession. Assessing the ethical requirements of the common good in response to ethical dilemmas presents an opportunity to constantly reflect on "what kind of society we want to become and how we are to achieve that society" (Markula, 2000, The Common Good, p. 4). In this way, through considering the common good, political and ethical issues are treated together (Rhodes, 1986). The ethical question of what a person ought to do in relation to others becomes a question of how society ought to be. The leader who considers the impact on the common good of every moral issue and ethical decision is thinking globally, but acting locally.

The preceding discussion has been an overview of many different ways to consider the nature of an ethical situation. At some point, however, it is important to take action.

Action

Action is the final component of moral citizenship. Action is a beginning and an ending. An ethical dilemma or quandary is resolved, and, in the process, new ethical insights and concerns are identified. As discussed earlier in this chapter and Chapter 6, action implies application of what is known, what is cared about, or what is reasoned to be the right course of action. Moral values and beliefs are only meaningful when they are transformed into action.

Taking action about an ethical dilemma or issue is the final step in being ethical by intention. Petrick and Quinn (1997, p. 100) note that intention may be at a different level of motivation than execution. However, "the desire to act ethically and to expend the requisite effort to do so makes the character difference in individual and collective moral performance." Ethical intention requires both a cognitive readiness as well as a volitional readiness. Cognitively, we are prepared to act based on the development of personal moral judgment, an understanding of how to think about ethical dilemmas, the organizational climate in relation to ethics, and an understanding of what is required for a future result. Volitional readiness is based on the involvement of the emotions and the level of caring about a particular concern. In addition, developing moral virtues, such as attending to one's conscience, becomes a motivating factor for the volition to act. A leader's moral passion to act on a moral vision provides the motivation to "summon up the will to act" (Petrick & Quinn, 1997, p. 102). The will to act moves leaders and constituents into the implementation phase of an ethical resolution or decision.

Implementation

Implementation of a decision that is the result of a reasoning process is the act of moving from thought to action (Goodpaster, 1983). Moral responsibility is manifested through implementation of some kind of action. The final task is determining how to make things happen. Goodpaster (1983, p. 9) notes that ". . . as the proverb has it, a certain road is 'paved with good intentions' . . . moral responsibility . . . includes a measure of seriousness about detail that makes the difference between wishful thinking and actual performance, between 'seeing it' and 'seeing it through.'"

Implementation includes several processes that help to take action. An *understanding of political, natural, and social forces* in the environment of the proposed action is important to have successful action (Goodpaster, 1983). Identifying stakeholders who may resist or lack understanding of the action and then strategizing an approach (for example, providing adequate information/education) can make a difference in rallying support and reducing barriers. Conversely, finding collaborators or advocacy groups to participate in moral action increases the potential power that can be wielded and promotes the probability of success. Using legal and regulatory bodies as potential rationale for the issue can help persuade others that a policy is necessary. For example, appeal processes in managed care organizations became more attractive to owners by identifying potential liability to the agency and the regulatory requirements that would be satisfied through a more ethical policy and procedure.

Perseverance in guiding the decision toward realization is also important. The route toward moral action is complex and not always direct. Leaders have described numerous punitive and resistive practices from others that impede ethical decisions and policies for a variety of reasons (Jackall, 1988; Manning, 1990). As discussed in Chapter 4, persistence and even stubbornness can be useful in developing influence in regard to particular actions. Here, leadership is a critical component.

Acting Civically

The action of moral citizenship is different from acting as a good person. Action as a moral citizen in an institution is political action that flows from the relationship with others; one is acting civically in reaction to an institution's unethical practices or to promote ethical practices (Neilsen, 1984). Civic action places responsibility on the decisionmaker to act toward the good of the organization and all who make up the community of the organization. Sometimes acting civically places the leader or constituents in loyal opposition with the organization (Tillich, 1952). The leaders take moral action against unethical practices and/or policies, not against the organization, but because of their loyalty to the organization. Ultimately, moral action is in the best interests of various stakeholder groups and the organization as well.

Leaders have special responsibilities to maintain and strengthen community foundations (Dobel, 1998). The civic leader evaluates action, and the effects of actions taken, on the results to the internal organizational community and the external community. Evaluation of ethical actions should be considered a routine component of a decision process. It provides opportunities for identifying any unanticipated consequences and additional moral problems. Routine evaluation helps leaders avoid reinventing the wheel by monitoring continuously the moral and ethical conditions of the organization that result from actions taken.

Consultation, dialogue, and interaction focus the action on the public good, rather than on private and/or personal good. Interaction with others provides the public space to discuss and decide, rather than acting in isolation. When leaders act in isolation, they are more susceptible to explicit and implicit coercion and immoral ideas and behaviors, factors that promote private interests (Arendt, 1963).

The freedom to comment and to give feedback in the organizational context is a critical variable in taking ethical action. In order for a leader or employee to serve as a moral citizen in an organization, there must be protected civil liberties (Arendt, 1963). Leaders and constituents experience great pressure to obey, to belong, and to be successful in their work. The courage to think and judge independently is the basis for acting civically with other managers and employees in order to resist immoral people, behaviors, and phenomena.

Freedom to comment supports two factors that lead to ethical actions and heightened moral sensitivity (Manning, 1990; 1997). First, to comment freely leads to a better quality of ethical action. Leaders and constituents must first interact, persuade, and debate complex moral issues in order to decide the right course of action; the freedom to comment starts a process that is ethical by intention. Individuals, units, and groups are alerted to potential immoral and unethical policies and practices through the feedback from individuals. Organizational practices can be evaluated openly, with a spirit of discovery rather than dread or avoidance. This process helps to reinforce a culture that informs all employees about right and wrong behavior.

Individuals and groups that take moral action, then, have the capacity to transform the organization. Stephen Rose (1995) argues that the soul of the human being carries action in it. Leaders and employees, as moral citizens, "can change history and produce history." The courage to be as oneself and the courage to be a part (of the organization) together make up the elements ". . . from which action flows" (Tillich, 1952).

Ethical Decision Framework

A framework that provides a guide to thinking about ethical situations can help to identify ethical situations as well as consider the many ramifications. Ethical leadership requires an understanding of complex situations with a myriad of emotional and intellectual data to be organized and applied. The following framework offers a structure to encourage awareness, feeling, thinking, and action in a systematic fashion. This framework is not all-inclusive, nor will it fit for every ethical dilemma. Hopefully, it will help to bring forward a rich reasoning process that is rational, experiential, respectful of self and others, and practical in relation to decisions and actions. This model incorporates material from several different sources (Johnson, 2001; Loewenberg, Dolgoff, & Harrington, 2000; Manning, 1990; 1997; Markula, Center for Applied Ethics, Decision Framework, 2000; Reamer, 1995; Rhodes, 1986).

Awareness: Recognize a Moral Issue

These questions help to recognize and identify the moral and ethical issue(s) (the *what* and the *why*) and begin to delineate the ethical aspects of the issue.

- Is there something wrong personally, interpersonally, organizationally, or socially that could be damaging to employees, consumers, community citizens, or other people? To animals, the environment, the organization, or society?
- Is there something missing that could be beneficial to the constituents mentioned previously, such as animals, the environment, the organization, or society?
- Does the issue go deeper than legal or institutional concerns? What are the implications for people as persons who have dignity, rights, and hopes for a better future?
- Have you defined the problem accurately? What if you stood on the other side of the fence?
- How did this situation occur in the first place?

Feeling: Care About Who Will Be Affected

These questions focus your attention on the well-being of the *other*—the individuals or groups who may be affected by your decisions and/or actions.

- What individuals and groups have an important stake in the outcome? What is at stake for each? Do some have a greater stake because they have a special need (for example, those who are poor or excluded) or because we have special obligations to them? What are those obligations? Are there other important stakeholders in addition to those directly involved? What is at stake for them?
- What values and perspectives are represented through these individuals and groups? What cultural traditions, norms, and beliefs are important to these stakeholders? What are their choices and/or preferences in regard to the issue?

- What is their personal experience in regard to the issue? How does their experience inform you?
- What are your values about the issue? How are your values influencing the way you think about the issue?
- What is your intention in making this decision? How does your intention compare with the likely results?
- What does the issue represent in terms of your moral vision, your cause, and your professional purpose?

Thinking: The Facts and the Wisdom to Use Them

This section helps you in the ethical reasoning process. The questions provide a format to think comprehensively and in collaboration with others.

- What are the relevant facts of the issue? What information needs to be obtained? What list of questions needs to be answered? By whom?
- To whom are you obligated? To whom do you feel loyal? Employee? Client? Agency?
- What is the symbolic potential of your action if understood? If misunderstood?
- What sources can you turn to for guidance? Code of ethics? Ethical theories and principles? Experts? Consultants? Peers? Constituents?
- What are the options/alternatives for acting?
- Have you discussed the issue with others? What are their perspectives about the moral issues? Have all the relevant people and groups been consulted? If you showed your list of options to someone you respect, what would that person say?
- How does the code of ethics inform you in relation to professional duties?

Evaluate the Alternatives from Various Moral Perspectives

These questions assist you in considering the moral implications of various alternatives from the perspective of ethical theory, principles, and philosophies.

- Which option will produce the most good and do the least harm?
- Which option respects the rights and dignity of all stakeholders? Even if not everyone gets all they want, will everyone still be treated fairly?
- Which option would promote the common good and help all participate more fully in the goods we share as a society, as a community, as an organization, or as a family?
- Which option would enable the deepening or development of those virtues or character traits that we value as individuals? As a profession? As employees? As a community? As a society?
- Which option would strengthen and honor relationships?
- Which option would build a caring community?
- Which option takes action against oppression?

■ Which option will be valid into the future?

Action: Make a Decision and Implement

After taking into account the following three questions you are ready to make a decision and take action.

■ Considering these perspectives, which of the options is the right thing to do?
■ If you told someone you respect why you chose this option, what would that person say?
■ Could you disclose, without qualm, your decision or action to your boss, CEO, the board of directors, your family, or society as a whole?

Take Action

In this section the questions precipitate a decision and help you consider your level of comfort with the decision. Would the decision "feel right" if you were to share it with significant others?

■ What are the political, natural, and social forces surrounding the proposed action?
■ Are there stakeholders that you need for support? Who could you include as collaborators in the action?
■ Who may resist the action? What strategies would help reduce or eliminate the resistance?

Reflect on the Decision and Action

This section promotes evaluation of the decision and action, the consequences of implementing the decision, and provides further learning for you and the organization. The results of reflection can be the basis for improved policies and practices.

■ How did it turn out for all concerned? If you had to do it over again, what, if anything, would you do differently?
■ What were the unanticipated consequences of the decision? What other moral or ethical problems have been identified as a result?
■ What new knowledge and understanding did you gain from responding to this issue?
■ How does the result inform you about needed policies and practices in the organization?

The use of a framework for decisionmaking may seem cumbersome and time consuming at first. However, with some practice, most of the topics and questions will become second nature; they will be internalized and routinely come to mind as leaders are confronted with the daily ethical problems of administration, management, and leadership.

Conclusion

This chapter concludes the framework of moral citizenship as an approach to considering ethical dilemmas and problems. Thinking, as the critical variable in a reasoning process, is emphasized. Thinking includes the aspects of rationality, which must be self-directed, and respect, which is other-directed. A comprehensive reasoning process includes a means of justification for an ethical decision, usually a combination of facts, logic, and decision premises. Decision premises (ethical principles, theories, and philosophical approaches) can inform leaders about many of the ethical aspects of a particular dilemma. However, the process of decisionmaking is also a part of thinking. The criteria to evaluate an adequate process include considering the quality, breadth, and honesty of the decision.

Taking action is more than simply implementing the decision. Activities and strategies that will help support the success of implementation are important. Equally important is the ability to assess potential resistance and variables that may act as barriers to the decision and also to find creative ways to change obstructions. Creating a public space for action to occur in relation to moral and ethical issues is part of the action of leadership. Public space provides the structure, time, and culture necessary for constituents to give feedback and facilitate ethical action. Ultimately, the willingness of a leader to act as institution citizen, sometimes in loyal opposition to particular individuals or groups, in order to promote the moral well-being of the organization is the true measure of ethical leadership.

The next section of the book moves the view from the leader as an individual decisionmaker to the leader's role in building an ethical organization. First, the nature of bureaucracy is considered, followed by chapters on ethical cultures and structures to promote ethical action.

QUESTIONS AND APPLICATIONS

1. Analyze the following ethical dilemma from the perspective of rationality and respect (Dilemma Tucker & Marcuson, 1998). A local nonprofit organization that networks with other service agencies in the area was designed to fill gaps in needed services for families. This agency has been in existence for several years and has gained the respect of the community. The staff of this agency can serve families who have a need that cannot be served in any other way through connecting these families with community volunteers who adopt them.

   The volunteer director of the agency works on a volunteer basis and contributes numerous hours each week to fulfill responsibilities associated with this position. To reduce her workload, the director of the agency applied to seven different foundations to request money for a part-time administrative assistant. The agency requested $10,000 from each of the foundations, with the hope that they would receive assistance from one of them. To the surprise of the director, three of the foundations accepted their proposal and awarded the agency with $10,000 for the salary of the part-time employee. The agency ended up with $30,000, which was three times as much as was needed for the salary. The granting foundations had different requirements for reporting on the use of the money. However, at least two of the foundations asked that the money be used in the manner for which it was requested.

- What are the known facts?
- What facts are missing that need to be obtained?
- Who are the potential stakeholders? (for example, agency, clients, public/community, or grantors?)
- What are the potential outcomes, both good and harm, for all stakeholders?
- Who would you seek out for input, advice, and consultation?
- What does your conscience say to you about this dilemma?
- What are the values and perspectives of those who could be affected by your decision?
- What ethical principles apply? What do they require in this situation?
- How do the ethical theories—the means or duty versus the ends or greatest good—apply to this situation? How would you link the two?

What would be your decision?

2. In order to take action, what political, natural, and social forces need to be considered?

3. What is your civic obligation for the good of the organization and the good of the community?

PART THREE

Building Ethical Organizations

The introduction to this section, Chapter 8, moves the reader from the individual leader to the context of leadership, the organizational system. The chapter provides a discussion of the nature of bureaucracy, the predominant organizational form of most human service organizations. The moral and ethical implications of this organizational form on personal morality and organizational behavior provide the background for the next two chapters. The characteristics of the bureaucratic form (for example, the organizational ideal, and principle of rationality) that have moral implications are explicated, followed by a discussion about the ethical implications for leaders.

Chapters 9 and 10 are focused on organizational culture as a "web of understanding" for ethical agreements. Chapter 9 focuses on a conceptualization of the nature of organizational culture as a place to shape ethical norms and behaviors. Development of culture, ethical climate, and the role of enactment (Morgan, 1997) are identified as culture-shaping strategies. Agency mission and explicit and implicit policies are examined as the message that is conveyed to employees about "how to be." This chapter emphasizes the importance of congruence between mission, policy, and practices. In addition, the argument for open feedback about ethical and unethical practices and policies is developed. Both congruence and feedback are integrated into Chapter 10 as critical components of ethical culture.

Chapter 10 turns to the tools and strategies that are useful in shaping and changing culture. The importance of institutionalizing values and the participation of constituents in a culture-changing process is emphasized. Analysis of cultures and the development of value statements and value program orientations are integrated with strategies to help achieve organizational integrity. Chapter 10 identifies various roles of leadership (for example, teacher, steward, and role model) as useful for leaders to be effective in the change process.

Chapter 11 challenges the reader to consider the opportunities that exist in the architecture of an organization that can promote ethical practices and norms. The leader, as architect, creates building blocks through the structure and process of the organization to promote ethical responsibility and responsiveness.

The role of communication as a change strategy, with mechanisms for feedback within the organizational structure, is critical to dialogue and reflection about ethical issues. Structures that enhance participation—of consumers, community citizens, and employees—are emphasized to keep the organization informed and honest. This section discusses the roles of whistleblowers, organizational dissenters, and civil disobedience. Components of an ethical work environment that provide both guidance and evaluation, such as codes of ethics, ethics audits, ethics review committees, and the ethics of governance, are discussed. The moral self-regulation of the organization rests on the previous dimensions and requires ongoing evaluation and monitoring of ethical practices and policies.

Chapter 12 concludes the book with an overview of the central themes and the integration with social work leadership. A challenge to professional leaders in human services is issued to consider their personal, professional, and organizational contributions to the common good.

8 Bureaucracy: Theories and Forms with Moral Implications

THE FOCUS OF THIS CHAPTER IS ON THE FOLLOWING AREAS:

- Bureaucracy as an organizational form
- The organizational ideal
- Characteristics of bureaucracy with moral implications
- Ethical leadership and bureaucracy

Weber's (1978) conceptualization of bureaucracy has become the dominant organizational form in the United States, as well as across the world. Bureaucracies exist in the public and private sectors and are prevalent in the delivery of human services. Most social workers and other professionals will work within a bureaucratic structure for at least part of their career. Leaders in human services will be responsible for the bureaucratic structures and processes of their organizations. The bureaucracy, with a capacity to organize and mobilize diverse specialists, authority, and communication networks in an organization, has been a critical factor in an enhanced standard of living and quality of life for people around the world. It is the "organizational motor of modern capitalism" (Sjoberg, Vaughan, & Williams, 1984, p. 442).

The bureaucratic form provides order and stability in this complex and changing society, yet, at the same time, seems to "... dehumanize all who come in contact with it" (Kweit & Kweit, 1981). Sjoberg, Vaughan, and Williams (1984, p. 441) argue that the process of bureaucratization, combined with centralization of power in politics and the economy, "... has generated the major moral problems of our time." This is an important concern for human service leaders because most social service organizations are based on a bureaucratic design.

Human service agencies are the nexus of the relationship between workplace conditions for social workers, the best interests of the client, broad issues of public and social policy, and the common good for society (Fisher & Karger, 1997). The ongoing tension that exists between the corporate need for profit and economic growth and the social and human needs of people are reflected in social service agencies' chronic state of being underfunded and understaffed, with ". . . adversarial policies toward clients and workers" (Fisher & Karger, 1997, p. 151). Social workers who have a commitment to the basic interests of those they serve are often ". . . trapped between implicit–and often repressive–goals of their agencies and the well-being of clients (Fisher & Karger, 1997, p. 150).

The working conditions of those who provide direct services to clients, as well as those who supervise service delivery, have a direct effect on clients (Fisher & Karger, 1997). The policies of the agency in relation to worker time available for clients, increased expectations of production and performance output, and a restricted range of service choices have a profound impact on the quality of service available to clients. The relationship between the provider and the client system is increasingly defined and controlled by agency policy that is directed toward increasing profits and decreasing costs. The range of choices for service, as well as access to service, is becoming more restricted.

Leaders in human services have administrative and moral responsibility for the decisions, policies, and practices that occur within their organizations. They determine the organizational requirements and are affected by them. The organizational requirements, in turn, affect all others, as discussed previously. The potential for harm and good exist as a result of actions and decisions by leaders within the bureaucratic structure. Social work leaders, then, are faced with a quandary. They have as their primary responsibility the well-being of the clients served by their agency. In addition, the employees under their responsibility and the community served are important constituents of their leadership. All are impacted by the nature of bureaucracies.

This chapter evaluates some of the characteristics of bureaucratic theory and form, as well as other administrative and organizational theories that have moral implications for these constituencies. This discussion is focused on the identification of moral issues. Chapters 9 and 10 will provide strategies, activities, structures and culture that promote ethical decisions and behaviors within the bureaucratic human service organization.

The Nature of Bureaucratic Theory and Design

The theory of bureaucracy has produced major transformations in the organization of work. Weber recognized the similarity between the way a machine routinizes production and the potential of the bureaucratic form to routinize the process of administration. Thus, organization as machine is an apropos metaphor for this model (Morgan, 1986). Morgan (1986, pp. 24–25) states:

> In his work we find the first comprehensive definition of bureaucracy as a form of organization that emphasizes precision, speed, clarity, regularity, reliability, and efficiency achieved through the creation of a fixed division of tasks, hierarchical supervision, and detailed rules and regulations.

Thus, Weber's contribution to efficiency was great; however, some of the previous characteristics of the form also produce moral issues as they are manipulated by human beings.

Features of Bureaucracy

The primary features of bureaucracy include a hierarchy of authority, a division of labor, a standardization of human activities, and an emphasis on efficiency that means choosing the most efficient means to reach an identified end (Weber, 1978). The hierarchy of authority provides for people at the top of the hierarchy to direct the organization and to make sure that rational and efficient means are used to reach the goals and objectives. Managers at lower levels of the organization supervise the delivery of services (or production of products) through a workforce that reflects a specialization of knowledge and technical understanding. The division of labor, according to specialization, occurs within the organization and also among organizations. Specialization helps to organize the various activities necessary for complex delivery of human services (Sjoberg, Vaughan, & Williams, 1984). Standardization and routinization provide the possibility of producing mass quantities of goods and services in efficient ways. All of these features, and the related functions, are directed toward the organizational ideal.

The Organizational Ideal

Bureaucracy is the manifestation of legal-rational authority; the attributes of bureaucracy are derived from legal-rational rules and the pursuit of maximum efficiency. Formal bureaucratic organizations have a central and defining characteristic in the use of a rational model of decisionmaking combined with a hierarchical system of authority that creates a logical order. Rationality is behavior that ". . . selects alternatives which are conducive to the achievement of previously selected goals" (Simon, 1965, p. 5). All decisions should flow from the organizational goals and objectives and be directed toward accomplishing the objectives. After the objectives of an organization have been decided on, all subsequent questions in the decisionmaking process are empirical questions of ways and means. The organization is presumed to have an ethical neutrality. All questions in the decision process relate to the objectives of the organization, and, therefore, are considered to be value free (Ladd, 1970).

Bureaucracy and the Relationship to Ethics

Organizational, sociological, and social work theorists have expressed concerns about the moral and ethical issues that are integrally connected to bureaucracy (Fisher & Karger, 1997; Jackall, 1988; Karger, 1981; Littrell, Sjoberg, & Zurcher, 1983; Rhodes, 1986; Sjoberg, Vaughan, & Williams, 1984). The following discussions of ethical issues and moral aspects of bureaucratic characteristics help to bring forward the nature of those concerns.

Organizations as Social Agents

Some aspects of the *organizational ideal* are incompatible with the principles of morality (Ladd, 1970). Because formal organization is a decisionmaking structure (Simon, 1965), there is a danger of decisions being attributed to the organization, rather than to the individuals who make them. From this perspective, administrators operate as instruments of the organization and can become separated from their own personal morality. The culture and ethos of the organization tend to absorb individuals so that they act, not on their own moral perceptions, but on the norms and values composing the ethics of the organization (McCoy, 1985). The results are an absence of moral responsibility on the part of individuals for their decisions and actions (Rhodes, 1986).

There has been debate in the fields of business ethics and organizational theory about whether organizations are moral agents. Goodpaster (1983) has argued that decisions, made for and in the name of the corporation, are corporate decisions. He developed the principle of moral projection that goes as follows:

> It is appropriate not only to describe organizations (and their characteristics) by analogy with individuals, it is also appropriate normatively to look for and to foster moral attributes in organizations by analogy with those we look for and foster in individuals (Goodpaster, 1983, p. 10).

Thus, according to the principle of moral projection, the expectations of institutions should be no more or less than expectations of individuals.

The alternative argument is that there is not such a thing as a corporate decision (Rankin, 1988). Because a corporation is defined as consisting of individuals, it is individuals only who can be called to account. The person-corporation analogy can have negative effects insofar as it encourages the view that the corporation deserves to be served and protected for its own sake. Rankin posits that the organization is a human tool with no intrinsic value.

> To the extent that employees (all the way up to the CEO) see themselves as serving the company in a sense where "The Company" is perceived as a superperson with a life and interest of its own; to that extent some morally important issues will be screened out of their considerations as irrelevant. If . . . they perceive their own security and advancement to be dependent on just such a view of their role, then even when moral considerations become obvious, they will be less likely to be acted upon because of conflict with self-interest (Rankin, 1988, p. 637).

In human service organizations this position is important to consider. If service employees see their role as serving the institution as the interest they are to serve, this would change the moral mandates about human service delivery.

The critical task for leadership is motivating people to develop habits of responsible action in their work roles (Rankin, 1988). The ideal is for employees to see themselves as "freely engaged in a labor whose outcome they recognize as valuable in human terms," rather than for the organization (Rankin, 1988, p. 637). Value that is placed on the importance of human relationships and accomplishing the mission of the organization provides individuals with a moral compass. It becomes more natural for them to use ordinary moral categories in noticing, evaluating, and choosing alternatives in the course of their work. The organization as person analogy distracts from that task.

Fact versus Value: The Criterion of Efficiency

There is also controversy about whether decisions are essentially factual, or based on normative values embedded in the organization and the decisionmaker. The contradictions between fact versus value in decisionmaking further promote the separation of individuals from their own morality. The issues of fact that are the foundation of decisions in an organization are determined by a principle that underlies all rational behavior: the criterion of efficiency. This simply means to take the shortest path and the cheapest means toward attainment of desired goals. The personal and professional values of the decisionmaker become subsumed in the pursuit of organizational objectives.

The industrial model of production has introduced the criterion of efficiency into social service organizations in a major way over the past 20 to 25 years (Fisher & Karger, 1997). The pressure to achieve the highest efficiency possible has resulted in some detrimental effects. Managed competition among human service organizations in the areas of health, mental health, criminal justice, and public welfare has resulted in ". . . higher caseloads for social workers, fewer resources, and more time-limited interventions" (Fisher & Karger, 1997, p. 152). Providers are expected to make decisions about rationing, often without clear agency policy or a community consensus about the nature of the rationing and the implications for the agency and society. Workers experience high levels of stress as they are confronted with the agency expectations of short-term intervention models and discharge planning that is not congruent with client needs, in contradiction with their professional values of looking out for the best interests of the client.

Human service employees are experiencing burnout, and employee morale is affected by policies that are directed by efficiency in conflict with appropriate standards of care. Burnout and low morale affect employee job satisfaction and, ultimately, the willingness of employees to remain in their agency. The turnover rate for direct service positions has been found to be 7 to 11 percent higher than the general economy. The high turnover rate in human services is due to ". . . large caseloads, standby duty, the high stress related to the job, insufficient salary and promotional opportunities, lack of agency and public support, inadequate training, and changes in the nature of job responsibilities" (Fisher & Karger, 1997, p. 152). Thus, the moral issues connected to a criterion of efficiency that subsumes other important professional and human service values has profound implications for leaders.

Value-free science.   The education of administrators and managers also contributes to an emphasis on efficiency, rather than the value issues embedded in professional practice. The adoption of administrative and organizational models from corporate businesses influence the purpose of the organization (Karger, 1981). The main aim of the organization becomes financial accountability and efficiency, rather than an orientation toward the meaning of the mission, and the responsibility to the people being served. Scientific management models that provide a theoretical approach to administration focus on the learning of operational skills rather than learning about a reasoning process, that is, the know how rather than the know why (Karger, 1981).

The characteristics of technology that underlie the scientific method are important to understand in relation to efficiency. Fisher & Karger (1997, p. 153) argue the following:

> ... Technology is driven by the desire to cut costs, specifically the costs of labor. Savings and cost containment are realized through increasing the scale and intensity of production. In theory, this scheme results in higher productivity by increasing the quantity of goods produced—in human service organizations, the number of clients processed. The goal of technology is, thus, to create the most goods or process the largest number of people at the lowest possible cost.

The industrial model of production, then, emphasizes a variety of "scientific" ways to evaluate the utilization of worker time to meet funder requirements for greater efficiency (Fisher & Karger, 1997). The time taken to accomplish a task becomes more important than the nature of what is accomplished for client well-being.

Alienation.   The sole standard for evaluating an organization, its activities, and its decisions is its effectiveness in achieving its objectives. Actions that are wrong by moral standards are not necessarily perceived as wrong in organizations if they are required to meet organizational goals. A double standard for leaders is developed. Organizational decisions (that have moral implications) are subject to the standard of rational efficiency, and the actions of individuals are subject to ordinary standards of morality. The leaders of an organization operate as vehicles or instruments of the organization. Thus, decisions are separated from the individual and instead become the decision of the organization. This separation of the individual from the decision is an example of the Marxian concept of alienation, whereby human reality and human need are made subservient to artificially created things (Sowell, 1985).

However, the practices and decisions of leaders are, in actuality, normative actions. Organizational and management theories impart both factual and normative information; the very choice and organization of collected facts demonstrates a normative orientation (Keeley, 1983). Also, organizational models have both normative and empirical implications. Scientific and ethical criteria can complement one another in the evaluation of alternative views. Science can indicate whether a model yields good (factually) solutions to specific problems, while ethics can indicate whether a model yields good (worthwhile or moral) problems in the beginning and provides for good (moral and ethical) results. Social work leaders can and should be guided by the organizational and management theories that provide effective, efficient provision of human services. Efficiency is an ethical issue in that it can result in cost savings. Resources can then be developed for more and better services to clients. However, leaders must also evaluate the methods, strategies, structures, and models of the organization that operate in the name of efficiency for the ethical and moral implications. Social work leaders have consistently reported conflict with the organizational ideal.

Social Workers and the Organizational Ideal

There is consistent and profound evidence that social workers experience some of the conflicts and contradictions described in the previous section, and that these conditions impact on ethical decisionmaking. Cossum (1992), in a review of research results on social work ethics, found that many studies reported conflict between the organizational requirements and professional practice. For example, some social workers experienced the organization as a force that constrained their intellectual and critical thinking abilities and sabotaged their professional duties (Kugelman-Jaffee, 1990). Felkenes' (1990) dissertation supported this finding. The obligations to the agency, and the restrictions placed on professionals by the agency, were the most primary factors in inhibiting professional practice. The authority of the organization in affecting professional practice was demonstrated by practitioners paying more attention to agency factors when employed there than when working outside of the agency.

Billingsly (1964) found that social work professionals were ". . . relatively more bureaucratic than professional in their moral evaluative orientations" (Cossum, 1992, p. 403). In this study, supervisors and direct service social workers were more apt to carry out agency policy than professional obligations when the two were in conflict. Social work field instructors also experienced a significant agency role in regard to their ethical practice (Congress, 1986). In addition, Congress found that the more complex and multidisciplinary agencies were less conducive to ethical decisionmaking. Conrad's (1988) research found that the ethical dilemmas related to the organizational setting were among the most serious. The conflicts identified by social workers between professional and organizational values created the most intense source of conflict for them. The use of lengthy waiting lists and policies that impeded adequate termination planning were examples of organizational efforts toward efficiency, in contradiction of professional values about the primary interests of the client. Also identified were conflicts between personal and organizational values. This discussion provides some general information about the experience of social workers in organizations. The following section explores the particular characteristics and attributes of the bureaucratic organization that have moral implications.

Characteristics of Bureaucracies and the Moral Impact

Bureaucratic organizations have a number of characteristics that are standard to a bureaucratic form of organization (refer to functions of structure, p. 233). The following discussion points out some of the typical characteristics and the associated moral issues that emanate from these characteristics (see Figure 8.1).

Rigidity of rules and regulations
Secrecy and hidden arrangements
Sacrifice of the disadvantaged
Mechanical decisionmaking structures and process for complex problems
Evaluation focused on efficiency and productivity
Moral anesthesia
Routinization and loss of purpose
Specialization that fragments service delivery
Language of technology, not people
Organizational climate that discourages ethical questions

FIGURE 8.1   Characteristics of Bureaucracy with Moral Impact

Rules and Regulations

The ideal type of bureaucracy does not take into account the variations in tasks that human service organizations have to perform. Excessive reliance on rules and regulations can reinforce rigidity as a defense against client needs and expectations. This leads to the formation of the bureaucratic personality (Hasenfeld, 1983). The leader with a bureaucratic personality uses the established rules and regulations to avoid the confrontations of employee and client needs that aren't a good fit with the existing system. In addition, reliance on rules can be dehumanizing to both clients and staff. The unique aspects, needs, and feelings of human beings are not taken into account in the rigid application of rules. One manager viewed the size of his bureaucratic organization as promoting rigidity (Manning, 1990, p. 208). He said, "the larger the system, the more inflexible it becomes . . . the rigidity of the system doesn't take into account the specific needs of the people provided services."

As bureaucracies discourage employees from questioning rules, goals, methods of evaluation, or organizational inconsistencies, the "givens" are no longer challenged or discussed. This discouragement is a barrier to professional behavior and to the examination of bias (Rhodes, 1986). Social workers and other professionals use discretion in relation to the applicability of rules and procedures in their work with clients and subordinates. If rules and procedures are not evaluated in relation to the values that are conveyed (for example, equity), clients are affected by the bias. The rules in a bureaucracy, then, can ". . . take on a life of their own . . . become the end itself" (Rhodes, 1986, p. 142).

The role of the professional staff can be adversely affected by the rigidity of rules as well. Professionals are educated toward a role that ". . . inherently calls for freedom from hierarchical authority, from rigid rules, and from regulations" (Hasenfeld, 1983). Ethical practices and decisions by professionals require the use of discretion and judgment, as well as the freedom to comment openly on unethical practices (Manning, 1990). Bureaucracies that require an adherence to rules, regardless of circumstances, place professional staff in the position of acting against professional requirements and sometimes against ethics.

Secrecy

Secrecy is inherent to the bureaucratic structure and leads to abuse of power (Sjoberg, Vaughan, & Williams, 1984). Leaders and other people in authority in complex organizations strive to build hidden arrangements to maintain and further their power. Those in command require and use information from subordinates for decision purposes, while preventing those at lower levels from sharing in the how and why of the decisions made. These hidden arrangements protect people in authority from being accountable to subordinates and to the public. The secrecy of decisions and resulting lack of accountability affects the well-being of large numbers of people in ways that are hidden from public scrutiny.

System loyalty is the product of an emphasis on secrecy (Sjoberg, Vaughan, & Williams, 1984). The loyalty of subordinates to those in authority is promoted by their dependency. Subordinates rely on the favors granted to them from those in authority to further their place and status in the organization. This further restricts their willingness to give feedback or to challenge unethical practices. People with authority hide information to abuse power, and people in lower levels hide information to avoid being abused by power. Sjoberg, Vaughan, and Williams (1984, p. 450) argue, "Actions based on loyalty to superiors and to the larger organization pose serious dangers to human dignity." Employees act in ways that are not congruent with their own authenticity, which results in feeling demeaned and alienated from their own morality.

Sacrifice of the Disadvantaged

A system of triage occurs in bureaucracies whereby disadvantaged individuals and groups are sacrificed in order to achieve broader organizational objectives. Those in upper level leadership positions know more about the rules and policies and are less constrained by them. They have the luxury of discretion to interpret the rules and also a more comprehensive understanding of the structures and processes under their authority (see Chapter 4, Ethical Decisions). Middle managers described decisions shaped by upper level administrators as decided through the good ol' boy network, the fiscal buddy network, and through friends in high places (Manning, 1990). The rule system becomes more rigid and complex for those at lower levels, and they are held more accountable for actions. The hierarchy of authority, then, ". . . produces fundamentally unequal relationships. . . ." (Sjoberg, Vaughan, & Williams, 1984, p. 447).

Leaders in upper levels of the hierarchy wield power in ways that can be harmful to those in lower level positions. An essential aspect of the administrative strategy of delegating authority is the ability to assign blame for mistakes or failures under the guise of delegating responsibility. Research into corporate practices in bureaucracies demonstrates that those below accept the blame for what goes wrong and those in authority deny responsibility (Jackall, 1988; Sjoberg, Vaughan, & Williams, 1984). The result furthers the secrecy discussed previously by those in lower level positions as they create hidden strategies to avoid blame and to protect themselves from the abuse of power.

The emphasis on efficiency and cost-effectiveness and the formal rationality of the bureaucratic organization leads to a kind of utilitarianism. The poor or underclass are expected to bear the greatest moral cost; the greatest good for the greatest number is defined by those who control and manage the bureaucratic structures (Sjoberg, Vaughan, & Williams, 1984). For example, in order to increase profits or reduce costs, many human service organizations now offer the lowest wages to those whom are most oppressed. The strategy of hiring temporary or contract workers in order to avoid the expense of benefits is also popular. The people who fill contract or temporary positions are also those who are most in need of the benefits, such as health care coverage, that can be gained through employment.

Decisionmaking Structures and Process

Decisions are conclusions, choices, or actions. They are directed toward what is, but also toward what ought to be. Therefore, decisions include both fact and value, as discussed in Chapters 6 and 7. Leaders' decisions are at the heart of ethical practices. The task of deciding is pervasive in any organization and is integrally tied to doing (Simon, 1957). Herbert Simon (1957), a well-known decision theorist, advanced the principle of bounded rationality. Bounded rationality describes the limitations to rationality in the decision process. The limitations include an individual's unconscious skills, habits, and reflexes; one's values and conceptions of purpose, which may diverge from the organizational goals; and the extent of knowledge and information of the decisionmaker. Simon argued, "The individual can be rational in terms of the organization's goals only to the extent that one is able to pursue a particular course of action, one has a correct conception of the goal of the action, and one is correctly informed about the conditions surrounding one's action (1957, p. 241) [inclusive language added]. Therefore, decisionmakers only satisfice when making decisions; they choose the first alternative possible that meets a subjective minimal standard, rather than searching for the most optimal decision. This position is based on the argument that human beings are limited by the cognitive capacities described previously. Satisficing rather than optimizing, however, does reduce the demands on the decisionmaker to find the best alternative (Filley, House, & Kerr, 1976). Leaders who satisfice in regard to decisions of a moral nature are vulnerable to missing information, which defines the complexity of moral and ethical decisions.

Bounded rationality and the limitations of human beings in regard to cognitive capacity is a pessimistic view (Morgan, 1986). Instead, Morgan argues that most organizations reflect a bounded rationality because of the bureaucratic structure, not because they are populated by people.

> Bureaucratization builds bounded rationality into its structure by design. The design reflects the limited capacities of a single individual to exercise control over activities and decision processes that require the contribution of a significant number of people (Morgan, 1986, p. 107).

The bureaucratic design reflects a mechanical and linear approach to complex problems and the required decisions. The hierarchical and mechanical structures of communication and authority fragment the attention and action of many individuals in an effort to manage and control the complicated situations that take place in an organization. This process of managing the events in organizations reduces the complexities of moral issues to incremental and fragmented examination by individuals, rather than a collaborative approach that allows for consideration of the totality of the issue.

Ethical decisions are by nature complex and contextual, as discussed in earlier chapters. The structures and processes for decisions in bureaucracies can constrain or enhance the decisionmaking process. Communication structures that guarantee collaboration and information sharing, for example, enhance the possibility of ethical decisions.

Social work leaders described some of the barriers to ethical decisionmaking in a qualitative study (Manning, 1990). One manager stated that the bureaucratic system ". . . placed such time consuming barriers to positive changes . . ." that it would affect her ". . . willingness to act, or to decide" (p. 205). She would find herself "not attending" to appropriate requests because it was difficult to challenge the bureaucracy. Others identified impediments to decisions as "the tremendous use of energy for justification and documentation" due to the "political realities" of a large bureaucracy (p. 205). In addition, "political expediency" required that managers be prepared to defend and justify decisions and actions at all levels of the bureaucracy (p. 205).

Managers and administrators complained of the incremental nature of the organization. They described the structure as keeping issues incremental and specific rather than promoting a broader view and analyzing issues for the symbolic meaning (p. 206). The structure was seen as fragmenting information and protecting decisionmakers from the whole picture (p. 206).

The structure of authority was experienced as a buffer to protect top level administrators from the dilemmas that occur at the level of providing direct services. This buffer would get in the way of dealing with the person or people who have the power to act. One manager (Manning, 1990, p. 206) noted that ". . . a flattened hierarchy is helpful . . . you can go directly to the person with power, the decision maker, and there is no middle person to filter the message . . . [I] can also report directly back to the staff."

Evaluation of Decisions and Programs

Unintended effects result from a lack of knowledge about the moral impacts and results of decisions. Bounded rationality, limited information, imperfect communication systems, functional specialization, multiple and conflicting goals and rewards, informal group norms, and environmental pressures all put ethical choices in a matrix of conflicting assumptions and criteria. All these conditions mean that people in a variety of positions make decisions that affect others without an ability to evaluate the effects of the decision directly. Analysis of ethical issues would be easier if immoral motives led to immoral effects and moral motives led to moral effects (Ritchie, 1988).

However, the issues are complex and affected by a multitude of factors. Due to the fragmented decision processes previously described (Decisionmaking Structures and Process, p.186), isolated individuals may have some perspective about the effects, but most in the organization will not have access to the information.

The mechanisms of evaluation turn the attention of the staff toward the organizational ideal, rather than client well-being. Formal evaluation procedures often focus on the efficiency and productivity of an organization, rather than the moral issues such as quality of service to consumers, access to services, accomplishing the organization's mission, and so forth. Evaluation is increasingly tied to revenue streams and the goal of increasing funds (Rhodes, 1986). Programs may offer needed services with excellent quality, but may be eliminated for fiscal reasons, based on evaluation objectives connected to fiscal issues.

Consumers of service are often not included in evaluation efforts. The lack of feedback from consumers seriously hinders an understanding of the organization's progress on realizing the mission of the agency. Evaluation without consumer participation also erodes the philosophy of client well-being as the reason for the agency's existence. Rhodes (1986, p. 143) sums it up by saying, ". . . bureaucratic structure operates steadily to direct workers to be responsive to their agency rather than to clients."

Moral Anesthesia

Leaders and constituents lose their moral sensitivity as they climb the bureaucratic ladder. Jackall (1988, p. 6) noted, "What's right in a corporation is not what is right in a person's house or church. What's right in a corporation is what the guy (usually) above you wants from you." The nature of bureaucracy shapes moral consciousness or lack of consciousness. The routines that provide for rational action to attain organizational goals, such as the proximity of authority that is based on most people having a subordinate status, the premium on achieving organizational goals, and the subtle measures of prestige and status, cause people to bracket their own personal morality. Instead, they follow the prevailing morality of their particular organizational situation (Jackall, 1988).

Immoral policies and decisions affect not only those directly impacted by the policy, but the corporate culture and those who carry out the policy (Brummer, 1985). As leaders and employees view their decisions as an "instrument of the organization," they are freed from the pushes and pulls of their own conscience (Rhodes, 1986, p. 186). They may want to provide more resources to a client or a supervisee from the standpoint of their personal morality, but the organizational policies do not allow it. Thus, the separation from personal morality is accompanied by a separation from the responsibility for the decisions being made; they are, after all, organizational decisions (Jackall, 1988; Karger, 1981; Manning, 1997; Rhodes, 1986; Sjoberg, Vaughan, & Williams, 1984).

Individuals isolate and alienate themselves to avoid feedback that may confront the process of moral anesthesia and in the process find themselves more distant from their own morality. Moral status and consequences become increasingly unclear as they are obscured by the bureaucratic structure. Therefore, explicit moral challenges are not the chief danger; instead, it is the "gradual erosion of one's ethical stance day by day" (Rhodes, 1986, p. 134). Alienation then affects one's commitment to the purpose of the organization.

Routinization and the Loss of Purpose

> We see the depths of passion whenever an organization invites its people to create a vision . . . But then we take this vital passion and institutionalize it. We create an organization. People who loved the purpose of an organization grow to disdain the institution that was created to fulfill it. Passion mutates into procedures, into rules and roles. Instead of purpose we focus on policies. Instead of being free to create, we impose constraints that squeeze the life out of us. The organization no longer lives. We see its bloated form and resent it for what it stops us from doing (Wheatley & Kellner-Rogers, 1999, p. 57).

The rigidity of rules and roles can circumvent the creativity and inspiration that promotes commitment to a cause. The bureaucratic potential to routinize and mechanize almost every aspect of human life can erode the human spirit and the capacity for spontaneous action (Morgan, 1986). A consistent finding in organizational studies is the relationship between job monotony and low job satisfaction. Job challenge is the best predictor of satisfaction (McNeely, 1992). McNeely suggests that leaders in human services should consider the pressures to adopt "highly routinized methods and procedures" in light of the long-term affects on worker job satisfaction (1992, p. 234).

Managers described the mechanical aspects of the bureaucracy as being "static" (Manning, 1990, pp. 207–208). The "same kind of rote exercises are done over and over," and the system "rewards stasis" rather than using creativity and new alternatives. One leader saw the system as created for the system, "caught up in self-perpetuation," rather than concerned with the needs of the consumers of services. In fact, it was noted that the involvement of consumers' perspectives in regard to decisions was viewed as "extremely threatening."

Routinization challenges the employee's sense of meaning and purpose as well. Fisher and Karger (1997) argue that the industrial model of production is antithetical to the values and philosophy of social work. Social work practice rests on the provider-client relationship and is labor intensive. The production model that is directed toward efficiency uses the strengths of the technology that is most efficient to provide the services to clients. Thus, if a particular technology is perceived as cost-effective, providers are expected to use that technology in interventions with clients, even though it may not be the most effective for particular people.

The industrial model of production forces a nonroutine professional model of service delivery that is individualized and labor-intensive into a "routinized and standardized format" (Fisher & Karger, 1997, p. 154). The result is the transformation of providers into machinelike components who become factors of production. This expropriation of skills removes the meaning from the work of providers and reinforces the feeling of workers that they are only replaceable commodities. This process results in the deskilling of professional workers; mechanical operations become the primary focus of the professional. Examples include time spent in mostly clerical roles: completing paperwork for reimbursement (for example, Medicaid, Supplemental Security Income), paperwork for discharge planning, and paperwork to document the quantity and types of services for billing purposes. Fisher and Karger (1997) note that resistance to these expectations is often met with sanction from agency leaders.

Specialization

The specialization of knowledge and expertise in human services can have moral implications for the consumers of services. Specialization allows workers to provide the best expertise to particular populations (for example, child/adolescent specialists in mental health), but it can also have negative results. Clients and their problems are often assigned to several different specialists who are responsible for only a part of the services delivered, rather than the whole (Rhodes, 1986). For example, in mental health, a person may receive services from an intake worker, crisis/emergency clinician, and outpatient clinician. Families with many problems are often involved with many different agencies. For example, social welfare, mental health, and criminal justice may all be involved with a family at the same time. Specialization can encourage a narrow focus on the part of agency personnel and reduce knowledge about implications related to the whole picture.

The results of specialization can precipitate consumers feeling fragmented and helpless. Quality of care can be affected, especially if there is inadequate communication and documentation among and between the caregivers involved. The labeling and shortcuts used to document people's experience in the case record can result in categorizing the consumer; caregivers think of the people being served by the nature of their label (for example, diagnosis) and the protocols associated with the label (Rhodes, 1986). Rhodes (1986, p. 141) said, "Bureaucratic aims of efficiency are served by this sort of 'management,' but in the process we may lose our original goals of bettering the lives of clients; both clients and workers feel depersonalized and have difficulty relating to each other."

Language

The language of bureaucracies, human service as well as corporations, conceals the ethical and moral dimensions of actions and decisions (Rhodes, 1986). Labels and diagnosis, levels of chronicity, and the sanitized language of technology provide cover for thinking about what is really going on. People become products or cases, and their experience in life becomes pain management or crisis management. Disagreements or ambivalence about treatment protocols become labels of noncompliant and resistive. Productivity and merit, usually defined in quantitative terms, take precedence over quality and effectiveness. The use of bureaucratized language serves a function for overwhelmed and burned-out providers. However, in doing so, the humanity of the people who are served and the provider's humanity are also diminished. The use of bureaucratized language also promotes compartmentalizing of personal morality in favor of organizational standards (Rhodes, 1986).

Organizational Climate

The level of ethical or unethical behavior depends, in part, on the atmosphere or climate of the organization (Longenecker, 1985). The leader must decide issues and make choices in an atmosphere "that encourages, discourages, or ignores the moral element in such decisions" (Longenecker, 1985, p. 65). Ethical climates in organizations are conceptualized as ". . . general and pervasive characteristics of organizations, affecting a broad range of decisions" (Victor & Cullen, 1988, p. 101). The climate informs the leaders and constituents about what they can do or ought to do regarding particular ethical situations, according to organizational norms. Three sources of ethical climate are identified by Victor and Cullen (1988): the larger social-cultural environment, the organizational form (for example, bureaucracy), and the unique characteristics of the organization's history and individuals' histories within the organization.

The bureaucratic design promotes a focus on meeting the objectives of the organization in the most efficient way possible. Thus, the beliefs of managers about how to reach the goals can result in using dubious tactics to get the job done (Toffler, 1986). The implicit messages that are conveyed through the climate about how to get things done are strong and powerful (Manning, 1990). Implicit messages and policies are conveyed through the leadership in unwritten and sometimes an unspoken manner. These implicit messages are guiding mechanisms that communicate how managers, administrators, and other employees are to behave and act, within and for the organization. Implicit policies are frequently incongruent with the explicit policies and the mission of an organization. They are also viewed as more powerful in shaping the behavior of leaders and constituents. An upper administrator noted that implicit messages have a "profound influence" on decisions made and the "way you make them" (Manning, 1990, p. 225). Decisions get made that are "stupid" or "not doable" because of unspoken policies of cost containment, or those who are impacted by the decision are not included in the decision process. Therefore, a philosophy is conveyed through decisions, without anyone really thinking about or understanding the effects of the decisions on the organization's ethical climate.

Implicit messages are subtle and therefore harder to challenge directly (Manning, 1990). A leader in human services described it this way. "It's the subtle communication that I worry about . . . If I feel I need to admit [pressure to increase the census], am I going to make a decision on the wrong side of things and respond to that? How objective am I going to be? Am I going to be influenced by the pressure?" Other managers described implicit policies "driven by money," for example, less quality in the credentials of personnel, use of students instead of employed staff, manipulation of insurance coverage, and so forth (Manning, 1990, p. 226). Implicit messages provide a form of guidance, but not the kind that would be communicated explicitly, through written policies, procedures, or rules. Instead, the word "pressure" is often linked to these kinds of messages (Manning, 1990).

Organizational values are often in conflict with professional values (for example, primacy of client needs in contradiction to the values of efficiency and profit in a competitive market). This creates a climate that can promote ethically questionable behavior. A manager (Manning, 1990, p. 227) gave a concrete example. She was instructed to provide programming for two different kinds of disorders on a unit that was only set up for one. She reiterated, "I said [to her administrators], so let me paraphrase what you said, 'You want me to admit people who I believe are inappropriate for treatment in this particular program?' and they said, 'No, but we don't want you to be sending any of our people anywhere else and you should have a fifty per cent conversion rate. . . .'" Other managers and supervisors reported simultaneous messages of valuing client care in conflict with valuing rewards and perks for upper administrative staff. Examples included the reduction in force of direct service staff positions and the lack of budget to repair patient units, while additional funds were allocated for marketing and to reimburse administrators for attendance at expensive out-of-state conferences and meetings. Patient care budgets were reduced at the same time as furniture was being purchased for administrative offices (Manning, 1990, pp. 227–228).

The top level administrators in the hierarchical arrangement of authority in a bureaucracy also have a critical impact on the organizational climate in regard to ethics. Toffler (1986) identifies top management's responsiveness to employees' ethical concerns as an important factor. Her research found that several managers had negative results when they raised ethical concerns with superiors. The company message was "We don't talk about those things around here" (Toffler, 1986, p. 27). These same companies had codes of ethics and policies that demanded ethical behavior on the part of employees. Manning (1990) found similar experiences. One manager described it this way (p. 225). "Be all things to all people, do the impossible, and don't complain, don't stir things up, do what you're told and find a way to do it . . . bringing up ethical dilemmas goes against that."

The implicit norms, procedures, and beliefs that are a part of organizational climate are essential to the conduct of business and to individual sanity. They can also become the mechanisms for stifling creativity, for discouraging challenges about unethical or questionable policies and practices, and for disregarding the not so usual situations that have ethical implications. Toffler (1986, p. 28) summarizes by saying, "When practices become so ingrained that people forget why they were established, or neglect to anticipate any but the expected outcomes, the way is laid for ethical problems to arise."

Leadership and Bureaucracy

The previous discussion demonstrates the moral implications of bureaucratic theory and design. Two points are important for ethical leaders. First, leaders must have a heightened consciousness of the pattern of interactions and relationships that naturally occur as a result of bureaucratic characteristics and attributes. Awareness of the characteristics and processes discussed previously (pp. 183–192) helps to anticipate and prevent the destructive effects. Second, as mentioned in Chapter 5, ethical challenges can be a constraint or an opportunity. The same is true of the ethical challenges of bureaucratic design. Goals, structures, and characteristics can be shaped and nurtured for organizations just as they are for individuals. After all, the organization is made up of people.

Changes in organizational goals and structures will come about from the experiences of people (Rankin, 1988). Leaders who focus attention on the meaning of employee and consumer experiences help to shape and give direction for desired moral changes at the organizational level. The creation of opportunities to interact about the nature of work and service experiences is the first step. Second, the opportunity to give feedback to decisionmaking bodies about the moral and ethical implications of experience provides the organization with an ongoing monitoring system for needed change in policies and practices.

Characteristics that promote ethical functioning can also be developed for organizations. Moral reasoning is an example of an important organizational characteristic that can be envisioned and nurtured through leadership (Goodpaster, 1983). Leaders can foster moral sensitivity and reasoning at the organizational level in any bureaucracy by making explicit provisions for the introduction of moral premises in the formal decisionmaking process (discussed further in Chapter 10).

Conclusion

The bureaucracy is a machine that has, as its most profound attribute, the ability to promote maximum efficiency in production or service. The structure, process, and function of this powerful machine have traditionally been viewed as ethically neutral. Those in leadership roles have learned to drive the machine using value-free science and technology. The same characteristics that advance efficiency also hold the potential of immoral and unethical activities and processes. Rules, hierarchy, routinization, and specialization help an organization accomplish goals in a rational, efficient manner. They also contribute to secrecy, sacrifice of the disadvantaged, abuse of power, and moral anesthesia at all levels of the organization. Ethical leadership in bureaucratic organizations must be concerned with the activities, messages, and results that emanate from bureaucratic characteristics. Further, leaders can create opportunities to shape moral characteristics of the organization that guide the practices and policies toward moral ends.

QUESTIONS AND APPLICATIONS

1. Analyze your organization in relation to the moral impact of the bureaucratic characteristics and the organizational ideal.
   - Is the culture of your organization one that promotes serving the company at the expense of client well-being or employee morality? Describe some examples.
   - What is the effect of the focus on efficiency in your organization? What is the level of turnover, burnout, and low morale? What are the reported causes of these conditions?

2. Read and discuss the section on characteristics and identify the moral impacts within your organization. Provide examples of the impacts on people, decisionmaking, evaluation, moral sensitivity, and so forth.

3. What are examples of language, buzz words, and labels used in your organization that have moral and ethical dimensions? What are the ethical implications of such language? How would you change the language used?

CHAPTER

9 Organizational Culture: The Tangled Web of Understanding

THE FOCUS IN THIS CHAPTER IS ON THE FOLLOWING AREAS:

- Organizational culture and ethics of leadership
- The definition and meaning of culture in organizations
- Rule following and enactment of culture
- Ethical climate: the message
- The freedom to comment
- The spiral of silence and the bystander effect
- Whistle-blowing and organizational loyalty

Organizational culture is a powerful force that can promote ethical activities and behaviors on the part of leaders and constituents in human service agencies. Organizational culture best captures *"How we do things around here"* (Deal, 1987). The nature of organizational culture is similar to an unwritten script for the behaviors and decisions of constituents and leaders. This script can embody moral and ethical proscriptions. The dialogue in the script that conveys the moral and ethical messages could be thought of as the ethical climate. The author(s) of the script include leaders and constituents. Culture contributes to the success or failure of the moral and ethical responsibilities tied to the mission, the values promoted through the organization, and the moral and ethical aspects of policies and practices.

Culture is the result of social interaction; it is a social construction whereby individuals socially create and re-create their reality in an organizational setting. Given this social construction, leaders can analyze and provide direction to the experience of constituents in shaping a new culture that is more constructive, ethical, and productive.

This chapter builds on the themes of some previous chapters: moral citizenship, the role of feedback, the organization as a social agent, and the relational nature of an organizational community. These themes are essential in thinking about the formation and function of ethical culture. First, moral citizenship is the embodiment of ethics by intention. It requires independent thinking and judgment and the ability to resist the activities in the organization that are harmful. To act as a loyal citizen requires membership in this community, the organization.

Constituent(s) have the opportunity to practice moral citizenship through the process of enactment which allows for every individual to influence the ethical culture of the organization. The critical ingredients in the enactment process are dialogue and feedback (also the critical ingredients in moral citizenship). The feedback loop in organizations provides the opportunity, expectation, and freedom of leaders and constituents to comment on the moral and ethical practices and policies of the organization (Manning, 1990). Thus, feedback provides an avenue to shape the ethical nature of the organization. The structural considerations of feedback are discussed in Chapter 10.

The purpose of this chapter is to provide an understanding of organizational culture as it applies to ethical issues for leaders. The definition and nature of culture in organizations and the relationship of culture to ethical leadership provides the background for the development of ethical cultures. The transformational nature of the leader's influence, the importance of congruence of messages within the culture, and the necessity of support for reflection are emphasized. In addition, the role of the leader as steward or servant is essential to shaping an ethical culture. Enactment as a process that can be used to shape ethical cultures is discussed.

Relationship of Culture to Ethical Leadership

The emphasis on the culture of an organization in this book is because it is through the culture that the web of meaning takes shape. The relationship of leaders to the people and processes of the organization is primary; the leader cannot create or shape the necessary values of an ethical culture alone. Think of the culture as an integral process that involves all constituents in the shaping of ethical norms and expectations. As the context and background for ethics, culture provides either support or obstructions to ethical decisions and practices. The following discussion highlights some of the reasons that emphasizing culture is important to ethical leadership (see Figure 9.1).

Leaders Are Not the Lone Ranger

Leaders who are committed to ethical leadership cannot control or manage organizational ethics by themselves (Ritchie, 1988). An organization's ethical stance, decisions, and actions are a reflection of all the individuals who make up the organization.

- Leaders are not the "Lone Ranger"
- Leaders affect the moral code
- Organizational culture is the context for ethics
- Organizational values influence personal conscience
- Values can be institutionalized through culture
- Decisionmaking rests on a culture of shared beliefs

FIGURE 9.1   Relationship of Culture to Ethical Leadership

"Values, goals, and actions do belong to people. And, while we attack, criticize, sue, and often hold organizations responsible for immoral actions, it is clearly *people* who state the values and goals and act on behalf of organizations" (Ritchie, 1988, p. 159). The organization, then, becomes the structure and process for the value commitments that provide the significance to individuals' actions. "There is no ethical 'Lone Ranger'" (de Vries, 1988).

The importance of membership and relationship is integral to this point. Both leaders and members must take the responsibility for managing the moral and ethical issues of the organization, in effect "disciplining the system" (Ritchie, 1988, p. 181). The inclusion of all members in the development of an ethical work culture provides a more comprehensive view. "We need not just rules and policies . . . but a way of thinking about organizations, leadership, and membership which respects and supports ethical relationships (Ritchie, 1988, p. 181). The collaborative creation of ethical culture, shared by all members, promotes a valuing of relationship and a climate that provides for less harmful effects from decisions. Further, the responsibility is truly shared.

Leaders Affect the Moral Code

Leaders are not the Lone Ranger, but they do have an enhanced ability to influence the values of the organization through the process of culture. Personal values are always a part of agency decisions. The leader puts a "moral stamp" on every decision, either directly or "by default" (Brummer, 1985, p. 87). The moral code of leaders, then, can permeate all levels of the agency and, in this way, help to enhance and support the moral sensitivities and activities of constituents. Thus, the leader's "moral stamp" is not only on a particular decision, but also on the entire organization. The ethics of the organization rely, in particular, on the commitment of leaders in high level positions to become moral leaders and moral models for others.

Organizational Culture Is the Context for Ethics

The degree of ethical or unethical behavior is dependent to some degree on the atmosphere or climate of the organization (Longenecker, 1985). Any leader or constituent ". . . must decide issues and make choices in an atmosphere that encourages, discourages, or ignores the moral element in such decisions" (Longenecker, 1985, p. 65). The influence of the organization is a powerful force in relation to ethical behavior. In addition, the administrative/managerial process itself is a contextual factor. The methods, procedures, and systems of managing all influence how constituents perceive what is valued, what is rewarded, and what to strive toward through activities and decisions. Leaders are responsible for articulating the "fundamental purposes or priorities of an organization . . . why an organization exists and the values which are important to its existence" (Longenecker, 1985, p. 66). Culture is a medium that can provide the processes to convey these important visions and values for leaders. In contrast, culture can also portray the negative and abusive messages that influence constituents and leaders toward unethical practices and decisions.

Organizational Values Influence Personal Conscience

Culture, as context, is a complex background for the value commitments of individuals. It has a major influence on how people perceive the freedom to act on their own personal values. Research studies support the assertion that organizational and group values assume greater emphasis than personal values (Bird & Waters, 1987; Carroll, 1975; England, 1967; Posner & Schmidt, 1987; Victor & Cullen, 1988). Bird and Waters (1987) found that managers experienced a standard of "organizational responsibility" communicated through the norms of the culture, whereby they felt an obligation to make decisions and do their work in a way that met the needs of the organization for efficiency (Bird & Waters, 1987, p. 9). Posner and Schmidt (1987), in a study of 1,500 managers, found that a person's level of authority in an organization made a difference in their perception that personal principles must be compromised in order to conform to organizational expectations. Top executives felt less pressured, whereas middle managers and supervisors felt pressured to compromise their personal values to meet an organizational demand. The power of the organization to influence individuals' value commitments, particularly those at lower levels in the hierarchy, is pervasive.

Value commitments of individuals are based on their conscience (Ritchie, 1988). As was clear in the preceding chapter on bureaucracy, it is difficult for the individual to stand only on their own conscience in the face of pressure to achieve the organizational ideal. Zaleznik notes that ". . . conscience is a fragile thing. It needs support from institutions and that support is weakening" (Ritchie, 1988, p. 161). An ethical organizational culture that promotes the freedom of constituents to listen to, and voice, their own conscience offers needed support. Further support can be developed through the institutionalization of particular values.

Ethical Organizations Institutionalize Important Values

Many complex forces in organizations shape actions and decisions. Internal factors, such as incentives, technology, research and evaluation, and employee relations, combine with external factors, such as the availability of resources, government, and other accrediting bodies regulations, the legal environment and pressures of competition to exert influence on decisions (Goodpaster, 1983). The leader's conscience about the administration of the organization ". . . does not translate automatically into running a conscientious corporation. The latter requires an 'institutionalization' of certain values, not simply the possession of those values in one part [or person] of the organization . . ." (p. 10). A leader's focus on the development of important values and characteristics that enhance the moral and ethical sensitivity and practice of leaders and constituents helps to form the moral "personality" of the organization, primarily shaped through culture.

Ethical Decisions Are Nonprogrammed Decisions

Ethical decisions are always made in a context of ambiguity and complexity, so they are nonprogrammed decisions. Programmed and nonprogrammed decisions are different. In programmed decisions, the choice is almost a foregone conclusion (Simon, 1957). Think of the analogy of driving a car. The person knows what to do automatically on every occasion of choice. Programmed decisions operate within an organizational framework; the organization influences the decisions of each of its members by ". . . supplying these decisions with their premises" (Azumi & Hage, 1972, p. 249).

Nonprogrammed decisions, which are most relevant to decisions about ethics, are defined as decisions where ". . . the alternatives of choice are not given in advance, but must be discovered" by a rational process of searching (Simon, 1957, p. 221). These decisions require much ". . . stirring about, deliberation, discussion, often vacillation," which are typical reactions to the complexity of ethical decisions. *Guides for action* that influence the choice in nonprogrammed decisions are not totally private to the individual. Instead, the guides are part of a common culture. Thus, aspects of the individual and the social context in which the decision is made are critical to the ultimate choice. Azumi and Hage, (1972, p. 250) explicate this further:

> In working organizations decisions are made either in the presence of others or with the knowledge that they will have to be implemented, or understood, or approved by others. The set of considerations called into relevance on any decision making occasion has therefore to be one shared with others or acceptable to them.

Organizations that facilitate nonprogrammed decisionmaking must establish and rely on a culture of shared beliefs about the common interests of the working community. Included would be the standards and criteria used to judge the appropriateness and relevance of decisions and what would be viewed as ethical and moral achievements for the organization. Norms and standards to evaluate individual contributions, expertise, and other matters in relation to ethics are also part of the culture. The cultural system, then, is expressed and visible in a code of conduct that is apparent to others, inside or outside of the organization, and helps to guide nonprogrammed ethical decisions. Understanding the nature of ethical cultures, then, is an important part of the knowledge of leaders.

The Nature of Organizational Culture

Different organizational theorists describe organizational culture in several ways. Morgan (1997) argues that traditionally we have seen culture in society as a *pattern of development* that is reflected through knowledge, ideology, values, laws, and day-to-day rituals. However, the more contemporary definition would be ". . . that different groups of people have different ways of life" (Morgan, 1977, p. 120). Organizations are now seen as minisocieties that have their own cultures and subcultures that are different from one another. Factors, such as the language used, patterns of interaction, rituals of the daily routine, and the images that are pursued in conversation, are examples of observable entities that have a historical explanation for how things happen and get done in that particular organization. "Shared values, shared beliefs, shared meaning, shared understanding, and shared sense making are all different ways of describing culture . . . we are really talking about a process of reality construction (Morgan, 1997, p. 138).

The culture of an organization is all encompassing, or "a tapestry of meaning" (Deal, 1987). Culture gives meaning to our human endeavors and also provides stability, certainty, and predictability (Deal, 1987). Organizational culture includes the shared beliefs, values, and basic assumptions that help everyone understand how the work of the organization is to be conducted (Nanus & Dobbs, 1999). The culture of an organization helps people cope with the daily situations of their work and provides a basis for making sense of behavior. Deal (1987) accentuates the power of culture in organizations by noting the analogy to primitive peoples' perception of their tribe.

Cultural Context

Organizations exist within a particular cultural context (Morgan, 1997). Therefore, what is culturally appropriate or relevant within the United States is very different from other countries. In the United States, competition, individualism, preoccupation with winning, an emphasis on consumerism, and so forth provide a different cultural context for organizational culture than other countries. This context makes the difference in success and failure of new ways of working within the organization and can shape the ethical culture as well. For example, the focus on efficiency, revenue generation, and cost-effectiveness can affect what is viewed as unethical or unethical practices. Profitmaking (sometimes at the level of greed) in our contemporary society appears to be promoted as the primary value that sets the scene for shaping the character of the organization. The most blatant current example is the culture of Enron, the energy firm that recently filed for bankruptcy. From accounts in the media, the culture of greed that was promoted throughout the organization affected people at every level; questionable accounting practices and decisions that had a dramatic negative impact on employees and shareholders were promulgated with few exceptions. This kind of widespread unethical practice in a corporation of that size can only be promoted through an organizational and societal culture that supports it. The questionable practices were perceived as normal in the organization.

Ethnocentrism

A characteristic of any organizational culture is ethnocentrism, the taken-for-granted codes of behavior we recognize as normal (Morgan, 1997). When people participate in activities that do not conform, they are viewed as abnormal. Ethnocentric views affect how people react to diversity in the workplace. It also affects how they respond to immoral situations or ethical dilemmas, as well as to different behaviors and activities on the part of other employees who do not seem to understand "the way we do things around here." A danger of ethnocentrism is the inability of those working in the culture to step outside of the norms and practices in order to evaluate the moral and ethical implications objectively. Instead, both leaders and constituents become socialized to "the way we do things here" and can collude or participate in immoral and unethical activities.

Development of Culture

Culture is not imposed on a social setting; it develops through social interaction (Morgan, 1997). This means that any individual at any level in the organization can influence the culture. Characteristics of culture develop over time in relation to the history of an organization; thus, the history of the organization can influence the present. Characteristics of the culture are generated through patterns of interactions between individuals, language used, images and themes explored in conversation, various rituals in the daily routines, and so forth. Leaders, most often those in the higher levels of the hierarchy, shape the values that guide an organization through the power to reward and punish. Often, competing subcultures and values are related to the organization's purpose. Sometimes there are divided loyalties among groups (Morgan, 1997), such as the following:

- Administrative expectations versus professional standards (for example, profit, cost savings versus service quality)
- Different professions with different professional values (for example, social work, business, medicine, psychology, and so forth)
- Different social or ethnic groupings (for example, social class differences, Caucasians and minority groups, groups with different ethnicity, and different sexual orientations)
- Occupational groupings (for example, union employees versus management or blue collar workers, paraprofessionals versus professional groups, and so forth)

The various subgroups and loyalties in the organization help to shape the culture of the organization, which can be identified through tangible cultural forms.

Tangible Cultural Forms.   Culture is developed and transmitted through a variety of activities and forms (Deal, 1987). The tangible characteristics of culture provide an opportunity to analyze the ethical messages conveyed as well as to promote ethics and values through the language, activities, and tasks of everyday work. The following examples illustrate some of the tangible forms of culture (Deal, 1987; Morgan, 1997):

- *Rituals*—Repetitive behavioral activities where values are expressed through implicit signals (for example, surgical scrub, roll call, report, and so forth).
- *Shared values*—Shorthand slogans that summarize deeply held values of the organization (for example, "we try harder," "minds to match our mountains").
- *Heroes and heroines*—Individuals who embody or represent core values and are recognized as such throughout the organization.
- *Ceremonies*—Periodic occasions in which values and heroes are put on display, acknowledged, or celebrated (for example, celebrating most productive unit, volunteer banquet and awards, and so forth).
- *Stories*—Concrete examples of values and heroes who triumph by following culturally prescribed ways.
- *Cultural network*—Collection of informal individuals—gossips, spies, storytellers—whose primary role is to reinforce and protect existing ways. No examples are needed. Everyone knows who they are. (For example, our faculty has the school historian who can offer the historical perspective in relation to any issue, the way we do things here.)
- *Physical impression*—Conveys value through facility and artifacts (For example, run down or dirty facilities for the serious mentally ill versus attractive, immaculate outpatient department with fruit on the coffee tables).
- *Language*—The buzzwords, cliches, catch phrases, and terminology that are used in everyday discourse (for example, in health and mental health, the language of diagnosis, such as the hip replacement down the hall).
- *Values/Beliefs/Norms*—The official and unofficial values, dos and don'ts, and standards of behavior.

All of these tangible cultural forms, each of which has the potential to transmit ethical and moral messages, culminate in the shaping of a comprehensive culture for the organization.

Rule Following.   The nature of culture is found in social norms and customs, or the rules of behavior (Morgan, 1997). If people follow the rules, they are successful in constructing the appropriate social reality. When one disrupts the norms, the ordered reality of life and work breaks down. For example, if an organization has an implicit dress code that includes suits and ties for men and dresses for women, there will be disruption if someone shows up for work in jeans. The rules about how to behave are communicated through formal and informal policies, leader and group behavior, verbal and nonverbal communication, and so forth. Leaders with authority in the organization influence rule following through rewards and punishments. For example, merit increases to individuals who support the leader's values or projects are an example of rewarding what the leader wants to be valued. The loss of prime office space or budget cuts for those individuals who resist or challenge leader initiatives are examples of punishments. Thus, what we take for granted about our work reality is actually based on skillful accomplishments that develop into normal patterns (Morgan, 1997). However, leaders are not the only ones who can influence culture and work climate. All of the constituents of an organization can influence what goes on around here through a process called enactment.

Enactment

Enactment is the process through which we can shape and structure reality (Morgan, 1997). Organizations are socially constructed realities that rest as much in the heads and minds of members as in concrete sets of rules and relations. The social construction of the situation influences what rules and codes of behavior are to be summoned. The first step in affecting changes in the ethical climate is to understand the common meanings that make up a shared sense of reality, for example, through an organizational values statement (see Chapter 10). Then, the shared reality can be shaped and changed through open discussion, feedback, and critical commentary.

A member can influence the culture and ethical climate of an agency by behaving differently. However, more directly, members can enact new norms and values by questioning, commenting, and challenging the prevailing norms, values, or behaviors. Initiating interaction promotes a process of dialogue that can lead to change. Leaders can provide structures for communication and interaction that lead to changes in the organizational culture and climate as well (see Chapter 11). Feedback and the freedom to comment openly is a critical component of establishing an ethical work climate (Manning, 1990).

Ethical Climate: The Message

The ethical climate of an organization can be thought of as one element of culture (Victor & Cullen, 1988) and is based on the organization's normative system (Schneider, 1983). Ethical climate is defined as "the range of perceptions that answer, for a member of an organization, the Socratic question: 'What should I do?' Included are the perceived prescriptions, proscriptions, and permissions regarding moral obligations in organizations" (Victor & Cullen, 1988, p. 101). The ethical climate, then, captures the organizational norms about practices and policies with ethical consequences. Employees perceive *the message*, or their moral duty toward others. Other *messages* include the restrictions and restraints of the organization (for example, what is considered harmful) and the opportunities (or lack of opportunities) for moral feedback through the ethical climate. The practices and policies convey particular norms and values that inform members of what they can do and what they ought to do in regard to their actions toward others. For example, the perceived support for initiating ethical questions or challenges, the tolerance for misappropriation of funds, and the decision process for ethical questions such as conflict of interest are indicative of particular aspects of ethical climate.

The ethical work climate is based on the prerequisite that the norms and values in the organization are institutionalized (Victor & Cullen, 1988). In other words, employees would perceive prevailing norms and values with a fair amount of consensus because the values and norms are embedded throughout the tangible cultural forms of the organization. In measuring ethical climate, employees' own behavior and values are not reported, but, rather, the practices and policies that they perceive to exist in the organization. As one leader noted, "Once a value system is in place at the team level, it comes naturally" (Manning, 1990, p. 230).

All employees carry the composite of messages through interactions and unspoken behaviors. The communication is also modeled through the leadership. The ethical climate is interdependent and reciprocal. All constituents have the potential to influence the climate at all levels of the organization, as was discussed in relation to enactment. Both employees and experts perceive that climate is most influenced by those at the top level of the organization (Manning, 1990; Wright, 1999).

Leaders Set the Tone

Leaders directly influence the organizational climate in relation to "how much unethical behavior will be present" (Wright, 1999, p. 67). In a criminal justice agency, ". . . excessive use of force, brutality, corruption, involvement in criminal activity, graft, employee theft, sexual misconduct, discrimination, racism, sexism, and harassment will vary directly with managerial attention to the promotion of ethical standards of practice among employees" (Wright, 1999, p. 67). The leadership's role and commitment to develop ethical accountability and an ethical culture is paramount. The CEO and other administrative and managerial leaders must "walk the walk" as well as "talk the talk." This means that ethical climate is determined by the ethical behavior of leaders, not just their rhetoric. For example, accepting gifts (for example, a bottle of whiskey) from vendors, taking home office supplies, flirting, excessive drinking, using support staff for personal business, and so forth are practices that "do not go unnoticed" by other employees (Wright, 1999, p. 68). There are occasions when leader behavior communicates a strong message about what behavior (and underlying values) are really acceptable. One administrator in mental health described her leadership philosophy this way. "How we operate affects the entire organization. Our philosophy and values drive us, [so] we don't have to think about ethics per se" (Manning, 1990, p. 232).

Elements of Ethical Climate

Three elements of ethical climate—mission, explicit policy, and implicit policy—were identified by human service leaders (Manning, 1990) as having a shaping influence on ethical or unethical practices. The integration of the real life experiences is useful, as well as important to consider as an illustration of the powerful effects of climate and the potential to shape climate by leaders. All of the following quotations that describe the actual experience of leaders are from this qualitative study (Manning, 1990), unless otherwise noted.

The Mission

The mission is the foundation of the ethical system in human service organizations. The mission statement is the central statement of the organization's purpose (Colorado Association of Nonprofit Organizations [CANPO], 1994). It is meant to guide and inspire the overall direction of the organization's work and the program goals and objectives that are developed to do the work. The mission is the human service organization's contract with the community; it states clearly what the public can expect in regard to the population served and the nature and meaning of the services provided. The mission provides the community with a statement of the ideal end that the organization hopes to achieve through its work.

Leaders referred to it as the one guide that could be counted on as "unchanging" and "clear." The mission was viewed as a shaper of decisions. One leader said, "Well, I kind of go back to the mission in terms of what is it that we're doing, what are we about, and where are we going, and what are the things that we believe in . . ." (p. 213). The mission shapes the goals, philosophy, and values of the agency, ". . . like going back to the constitution . . . never sacrifice the mission" (p. 214). The mission provides leaders and constituents with a clear mandate that helps determine the boundaries of service delivery and serves as an indicator about "when to take a stand." It is particularly helpful in making rationing decisions about services, such as access to services, programs for unique needs, and so forth. The mission is also a backup system for inappropriate requests. One manager (p. 214) said, "Go back to the mission, this is what we're here to do." It was also used as a source of support in the face of unethical actions or decisions that were "out of sync" with the mission.

Explicit Policy

Explicit policies also function as guides to behavior and decisions. Policy is usually documented, is sometimes verbal, and is derived from the mission. Formal policies are usually organized around particular functions, such as personnel policies, clinical policies, admission policies, financial policies, ethics policies, and so forth. Leaders viewed the guiding function of explicit policy as "weak" (p. 216). It was not viewed as particularly relevant to professional behavior, and many leaders were not even aware of what was in the policy manual of the organization. There was general agreement that explicit policy reflects legal requirements that have been translated into the necessary policy for agency use, usually protection from liability. One manager related an experience over inequities in salary. "I thought that this is a really interesting process, where you don't think so much about the ethics of the situation as opposed to the legalities of the situation." They only became concerned when issues of legality were confronted in the policies.

Leaders in the upper level of the hierarchy usually develop explicit policy. Middle managers and supervisors experienced less direct involvement in policy development. One person (p. 218) said, "Corporate policy is developed in a way that the manager has no control." Constituents and leaders at lower levels may offer less support for ethical standards and expectations if there is a lack of representation in the policy development process. Policies developed without their input may have little bearing on the actual situations they face, and lack of participation affects a person's sense of control and commitment. The following were identified as functions of policy in regard to ethical issues.

Policy to Express Legal Requirements. *Legal requirements* can be used to define the parameters of what is considered ethical. Executive directors shared conflicting perspectives about the role of the law in ethical climate. One director (p. 217) stated, "Ethics can never be above the law anyway, so what does it matter?" Another said, "I am concerned with how highly structured some of our own rules and regs are regarding the kind of canned judgment they represent . . . in the process of assuring protections we have gradually reduced the role of judgment to the point that it places people at risk." To one leader, the law was the highest authority, and, to another, legal requirements can act as a barrier to ethics. Each leader's perspective shapes the ethical climate of their agencies.

Policy as a Protection Against Liability.   *Protection against liability* was a primary concern. Thus, policies are available to "keep bases covered" though they are not usually under the heading of "Ethics" (p. 218). Leaders (p. 218) described policies that "spell out anything where you can be sued . . . everyone is scared of being sued." Fee schedules, informed consent, research, and confidentiality are examples. Documentation of standards and requirements to address liability add to individual and agency accountability and provide explicit messages to employees.

Policy for the "Thou Shalt Not" in Organizations.   Explicit policies are often directed toward the negative, the *"Thou shalt not"* pronouncements. Restrictions rather than positive and proactive designations for ethical issues were the rule. One manager (p. 217) gave examples: ". . . don't get drunk . . . don't have sex with clients. I think having general written guidelines in more proactive areas is useful and it's something that is a little harder to develop than the prohibitions of the stuff that is obviously unethical and not appropriate." The tendency to develop prohibitions may be connected to the legal requirements previously discussed. Also, as this leader pointed out, it is more difficult to think through and document the positive exhortations for ethical behavior.

Professional and Organizational Standards of Care.   *Standards of care* are explicit policies that convey a positive message about the primary well-being of the clients who are being served. Standards of care promote the basic minimums about what clients can expect and that caregivers should provide in the intervention process, from engagement with the agency to termination. These standards are useful in providing clarity and administrative support in decisions involving client interventions and client rights, the "clinical mantle" (p. 219). Standards of care are also ensured through policies that cover professional privilege, service agreements, professional standards and the code of ethics from various disciplines represented in the organization.

Justification and Protection for Leaders.   Explicit policy can be used in a variety of ways to *justify decisions* and to *protect leaders* in the case of unpopular decisions. A director (p. 219) described being sued: ". . . and then when I go to court . . . his peers determine that this was so and our policy says that this is so, and then I just follow the policy. That's being ethical because I follow the policies." Another manager revealed that policies are used less to guide and more to ". . . get rid of someone." The policies are a necessary backup to personnel because it is difficult to get rid of dysfunctional staff. They have to have an act of commission rather than omission, so policies help. Policy and the motivation for using policy in particular situations convey a strong message about the ethics of the organization. In the first instance, policy served to protect against liability, but may have promoted what is morally right. In the second, the use of policy conveyed powerful messages about the value of employees, due process, and fairness.

Clarity Through Written Guidelines.   The documentation of policy does provide *clarity through written guidelines.* The policies that are delineated and accessible to leaders and constituents provide a level of guidance for the major ethical issues the organization has identified (such as conflict of interest, involvement with clients, confidentiality, and so forth). However, leaders have also identified a danger of relying on policy to create distance from the emotional and intimate elements of interacting with others in relation to issues that are ambiguous and complex. One person (p. 221) said, We are engaged in an industry of being intimate [human services], while being objective . . . too many policies affect intimacy and increase objectivity." A well-known ethicist has expressed the same concern. Toulmin (1981) argues that "the ethics of strangers"—objective and rule driven—is not conducive to participation and trust. The ethics of intimacy relies on dialogue, relationship, and a sense of being in a community together.

Implicit Policy

The implicit messages that are conveyed through the climate of how we get things done here are strong and powerful (Manning, 1990). Implicit messages and policies are conveyed through the leadership in *unwritten* and sometimes an *unspoken* manner. These implicit messages are *guiding mechanisms* that communicate what is valued and how leaders and constituents are to behave and act, within and for the organization. Implicit policies were described as frequently incongruent with the explicit policies and the mission of an organization. They were also viewed as more powerful in shaping the behavior of leaders and constituents. An upper administrator noted that implicit messages have a "profound influence" on decisions made and the "way you make them" (p. 225). Decisions get made that are stupid or not doable because of unspoken policies of cost containment, or those who are impacted by the decision are not included in the decision process. Therefore, a philosophy is conveyed through decisions without anyone really thinking about or understanding the effects of the decisions on the organization's ethical climate.

A Form of Guidance.   Implicit messages are *subtle* and therefore harder to challenge directly. A leader in human services described it this way. "It's the subtle communication that I worry about . . . If I feel I need to admit [patients to increase the census], am I going to make a decision on the wrong side of things and respond to that? How objective am I going to be? Am I going to be influenced by the pressure?" Other managers described implicit policies that are driven by money. For example, managers would lower the qualifications for new personnel (for example, hire paraprofessionals rather than professional staff), use students instead of employed staff, manipulate insurance coverage, and so forth to save money (p. 226). Implicit messages *provide a form of guidance*, but not the kind that would be communicated explicitly through written policies, procedures, or rules. Instead, the word *"pressure"* is often linked to these kinds of messages.

Implicit messages can and do *convey ethical expectations*. Sometimes they are spoken, and often they are modeled, but usually ethical messages were not found in written form. As ethical messages are communicated, they shape the ethical climate of the agency. One administrator (p. 223) explained, "I know one thing that I try to communicate that is unwritten, but I try to teach people . . . try to get them around to my way of thinking . . . a sense of empathy for clients. It has to do with how we treat people . . . to treat people with respect."

To Avoid Accountability.   In contrast, messages are also communicated implicitly to *avoid accountability*. These messages convey expectations that may be unworkable, irrational, inappropriate, unethical, and hidden from public view. One person described the pressure to admit clients inappropriately to increase the census (p. 224). Another said, "there's all this unwritten . . . policy . . . about six to eight visits, and who's going to be there for you when, on what would have been their ninth visit, they run out and shot somebody? You'll be out there alone (p. 224)." Implicit policy can put pressure on others to behave unethically without the leader taking responsibility for the message. These covert messages shape ethical climate to include secrecy and hidden practices that cannot be evaluated or regulated by others in the organization or by the public.

Delegation of Blame.   *Delegation of blame* was also a function of implicit messages due to the lack of accountability. Techniques and tactics to increase revenue or cut costs that may not be popular with the public can be enacted through lower level employees and managers without the organization taking responsibility explicitly through written policy. Because middle managers and supervisors are in the position of passing on the implicit expectations to direct service staff, they are more vulnerable to the ethical nature of the expectation and the accountability for it. For example, one manager (p. 228) said, ". . . not only [is it] not stated in policy, but its not going to be . . . and [I'm told] 'don't you put that in writing because we'll get nailed on that.' So [I] kind of get a very vague kind of policy that you can justify anything you want to do under."

Disapproval and Devaluing of Constituents.   Implicit messages are often used to *convey disapproval* of activities or decisions or to *convey devaluing of staff*. Leaders can simply not attend to ethical issues they don't want to confront directly. The message is "leave it alone." Upper level administrators have authority to impact budgets and other distributions of desired resources. After disagreeing with a superior about an ethical issue, a manager (p. 229) reported, "It got to the point where if you fought what they were doing, then your group suffered by not getting the resources, because then you were not their favorite group. Like one year I got half of everyone else's operating budget. It was a punishment. Oh yeah, it was an out and out punishment." Implicit policy is also a means to get rid of employees who do not hold values that are congruent with organization's values. A high level administrator (p. 229) said, "a manager is in trouble who has a set of values or mode of operation that is different from the main line . . . we will eventually get them to leave." Inducing employees to leave happens through unwritten activities and decisions that have the ability to make work life miserable and untenable.

The Importance of Congruence

A major factor in shaping an ethical climate is congruence between what is conveyed formally and explicitly by the organization and what is conveyed implicitly. Conflicting messages contribute to feelings of confusion and alienation about the purpose of the agency and each individual's responsibility in relation to purpose. One manager (p. 225) described the explicit message of "we serve everyone" that was written in the mission statement and the implicit message from administration that said, "Offer less services to indigent clients at sites where you want to attract wealthy, upwardly mobile clients." This contradiction between mission and revenue generation is a critical issue about values, as well as survival of the organization. A manager argued, "We need a clear message about what to expect in terms of the mission and boundaries . . . then we can decide whether to work here (p. 231)."

Leaders in the for-profit sector must come to terms with the conflicts between excessive levels of profit and quality service delivery to consumers and then provide a congruent message to employees and consumers. The atmosphere in the for-profit sector of human services has followed other businesses and corporations in society; the drive for increased profits has overtaken other values and affects the ethical climate of these organizations. One leader (p. 231) in a for-profit described this conflict "I can't buy into the organizational goals because of greed and the profit motive . . . it's not good business and it's not a money issue." Another (p. 232) described the "schizophrenic vision" at her organization: ". . . corporate zeal . . . and a high profit margin . . . They don't have a clue as to what goes into that . . . but the clinicians do." Congruent messages between what an agency communicates publicly and what is communicated implicitly rest on a well-defined balance of the profit motive and quality service. In this balance, profit does not accrue at the expense of employees and quality of service to consumers.

Conflicting messages also inform employees about the openness of the system to feedback and the expectations of individuals to give feedback about unethical practices. An "open door" policy may be conveyed verbally by the director, but, if individuals attempt to go through the door and discuss sensitive ethical issues, they may be instructed to go through the line of command. The *communication system* is the route for feedback about ethical concerns. The implicit messages of the organization convey what can travel up and down that route. A middle manager (p. 233) said, "Part of it . . . is giving your staff the latitude and the permission to bring problems to your attention. If you give the staff the message that you don't want to hear it . . . then you won't hear a lot of things . . . cause if you don't hear them, you can't do anything about them." Leaders' sensitivity to the messages they convey and a commitment to communicating clear, overt and congruent messages through implicit and explicit policy help shape ethical climate and moral commitment for constituents.

The Freedom to Comment

The freedom to comment on unethical practices and/or the daily moral and ethical questions is the critical factor in developing and maintaining an ethical climate. Without permission to respond, constituents are doomed to collude in existing practices, ethical or unethical, or to submit to the manipulations of well-meaning or unethical leaders with their own moral and ethical agendas. The organization, as argued earlier (see development of culture), is a particularly social enterprise and individuals who spend considerable time there are socialized by the organization. Niebuhr (1960, p. 257) notes that ethical behavior toward others is more difficult in social groups (like the organization). "In every human group there is less reason to guide and to check impulse, less capacity for self-transcendence, less ability to comprehend the needs of others." People strongly want to be part of a group, and the fears of isolation and rejection act as inhibitors to taking moral risks. Further, organizations and leaders, because of the pervasive inequality in the distribution of power, are inherently at risk of immoral behavior (Ritchie, 1988). The risks of real punishment—loss of job security, salary, and other benefits, not to mention the risk to career development—can restrain the moral tendencies of employees and their willingness to give feedback. These issues are especially salient in regard to whistleblowers.

The Spiral of Silence

The inaction of individuals and their reluctance to comment about moral and ethical issues promotes a process that goes beyond the individual. Noelle-Neuman (1997) has proposed a theory called the spiral of silence. She suggests that people are able to intuitively figure out what their neighbors or peers think about potentially conflictual issues. When people think their opinion is a minority view, they are less likely to express it. Neuman develops this thesis further by asserting that the majority becomes stronger and more powerful as those with a different view withdraw. Thus, the spiral of silence feeds on itself (Alter, 2000). A recent news event in the field of business surrounding the Enron scandal is an example. It appears that many individuals had knowledge of questionable ethical practices and even illegal behavior, yet, to date, only one person took any formal action. The spiral of silence was strengthened, and an organizational climate that promoted silence was further reinforced.

The Bystander Effect

Bly (1996, p. 375) has titled a chapter in her book, "Evil in the Comfortable Herd." She states that the "ethical core of the whole issue is: can we be brave enough to be unpopular?" The bystander effect is connected to the spiral of silence. People become immobilized when confronted by evil or unethical practices and take their cue from other bystanders. If the group is not reacting or acting, the individual behaves accordingly. Therefore, the group effect can have a powerful shaping influence on the norms in an organization about giving feedback and taking action in relation to moral challenges.

The nature of ethical climate that develops can be based on a spiral of silence or the freedom to comment. Leaders interested in developing a climate that supports feedback must actively and formally build processes for feedback into the design (see Chapters 10 and 11). Leaders also must model a genuine interest in hearing about questionable practices and moral quandaries. In a study with 50 middle managers, every one had experienced a request by a superior to do something "immoral, illegal, or unethical." However, two-thirds of the group felt the boss did not intend or was unaware of the negative impact (Ritchie, 1988, p. 167). Although inadequate information, pressures of time, and differences of opinion were relevant, the most relevant concern was that ". . . the boss was not sensitive to the functional or ethical perspective of the subordinate." The leader's style, openness, and philosophy about feedback is connected to creating a climate that nurtures feedback. However, many organizations are ambivalent about feedback, and this is evident in the reaction to whistleblowers.

Whistleblowers in Organizations

Whistleblowers are viewed in two different ways: as *dissidents or reformers* (Gummer, 1996, p. 95). When viewed as a dissident, the person is perceived as disrupting the status quo in the organization and interfering with stability. Gummer notes that this is the primary view in bureaucratic organizations that have "formalized rules and procedures" (1996, p. 95). Even though rules and policies may prohibit unethical practices and various kinds of wrongdoing, the behavior of the whistleblower is seen as illegitimate.

The second perspective is that whistleblowers are reformers. From this view, information that is essential to the organization about policies and practices that could be harmful—to constituents, clients, the community, etc. and to the organization in terms of reputation—is brought forward through feedback. This is seen as help to the organization to increase effectiveness by ". . . bringing forward problems and potential solutions to mangement's attention" (Gummer, 1996, p. 96). Whistle-blowers who are viewed as an attribute to the organization are reflective of ethical climates that are more positive, in contrast the dissident view, which encourages further wrongdoing and negative effects on the ethical climate.

The incidence and seriousness of wrongdoing in organizations does have a relationship to the organization's perspective about whistle-blowers (Gummer, 1996, p. 97). These researchers found that ". . . values encouraging whistleblowing and protection from retaliation are associated with less serious wrongdoing." It is apparent that to promote an atmosphere of feedback in concert with expectations of ethical practices there must be a supportive environment for people who come forward with concerns for the organization. Further, that support must be in the form of protection. Nothing gives a stronger message to constituents and leaders than to punish, discipline, or fire someone who has identified an ethical concern. However, where whistleblowing is concerned, issues related to loyalty—to leaders and to the organization—become a concern.

Organizational Loyalty

Leader and employee loyalty to the organization is also a concern in regard to feedback. People who criticize or resist or question organizational policy or practice are sometimes thought of as disloyal. Levy (1979) argues that the agency can expect loyalty from employees, but that loyalty does not abrogate the freedom and responsibility of the worker to initiate positive action in regard to ethical issues and to comment on the ethical and moral issues of agency policies and practices. This form of loyalty, provided through each leader and constituent acting as "institution citizen in loyal opposition," promotes speaking out, challenging, and questioning the nature of the organization's functioning. These activities are representative of loyalty, but a loyalty that is in the best interests of all concerned, especially the organization (Manning, 1990; Tillich, 1952). Townsend (1998, p. 170) affirms this kind of loyalty through behavior she describes as "constructively oppositional." Rather than an oxymoron, this kind of behavior initiates needed change in the system.

Equally important, as employees give feedback, the separation between "their personal integrity and their professional lives" is abolished; accepting responsibility for the "ethical and political dimensions of their work" provides leaders and employees with moral agency (Rhodes, 1986, p. 154). The feedback from individuals about rules, goals, and methods of intervention and evaluation prevents moral detachment and encourages the empowerment of leaders, employees, and consumers rather than empowering the bureaucracy (Rhodes, 1986).

Leaders who want to develop an ethical climate beyond their own moral obligations must institute "the consent of the governed" and "a system of checks and balances" as the most positive form of control that is inclusive of all constituents (Ritchie, 1988, p. 169). The involvement of all constituents in the development and shaping of an ethical climate provides the consent of the governed. They then feel responsible and accountable for the decisions and actions that take place there. Democratic participation will not totally eliminate the power imbalances, the exploitation, and the reality of administrative and management control functions. However, an egalitarian system of feedback is an important first step in managing the inherent manipulation in organizations "within a given value system" (Ritchie, 1988, p. 169). The "checks and balances" rest then, on participation and feedback, along with organizational structures and processes that provide formal feedback mechanisms to leaders (see Chapter 11).

Conclusion

Organizational culture can be effective in unifying the members of an organization toward ethical goals and commitments. Evidence of a strong culture rests in the support, loyalty, and trust of employees; "these form the cement that binds an organization together" (Nanus & Dobbs, 1999, p. 156). Leaders cannot make an organization ethical by themselves. Leaders must understand the nature of culture and the role of ethical climates in order to help with the construction of cultures and climates that nurture and support ethical understanding and reflection for all constituents. The emphasis on congruence of the mission, explicit policy, and implicit policy is the beginning of clarity for ethical expectations of members. The importance of a feedback system that provides the opportunity to reflect on ethical and unethical policies and practices is necessary for leaders to know and understand the ethical challenges of the organization. The next chapter will focus on the tools and strategies of leadership that enhance the development of culture.

QUESTIONS AND APPLICATIONS

1. Identify particular historical influences at your agency that have shaped the current culture. What divided loyalties exist in your agency? Discuss.

2. Identify examples of tangible activities and forms of culture (Figure 9.1) from your organization. What ethical and value messages are conveyed through these forms?

3. What are examples of rewards or punishments in your agency in response to ethical and moral issues that you have observed or have experienced personally?

4. Choose one value (empowerment, collaboration, openness, loyalty, fairness, commitment, and so forth) that you believe would enhance the ethical culture of your organization. Brainstorm strategies, behaviors, policies, and so forth that would lead to the enactment of that value in your organization.

5. Think about the mission, explicit policies, and implicit policies in your organization. What is your analysis of the congruence or incongruence between them?

6. Identify and discuss three implicit policies that are conveyed by leaders in your agency that promote unethical or questionable practices. Identify three implicit messages that you communicate that undermine ethical practice.

CHAPTER

10 Tools and Strategies to Shape Ethical Cultures

THE FOCUS IN THIS CHAPTER IS ON THE FOLLOWING AREAS:

- Leader roles and behaviors that shape ethical climate
- Program orientations for ethical climates
- Analysis of culture through metaphor
- Organizational value statements
- Building organizational cultures with integrity

Culture is inclusive of ethical climate; both are part of *a web of understanding*. In fact, "our worlds are often tangled webs" (de Vries, 1988, p. 147). Leaders are the force that help to provide direction in understanding the nature of the web by untangling the web and weaving new webs as they are needed for a more ethical climate. Margaret Wheatley describes the lesson of the participative universe: "Nothing lives alone" (1999, p. 145). Everything that is important comes into form because of relationships. We cocreate our world. In order to effect change then, the webs of relationships are the focus of the change effort. Wheatley (1999) reinforces two important metaphors that are relevant to shaping ethical meaning through the organizational culture. First, organizations are like a spider web: resilient and open to repair through reweaving the parts that are damaged. Second, from biology, a system can be restored to health by "connecting it to more of itself. In other words, creating stronger relationships that, in turn, promote learning "about itself from itself." The attention to relationships (enhancing connections) and increasing the possibility of learning valuable insights from all leaders and constituents (systems of feedback) are themes that will be repeated throughout this section on shaping ethical culture (and will reappear in Chapter 11).

In addition, change is a process, not a light switch. Barbara Kingsolver (1993), in one of her novels, notes that you "cannot turn a mile long train like a pony." The momentum that has developed in the history of an organization, resulting in a particular culture, is a force to understand and respect. Leaders must be sensitive and responsive to the organization's culture, but not act precipitously to change it (Nanus & Dobbs, 1999).

The previous chapter delineated the nature of culture and ethical climate as the context for ethical policies and practices. Culture and climate are social constructions that can be shaped and developed. For purposes of the discussion, culture and climate will be used interchangeably. This chapter builds on the conceptual ideas of Chapter 9 through the metaphor of the web. In addition, the role of the leader is accentuated. The ultimate responsibility for the success or failure in relation to culture rests on the involvement commitment of leaders. Tools and strategies that are helpful to leaders and constituents to analyze, shape, and enact ethical organizational cultures will be discussed.

The importance of leadership that is connected to a moral vision cannot be under-estimated in relation to ethical culture. Leadership has to come first. Messages about ethical vision and goals are uplifting and give all constituents an opportunity to reach beyond current practices to a better, more ethical future. However, it is difficult for constituents to take ethical risks in the face of leaders who remain uncommitted. For leaders to be transformational, they must ". . . have the vision to see beyond the horizon, along with sensitivity to really feel human needs, plus an almost contradictory toughness to build an organization capable of translating the vision and sensitivity into change" (Zdenek, 2002, p. 6). The leader is the key; "employees pay attention to what bosses care about" (Wright, 1999, p. 68). The old adage, "The buck stops here," is relevant. The leader is responsible for what constituents perceive as valued in the organization through the modeling of the leader. Also, the commitment of leadership to providing the support and resources necessary is critical to the success in shaping an ethical culture. The leader as steward or servant to constituents is an attitude that helps greatly in shaping ethical cultures. Therefore, leadership roles and behaviors are discussed as the first strategies. Leaders demonstrate their ethical commitments through behaviors and roles.

Leader Behaviors that Shape Culture

Leaders behave in ways that intentionally or unintentionally convey particular messages to constituents. Awareness of the power of behavior in conveying particular values and expectations is important. The role of steward and servant leader sets the attitudinal perspectives for a culture of communication, role modeling, activities, and behaviors that shape culture (see Figure 10.1).

Leader as Steward

The steward role is "the subtlest role of leadership" according to Senge (1990, p. 12). This role is a matter of attitude and is critical for any leader who is trying to develop a learning organization (see Chapter 11). Leaders who take the role of steward are putting themselves in a servant role. Greenleaf (Senge, 1990, p. 12) explains:

- Create a culture of communication
- Act as an ethical role model
- Pay attention to important organizational values
- Attend to crisis by preserving important values and apportioning responsibility
- Reward, recognize, and promote those with characteristics and behaviors that are desired and necessary for an ethical climate
- Stretch the boundaries of moral responsibility
- Be a voice for the unseen and the voiceless

FIGURE 10.1   Leader Behaviors that Shape Ethical Cultures

> The servant leader is servant first . . . It begins with the natural feeling that one wants to serve, to serve *first*. This conscious choice brings one to aspire to lead. That person is sharply different from one who is leader first, perhaps because of the need to assuage an unusual power drive or to acquire material possessions.

The leader as steward is doing the work for two reasons: to make a positive difference for the people who are their constituents and to be the shepherd for the mission and purpose that is the basis of the organization. To do the first, the leader must have a sensitivity and a keen appreciation for the effects of leadership on others. Employees and consumers can suffer from destructive, inept, or misdirected leadership. In addition, the work of engaging in shaping ethical cultures and learning to learn for the organization places constituents in a vulnerable position. Their "commitment and shared ownership" places them squarely in the forefront of responsibility, along with the leadership (Senge, 1990, p. 13).

The second part of stewardship, the connection to the purpose, emanates from the leader's sense of moral vision and commitment. The servant leader is engaged in something larger than the organization's profit or material success. Servant leaders are invested in changing the way the organization operates and conducts its work toward more productiveness and effectiveness. In this regard, the way the organization works with ethics and moral issues would be a primary focus of the servant leader. One of the most important activities, then, for a servant leader is that of communication with constituents.

Culture of Communication

The *culture of communication* sends a message about dialogue and feedback. Upper level leaders are viewed as setting the tone for the agency. One administrator noted that "how we operate affects the entire organization . . ." (Manning, 1990, p. 232). Leaders have identified several ways they create an ethical climate, primarily through use of self. Communication can create opportunities or act as a barrier for ethical and moral issues to be discussed. One leader said, "If you don't want to hear it, then you won't" (Manning, 1990, p. 233). Another manager said that the response, figuratively, to her concerns about unethical or questionable agency practices was "shut up."

Leaders can use the system of communication to identify ethical issues for problem-solving and resolution. One leader (p. 233) described it this way: "If you don't set the tone or create the opportunity, what you have are people talking about these issues, like in their offices behind closed doors. I think that's great, too . . . But . . . it needs to come to an arena where it can be responded to and dealt with." The culture of communication that is shaped by leadership gives permission for the level of challenge and feedback that will be accepted and also a message about the leader's willingness to engage in ethical concerns.

Leaders as Role Models

Leaders are *role models*. The values and beliefs that are modeled are an important activity in establishing ethical culture. One leader noted, "the modeling impact is greater than anything" (Manning, 1990, p. 233). Leaders can teach about ethics through their own example. Friedman (1990, p. 111) makes the point that "other people's ethical beliefs and standards cannot be controlled, regulated, legislated, or managed . . . many people don't even like to be rubbed the right way." Ordering people to be ethical will not work. Instead, leaders must think about how they send the invitation. The manner with which leaders treat employees and consumers, respond to concerns, and develop an atmosphere of trust will send a message to others about what is valued. Leaders will have to act directly to prevent unethical behavior. However, to accentuate the ethical behavior of constituents, an atmosphere that supports and rewards such behavior is necessary.

The leader can model permission for constituents to *participate in the ethical decision process*. That can include the permission to comment on the leader's behavior as well as the reverse. A manager (Manning, 1990, p. 234) said, "If they think that I really screwed up, all five of them will be in here . . . and if they screw up all five of us will go to them too." An atmosphere of participation allows for employees to participate in the decisions that affect them and to *take risks* and *make mistakes*. For example, "part of setting the tone . . . is openness; for people to make mistakes but to learn from those mistakes . . . setting an environment where people are not afraid to take risks or to ask about decisions they may need to make . . . but yet make their own decisions" (Manning, 1990, p. 234).

Leaders and constituents can model ethical behavior and can also *provide mentoring* to each other (Manning, 1990). Ethical behavior is enacted through a process and is not a "pat solution . . . Ethics simply establish a moral framework for decision making by providing guidance, clarification, and insight" (Friedman, 1990, p. 111). An organizational culture that promotes seeking advice and consultation is supporting all constituents in the development of ethical skills and understanding. A leader in mental health (Manning, 1999, p. 234) described his experience:

> That whole modeling issue . . . it's true for most of us, it's less what we've read and more what we've experienced in some fashion. The people who have been most important in my life have been the people who I could count on in terms of consistency and . . . honesty . . . fairness and equity, and the other kinds of values that I feel are real important.

Leaders reported the importance of *being present* and *visible* with an *open door policy*. In addition, the ethical treatment of constituents was related as a primary method of establishing an ethical climate: "It is easy to be unethical yourself when you're treated unethically. I treat people ethically. My team leaders see I'll do it [the right thing] and they say, 'OK, now I can do it.' So you empower people with ethics" (Manning, 1990, p. 236).

Leaders as role models convey messages about how to be in all of their daily activities, decisions, and behaviors. In order to change organizational culture, leaders must consider the "complex interplay of formal and informal systems" that support either ethical or unethical behavior (Sims, 2000, p. 66).

Leader Activities that Shape Culture

Several primary mechanisms assist leaders in thinking about how culture is shaped, based on their decisions and behaviors (Friedman, 1990; Manning, 1990; Schein, 1985; Sims, 2000). These mechanisms emphasize institutional as well as individual processes.

What leaders pay attention to, including what they ask about, measure, praise, or criticize, have an influence on the ethical nature of culture. Attention is what the leader emphasizes to employees that they should concentrate on, which communicates the leader's and the organization's values. "When things go wrong, you can't turn a blind eye. Leadership must enforce values . . . I don't just mean compliance with the law. I also mean issues of diversity, the treatment of women . . ." (Sims, 2000, p. 68).

How leaders react to crisis, especially how responsibility is apportioned and what they seek to preserve, provides constituents with a view of what is valued by leaders through their emotionality, which brings values to the surface. In response to the Salomon scandal in business, acting CEO Buffet provided full disclosure of the firm's wrongdoing. He sent a directive to employees that asked them to evaluate any of their actions by considering if they would be willing to see it described on the front page of the local paper and read by "spouse, children and friends." He said, "We simply want no part of any activities that pass legal tests but that we as citizens, would find offensive" (Sims, 2000, p. 69).

How the leader behaves as a role model, exemplifying certain values in speech and actions and demonstrating such qualities as empathy, loyalty, and self-sacrifice is the third mechanism. Refer to the discussion, "Leaders as Role Models," about role modeling for the numerous examples of values that are communicated through leader behavior.

Whom the leader chooses to reward, recognize, or promote, and especially what characteristics or behaviors seemed to elicit those rewards is the fourth mechanism. The leader's allocation of rewards communicates to constituents what is desired and necessary to succeed in the organization. A manager (describing who would be promoted in a mental health center) said, "The one who makes the least noise or creates the least problems . . . if you're in that position, then you have to act unethically at times" (Manning, 1990, p. 238). In this organization the leadership promoted a value of compliance rather than feedback.

The last mechanism involves *whom the leader hires and fires*, which provides tangible evidence of the skill and attitudes that are valued and expected to contribute to the success of the organization. The choice of hiring ambitious, aggressive people who will do anything to achieve success, at the cost of harming others, conveys a different message than hiring fair, prudent managers who demonstrate ethical integrity. Similarly, disciplining those who violate ethical standards and firing individuals who have acted grossly unethical or who cannot participate voluntarily in an ethical climate is a message.

Stretch the Boundaries of Moral Responsibility

It is easy for leaders to focus on the ethical events that stand out, the isolated incidents involving employees, clients, or organizational issues. However, it is "what we don't see and don't do" that can be just as "ethically problematic" (Friedman, 1990, p. 111). Leaders have to *stretch the boundaries of moral responsibility* in order to think about the populations not served, the needed services that are not delivered, and the funds not available. Friedman (1990, p. 111) argues that, "there is no ethical difference between crimes of omission and crimes of commission. What we do not notice can be just as ethically questionable as what we do notice and act on." Both *omission* and *commission* reinforce values and norms to the constituents of the organization.

Leaders also convey messages about *the scope and breadth of ethical responsibility.* "We are responsible for both identified and statistical lives" (Friedman, 1990, p. 112). It is a common occurrence that those who are invisible are not retained in the awareness of leader's conscious agendas. Thus, it is easy to neglect the unnamed. Rather than only directing energies toward services that are currently covered and available, leaders must take the time to pursue coverage, funding, and support for programs, services, and coverages that are not available. The mental health system is an example of a system that no longer has a safety net for the uninsured and the working poor. Only those with health insurance, Medicaid/Medicare, and/or the ability to pay for services have access, yet the philosophical and ethical foundation of community mental health services is access for all that need mental health, within the community where they live. Friedman poignantly notes (1990, p. 212), "Statistical lives are not less valuable because we have not put names to them; after all, each of us is only a statistic to most of the world." A consciousness about statistical lives motivates political action and advocacy in collaboration with other leaders in the field.

A related leadership behavior is to have an awareness of and be *"the voice"* for the *"voiceless and unseen"* in the organization (Friedman, 1990, p. 212). Employees, who have the least status and the lowest positions are often without power or participation in decisions that impact their well-being. Friedman makes the point that everyone in an organization, from janitors to security guards, from finance and medical records to maintenance, is also a provider to clients. The powerful mechanism of parallel process is relevant here. How employees, especially those with the least power, are treated, will make a difference in how they behave with clients. Leaders have the ability to deepen values about respect and fairness and compassion and equality through their ethical treatment of those who are traditionally unseen. These leader behaviors take place within the context of a particular role. Thinking about the opportunities that exist within role is also important to shaping culture.

Leadership Role Activities and Relationship to Culture

The leader's role, as envisioned in transformational leadership, is uniquely integrated with the necessary aspects for building ethical cultures. Leaders are responsible for particular role activities in regard to shaping culture (see Figure 10.2). Paine (1997) suggests four aspects of the leader's role that help to develop and maintain culture: developing an ethical framework, aligning the organization, leading by example, and addressing external challenges.

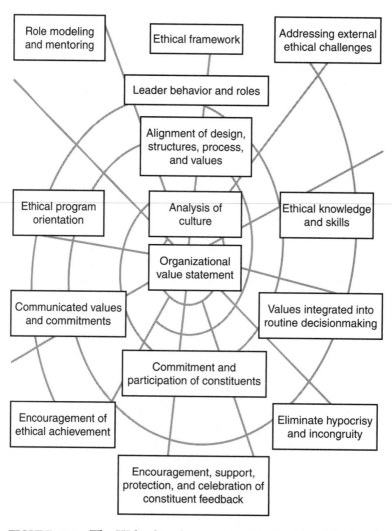

FIGURE 10.2   The Web of Understanding: The Building Blocks of Ethical Culture

Building Ethical Frameworks

First, leaders must develop an *ethical framework*. The framework is similar to a compass; it is used to *guide* "planning, decision making, and the assessment of performance" (Sims, 2000, p. 76). The ethical framework includes the organization's mission, value statement, and ethical code. It also includes the leader's moral vision discussed earlier (see Chapters 3 and 5). The moral vision is the leader's commitment to a moral future that can be enacted through the mission and purpose(s) of the organization. Contributions to the common good, the environment, the well-being of oppressed populations, sustainability, and so forth are large order examples of moral vision. However, moral vision also includes the moral commitments connected directly to the agency mission. A final component of the ethical framework has to be the moral identity of the leader (discussed in Chapter 5) that provides the moral commitment of the leader; the motivation to commit to "I want" and "I will" behavior, rather than just "I think" or "I wish." The ethical framework communicates to other stakeholders the organization's ethical stance.

Alignment of the Organization

Second, leaders must *align the organization* by attending to organizational design, structures, and processes (for example, com-munication, authority, supervision, performance evaluation, resource allocation, planning and goal setting, and policy and procedures), according to the values and ethical framework of the organization (discussed further in this chapter). Leaders are responsible for establishing, monitoring, and maintaining congruence between the ethical framework and the organizational structures and processes. Policies must create an ethical workplace where people perceive a general sense of fairness; equal treatment, equal application of policy, and equitability are key issues (McClenahen, 1999). Transformational leaders will develop participatory structures that include representatives from all constituencies to help in maintaining the alignment process.

For example, a value of equal opportunity would not only be identified, but would be integrated into personnel policies and procedures, the hiring and promotion process, and decisions and actions. An institution of higher education was recently offered a gift of membership to a men's-only golf club for students to use for practice. Women students would not be able to practice there. Acceptance of the gift is incongruent with the goals and policies of the institution. The leaders were ethically obligated to refuse the gift or to ask that both men and women be allowed to play there. The gift offered a substantial material resource but would have been contradictory to the ethical culture. The leadership, after hearing from multiple voices (faculty and staff) refused the offer of the golf club membership.

An important component of aligning the organization is a long-term strategic and ethical plan to continue to create and maintain an ethical culture (Sims, 2000). The planning process is an opportunity to identify the strengths and deficits of the organization and the opportunities and constraints (internal and external) that impede ethical behavior and activities. Formal goals and objectives can be devised and measured as a way to institutionalize ethics into the routine functions of the organization. Training programs and staff development activities for leaders and constituents that focus on ethical reasoning and decisionmaking can be formalized in the planning process. Budget resources can be allocated and persons accountable to carry the activities through to fruition can be assigned. Resources should be spent where there will be the best outcome, that is, where the effect is based on the constituents' feelings about and understanding of ethics (for example, retreats to develop values consensus rather than the development of rules and requirements) (McClenahen, 1999).

Leading by Example

Leading by example is the third aspect for leaders. The organization's ethical starting point is "most powerfully defined through the behavior of [those] invested with great authority. Their behavior sends a message clearer than any in a corporate ethics statement. Leaders must walk the talk, practice what they preach, live out what they say (McClenahen, 1999, p. 76). As was discussed earlier in regard to leader activities, pp. 215–222, the leader's behavior is critical to the messages that are communicated about what to value, what is valued, and what will be rewarded and reinforced.

Address External Ethical Challenges

The fourth aspect is the leader's role in *addressing the external ethical challenges* that are inherent in human service delivery systems and environments. These challenges pose conflicts and impediments to employee behavior. Many examples have been discussed in relation to the force of revenue generation and cost efficiency, the privatization movement and the attacks on quality of services, and the lack of access to basic and necessary services for stigmatized and oppressed populations, to name just a few. Confronting the ethical challenges imposed by the external environment takes courage. Friedman (1990, p. 113) argues that embracing ethics requires taking risks. "Risk-taking behavior means going against the odds." The leader's willingness to address these external challenges in human services plays an important role in organizational culture. One of the greatest risks, according to Friedman (1990, p. 113), ". . . is the poisoning of the culture in which one works, of which we want to be proud. An ethical corporate culture cannot rest on cowardice."

The ideal of organizational culture, then, is one that rests on integrity of leaders and constituents. The lens that provides the focus on how ethics are imbued to members makes a difference in how they are received and used. As leaders move from their own roles and behaviors to a focus on the organization, an ethical program orientation must be considered.

Program Orientations for Ethical Cultures

There are two schools of thought in relation to ethical program orientations: compliance-based programs and value-based programs. The climate of an organization, based on a foundation of collective values, has been identified as a more important factor in determining ethical behavior than structures and strategies. Written codes, ethical compliance hotlines, and ethics programs that emphasize rules, legal compliance, control, and discipline can provide some positive guidance, but are not as effective as climate (McClenahen, 1999; Paine, 1994; Weaver & Trevino, 1999). Organizations that emphasize values, counseling, and responsible conduct are more likely to have lasting impact than compliance-based programs (Paine, 1994).

Compliance Programs

A compliance program does help to define expectations, but they are imposed from outside the employee and present a top-down imposition (Weaver & Trevino, 1999). These programs are oriented toward rule compliance achieved through coercion and punishment. Standards and rules are written in terms of legal compliance, and communication with employees is in regard to learning the rules. There may be orientations or seminars to teach employees the proscribed rules and/or the organization's ethical code. The focus would be information dissemination rather than critical discussion and evaluation. This approach does little to generate "moral imagination or commitment," rather it promotes a more "minimalist" motivation of "don't get caught" (Paine, 1994, p. 1).

Value-Based Programs

A value-based program influences employees by encouraging the development of meaningful, shared ethical values and emphasizing activities that help employees in decisionmaking through advice, support, and consensus. This program assumes that employees want to be ethical and are committed to ethical behavior. The values orientation makes awareness of ethical issues an in-role behavior and helps to reduce the tendency of employees to develop moral muteness, in which they choose to remain silent about ethical issues and challenges. An additional strength of the values orientation is that it supports the aspirations of employees so that the organization "embodies a collective commitment that applies equally to all persons" (Weaver & Trevino, 1999, p. 4). The collective commitment reflects the shared interests and collective vision promoted through the transformational leadership paradigm (discussed in Chapter 3).

The values orientation is most congruent with human service organizations. It is also directly related to the metaphors of re-weaving and restoring using relationship and organizational learning for repair of a nonexistent or ineffective ethical climate. Finally, the values orientation relies on dialogue and feedback to develop and sustain a foundation of ethics.

A values program is a step toward cultivating the habit of ethical behavior for leaders and employees, based on a clear understanding of what is required ethically in performing tasks and providing services. The institutionalized values of the organization become internalized to each member, integrating with personal and professional values. The result is what Aristotle argued. "We are what we repeatedly do."

Member's behavior in regard to ethics becomes more a matter of habit, rather than an isolated act (Kelly, 2000).

The tools that work best in reducing unethical conduct—being consistent in policy and actions, rewarding ethical conduct, treating employees fairly, and providing leadership—are part of establishing an ethical climate. Ethicists in business have emphasized the results of research that promote the adage "actions speak louder than words" (McClenahen, 1999). One trainer stated, ". . . We have learned to minimize . . . walking people through some booklet and the policies in detail . . . It's what people are thinking that you have to get behind and try to understand, because perceptions are reality when it comes to a lot of this [ethical or unethical] conduct" (McClenahen, 1999, p. 2).

The first step in shaping the values orientation is to analyze the current organizational culture in relation to values and beliefs. The process of shaping culture rests on an assessment of the meaning of the current culture—or the groundwork for enactment. Therefore, it is important to analyze organizational culture as a prerequisite to change. Metaphor is a useful tool for analysis (Morgan, 1997).

Analysis of Culture: The Metaphor

Organizations have shared systems of values and beliefs that take on the form of identity (Ritchie, 1988). This identity becomes a symbol of meaning that is important to leaders and constituents. People in human service organizations are most often there because of the meaning they attach to the purpose or mission of the organization. The values that are actualized through the work of the organization, then, are equally meaningful. The organization has the opportunity to "unite its work force around a strong set of ethical values," which are incorporated through the culture (Ritchie, 1988, p. 178).

Metaphor is a useful tool to learn to read an organization in respect to climate and culture. The nature of a metaphor is that it has a capacity to organize complex information and also to help identify the different dimensions of a situation (Morgan, 1997). Metaphors can be a method of analysis and can also provide direction for shaping the ethical climate; "metaphors create ways of seeing and shaping organizational life" (Morgan, 1997, p. 349). Using metaphors to describe or capture the characteristics, norms, values, and so forth of the organization that are significant to ethical climate provides important information about where people are and where they would like to go. For example, the metaphor of education may describe an organizational commitment to lifelong learning. "Life is a learning experience" (Ritchie, 1988, p. 179). Values in this organization would probably include the importance of reflecting, learning new knowledge, developing strategies like double-loop learning, and continuing education for all constituents. The metaphor of music promotes such values as ". . . harmony, balance, rhythm" and the importance of "inspiration and passion" being a part of organizational life (Ritchie, 1988, p. 179). Leadership, through this metaphor, could be similar to the conductor, leading from the front with a great deal of direction, or a jazz leader, who leads from within the group, encouraging participation, creativity, and innovation.

The use of metaphor can provide the following kinds of information (Morgan, 1997):

- Help understand the symbolic significance of organizational life
- Provide a new focus and an avenue for the creation of organized action to shape culture
- Determine how reality in the organization is defined by constituents
- Learn about situations from different standpoints
- Follow a powerful image to its logical conclusion (for example, Morgan's (1997) metaphors of organization as machine, as brain, or as prison)
- Provide images that are theories or conceptual frameworks for the organization

Leaders who learn to read the situation from different points of view have an advantage over those committed to a fixed position (Morgan, 1997).

Different lens or perspectives identify limitations of a given perspective, how the situation and problems can be framed and reframed in different ways, and the possibility of new solutions. From this perspective, leaders and constituents can apply different metaphors to the organizational culture to accentuate what exists, what is missing, and what would strengthen the ethical climate. For example, managers and administrators developed metaphors or analogies to describe the ethical culture in their organization (Manning, 1990). The metaphors included examples such as "dream into nightmare"; "blind people touching an elephant"; "Russian roulette"; "the noose and the guillotine." These metaphors can be used to unravel multiple patterns of significance and the interrelationship among those patterns (Morgan, 1997). For instance, the Russian roulette metaphor captures the experience of a leader who never knew when punishment would ensue in response to an ethical dilemma. Patterns of power and authority, communication, nature of supervisory relationship, and so forth could be explored in relation to this metaphor for an organization.

A simple exercise to elicit metaphors from any individual or group that can help uncover the ethical climate is to ask each individual to create a metaphor in reaction to one or both of the following statements (Twinam, 1990):

- Making an ethical decision in my organization is (or is like)
- Working with moral and ethical issues in our agency is (or is like)

Write the metaphors on a blackboard or flipchart board and ask each person to interpret the metaphor in relation to ethical climate. Look for common themes that help elucidate characteristics of the climate. Use the discussion as a starting point for reviewing and shaping the climate for ethical decisionmaking. Shaping the climate, however, must start with the identification of core values to guide the organization in decisionmaking.

Values for an Ethical Culture

The heart of any organization, and particularly human service organizations, is values (Zdenek, 2002). The adopted values are the explicit meanings and principles that the organization is trying to achieve. The articulated values of an organization lead to shared meanings, referred to as emergent understandings, that are constructed by the members of a group as they interact together (Schein, 1985). These meanings should be congruent with the mission and should reflect "a consensus of the ethical culture" of the organization as a whole (CANPO, 1994). Values, then, can be useful in building an ethical culture in an organization. A values statement for the organization can be described as the organization's "manifesto." A code of ethics for the organization can then be developed that puts those values into action.

The values statement must reflect a consensus of the different groups who make up the organization—administrators, employees, board members, consumers, and volunteers (CANPO, 1994). This creates an opportunity for all stakeholders to explore differences, find common understandings, and celebrate a renewed commitment to the mission. Therefore, participation of as many members as possible is important. "The greater the participation in their formulation, the greater the emotional investment and sense of ownership by the organization's stakeholders" (CANPO, 1994, p. 4). Similar to the mission, the values statement should articulate the essence of the organization that the leader(s) wants to develop and nurture.

Developing a Values Statement

The steps for developing a values statement are similar to any major planning activity. First, *decide who should be involved*. Leadership, board members, and at least representatives of all stakeholder groups are important in order to contribute different perspectives to the process. Because a major challenge that human service organizations face is the "growing diversity of society," the participation of members who represent gender, race/ethnicity, language, special interest groups, and so forth will strengthen the overall result (Zdenek, 2002, p. 5). The organization's ability to serve diverse communities is based on finding a base of shared values and assumptions that are relevant and responsive to diverse constituencies.

Establish a timeline and a process for members to interact together about the different value perspectives. Develop a plan for the facilitation of the process, which could include the use of an outside consultant (particularly important for equal participation of all members and in regard to handling conflicts). The dialogue that ensues "opens the space for multiple realities and perspectives" (Allen, 1993). Based on the constructivist approach, the commitment to dialogue is based on the assumption that every person's reality is valid. The dialogue of a value statement activity helps to bring forward "subjugated knowledge . . . the untold stories and ways of thinking and being that have never been admitted to the mainstream conversation" (Allen, 1993, p. 38). This approach is respectful of diversity and provides an avenue for different perspectives, which is important to shaping an ethical culture that is inclusive of all groups.

This kind of process will involve a *commitment of time*. The format could range from a day-long meeting with everyone represented to several short meetings among stakeholder groups, with representatives bringing the results to a larger meeting. Prepare members for the meeting process (CANPO, 1994): (a) supply each with a mission statement and any previous value statements, (b) ask each participant to think about their own personal values as well as organizational values, and (c) encourage all participants to bring any materials to the meeting they believe would be useful (for example, articles, other organizations' value statements, and so forth). CANPO suggests providing a questionnaire to be prepared ahead of time that asks the following questions:

- What principles/qualities do you hold in regard within the organization?
- How are these values reflected or acted on in our organization?
- How do these values reflect or conflict with your personal values?

Allen (2002) has some other perspectives that may also be useful:

- What core values might inspire collective action?
- What differences exist in the ways subgroups view organizational values?
- What norms or values stand in the way of, or support, the mission?

The answers to these questions can be the start of developing lists of common values. The emphasis should be on consensus of the values to be included. Areas of disagreement can be used as the identification of underlying difficulties to be addressed.

The following questions can be useful in clarifying which values should be included in a values statement (CANPO, 1994, pp. 6, 7):

- What values motivated formulation of the mission in the first place?
- What values must be prominent in society for the mission to succeed? What are the values of the ideal society toward which the organization is making a contribution?
- What values important to the nonprofit (public or private?) sector ought to be included in the values statement (for example, community, diversity, tolerance, efficiency, and so forth)?
- What values ought to guide the personal conduct and day-to-day operation of the organization?
- What other values (for example, ecological, social, or spiritual) should the organization respect?

The final step is formulating the statement. A person or small group that develops a draft to bring back to the large group can facilitate this. The final statement should be short (one to three pages), and forceful. Sentences using active verbs such as "We value honesty" are powerful for people internal to the organization and those in the community. The values statement should be congruent with the work of the organization, rather than a generalized listing of values that are important, but not relevant. An important evaluative tool is to consider the statement's future orientation.

Could the values statement outlive the individuals who wrote it? Always return to the mission to work with drafting problems or difficulties. The group can assess the first draft by considering the following questions (CANPO, 1994, p. 8):

- Do we believe in this statement?
- What if only some believe in this statement?
- How will we ensure that our values are acted upon?
- What do we do if our actions are incongruent with our values?

It is the last two questions that lead to the development of a code of ethics for the organization (discussed in Chapter 11, see also Appendix A).

The process of developing a values statement is a concrete example of reweaving and restoring the ethical climate of an organization. Relationships are developed that did not exist previously, and the identification of common values as well as differences in values leads to a consensus of values that restores the ethical climate. The organization learns from itself based on the contributions of leaders and constituents. A consensus of values is the foundation for culture change. The role of all constituents in the socialization of an organization's members is crucial to the success of organizational integrity.

Cultures Based on Integrity

An ethical culture based on integrity is indispensable to human service organizations because, as Friedman (1990, p. 18) argues in this way:

> . . . they are held to a higher standard. Much more is expected of them . . . From people who hold other people's lives in their hands, the public expects a whole lot . . . only by fulfilling the public's expectations of proper ethical behavior can such organizations retain the unique privileges society has given them. Thus ethical management is good management, and ethical corporate culture is a good corporate culture–and both are critical to the provider's survival.

The elements of an ethical culture that build integrity are also the responsibility of all stakeholders, not just leaders. Integrity helps to promote the integration of the organization and to provide a sense of balance for constituents and leaders. The following elements are tools that contribute to the shaping, monitoring, and evaluation of ethical cultures (see Figure 10.2, p. 220).

Sensible, clearly communicated values and commitments that articulate the obligations of the organization to external stakeholders (funders, other organizations, consumer groups, advocacy groups, or political entities) are the organization's message to the outside world (Paine, 1994). Based on the values-statement process, all constituents are aware of, and are committed to, the vision they developed.

Values are part of the routine decisionmaking process and are factored into every important organizational activity (Paine, 1994). Ethics and values are considered as an integral part of the management systems of planning, goal setting, budgeting, sharing and disseminating of information, evaluating, and so forth. Thus the values are *embedded values* (de Vries, 1988). Constituents consider the values as they make decisions and carry out the tasks of human service delivery.

However, people can only be fully congruent with the structures of embedded values when they are encouraged to "reflect on and evaluate those values at the same time. Otherwise those values are mere habits and prejudices" (de Vries, 1988, p. 141). Therefore, the other needed ingredient is *embedded reflection*. Embedded reflection becomes part of the learning activities for all members as they consider, discuss, and disagree about the nature of the embedded values. Embedded reflection must be cultivated and nurtured as part of the ethical climate.

Systems and structures support and reinforce organizational commitments (Paine, 1994). The design and process of the organization is used to pursue the ethical commitments identified in the ethical framework. If participation is valued, structures that formally provide for participation from employees, consumers, and community citizens reflect that value (see Chapter 11). If feedback is encouraged and desired, policies and structures that encourage and reward feedback are evident. Values, such as diversity, equal opportunity, and so forth, are clearly identifiable through policies that articulate hiring and promotion practices and in the objective data about the demographics of the workplace.

Leaders and constituents in the organization have the knowledge and skills they need to make ethical decisions (Paine, 1994). Ethics is not considered a by-the-seat-of-your-pants activity. The organization invests in the education necessary for all members to be ethical and to know when they need consultation and advice; education is for "the process of moving from cocksure ignorance to thoughtful uncertainty" (Friedman, 1990, p. 20). The commitment of leadership to ethics training and learning will be reflected in the budget as well as in activities.

All *constituents who bring forward ethical issues, concerns, and challenges are encouraged, protected, and responded to* (Friedman, 1990; Manning, 1990). Feedback is celebrated. As argued throughout this chapter, ethical culture rests on the opportunity and support for issues to be discussed, debated, and resolved openly. People must perceive permission, but also be openly rewarded for taking the risks to be in loyal opposition.

The organization *encourages ethical achievement rather than avoidance of ethical failure* (Friedman, 1990). Members are acknowledged for thinking about ethics, initiating ethical practices, commenting on moral issues to be considered, and so forth. Organizational assessment is not just focused on ethical wrongs, but also ethical rights. The practices and policies that may be unethical are not ignored, but are not the only focus.

The organization *avoids hypocrisy and incongruity between mission and policy and between stated values and behavior* (Friedman, 1990; Manning, 1990). The statement of mission is factual and true. The description of services to others through marketing and public relations efforts are accurate and do not mislead or misrepresent. Friedman (1990, p. 19) also notes that "it is not healthy to have two standards: one for how patients are treated and another for how employees are treated."

Maintaining a culture that has integrity means being on the lookout for warning signs that may be putting an organization at ethical risk. Cooke (1991) has suggested several points to consider as early warning signs. They include a short-term revenue emphasis, arbitrary performance-appraisal standards, and internal environments that discourage ethical behavior and ethical problems being brought forward to experts and leaders. For-profit organizations need to be alert to the red flag of making the shareholder's wealth the primary priority over and above ethical concerns.

Conclusion

Shaping ethical cultures begins with leadership and the messages conveyed through leader behavior. Leaders set the tone. The ethical framework that guides the transformational leaders is enacted through their roles and responsibilities; they have an ongoing opportunity to cocreate ethical culture with constituents. The constituents of the organization, through the development of a values statement and value orientation, can *reweave* the moral and ethical messages that underlie all processes at work. Establishing organizational integrity through "connecting the organization more to itself" through relationships and dialogue provides the opportunity to repair the ethical failures and to promote a culture of feedback. Aligning the values of the organization with the structures and processes and then continuously evaluating the congruence between mission, policy, structures, values, behavior, and decisions provides the compass to stay on course. The following chapter will focus on tools and strategies through the architecture of the organization to promote congruence with the ethical cultures that develop.

QUESTIONS AND APPLICATIONS

1. Analyze the ethical culture in your agency (if possible with other constituents) by completing the following statement with a metaphor or analogy: Working in my (our) organization is (or is like) . . . Then, answer the following questions:

   ■ What characteristics or attributes of organizational culture are evident in the metaphor(s)?
   ■ What values in the organization are conveyed through metaphor(s)?
   ■ If you were having a conversation with the situation conveyed through the metaphor, how could it be understood from other vantage points, roles, or hierarchical levels?
   ■ What values are missing? What values would the group want to create?

2. Reflect on your ethical framework as a leader. What is your moral vision? What ethical future do you envision for the work of the organization? Develop a one-page essay that describes your ethical framework.

3. Analyze the ethical culture and climate of your organization based on values, program orientation, and the elements of organizational integrity. What would you recommend based on your analysis?

11 The Feedback Loop: Leaders as Architects of Ethical Organizations

THE FOCUS IN THIS CHAPTER IS ON THE FOLLOWING AREAS:

- Leaders as architects of ethical organizations
- The role of structure in organizational design
- Participation as the change strategy
- Feedback loops: self-regulation and information nets
- Introduction of moral premises: codes of ethics, professional standards, and ethics advisory boards and committees
- Ethical oversight: governance ethics, ethics audits

Ethical leadership is intertwined with ethical organizations. That is to say, the organization is the repository of leaders and constituents and their purposes, actions, decisions, and moral agency. The previous chapter discussed the role of culture, the powerful shaping influence that exists through culture, and its relationship to ethical leadership. The purpose of this chapter is to concentrate on leaders as ". . . architects of responsible institutions . . . through the powerful sources of influence available to them" (Goodpaster, 1983, p. 20). Leaders can build an organizational design that helps promote and facilitate ethical actions, policies, and practices. Their sources of influence include planning and goal setting, modifying and creating structures of participation and feedback, introducing measurement and self-regulating mechanisms, and introducing moral premises into the organization through various structures and strategies.

However, "few acts of leadership have a more enduring impact on an organization than building a foundation of purpose and core values" (Senge, 1990, p. 10). Therefore, organizational design is not just about drawing the organizational chart.

The fundamental task is ". . . designing the governing ideas of purpose, vision, and core values by which people will live" (Senge, 1990, p. 10). Design reflects what is implied—the fundamental assumptions that are communicated by the lines and boxes and the vertical, horizontal, and circular relationships of the organizational chart. Further, though lines and boxes show the graphic representation of design, the social architecture is "rarely visible"; the functions "take place behind the scenes" (Senge, 1990, p. 10).

The structure of an organization provides the form to accomplish the organization's purpose. In this case, it is the moral and ethical purpose that is promoted through a moral vision and the transformation of the organization toward higher ethical practices. For leaders to use structure effectively to facilitate a moral vision, they must develop two complementary aspects: the ability to see into the moral future (the leader's and organization's moral vision) and the ability to see into and know the current organization's structure and functioning (Shandler, 1986). Understanding the current structure, which can be murky and muddled, provides the leader with the information necessary to modify and/or create new structures that are more conducive to accomplishing the moral purpose. The purpose of this chapter is to (a) stimulate the thinking of leaders about current and new structures that accentuate constituents' collaboration and ownership of the organization's ethical performance, (b) introduce moral premises for decisionmaking through design, and (c) develop moral and ethical oversight using the structures of the organization. The role of feedback and participation are central themes, connecting the organization's current functioning to the desired future. Before looking at designing new structures, the nature of organizational design will be discussed briefly.

The Nature of Structure and Organizational Design

The structure of an organization refers to the formal organizational design; the form provides a way for the organization to operate. The design typically includes the organization chart, standard operating procedures, and job descriptions that correlate with the chart (Connors, 1988). In addition, goals, policies and procedures add to the structure of an organization (Shandler, 1986). The design is based on underlying assumptions, principles, and values that predicate how authority, communication, and decisions will take place. For example, values of empowerment, participation, and entrepreneurial activity may be reflected in an organic design, whereas values of rational law, formal procedures and rules, and hierarchical authority would typically be promoted through a bureaucracy. The processes and form should be congruent with the ideology of the organization. The construction of both is a conscious political act (Alter, 1997). The mission and purpose of an organization, combined with the identified values (for example, values statement) provide the ideology. Particular designs are more effective in interaction with particular environments. Bureaucratic designs are organized to operate within very stable, predictable environments. Organic networks are organized for flexibility and change in relation to turbulent, chaotic environments.

The form of an organization typically follows function (Nanus & Dobbs, 1999). The design is developed and elaborated to support the functions necessary to meet the organizational purpose and goals. Human service agencies usually organize themselves around the delivery of services that are necessary to meet the mission of the agency. The type of service (for example, inpatient or outpatient), client populations (children, adults, and so forth), substantive area (child protection or social welfare) or geographic location where services are delivered (East office, West office, and so forth) are examples.

Functions of Structure

Structure emphasizes particular functions that are necessary to accomplish the mission and goals of the agency. For purposes of this discussion, the functions are described according to their relevance to addressing moral and ethical challenges. Each of the functions corresponds with opportunities to revise or create new structures that promote or support ethical actions and reflection. The following sections describe critical functions that help the agency do its work.

The Division and Distribution of Authority.   Authority provides particular individuals with the legitimate power and means to take responsibility for particular areas of work and the work of others. Authority carries with it the accountability for the results. Authority can be distributed through a hierarchical arrangement in the structure, such as in a bureaucracy, or through the delegation of authority horizontally to particular individuals or groups, as in an organic network. As mentioned in Chapter 4 in regard to power, the use and abuse of power is at the heart of ethics and leadership. Structures that empower constituents and that distribute decision power increase the transformational potential of leadership.

The Division and Distribution of Work.   Organizations must provide a way to divide and accomplish the work. This is called departmentation. The organization is divided, usually through centralization or decentralization, into units, departments, teams, and so forth, that provide particular services or tasks that are critical to reaching the goals and mission. It is important to assess if the design of the organization is connected to the goals. A certain amount of centralization is required in order to coordinate tasks and to act as a unified entity. However, decentralization is also required to accomplish the work. In decentralization, the work is often organized around function (for example, medical records), client groups (for example, child/family), geography (for example, South office or North office), or type of service delivery (for example, inpatient, crisis/emergency, and so forth).

The nature of departmentation also has moral effects, such as on the continuity and quality of care that consumers receive (refer to Chapter 8). Human service agencies that have emphasized specialization may have fragmented systems of care for those individuals who need access from one specialization to another (Rhodes, 1986). In addition, departmentation can either facilitate or obstruct the relationships and interaction among employees about issues of ethics.

Formal Lines of Communication.   The design structures the formal lines of communication, both vertically and horizontally. The formal lines of communication provide the route whereby information that is necessary to particular individuals or groups is conveyed through appropriate channels. The information can be conveyed through rigid, formalized procedures and processes or can be more expansive, spontaneous, and interactive, depending on the particular design, and underlying assumptions of what the design should accomplish. Informal communication happens in any organization apart from the formal lines established in the design and does not follow any prescribed pattern. Both formal and informal communication processes are critical in regard to ethics. As discussed in Chapter 10, the message that is conveyed about how we do things here flows through both formal and informal channels. However, as was emphasized in the discussion about implicit messages in Chapter 9, the informal channels of communication carry some of the most powerful and influential messages (Manning, 1990).

Decision Processes.   Decisions are connected to the distribution of authority. Organizations can keep the decision processes within hierarchical areas of influence, whereby decisions often have to be "delegated upward for action" (Morgan, 1989, p. 65). In contrast, organizations that want to create innovative, entrepreneurial activity delegate decisionmaking to the individual(s) who are most familiar or most knowledgeable about the issue. Decision processes are opportunities to introduce a consideration of the moral premises of decisions. Leaders at all levels can make discussions about moral and ethical implications a matter of routine. In this way, the moral and ethical impacts of a decision are explored and a norm of considering moral issues routinely is reinforced and institutionalized.

The access to decisionmaking in regard to ethical issues is of paramount concern. Those with the most authority sometimes have the least information about the issue. Employees with less decision power sometimes have a unique contribution to understanding the nature of the ethical issue. The structure of the decisionmaking system must accommodate for the differences in perspective, different levels of ethical knowledge and skills, and different levels of awareness of ethical issues. Thus, the structure must allow for some inclusion of all perspectives relevant to the dilemma for the best ethical reasoning process.

Design Issues that Go Beyond Function

Beyond the standard organization of authority, communication, and departmentation, the architecture can promote a number of positive processes. Some of these processes also accentuate ethical sensitivity and behavior. The design ideas in the following sections not only improve the functioning of an organization, but also provide the mechanisms for ethical action.

Collegiality, Interdependence, and Teamwork

Nanus and Dobbs (1999) argue that collegiality and teamwork are critical processes that can be influenced by design. The importance of interconnection and the recognition of leaders' and constituents' interdependence on each other in regard to ethics cannot be overstated. Two aspects of work relationships are helpful to consider. First, friendship is inseparable from moral work. Both Socrates and Aristotle argued that true friends, who care about what is best for each other, would want to be reciprocal in providing aid. In addition, people contribute differently and it is the differences that allow for the complementary aid, ". . . each contributing to the other what the other cannot self-supply" (Norton, 1976, p. 57). Structures to encourage teamwork and collaboration reinforce the sense of community with one another that help people care about moral issues.

Collaboration also increases the collective awareness and ownership of ethical problems (as discussed in Chapter 4). Collaboration provides for the diverse strengths and contributions of very different people in the analysis and resolution of complex ethical problems. Structures can be developed easily that facilitate interaction and dialogue in regard to work issues. Team meetings, case conferences, quality circles, and ad hoc and ongoing committees are just a few examples of structures that promote relationship and interdependency.

Designs that Facilitate Integration

Teamwork and collaboration supply the organization with the mechanisms for *integration*; core values, the ethical message, and the culture of the organization are fostered through the interactions of leaders and constituents. Norton (1976) projects Plato's image of ". . . chariot, charioteer, and two contrary-minded horses" as a metaphor for the fragmentation people experience through unconnected roles, competing emotional and psychological abilities, and the conflict of complex choices. The classical Greek philosophers argued that *integration* is the primary challenge to worthwhile living. Thus, the leader in an organization has a primary responsibility to promote opportunities for integration into the design of the organization.

Integration can be facilitated by structures that support opportunities for communication with those in a constituents' immediate work area, across departments or units, and through committees and groups with representatives of all stakeholders in the organization. The structures can be formal, such as various task groups (for example, developing a policy on ethics), freestanding committees (for example, ethics committee), or project groups (for example, development of an ethics award). Informal opportunities for integration could include celebrations and rituals and time and place for informal interaction. These homogeneous and heterogeneous groupings encourage relationship and community building and offer openings for the diverse strengths of the collective to be employed in the identification of ethical issues and the resolution of ethical dilemmas.

Finally, formal policies of the organization (human resource policies and clinical policies) should reinforce the notion of respect for the integration of work life with the other dimensions of life, such as family, interests and hobbies, and civic and religious/spiritual commitments (Norton, 1976). Performance evaluation and supervisory expectations should not reflect an excessive anticipation of overtime hours and overwork at the expense of an employees' balance in life. Similarly, consumers of services have more in their life than treatment, interventions, and services. Attention to conveying respect through policies that enhance the quality of life can be developed through design.

Designs that Invite the Environment into the Organization

Open, flexible, and responsive designs offer opportunities to include the external environment (Nanus & Dobbs, 1999). Leaders that develop linkages and connections with community groups and representatives have an opportunity to position themselves in relation to ethical challenges. Relationships with community help with ethical success in several ways. Community members are often tuned in to potential economic and political factors that can precipitate ethical quandaries (for example, funding cuts, political pressure, and so forth). Their perspectives, as well as their relationships with important constituencies, can provide support. Second, outreach and involvement with the community that the agency serves is an ethical act. The "Africentric value of blending individual and community in one's identity" is an example (Arches, 1997, p. 120). African American and feminist leaders in human services gave examples of outreach to the agency's community in order to serve the well-being of the community. Examples such as hiring community members for staff positions, developing advocacy programs, and having retreat days that include community members resulted in dedicated staff and a high energy level. "If there's one thing that keeps us going, it's our commitment to the agency and the community" (Arches, 1997, p. 121).

The designs of agencies can accommodate different community emphases (Arches, 1997). Bureaucratic designs can build community through recognition of community needs in goal setting, planning, providing space for social interaction with and for the community, and including community representatives in problem solving. Collective models can "structurally include the community through hiring, strategic planning, and community-driven programs. . . ." (Arches, 1997, p. 123). Both types of design can celebrate community through rituals and events that integrate the community with the organization. Any organizational design can include community representatives in developing the organization's values statement and code of ethics and participating in the ethics audit of the organization's ethical performance.

Designs that Emphasize an Ethical Project

The architecture of organizations include the forms for programs and service delivery. This architecture can provide innovative or needed ethical projects, such as developing a unique service system or serving a currently underserved population (Nanus & Dobbs, 1999). Health care systems can identify a particular group that experiences difficulty accessing preventative health care and provide services to that group. For example, women with serious mental illness who do not have insurance coverage could be provided with mammograms. The development of pro bono programs (for example, counseling or case management) as an adjunct service for those without the means to pay for it and who are not covered by public entitlements could be an enactment of the organizations' ethical vision. There are many design possibilities to consider, but more important, designs that enhance the ability of people to create and innovate new designs in response to the changing ethical environment is helpful to leaders and the organization.

The Learning Organization

Learning organizations are where people learn together, based on a fluid flow of information, feedback, and collaboration among employees (Nanus & Dobbs, 1999). Building and sustaining an organization that is attune to ethics and the moral issues of human services require an effort by all members and an effort that is continuous. The ideal of the learning organization provides some helpful strategies. The learning organization is based on the assumption that human beings have an inherent capacity for learning (Senge, 1990). Organizational success is based on *generative* learning, which is creative and requires an ability to see the systems that control events. The ability to discern the underlying systems that are the source of ongoing or consistent unethical practices makes it possible to eliminate the underlying causes. Another assumption is that individuals at all levels of the organization are in the best position to generate learning and will feel a deep satisfaction in doing so. Leaders of learning organizations then "are responsible for *building organizations* where people are continually expanding their capabilities to shape their future," that is, *leaders are responsible for learning* (Senge, 1990, p. 9). The metaphor of the learning organization is useful when considering the structures necessary for ethical actions and behaviors. The following section discusses design tasks for leaders related to the focus on ethical leadership. A framework is introduced for building ethical structures that includes culture, participation, and feedback (See Figure 11.1).

The Governing Ideas

The first design task is to develop the governing ideas of the organization. As discussed in Chapters 9 and 10, the ethical culture (the mission, purpose, vision, and values of the organization) has to be a clear, explicit guide. The culture contains the guiding ideas of the organization, which includes the leader's moral vision that is in concert with the constituents' vision. As argued in the previous chapters, the guiding ideas contain the moral and ethical mandate of the organization. (Refer especially to Chapters 9 and 10.) Some of the structural elements discussed later such as codes of ethics, standards, advisory committees, and ethics audits also contribute to the message about ethics.

Governing Ideas into Real-Life Decisions

The second design task focuses on the policies and procedures that translate the guiding ideas of governance into the real-life decisions (Senge, 1990). Policies are the rules that guide decisions, and policymaking should be a separate activity from decisionmak-

I. Governing Ideas
Mission, Moral vision, and Values Statement

II. From Ideas to Decisions
Policies, Procedures, Standards, and Code of
Ethics

III. Effective Learning Processes
Effective Participation
  Reciprocity between constituents and leaders
  Involvement affects the outcome of decisinos
  Participation and decisions are legitimate actions
  Reciprocal climate of trust, honesty, & confidence
The Feedback Loop
  Freedom of action
  Systems of accountability
  Enhancement of learning
  The information net

IV. Moral Premises into Design
Organizational Code of Ethics
Ethical advisory groups and committees

V. Structures for Ethical Oversight
Ethics of Governance—The Board of Directors
The Ethics Audit

FIGURE 11.1   Framework for Building Ethical Structures

ing. Policies, whether explicit and documented, or implicit and conveyed through the climate, should be congruent with the governing ideas. Policies and strategies cannot be prescriptions when it comes to ethics. Instead, policies should help foster strategic thinking, which is based on developing the insight to understand complexity, always an issue in analyzing and understanding ethical issues. In addition, an underlying assumption of the learning organization is that constituents from all levels be engaged in the policy development process, so *structures of participation* are important (p. 240).

Policies about ethical conduct and practice in organizations can provide many ways to think strategically about moral and ethical issues. The social work code of ethics (NASW, 1996) contains standards for social workers that apply to agency policy (see Appendix C). Also, professional organizations (for example, NASW) distribute standards of care to guide practice. Standards of care serve three purposes for the organization (Jayaratne, Croxton, & Mattison, 1997). These include "an internal monitoring" function for the profession, a "quality control" mechanism for practitioners in the organization, and as criteria that are used in courts in the case of liability or malpractice suits against individuals and the organization (Jayaratne, Croxton, & Mattison, 1997, pp. 187–188). Standards such as conflicts of interest, private conduct, dishonesty, fraud, deception, sexual harassment, solicitation of clients, and so forth are ethical issues that must be addressed through policy (Reamer, 1998). However, a chronic problem for the professions is that standards of care are often outdated and "out of touch with the realities of practice" (Jayaratne, Croxton, &

Mattison, 1997, p. 196). As with codes of ethics (discussed later in this chapter), leaders and constituents in the profession must participate in ongoing revision and development of standards to make them meaningful to guide practice in the organization.

Policies in human services, because they reflect the thinking and guide the behavior of many different work groups and disciplines, have to be developed in a participatory way. Finally, policies are not static, but dynamic. Leaders can design structures for the policymaking process in regard to ethical conduct, but also must create structures for assessing and reshaping policy as the organization is challenged by new ethical and moral dilemmas.

Morgan (1997) argues that most organizations modeled on a bureaucratic design operate in a way that actually obstructs the learning process. The bureaucratic design fragments and isolates the flow of thought and action. People are divided from one another and sometimes experience political systems that provide additional barriers to organizational learning. Employees are not encouraged to challenge or question norms, policies, or actions and are rewarded for their silence. The organization uses single loop learning effectively, but may actually be on the wrong course. What is needed are more effective learning processes.

Effective Learning Processes

The third design responsibility is the design of effective learning processes. To do so means that the leader becomes a teacher (Senge, 1990, p. 11), "not as authoritarian expert whose job it is to teach people the 'correct' view of reality . . ." but by helping oneself and constituents achieve "accurate, insightful, and more empowering views of reality." The teaching role of the leader is directed toward helping others identify the mental models, the assumptions or worldview they carry in their head about how things work. These mental models shape and influence how problems, dilemmas, and ethical challenges are perceived, and how leaders and constituents think about opportunities, alternatives, and eventual choices and actions. Our mental models are mostly silent, so, unless they are identified and made explicit, the validity is impossible to challenge, and it is difficult to develop more "accurate assumptions" (Senge, 1990, p. 12). For example, in human services there is such an emphasis on cost-efficiency and revenue production that employees may have a mental model that money and resources are more important than client well-being. This kind of mental model has a dramatic effect on the awareness and processing of ethical dilemmas.

The activity of creating consciousness about mental models is directed toward restructuring their views of reality through understanding the underlying causes and reshaping the future. Leaders can focus attention on three levels of reality: events, patterns of behavior, and systemic structures (Senge, 1990). Events are the who did what to whom category, that is primarily *reactive*, and focused on a limited view of the ethical problem (for example, a clinician met with a client for only 30 minutes, but filled out paperwork that billed Medicaid for a 60 minute session).

Patterns of behavior are a more useful focus because they provide a more long-term view, with some analysis of the context of the patterns that help with understanding and with a *responsive* stance for change. For example, it is brought to the attention of administration that clinicians across units are routinely billing Medicaid for more time than is spent with client systems. The analysis of system structures is the most powerful because it addresses the underlying causes of behavior and results in efforts that are *generative*, changing the way the system works so patterns of behavior change. The system structure with the previous examples may be an incentive system that rewards employees for the highest number of billable hours or implicit messages from supervisors that push clinicians to increase revenue generation for their unit. Understanding the system structures could promote changes to the system that then eliminates the unethical activities.

Generative changes can be initiated by *double loop learning* (Morgan, 1997, p. 86). Single loop learning is a well-known strategy to keep organizations on track. Scanning the environment, comparing the information to existing norms, and then initiating action make up the loop. Single loop learning is the usual function in organizations and typically relies on the management information system for data. An additional step in that process is added for double loop learning: questioning whether operating norms are appropriate. The structures that promote this evaluation or questioning have to involve the thinking and reasoning of human beings. An ethical learning organization must not only scan the environment, but develop "an ability to question, challenge, and change operating norms and assumptions" (Morgan, 1997, p. 90). For the above example, the incentive system and productivity requirements would be assessed in regard to the potential for unethical practices. As challenges and questions occur, leaders must facilitate a new pattern to emerge, based on the learning that has occurred. Structures of participation are necessary for this process.

Structures for Participation: The Quantum Wave of Potentials

Information and participation remind us again of the world of quantum physics. Wheatley (1999, p. 66) suggests that the focus on objective, hard data and firm numbers in organizations is an avoidance of "coming to terms with the murky, fuzzy world that the observation dilemma exposes," the dilemma of the subjective choice of the observer about what to observe. With social constructions, the choice of what to observe is made through each person's lens that filters and selects based on individual socialization, yet, as Wheatley acknowledges, objective information is necessary. Participation is the key. Participation expands the data, interpretation of the data, and views of the meaning of the data exponentially. This is very helpful when it comes to understanding the ethical implications of complex issues, as Wheatley explains (1999, pp. 66–67):

> Think of organizational data for a metaphoric moment as a quantum wave function, moving through space, rich in potential interpretations. If this wave of potentials meets up with only one observer, it collapses into only one interpretation, responding to the expectations of that particular person. All other potentials disappear from view and are lost by that solo act of observation. This one interpretation is then passed down to others in the organization.

Consider how different it is . . . when data is recognized as a wave, rich in potential interpretations, and completely dependent on observers to evoke different meanings. If such data is free to move, it will meet up with many diverse observers. As each observer interacts with the data, he or she develops their own interpretation. We can expect these interpretations to be different, because people are. Instead of losing so many of the potentials contained in the data, multiple observers elicit multiple and varying responses, giving a genuine richness to the observations. An organization rich with many interpretations develops a wiser sense of what is going on and what needs to be done. Such organizations become more intelligent.

Leaders can design structures and cultures in their organizations that promote this participation and enrich the ethical analysis and reasoning process of themselves and constituents. An example of a design that promotes relationship and participation is the web design.

The Web

The web is an innovative design that builds on the new science of quantum physics and chaos theory (Helgesen, 1990; Wheatley, 1999). Consider the spider and its web metaphor as this design is discussed. The web design is based on the science and art of architecture. The idea is to skillfully relate individual parts of the organization to the greater whole, with the goal of creating a form that is unique to a particular agency in order to exercise a specific set of functions. The web can be an entire organizational structure or an internal web of a larger structure, such as a bureaucracy. The web is both a pattern and a process. The following principles and assumptions guide the creation of a web design:

- The web builds from the center out, in a never-ending process.
- The tools to build it are not coercive or authoritative, but use access and engagement in dialogue instead.
- Both the periphery and the center are interdependent parts of a fabric that strengthen each other and the whole.
- The leader in a web-like structure manifests strength through yielding and augmenting the influence of others (for example, as servant leader).
- Channels of communication permit the various parts of the organization to communicate directly.
- The web transfers expertise to where it is needed; everyone who has access to the system is an expert.
- The web increases decisionmaking capacity to all participants; the direct connections are in disregard of rank or division. Thus, it provides the means to a more humane and participative workplace.

The web design functions as a way to enhance the process of communication in an organization. The following characteristics demonstrate the web as process (Helgesen, 1990; Wheatley, 1999):

- Webs operate by means of open communication across levels.
- Webs blur distinctions between conception and execution. There doesn't have to be a division of labor between thinking and doing.
- Webs create lasting networks that redistribute power in an organization. It links people in unorthodox ways, maintains new links, and provides allies and contacts, diffusing power toward the edges.
- Webs serve as a vehicle for constant reorganization; they are permeable around the edges and make opportunities for what the Japanese call "Kaizen," the process of making continual improvements.
- Webs embrace the world outside the organization. Connections can be made to entities and organizations outside of the boundaries of the organization.
- Webs evolve through trial and error. They are like pattern language in architecture. They evolve piecemeal rather than through a grand scheme and through small decisions rather than large reorganizations.

The web design, or some elements of it, provides rich opportunities for participation. However, participation, to be meaningful from an ethical perspective, must be effective.

Effective Participation

Effective participation does not necessarily happen naturally, for example, if leaders just get out of the way and people participate at will. Ritchie (1988) suggests that certain conditions must exist to facilitate effective participation. These conditions rest on *reciprocity between constituents and leaders*. For example, individuals need relevant skills and information to be effective in their participation. Access to information, the contextual picture, and an understanding of any intervening variables, such as resources, political issues, and so forth must be made available just as it would be to leaders in the organization. There must be assurances that participants will be listened to and their contributions will honestly be considered. That assurance usually happens through experience.

Constituents must trust that their *involvement will really affect the outcome* of decisions. Nothing is more discouraging of participation than being asked for input after a decision is already made, or as a token gesture from leaders, without any expectation that the input will be used. Further, asking for participation when there is not the intent to honor and use it ". . . is more than bad management. They insult, demean, and abuse the members of the organization the leader is supposed to respect . . ." (Ritchie, 1988, pp. 170–171).

Individuals must perceive their *participation and decisionmaking as part of legitimate actions*, that is, there is not a moral, ethical, or legal problem that is hidden from them. They are not being asked to collude in unethical practices through their participation. In this regard, the ability to ask questions and give feedback is critical. As was mentioned earlier in the chapter on culture, many constituents have been asked to participate in unethical actions because of unaware or uninformed superiors or for deliberately wrong ends.

Finally, a *reciprocal climate of trust, honesty, and confidence* should exist between leaders and constituents, such that the value of participation is reinforced and has a positive effect on all involved. Burn's (1978, p. 20) vision of transforming leadership captures this relationship. Leaders and constituents, through their participation together, "raise one another to higher levels of motivation and morality . . . transformational leadership ultimately becomes moral in that it raises the level of human conduct and ethical aspiration of both the leader and led, and thus has a transforming effect on both." Participation, then, has a powerful effect on leaders and constituents.

Participation also advances important values that enhance the moral functioning of the organization. Democracy and other significant moral goods are embedded in structures that enhance participation.

Participation as Democracy

It is important for human service organizations to operate as a "humane and democratic organizational form" (Fisher & Karger, 1997, p. 156). Democracy is dependent upon increasing citizens' sense of power in the local and immediate parts of their lives, of which employment occupies a large role (McCall, 2001). The workplace is an important example of an environment where people learn how to be potent and effective or impotent and powerless based on their participation. Human service organizations impact the empowerment of consumers of service as well as employees. Therefore, structures and strategies that enhance participation also help to encourage constituents toward greater civic involvement (McCall, 2001). This participation, then, strengthens the larger democracy. In addition, no matter what the motives of leaders, and, under the best intentions of administrators, the power that is used and/or abused must be "managed and restrained" (Ritchie, 1988, p. 169). The way to manage and restrain power is through a democratic structure, which promotes the participation of all constituents.

Cox and Joseph (1998, p. 168) argue eloquently for a "visionary" empowerment-oriented workplace for human services in particular. Empowered workplaces lead to increased effectiveness that is "superior to that of the . . . authoritarian model"; this type of workplace also enacts the "basic ethics and commitments of a social work" that emphasizes "self-determination and collective action." Many human service organizations are in a unique position to promote empowerment and participation as part of the organizational design because of the nature of their work (Gutierrez, Parsons, & Cox, 1998). However, traditional hierarchical arrangements of many social service organizations create adversarial relationships between those with more legitimated power and workers at lower levels, which are not ethical work relationships (Fisher & Karger, 1997).

Design formats that are democratic and empowering include collegial work designs that emphasize participation in decision processes and collaboration at all levels. Allowing *flexibility* for workers to create the roles that are necessary for client well-being, such as advocacy as well as treatment, also enhances the empowerment of workers and clients (Gutierrez, Parsons, & Cox, 1998). Participative organizational technologies and evaluation designs that seek *input from all stakeholders*—clients, employees, and the public to which the agency is accountable—increase involvement in critical decisions about the ethics of intervention models (Fisher & Karger, 1997).

Research on empowerment in organizations also supports the role that organizational practices can play in empowering members (Conger & Kanungo, 1988; Heil, 1991). However, leaders can create empowering structures that ultimately undermine empowerment if members do not share real decisionmaking power (Gruber & Trickett, 1987). There is a large benefit to the organization in empowering all constituents. Empowerment theorists argue, "Organized as a vehicle for the empowerment of staff, clients, and the community, it maximizes the power of its workers and constituents to participate fully in the governance of the organization" (Gutierrez, Parsons, & Cox, 1998, p. 227). Participation also promotes other moral values.

Moral Significance of Participation

The *moral right to participate* as an employee or other constituent of the organization is argued by McCall (2001). He notes many forms of participation are possible in an organization, and can be structured formally and informally. Advisory mechanisms (for example, quality circles) or more potent mechanisms that delegate actual control over decisions (policymaking committees or employee stock ownership plans) are examples. Participation in decisionmaking can also take different forms. Employees can make decisions themselves, or decisions can be representative, that is, made by a group or committee made up of representatives of different employee groups, work units, and so forth.

McCall (2001) defends employee participation on many grounds, including dignity, fairness, self-respect, health, and democracy. *Dignity* is viewed as connected to the belief that human beings have inherent value and must be treated with dignity. Dignity rests on the ability to be self-determined and to choose freely how to live, especially at work, where people spend over one-third of their lives. Therefore, employees should, "have some ability to exercise control over their work lives" (McCall, 2001, p. 197). This confronts the traditional hierarchical patterns of thinking of employees as resources to be managed for organizational goals.

Fairness requires the organization to have a commitment to equality such that decisions that affect employees' interests be made fairly. Policymaking is an area that has great impact on the individuals in an organization. Fairness would support the inclusion of employees or their representatives in the decision process. The mechanisms of participation must include real authority, particularly when there is opposition from those with more institutional power. McCall notes, "employees deserve an amount of authority that enables them to resist policies that unfairly damage their interests . . . a right to co-determine policy at all levels" (2001, p. 197).

Self-respect is based on the relationships that a person has and the reciprocal responses from others within those relationships. Departmentation and systems of authority in modern organizations restrain people from exercising autonomy and feeling their contributions are influential. As discussed in Chapter 4, the consequence can be burnout and alienation. These results are less likely when people participate in decision processes and use their discretion and judgment. These activities reinforce a sense of self-worth and a sense of making a difference.

Finally, *health* is important to participation. The stress that develops because of alienation (prevalent in our society) can lead to physical and emotional problems. Research studies (presented by McCall, 2001) support that there is a relationship between perceived control over one's work environment and stress, that is, as employees have more control over their work life and environment, work-related stress is reduced. In addition, there is an increase in job satisfaction when employees feel a sense of influence over policies. Finally, participation from employees in regard to health and safety factors increases the development of more effective measures to enhance health and safety at work. The argument about the moral significance of effective, democratic participation promotes many reasons for developing structures in the organization that enhance participation. Participation is most useful in regard to ethical issues when feedback is the norm and the function of participatory structures.

The Feedback Loop

Designing structures for feedback at all levels of the organization has the potential to enhance empowerment of leaders and constituents and to promote ethical practices and policies. In a study on ethical decisions (Manning, 1990), the permission to comment was fundamentally connected to the prospect of ethical action and decisions. Managers and administrators who could comment and react openly to ethical challenges responded to complex ethical issues (with the same scarcity of resources) in a more effective manner than managers who perceived restraint or restrictions to their participation or feedback.

The freedom and opportunity to comment supports several critical factors that lead to more ethical behavior in organizations.

Freedom of Action

First, the freedom to comment leads to freedom of action (Manning, 1990). Leaders and constituents must first relate, discuss, and interact in order to move to a decision that is ethical by intention. When people are prohibited from expressing their values and opinions, they separate themselves from the values and feelings that inform them. Thus, they become co-opted by the requirements of the organization and alienated from their own morality. This leads to further isolation and reinforces not acting, rather than action. The result of not acting is also a loss to the organization. Critical information that has ethical, legal, and social implications remains hidden and secret, reinforcing the possibility of corruption and harmful behaviors.

Systems of Accountability

Second, the freedom to comment using feedback structures establishes a system of accountability and promotes self-regulation within the organization (Manning, 1990). The self-regulation of constituents, leaders, and the organization as a whole is reinforced. Individuals and the organization are held accountable for ethical or unethical actions and behaviors, and, in turn, the organizational practices and policies are examined openly. A system of accountability is especially important since many people in organizations, particularly those with the least power, assume their ability to influence is minimal (Brummer, 1985). However, internal challenge and whistleblowing are important self-correcting activities that are needed for ethical organizations. The behavior of each individual is reflective of the behavior of the organization, and vice versa. "Every decision to abide by or ignore the demands of conscience is a choice and, as such, involves the initiation of a policy or precedent of choice by the subordinate" (Brummer, 1985, p. 86). The decisions of every constituent provide an example, just as the leader's decisions do, and thus contribute to an atmosphere of self-correction or avoidance. A leader, constituent, or organization that is accountable to others for decisions, messages, policies, and so forth will act more on intention, than by accident.

Enhancement of Learning

Third, the design of structures to facilitate feedback enhances the learning of the organization. Causes and consequences of ethical problems are understood more comprehensively, and constituents and leaders are more able to see the systemic effects that need to be corrected or modified. Also, new policies, structures, or strategies can be devised for themes or patterns of moral issues that have not been a concern or received attention previously.

The social constructions discussed in Chapter 10 on culture become relevant again as the motivation for structures that promote feedback. Everything is a social construction that is *interpreted* by human beings, so ". . . there can be no escaping evaluation . . ." because evaluating ethical decisions and the moral consequences of those decisions provides the basis for "understanding the many ways in which narrow interpretation and its moral consequences are institutionalized" (King, 1986, p. 5). In other words, without consistent and structured opportunities for evaluation of the moral and ethical impact of daily decisions and action, there is a great risk of perpetrating harm. For example, harm can occur because leaders and constituents perceive their action in relation to the pursuit of organizational goals (the organizational ideal), or because it is what everyone else is doing (multiple moralities), or because they think about the issue simplistically or narrowly (which leads to behavioral stupidity).

Evaluation, in the form of feedback and dialogue, helps to create a social reality that supports ethical reflection and learning. Structures of feedback can open the door to new learning, rather than remaining constrained by narrow, rationalistic theories that do not attend to moral and ethical issues. They can provide an opportunity to recognize the "incompleteness of even our best policies . . . reflect creatively and self-critically on our own good decisions [and] policies, and seek knowledge beyond our well-trained expectations" (de Vries, 1988, p. 148). This form of ethical evaluation creates information.

The Information Net

A morally responsible organization has, as a central characteristic, an *information net* that is available in the areas of operation that "significantly affect the lives of others (consumers, the general public, future generations, workers, shareholders, managers themselves, etc.)" (Goodpaster, 1983, p. 11). The metaphor of a net, woven in a way that it can capture, store, and use the feedback about moral and ethical issues of the organization, is a useful strategy to evaluate what may have a moral impact on others. The data that is collected by organizations is voluminous. It is gathered in respect to performance, outcomes, marketing, finance, personnel, standards, and so forth and then processed through the organization and often forgotten. The perception of data that is gathered and analyzed by leaders and constituents makes a difference in the usefulness of the data in regard to ethical issues. *Perceptual selectivity* in regard to what data is gathered and what is considered for action comes into play (Goodpaster, 1983, p. 11).

Perception is critical in the arena of moral and ethical activity because it is the beginning of responsibility (Goodpaster, 1983). The availability of data affects perceptions about the data. Data about worker safety issues, such as assaults in a mental health or criminal justice facility, or the effects of a particular technology on consumer health or the dignity of consumers, may not be gathered at all, or gathered and lost in the system. Therefore, the data is not evaluated for moral and ethical issues. The result is selectivity in moral perception on the part of the organization. Leaders can reduce selectivity of perception by designing structures that provide information gathering, as well as information processing. Both are critical feedback mechanisms for identifying the ethical issues that emanate from the delivery of human services.

Nanus and Dobbs (1999) recommend that leaders consider designs that use information and communication technology to the fullest extent possible rather than traditional designs that compartmentalize information and isolate employees from one another and from data that is available. An information net that is responsive to the moral and ethical questions of leaders and constituents can greatly facilitate the evaluation of moral and ethical impacts on various stakeholders. For example, program evaluation processes that focus on the moral premises of both technology and intervention models provide information to evaluate choices of models. Access of all stakeholders (board members, employees, consumers, and community citizens) to computer technology and the available data promotes face-to-face and electronic conversations about the meaning of the data in regard to organizational practices. Open access also conveys an openness to the organization's public to give feedback and to evaluate the data from their perspective. The production of information as well as access to information is integrally connected to the participation of all stakeholders. Information is also imperative for moral premises that can guide decisionmaking.

The Introduction of Moral Premises to Design

Organizations can develop moral reasoning as a formal characteristic by making moral premises an ongoing part of the decisionmaking processes (Goodpaster, 1983). Premises that underlie decisions are more commonly thought of in economic or technological or marketing concerns in organizations. In these areas, a systematic and *self-*

conscious approach is prescribed. The organization looks out for itself in order to make key economic decisions that will be most beneficial. However, developing moral premises for decisions makes the moral and ethical issues overt as well, not as a form of dilution of the corporate purpose, but "as an indispensable safeguard for the humanity of those purposes" (Goodpaster, p. 12). The following are a few examples of the introduction of moral premises through policies, structures, activities, and people (Goodpaster, 1983; Reamer, 2001):

- Development of organizational codes of ethics
- Institutionalization by top-level leaders of moral responsibility through setting goals, designing structures, and introducing evaluation criteria
- Interest and vigilance in relation to moral and ethical issues by the board of directors
- Education and training programs on ethical reasoning and decisionmaking and the moral aspects of functional specialties (for example, service delivery, marketing, production, finance, monitoring, and human resources management)
- Incentives and acknowledgement for leaders and constituents for success with morally motivated goals (for example, affirmative action)
- An emphasis on employee and consumer health and well-being
- Board, staff, and consumer committees and/or representative committees to monitor and shape areas of moral and ethical significance
- Upper level leaders given responsibility and accountability for organizational ethics in policy, administration, management, and service delivery
- An emphasis on internal dialogue about the moral aspects of the organization's performance
- Identified standards of practice for services rendered
- Structures for ethical oversight (for example, ethics audits)

The following discussion will highlight two structures that provide moral premises for the organization: organizational codes of ethics and ethics advisory boards and committees.

Organizational Codes of Ethics

Business and social organizations develop organizational codes of ethics in order to delineate the moral framework that guides the conduct of executives and other members of the organization (Levy, 1982). The code of ethics for business and social organizations is derived from the moral norms of society. However, expectations of social organizations also are derived from "occupational and social service norms" (Levy, 1982, p. 77). Therefore, human service organizations have professional and social service ethical obligations as well. The code may reflect a variety of norms and values that support the ethical functioning of members of the organization, the obligations to society, and obligations derived from professional standards of behavior. An explicit code of ethics is a step toward transforming "moral ambiguity" in the organizational environment into organizational "self-commitment" (Wieland, 2001, p. 81).

The code of ethics for an organization provides the operating instructions for the values and norms, reflected in a values statement (discussed in Chapter 10), if one has been developed (CANPO, 1994). The code of ethics answers the question, "How will we ensure that our values are acted upon?" (CANPO, 1994, p. 8). The code provides more concrete guidance for what is expected from members of the organization than a values statement, but is not as specific as a rule or policy. However, a code of ethics is specific enough that it may be used to support grounds for personnel actions. The code helps to organize a variety of spoken and unspoken policies, as well as written policies, into one "authoritative document" that is "a tangible outcome" of the mission statement (CANPO, 1994, Refer to Model Code, Appendix A).

There are some drawbacks to developing a code of ethics (CANPO, 1994). In some occasions, the necessity of doing the humane, right thing may require the use of individual and/or professional discretion and judgment that results in a decision that is outside the code. Because formal standards and written documents are often examined in regard to liability and malpractice issues, deciding something that is in conflict with the code could result in legal action, even though the code is not a legal document (CANPO, 1994). Another criticism of codes (and other written guidelines) is that it "can become a substitute for thinking" (CANPO, 1994, p. 9). It is not uncommon for codes to be viewed as prescriptions for behaviors and decisions, even though they are not specific enough for definitive guides to action. The code of ethics may dissuade people from using judgment and discretion when needed. In addition, the existence of a code (or written policy) sometimes relieves the organization of thinking further about complex ethical challenges. The "thou shalt not lie, cheat, or steal" seems to cover the ethical bases, and there is little consideration or commitment to examining further the moral and ethical challenges that do not lend themselves well to guides for action. Finally, the organizational literature reports that codes do not appear to be the defining issue, alone, in leaders and constituents acting ethically (Matthews, 1988, p. 133).

Developing a Code of Ethics. A code of ethics is a collective document; therefore, the thinking of many different stakeholders should be represented. Participation in creating the code will promote a greater degree of commitment and ownership for the finished product. A code is more effective when it has a balance of positive affirmations and ideals, as well as prohibitions of particular actions and behaviors. Even though a code of ethics exists to provide guidance, it is helpful to clarify what particular statements mean. For example, the statement that "constituents should avoid conflicts of interest" may be too vague. A statement of "what constitutes a conflict of interest is also needed" (CANPO, 1994, p. 12). The following steps (CANPO, 1994), adjusted to each organizational style and needs, are a process to develop a code. (Refer to model code of ethics in Appendix A.)

Think about primary categories that are necessary to guide constituents in relation to possible unethical or illegal activity. The statements in the code are not about existent facts, but are more in the form of a *promise:* "self-commitment to and self-organization of a performance promise" (Wieland, 2001, p. 82). The promise creates behavioral expectations and behavioral standards for all constituents and informs the public about what can be expected from the organization in terms of ethical conduct. Areas such as "fiscal management; purchasing and acquisition; fund raising; grant writing; public relations; volunteer management; the appointment, termination, evaluation and compensation of board, staff and volunteers; board duties and responsibilities; staff duties and responsibilities; board-staff relations; responsibilities to clients and the community; responsibilities to society; and advocacy" are potential areas for ethical guidelines (CANPO, 1994, pp. 11–12).

In addition, Matthews (1988, p. 138) recommends discussing the following areas in the code that help to inform the ethical culture of the organization:

1. Extremely important in the written code is the concept of [leaders and] senior executives as role models. This should be stressed throughout the code.
2. A discussion of the importance of the reputation of the organization is also an integral part of the code . . . .
3. The basis of the code should be ethics as well as law . . . [people] should engage in law-abiding and ethical conduct not because of legal imperatives, but because it is *unthinkable* to do otherwise.
4. Social responsibility to consumers and the general public should be stressed throughout the code.
5. Trust is also a necessary ingredient in the employer-employee relationship and should be addressed directly in the written code.

These five areas are useful in thinking about the underlying assumptions of the code and for communicating to all leaders and constituents the message that is embedded in the code. The message is that leaders set the tone, the organization as an entity is affected by ethical and unethical behavior of all constituents, and an ethical organization made up of ethical leaders and constituents is based on trustworthiness internally and with the public.

Work with all stakeholder groups for a commitment to develop a code (consumers, volunteers, board members, administration, staff, and community representatives at a minimum). Ask each group to create a draft of statements separately that cover the ethical issues in their area for the code. Remind groups to think about the mechanisms available to receive guidance about possible illegal or unethical activity (Matthews, 1988). Provide a timeline and ask that one person in each group be responsible for writing the draft. Circulate examples of codes of ethics and the organizational values statement, if there is one. The values statement and the code of ethics should be congruent, and there should be a clear relationship between the two.

Set aside time, perhaps a full day, for representatives of each group to meet together with their drafts (or the entire organization if small in size) to share perspectives and to begin the development of agreed-on guidelines. An outside consultant or facilitator can be helpful in working through disagreements and/or conflicts, as well as encouraging more reluctant members to share their views. This is particularly useful if there are differences in the level of authority between members (for example, volunteers and administrators, direct service staff and executive director, consumers of services and board members). Ask for someone to volunteer to do the wordsmithing during the day and to develop a draft of the group's work at the end of the day.

Plan for the next steps, including timeline, the structure of how the draft will be revised and refined, and the process of approval throughout the organization. A task force could be developed, with representatives from all groups, or a committee from the board may take on the responsibility. The board is ultimately responsible for approving the code when completed.

Review the first draft to make sure that all the moral and ethical concerns of the organization are addressed. All involved stakeholders should have an opportunity to review the final version and to give feedback before approval from the board.

Mechanisms for guidance are important for constituents in addition to the code of ethics. The code of ethics provides the opportunity for all constituents to participate in developing the moral premises that guide the operations of the organizations, but mechanisms for constituents to receive guidance are an important consideration. Some organizations suggest the legal counsel of the organization; sometimes senior administrators and managers are available. An *open door policy* whereby anyone can take questions or concerns to upper level administrators or the executive director may be helpful. However, some employees may find it intimidating to express their concerns to a particular executive (Matthews, 1988). The recommendation of seeking help from a direct supervisor may be problematic because the person who may be requesting or implying unethical conduct is often an employee's direct supervisor (Matthews, 1988). When there is disagreement on interpretation, or people are faced with ethical dilemmas that do not lend themselves readily to the guidelines of the code, ethics committees or advisory boards may be helpful.

Ethics Advisory Boards and Committees

Boards or committees, whose task is to aid in the analysis and resolution of complicated ethical dilemmas, can add another dimension of thinking about and communicating moral premises through structures. Ethics committees may also be viewed as having an ethical oversight function. However, their contributions in regard to case consultation, policy, and education also introduce moral premises. Ethics committees are a phenomenon that have arisen particularly in the health care arena and are often located in hospitals or other health care institutions.

The functions of ethics committees have centered on three activities: (1) case consultation, (2) policy development, and (3) education (Csikai & Sales, 1998; Hoffman, 1993). Case consultation provides an opportunity to review ethical dilemmas as they occur or in retrospect. Policy development provides the organization with an opportunity for the committee to consider existing policies that affect ethical and moral issues, change them if necessary, and create new policies for consideration, based on the ethical challenges that emerge for the organization. Education is focused on identifying emerging ethical issues and then informing relevant stakeholders in the organization and community as to the nature of the issues. Education could also include organizing educational seminars or workshops around particular ethical topics or concerns (Csikai & Sales, 1998).

The functions of such committees are consistent in the literature. However, there is considerable disagreement about the nature of the purpose of the committees. Hoffman (1993) argues that function has become confused with purpose and that many committees do not define and articulate their purpose clearly. The initial purpose was to protect the patient's interests. However, this is not always the case; committees' purposes may actually be assisting the patients' family or to "manage risk and protect the interests of the institution . . . and other health care providers" or ensuring that the allocation of medical resources is done in a fair manner (Hoffman, 1993, pp. 682–683). The duality or multiplicity of purposes creates confusion for the committees, who sometimes respond to the confusion by not identifying explicitly the goals that guide their work. A lack of explicit purpose and goals that guide the committees' functions also jeopardizes any attempt to evaluate their efficacy for the organization.

An additional risk is embedded in the committee and its relationship with the organization. Levine (Hoffman, 1993, p. 679) argues the following:

> . . . Ethics committees, like any institutional arrangement, can be used for ill as well as for good. They are in essence a procedural mechanism that can aid those faced with difficult ethical decisions; their presence does not guarantee that they will be used constructively or that the most appropriate decision will be made.

The use of ethics committees and advisory boards, then, must be clearly defined as to purpose. Committees must function autonomously, free from organizational pressure. The results of their work should not be dictated by those in authority, nor used for inappropriate organizational practices. For example, a committee should not be expected to give legitimacy to a questionable practice or policy to help protect top level administrators and/or the organization. Finally, thoughtful consideration must be given to the composition of the committee so that, whatever the defined purpose, people have the best qualifications to accomplish the purpose.

The definition of purpose must be followed by a definition of access and jurisdiction (Fost & Cranford, 1985). If case consultation is a function, potential users must know about the committee (the purpose) and the procedure for accessing the committee. Identification of potential users (for example, consumers, providers, staff, board members, administrators, and so forth) and avenues to inform them about access must be developed (Hoffman, 1993). In addition, the jurisdiction of the committee will determine if community representatives are important. For example, if policy development is identified as an important function, representatives from outside the organization may be invited to participate. Similarly, if education of organizational staff or those who receive services from the organization is a priority, the appropriate staff, consumers, family members, and so forth must be assured of access to the educational activities.

The quality of an ethics committee is difficult to define (Hoffman, 1993). The structure of the committee is made up by those who serve, and "their qualifications and expertise" (Hoffman, 1993, p. 683). Thus, the point mentioned earlier about purpose and the relationship to credentials and abilities is imperative. Quality is also related to the institutional support for the committee's functions. Access to adequate space, budget resources to support the activities identified earlier, and support staff to help with planning and carrying out functions beyond committee meetings is important. The organization's commitment of time, space, resources, and interest will define the quality of what can be accomplished and will be seen as an indicator of the organization's investment in a quality structure.

Ethics committees can be adapted and changed beyond the bioethical model found in health care. Organizations could create innovations that provide for participation of representatives from all stakeholder groups through a committee charged with double loop learning processes. To do so, the committee should have the authority to evaluate the ongoing ethical culture, suggest policy on ethical standards, and arrange for continuing education for organizational members on ethics. Monitoring the ethical patterns and themes and analyzing the underlying systems issues that cause moral and ethical problems for the organization can promote generative responses that move the ethical climate forward. The ethics committee is a structure that promotes the process of thinking about and working with ethical issues. Other structures, such as the formal ethics audit, can introduce ethical oversight to the organization.

Structures for Ethical Oversight

This chapter has discussed many important factors related to the design of an organization that can enhance the overall ethical quality of everyone's performance. The final theme is one of oversight. How does an organization ensure that ethical guidelines and codes, policies, and practices are being met? Two potential structures for oversight include boards of directors and a formal ethics audit. Both can help to review and assess what currently exists and what is needed.

The Ethics of Governance: Oversight by the Board of Directors

Board of directors have the primary responsibility for the purpose, direction, and policies of the organization. They ultimately are the "custodians" of the organization's values (Goodpaster, 1983, p. 20). Ethical leadership entails working with the board toward their involvement in the moral vision and their commitment to their role in the creation of ethical cultures and structures. Board involvement communicates a powerful message to all other constituents of the organization. The type of organization, whether profit or nonprofit, does not change the fact that the board is responsible for the interests of a wide range of stakeholders, such as consumers of service, employees, suppliers, the community, and, if for-profit, the shareholders (Collier & Roberts, 2001). From this perspective, board members or directors are in the role of stewards of a social institution (Collier & Roberts, 2001; Kay, 1996). Not only does the board have responsibility for the competing interests of stakeholders, but also for the effects of the organization on the community within which it operates. Therefore, board of directors must "increase both their vigilance and their effect" through their governance roles (Goodpaster, 1983, p. 20).

The stakeholders are often thought of as having competing interests, such as the common view that the shareholders of for-profit organizations are the most important interest. However, a more helpful approach, suggested by Collier and Roberts (2001), is that the different interests are a property of moral relatedness. Corporate governance, then, is "about the way in which we seek to manage the interdependencies in which we are all immersed" (Collier & Roberts, 2001, p. 70). The board of directors, from this perspective, is responsible for the moral and ethical performance of the organization through oversight of the changes in conduct that are necessary "across multiple chains of interdependent relationships" (Collier & Roberts, 2001, p. 70).

This approach encompasses ethical cultures and structures, the policymaking responsibilities, and long-term planning and evaluation. Every point of the chain (for example, different stakeholder groups) is a potential opportunity and responsibility for ethical questions and ethical conduct. Board of directors must have more than good intentions; they must develop the mechanisms to evaluate and change the organizational activities that produce immoral or unethical effects, whether they are clinical, economic, social, or environmental. They must also promote their moral commitment to all of the stakeholder groups and society.

The ethics of governance charges boards of directors with the responsibilities of oversight for the ethical policies and practices of the organization. "Codes of ethics, ethics management systems, and corporate ethical programs" are typical governance structures by which the organization monitors, protects, and develops the "integrity of their transactions" (Wieland, 2001, p. 73). The board's involvement in initiating and participating in the development of these structures is crucial. Leaders in higher level positions, the executive director or chief operating officer, and upper administrators must work closely with the board in this process. New boards and boards who have not experienced ethical governance before may need assistance from organizational leadership. If necessary, leaders should educate the board about these governance activities and provide support for carrying them out. Board of directors, as well as agency staff, should also be involved in an ethics audit.

The Ethics Audit

The nature and degree of ethical issues and challenges in the organization is complex. Ethical expectations and standards are interrelated with many different constituencies, and service delivery is affected by professional, legal, and ethical obligations. The ethics audit (see example in Appendix B) provides leaders and constituents with a "comprehensive assessment of an organization's performance according to predetermined ethical criteria" (CANPO, 1994, p. 29). The process could be compared with a financial audit. There is not always a clear understanding of the rights and wrongs that may be taking place, but the questions of the audit can raise flags that alert leaders to investigate and revise policies and procedures more closely (CANPO, 1994, p. 30). Audits can be organized according to areas of accountability (for example, board, staff, clients, volunteers, donors/recipients, and so forth) as in the CANPO audit. Ethics audits can also be specific to particular professional values and obligations.

For social service organizations and social work leaders, Reamer's *Social Work Ethics Audit* (2001) is directly related to the ethical concerns and obligations of social workers. The audit provides leaders and constituents with a tool to ". . . examine their ethics-related practices, policies, and procedures." The purpose of the audit process is to do the following (Reamer, 2001, p. 3):

- *Identify pertinent ethical issues in their practice settings.*
- *Review and assess the adequacy of their current practices.*
- *Design a practical strategy to modify current practices a needed.*
- *Monitor the implementation of this quality assurance strategy.*

The social work audit is focused on the "essential or core knowledge of the profession." Reamer (2001, p. 5) identifies two key areas that are fundamental to the social work audit: (1) "ethics related risks in practice settings" that have been compiled from ethics complaints and (2) "current agency policies and procedures for handling ethical issues, dilemmas, and decisions." Reamer notes that an ethics audit helps to evaluate whether the agency has adequate policies and practices to protect clients, employees, and the agency from complaints about ethical violations and liability in regard to ethics issues. The element of prevention that occurs from using an ethics audit is a type of "risk management" that strengthens the agency's ethical culture, structure, and governance (Reamer, 2001).

Conducting the audit can occur through a retreat format that is inclusive of all constituents or representatives of particular constituent groups (consumers, volunteers, direct service staff, support staff administration, board members, and so forth). The existing structures of the organization, such as board meetings, team meetings, consumer groups, and so forth could be used, with the audit as the main agenda item over several meetings. Each stakeholder group would then provide their contributions to upper level administrators and the board, or an ad hoc committee of the board, for decisions. Providing the questionnaire ahead of time to all participants is helpful in enhancing the reflection and awareness of the items. Also, CANPO recommends soliciting responses and perspectives from individuals external to the organization. Representatives of other agencies, political leaders, accrediting and regulatory agencies, community leaders, and advocacy groups come to mind. For example, a mental health center would want feedback from groups such as the Alliance for the Mentally Ill.

The purpose of the audit is not punishment or retribution, but an opportunity to evaluate the existing policies and practices that influence organizational and individual ethical behavior (CANPO, 1994). The audit can result in the realization that the agency has some outstanding areas of ethical performance. It can also help to improve the areas that need attention.

Conclusion

Organizational design can be a powerful tool to enhance the organization's ability to accomplish the mission and ethical goals. Through reorganization, revision, modification, or the addition of a new structure or process (for example, a task force, committee, or community coalition), the moral and ethical vitality and energy of the organization can be increased. Design should be conceptualized as a continuum of possibilities that are dynamic, rather than static. Design should reflect the governing ideas of the organization (values, vision, and ideology). Further, designs and structures should be responsive to ethical challenges internally and to the external environment in which the organization exists and interacts. The leader as architect, in collaboration with all constituents, can create the most effective structures for ethical performance and effectiveness.

QUESTIONS AND APPLICATIONS

1. Share your organizational chart with someone. Identify the underlying values, assumptions, and philosophy that are attached to the type of design of your organization. What are the implications of your organizational design on participation of all constituents and feedback loops for all constituents? How would you develop formal and informal structures to increase participation and feedback?

2. In collaboration with two or three others, identify some key assumptions, values, and principles you want to reflect in an organizational design. Develop a design based on those assumptions and present it in a graphic design, such as a chart or picture. Account for the division of work, distribution of authority, communication, and decision processes. Also consider structures for participation, self-regulation, and feedback in the design. How does this design differ from your current organization? What accounts for the difference?
   - How would you enhance collegiality, interdependence, and teamwork through such a design?
   - How could you facility integration through your design?
   - How does your design accommodate the environment and community?

3. How would you incorporate the mechanisms of a learning organization into your design? How would you orient the organizational learning toward ethical and moral issues?

4. What do you see as the important moral premises that should be introduced into the design? How would you include them in the organizational structure?

5. What mechanisms of ethical oversight would be useful in your agency? Why? How would you structure ethical oversight through the design?

12 Ethical Leadership for the Future: Contributions to the Common Good

Leaders in human services have the opportunity to help shape the nature of society in the new millenium. The human service delivery sector is ideally situated to enrich society's understanding and responsiveness to the complex and diverse experiences of being human. The actions and decisions of human service leaders and constituents convey a powerful message to society about the needs and well-being of those who seek services, as well as the responsibility and accountability of those who provide services. We are living in an age where people in need are quickly becoming commodities to be exploited—the means to a profit-oriented end—rather than as subjects who are ends in themselves, to be respected and empowered. Human service leaders who are ethical by intention can change that trend.

However, beyond opportunity, or possibility, or potential, there is a moral necessity to contribute to the common good through the social responsibility that is attached to leadership and to organizations as primary entities in society. The human services sector (public, non-profit, and for-profit organizations) contributes greatly to the primary values that are promoted through our culture. Within this sector, leaders influence the thinking and understanding of a variety of stakeholders—consumers of service, employees, community citizens, shareholders, and policymakers. Leaders also have a significant impact on the well-being of those same stakeholders. The activities and decisions that take place in the organization reflect the nature of the community where it is located. In turn, the community reflects the nature of its institutions and organizations. Thus, the organization, as a microcosm of society, acts as a fertile greenhouse where primary values such as democracy, empowerment, service, justice, and integrity can be nurtured and promoted.

Ethical leadership contributes to the common good in several ways—through political advocacy, social reconstruction, moral citizenship, empowerment of various constituencies, and development of community (internally and externally), to name just a few. These are discussed below. But first, a brief discussion of the common good is provided.

The Common Good

There have been frequent discussions and analyses in news columns, editorials, and professional articles on the social challenges confronting American society in recent years in reference to the materialism and greed that permeates our culture. As a result, well-known ethicists and other leaders have initiated a call for an emphasis on the ethic of the common good rather than the current prominence of the ethic of individual rights (Markula Center for Ethics, 2000). The common good simply means "certain general conditions that are . . . equally to everyone's advantage" (Markula, 2000, p. 1). The social systems, institutions, and environments that people depend on should work in a way that contributes to the benefit of all people, not just a select few (for a more detailed discussion, refer to Chapter 7). Lewis (1989) argues that ethical organizations will give precedence to the common good—even beyond consumers' interests and needs. The challenge is to conceptualize service as an avenue to maximize the good of the community, not only to serve individual needs. In doing so, Lewis (1989) points out that altruism—"caring for one's own" (in this instance the larger community) is necessary. All human service organizations, public, non-profit and for-profit, have an obligation to contribute to the common good. For-profit organizations have a responsibility to promote the financial gain of their shareholders, but this does not prohibit, and should not be "detrimental to the common good" (Lewis, 1989, p. 9).

The notion of a common or collective good is complex, and few "purely public goods" exist (Howe, 1980, p. 181). However, services that are provided through human service organizations do benefit others, beyond the service recipient. Economists call this dynamic "externalities" (Howe, 1980, p. 181). For example, services, policy advocacy, and education efforts provided through domestic violence shelters and agencies not only benefit individual women and children, but also have a positive effect on the reduction of violence in the larger community. Values are communicated that have a shaping influence on the community culture about domestic violence. Further, feedback about the nature of the social problem impacts the understanding, and subsequently the activities, of policymakers and community citizens. The common good, then, is the ultimate concern of ethical leaders in human services. The common good is integrally connected to political action and advocacy.

Political Advocacy

A mission for leadership in the 21st century was created from the topics of concern expressed by social work leaders (Rank & Hutchison, 2000). Four topics were accentuated: political advocacy, social reconstruction, vision, and professional identity. These topics resulted in the following mission statement for leadership. The mission states: "Articulate a vision to create processes of political advocacy in order to effect social reconstruction on behalf of those, who for various reasons, cannot participate in the economic prosperity of the global economy" (Rank & Hutchison, 2000, p. 502). This mission for leadership reflects a fundamental moral mandate for leaders to actively initiate and participate in social change efforts, thus contributing to the common good through their leadership.

Political advocacy, which was identified most often by social work leaders as needed in leadership, is directly connected to the social responsibility for social and economic justice—both which contribute to the common good. Leaders are challenged to pursue a fundamental impact on public policy and the decisions of policymakers, such that the impact enhances social and economic justice. The social responsibility inherent in this theme is intimately connected to ethical leadership. Leaders are policymakers. The policies regarding delivery of services and human resources communicate underlying themes about distribution of power, choice, and opportunity. In turn the actions and decisions of leaders have a profound influence on policymakers at the community level. Ethical leaders are actively involved with the key leaders and policymakers in their external environment. They have developed the necessary reputation and integrity to initiate and influence policies that enhance the social and economic well-being of all citizens, particularly those most in need.

Political advocacy is also directly related to the consensus of communities regarding social issues. As Hardin (1990, p. 539) argues, "If our ethical requirements are largely determined by our roles in relevant institutions, then they are largely determined by political decisions about what those institutions should be and do . . . policies on welfare should be determined by the polity." Thus, the larger society must be influenced by feedback from institutions and institutional leaders, such that the needs, conditions, and priorities of those who receive services are represented, and institutional reforms are demanded and initiated by an informed community. A community consensus concerning complex social problems can be developed only through an informed public, thus the ethic of feedback through political advocacy is central to ethical leadership and the common good. Motivating and mobilizing the community is relevant to another theme of leadership identified by social work leaders—social reconstruction.

Social Reconstruction and Social Change

The second important theme that is congruent with ethical leadership is social reconstruction—the promotion of "social change on a broad scale and the redistribution of wealth" (p. 498). The policies and decisions made on a daily basis have an impact on social change and social reconstruction, both internally and externally. Lewis (1989) relates this idea to the altruism that underlies the commitment to the common good of non-profit organizations. He argues that there are certain obligations and duties that are an ethical commitment. They include the duty to make distributive decisions that give precedence to the common good—assessing what will provide for the least advantaged in a particular pool of consumers. In addition, quality-of-life decisions should be considered and carry as much emphasis as other types of outcomes (financial and clinical). These duties lead to social reconstruction at the organizational level as well as within a particular community.

The decisions and activities that take place within an organization also contribute to social reconstruction. Leaders who design structures that promote the sharing of power in organizations and thus the participation of all stakeholders (for example, consumers) in meaningful ways are participating in social reconstruction. Leaders who emphasize ethical behaviors and decisions, who demonstrate a commitment to service and duty, and who act as a voice for the most vulnerable, are contributing to social change. Leaders who design and construct ethical organizational cultures that provide for feedback within the organization and to the larger community are promoting social reconstruction, starting at the level of the organization. The direction of social change or reconstruction rests on the moral vision of the leader and constituents.

Moral Vision

The above themes, connected to a moral mandate toward enhancing the common good, can be actualized only through a redefinition of social work leadership—leadership that is based on a foundation of moral and ethical will and directed by a moral vision. Only the moral nature, intentions, and contributions of the organization to the common good of society justify the survival of human service organizations. The moral intentions are articulated through the organizational mission. However, leaders also must articulate a moral vision that has the capacity for advocacy and action toward social reconstruction. Green (1987, p. 187) points out that the future tense of a vision is important in relation to the clarity of direction that is identified. He notes,

> The point is . . . having given us a vision, a glimpse of an alternative context for living and acting with its own resources, its own risks, its own advantages, they invite our entrance into that future now. Leaders without vision, without rootedness, and without imagination are dangerous or at best inept. Where would they lead us? Nowhere. Nowhere at least that anyone should want to go.

Moral vision then, must be a public vision, open to comment from stakeholders and the public, and in interaction with constituents' aspirations.

The moral vision is about more than just the leader, though it must start with the leader. Leaders in human services must first of all develop a moral identity—their starting point that defines the moral direction of their personal and professional lives. The moral identity of the person walks hand in hand with the leader's professional identity and values. The moral vision that is enacted through leadership must be articulated internally and externally to all constituents, so that there is clarity in regard to the leader's professional values and moral goals. The leader's moral vision is a starting point for a shared vision, whereby the vision reflects what is meaningful to all constituents.

Ethical leaders develop the leadership of constituents. As constituents identify with a mutual vision, the power to promote and fulfill the vision is exponential. The moral vision then is communicated through, and congruent with, all of the structures and processes of the organization. The moral vision becomes the constitution for the organization's contribution to constituents and to the common good.

Moral Citizenship: Values and Ethics in Action

Leaders must be proactive if they are to make a difference. The ability to be proactive was one of the five themes identified by Rank and Hutchison (2000) as critical to leadership. To be proactive is to be ethical by intention. The intentional activity that is essential to being proactive is the essence of moral citizenship (discussed in Chapters 6 and 7). Leaders can develop organizational cultures that promote independent thinking and the responsibility to give feedback—within the organization and to the larger society. Employees, consumers, and other stakeholders who have the skills to think independently and take responsibility for their own and others' actions are improving their abilities to act as a citizen, both in the institution and in the community. This, in turn, contributes to the common good.

Communication is the critical ingredient to moral citizenship through participation and feedback. An organization and a society that accentuate moral citizenship and "loyal opposition" have created a strong system of self-regulation, such that the moral nature of everyone is enhanced and embraced. Loyal opposition requires leaders and constituents to speak out when confronted with potential or actual unethical policies and practices. The underlying motivation for doing so is to help the organization, as well as those affected by the unethical behaviors. Organizations that are aware of unethical policies and practices have the opportunity and responsibility to change them. The numerous examples in the media regarding Enron and other corporations engaged in illegal or unethical practices, and the failures within the bureaucracy of the FBI and other federal agencies, portray the results of closed ethical systems and cultures. The resulting damage to these entities and to the general public conveys the importance, morally as well as practically, for constituents to give feedback, and for leaders to insist on it.

Therefore, leaders at all levels of the organization (board, administrative, managerial, supervisory, and so forth) must nurture and structure opportunities for participation, particularly in the form of feedback about moral and ethical practices and policies. This is the political nature of ethics. Leaders and constituents must give feedback and participate in the resolution of ethical challenges, even when there is great risk to their own economic or psychological well-being. A leader who is unable or unwilling to model that level of participation will engender constituents who do the same. The result of an avoidance of ethical and moral issues is the propagation of alienation, a withdrawal from the moral aspects of life, which has negative effects on constituents, the organization, and the common good.

Leaders must design processes and structures for feedback, and assess the organizational structure for barriers and impediments to ethical action. As Christensen (1995, p. 226) notes, "Enumerating ethical principles and good practices is not enough to help us identify those organizations that are best suited to promote the provision of . . . care in an atmosphere relatively untainted by financial conflicts of interest . . . Structure determines in large part the nature of the conflicts providers have to face, and it can also impact the quality of the care delivered."

Leaders as architects can make the structural difference in designs that enhance rather than impede ethical service delivery.

Empowerment and the Common Good

Empowerment of constituents—consumers of service, providers of service, other employees, board members, and community citizens is a necessary part of ethical leadership. The sharing of power creates power toward accomplishing the moral vision and developing the skills of constituents that are necessary for organizational success. Constituents that are empowered to participate, to give feedback, and to take responsibility for ethical issues are developing their skills for citizenship in the community. Thus, empowerment is directly associated with the common good.

Leaders can influence characteristics of their organizations that facilitate empowerment of constituents. Research on empowering community settings produced four characteristics (Maton & Salem, 1995). First, it is important to have a belief system that inspires growth, is strength-based, and focused beyond the individual self. This characteristic connects with the necessity of a moral vision that is meaningful to constituents; a vision that allows them to contribute to the fulfillment of the vision with their own unique strengths and contributions. Second, there are role structures that create opportunities for growth and development as well as participation and skill building. The authors note that these role structures should be pervasive, highly accessible, and multi-functional. Thus, the opportunities for empowerment are also the same opportunities that have been discussed as necessary for ethical actions and behaviors for individuals and organizations.

The third characteristic that facilitates empowerment is a support system that is encompassing, peer-based, and provides a sense of community. The support system that is in place is critical to constituents' and leaders' willingness to take risks and give feedback. Further, support systems generate interaction and involvement, which in turn help to identify potential ethical challenges, as well as provide the support necessary to resolve them. Empowerment leads to increased motivation and a sense of community.

The final characteristic is leadership—leadership that is inspiring, talented, shared, and committed to both the organization and the constituents. Leaders who role model the behaviors that are empowering to others—risk-taking, integrity, competency, responsibility, and action—help to teach and support those same behaviors in constituents. Leaders who share their power with constituents provide the opportunities for constituents to make mistakes, take risks, accept responsibility, and contribute on many levels to the ethical performance of the organization. Sharing of power leads to more democratic actions within the system, and contributes to furthering democracy in the community. Empowered constituents are empowered citizens; increased citizenship contributes greatly to the common good. Empowerment of constituents leads to increased motivation to do the right thing and contributes to an individual's sense of belonging to a community.

Developing Community

Leaders should help to develop a sense of community within the organization and within the external environment in order to promote an ethical workplace. A community, from the perspective of organizations, is "a framework of shared beliefs, interests, and commitments uniting a set of varied groups and activities . . . that establish a common faith or fate, a personal identity, a sense of belonging, and a supportive structure of activities and relationships" (Selznick, 1992, pp. 358–359). The experience of community provides the context for moral action to take place, and for the commitment necessary to stay the course in response to what are perceived as intractable moral and ethical problems.

The motivations of the diverse stakeholders involved in organizations to take moral action are complex and varied. Wheatley (1988) argues that the emphasis on self-actualization in organizations has been misdirected. Instead, the meaning of work, and making a contribution through work, motivates people. People must experience a connectedness to a greater whole, something beyond them that has meaning. The meaning they construct, in collaboration with others, provides the inspiration to strive toward higher ethical goals. The existence of a sense of community, then, provides a medium to "view ourselves as part of something beyond ourselves . . . The very act of meaning making, of assuming responsibility for making choices about one's behavior, is motivating. Ethical inquiry, then, is a strong motivator" (Wheatley, 1988, p. 141).

Developing community in organizations provides the opportunity to practice the ethics of intimates as opposed to the ethics of strangers (as discussed in Chapter 3). The fast pace of our information society promotes doing more and doing it faster. Wheatley (2001) argues that organizations and society are on a destructive path where working 24/7 is seen as a benefit and the time for relationships is being eroded. The time of friendships and relationships must be reclaimed (Wheatley, 2001). Relationships and dialogue are critical to the effective solution of ethical dilemmas. The interactions of the people involved—with one another, with their professions, and with their personal lives bring forward the answers to complex dilemmas (Wheatley, 1988). Constituents and leaders cannot fully understand the nature of moral and ethical issues without reflection and discussion with others. Developing a sense of community in organizations provides a venue where trust and collaboration support the necessary reflection and interaction.

Leaders in organizations that visualize the organization as part of a larger community will consider the impact of decisions in relation to the larger community. Myopic and narrow ethical analysis and problem solving can be replaced with a broader vision. Analysis of the impact of policies and decisions with ethical implications must be sensitive to the repercussions of time, complexity, and impact on other systems and constituencies. The sensitivity of leaders to organizations' social responsibility to the community promotes an attention to the common good.

Conclusion

Ethical leadership in human services must be based on the values of a "helping profession." Wheatley (2001) notes that "a leader is someone who feels called to serve." Ethical leaders are not value neutral, but value promoting. The nature of those values must be clear in every action. The essence of ethical leadership is enacting professional values through every decision and action—values that contribute to the common good. As Bertha Reynolds (1963, pp. 283–284) articulated the following so well:

> The way we do our professional work contributes inescapably to the outcome of that struggle. If we think social work is not a force in the battle of ideas, the enemies of the people know better. Either we serve the people's need or we evade them. Either we make democracy real or we reduce it to an abstraction, which the foes of democracy do not object to at all. Either we use all that science can teach to help people to build a genuinely good life for themselves, or we build a professional cult that takes the place of interrelation with other advances in human knowledge.

This is the nature of ethical leadership; either we mean it or we don't. Ethical leaders and constituents have the power to transform both the organization and their communities. The values that are conveyed through each action and interaction can lead to a moral and ethical workplace, and contribute to a moral and ethical society.

Leaders, to provide ethical leadership, must see their role beyond the individual accomplishment of role responsibilities and organizational objectives. They must consider the theories that inform their leadership and what is conveyed through underlying values and assumptions. Transformational leadership (discussed in Chapter 3) provides a paradigm that incorporates ethics and moral action into the day-to-day leadership responsibilities. Ethical action must include more than the leader. Constituents and stakeholders are important to the development of ethical cultures and structures.

Ethical leaders will act as an architect, designing and shaping the structures and processes of the organization in ways that enhance and promote a moral vision and ethical action. Ethical leaders will view ethics as the essence of their leadership; as the heart of the matter, as the nature of leading, as a permanent fixture, as the utmost importance, and as a motivator for new energy and contributions. Ethics as the essence of leadership will be evident in the daily activities and decisions. As Chekov noted, "Any idiot can handle a crisis; it's this day-to-day living that wears you down" (Curtain, 2000, p. 58). The ethical dilemmas of daily practice are not in the headlines, but ". . . do constitute the fabric of our daily lives. . . ." (Curtain, 2000, p. 58). Ethical leadership is concerned with the weaving and re-weaving of that fabric, with the ongoing and ultimate goal of adding to the common good of our world community.

APPENDIX A

The Community Services Code of Ethics (*Adopted August 30, 1993*)

The mission and values statement of Community Services, together with a general consensus within our agency on desirable and acceptable moral behavior, obligate our board, our staff, and our volunteers to observe the following standards of conduct in the performance of our work:

Obedience to the Law

- Whatever our personal feelings about the justice and appropriateness of particular laws, all board members, staff, and volunteers are to obey all laws in the performance of their work on behalf of Community Services.
- All funds are to be solicited in full compliance with the relevant laws and tax regulations.
- Our agency's financial activity is to be reported in compliance with all required laws and regulations.
- Where laws clearly conflict with the welfare of our agency, our clients, or the community we serve, we will attempt to change the offending laws through legislative action or, if necessary, through the recognized judicial process.

Commitment to Diversity

The selection of board members, staff members and volunteers, and the delivery of programs and services by Community Services are to be carried out without regard to race, religion, ethnicity, economic status, gender, age, sexual orientation, or physical ability.

Discrimination and Harassment

All Community Services employees, board members, and volunteers are to refrain from any sort of discrimination and harassment of any clients or co-workers based on

Reprinted with permission from Rigg, M. & Allen, M. (1994). The ethics audit checklist. *In Conducting an ethics audit: A checklist for nonprofits* (pp. 19–27). Colorado Association for Nonprofit Organizations (CANPO).

race, religion, ethnicity, economic status, gender, age, sexual orientation, or physical ability.

Communication of Information

- Our commitment to openness and honesty requires, as a minimum, that all financial records and records of organizational activity be open to all donors, funders, and the general public.
- All staff and volunteers are to be open and honest in the communication of information with their clients, the community, and the general public, withholding information only in the greater interest or when perceived as absolutely necessary to the welfare of our agency. This includes information contained in marketing, fund raising, and public relations materials.
- Board members, staff, and volunteers are to be open and honest in their working relationships with one another.
- No information about the agency or its programs relevant to the performance of an individual's responsibilities is to be withheld from that individual.
- Specific efforts are to be undertaken to ensure that volunteers are given complete and accurate information about the agency and the particular projects in which they are involved.
- Any important decisions made, actions taken, or information presented at board and staff meetings are to be communicated promptly to the staff and to the board, respectively.
- Any information shared in confidence between client and staff or between agency staff, board, or volunteers is to remain confidential unless, in the considered judgment of the confidant, serious harm to an individual, to the community, or to the agency would be prevented by breaking the confidence.

Conflicts of Interest

- As much as possible, conflicts of interest affecting board, staff, and volunteers are to be avoided. Resolution of any such conflict may necessitate the termination of a professional relationship with a particular vendor or client, abstention from a vote or from involvement with a particular project, or, in the extreme, resignation of one's position with the organization.
- While friendships are encouraged between participants in the agency and between agency participants and the broader community, romantic entanglements between agency participants are not encouraged and are prohibited between agency professionals and their clients.
- Board and staff members are not to allow personal relationships to influence decisions regarding staff hiring and evaluation, the choice of vendors, or the provision of programs and services.

Responsibilities of and toward Clients and the Public

- The integrity, dignity, and autonomy of the organization's clients and public are to be respected fully at all times in the delivery of services and the presentation of programs.
- Services are to be delivered honestly, openly, and professionally and with compassion and respect for the clients served.
- The aim of all agency services and programs is to be the enhancement of the integrity, autonomy and knowledge of the clients, the client's family, the community, and the public.
- Confidentiality in the relationship with all clients is to be respected and maintained unless serious harm to the clients, to other individuals, to the community, or the agency would be averted by breaking the confidence.
- Clients are expected to be responsible in honoring commitments they have made to enhance the effectiveness of services received, including showing up promptly for scheduled appointments, and to pay, as arranged, for services rendered.

Responsibilities of Board Members

- Board members are entrusted with the moral well-being of Community Services and are expected to demonstrate the highest moral integrity and leadership both in their work on behalf of the organization and in their private lives.
- Board members are entrusted with the financial well-being of the organization and are expected to exercise that responsibility with the greatest integrity and concern.
- Board members are expected to perform fully and capably the responsibilities of their respective board positions.
- Board members are expected to recognize the volunteer nature of their commitment and not to expect any perquisites or any financial gain from their involvement in the organization.
- Board members are to be given all information relevant to the performance of their responsibilities and are not be deprived of any information that would compromise their integrity or autonomy, or affect their ability to perform their duties.
- When necessary, board members are to be given training to enhance their effectiveness.
- The performance of board members is to be evaluated on an individual basis much like the work of paid staff. Exemplary board performance is to be recognized, and poor performance is to be pointed out with the goal of enhancing future performance.

- Board members may be dismissed for dereliction of duty, for continued poor performance, for serious breach of law or of ethics, or because of irreconcilable personality conflicts with other members which interfere with their governance duties. Dismissal of a board member should be done with compassion and fairness and discussed fully with the board member concerned.
- Board membership is to be open to as diverse a constituency from the community as possible.
- No one should be precluded from participation on the board because of financial circumstances.
- No board member should be expected to bear extraordinary personal expenses in the performance of his or her board duties beyond whatever monetary contribution to the organization the board member might care to make.

Professional and Staff Responsibilities

- All staff members are to honor their responsibility to the code of ethics governing their particular profession unless their professional code is in some way superseded by the Community Services Code of Ethics.
- In the event that a code of professional conduct should conflict with Community Services' code of ethics or with agency practices or policies, such a conflict is to be brought to the immediate attention of the agency's executive director.
- In general, the agency considers job responsibilities and the professional relationship between agency professionals and their clients to be primary, and no other responsibilities or collateral relationship between agency professionals and their clients are to interfere with job responsibilities or with a professional/client relationship.
- Staff are encouraged to discuss any conflict between personal and professional responsibilities with their supervisor or with the executive director.
- All staff are responsible for performing their work as efficiently and professionally as possible. Expenses are to be kept as low as possible.
- Staff are responsible for keeping track of non-job-related use of office supplies and equipment and for reimbursing the agency for any costs incurred, in accordance with the current agency policy.
- Staff are encouraged to spend time during the day interacting casually with other staff, board members, and volunteers as long as such socializing does not prevent staff from carrying out their required responsibilities in a timely manner.
- Staff may pursue personal matters during the work day, but they are to keep such activities to a minimum and not allow them to interfere with the expeditious performance of their job responsibilities.

Staff Hiring, Evaluation, and Compensation

- Staff are to be hired in as fair and open a process as possible that respects the autonomy and dignity of all job applicants.

- Only background information relevant to job performance is to be elicited from candidates; no other information is deemed appropriate to the hiring process.
- Hiring is to be done in compliance with affirmative action guidelines so that the pool of candidates for a particular position reflects, as much as possible, the broad diversity of the community regarding race, religion, ethnicity, economic status, gender, age, sexual orientation, and physical ability.
- In all cases, the candidate who demonstrates the greatest promise for success is to be offered the position.
- Staff performance is to be evaluated fairly and honestly. Evaluation is to be based primarily on job performance and on the contribution the staff member makes to the building of community within the work place.
- In general, staff are encouraged to share any work-related dissatisfaction, problems, or grievances with their supervisor or with the executive director.
- Paid staff are encouraged in general to further their skills and education. They are especially encouraged to pursue training, at the agency's expense or on job release time, to improve areas of job performance that are deficient or in order to enhance their work-related skills and knowledge.
- Salary levels are to be set fairly and appropriately. The only relevant salary considerations are (1) level of job responsibility and technical sophistication, (2) prior education and experience, (3) seniority, (4) job performance, and (5) comparable market salary.
- Efforts will be made to compensate employees as generously as possible consistent with relevant salary considerations and the long-term financial well-being of the agency.
- The salary differential between the highest-paid and lowest-paid employees is to be reasonable and not excessive and based only on the relevant salary considerations enumerated above.
- Termination of staff members is to be undertaken as a last resort and, when necessary, to be done fairly and compassionately and discussed thoroughly with the staff member.
- Employees who are terminated are to be compensated fairly and promptly for salary outstanding.

Responsibilities of and toward Volunteers

- Volunteer participation in the organization is to be open to as diverse a constituency from the community as possible.
- Volunteers and donors are to be treated with the same dignity and respect as board members and paid staff.
- Volunteers are to be given all information relevant to the performance of their responsibilities and are not to be deprived of any information that would compromise their integrity or autonomy or might affect their decision to participate in a particular project.

- When necessary, volunteers are to be given training to enhance their effectiveness.
- Volunteers are to be given clear job definitions and expectations.
- The performance of volunteers is to be evaluated on an individual basis much like the work of paid staff. Exemplary job performance by volunteers is to be recognized, and poor performance is to be pointed out with the goal of enhancing future performance.
- Volunteers may be dismissed for continued poor performance, for serious breach of the law or of ethics, because of irreconcilable personality conflicts, or out of financial necessity. Dismissal of a volunteer should be done with compassion and fairness and discussed fully with the volunteer concerned.
- Volunteers are expected to perform the responsibilities they agreed to assume promptly and capably and to inform the organization if other commitments conflict with their organizational responsibilities.
- Volunteers are encouraged to discuss any problems they encounter with the volunteer or project coordinator or, if necessary, with the executive director.
- Whenever possible, volunteers are to be invited to participate in organizational programs and activities out of gratitude for their contribution and in an effort to strengthen the organization's sense of community.
- Volunteers are asked to recognize the volunteer nature of their contribution to the organization and not to expect perquisites in exchange for the performance of their organizational responsibilities.
- Volunteers are to be reimbursed promptly and completely for any previously authorized out-of-pocket expenses incurred in the performance of their work on behalf of the organization.

Solicitation and Investment of Funds

- The solicitation of funds on behalf of Community Services is to be carried out according to the highest ethical standards and in full compliance with the laws and regulations governing fund raising in nonprofit organizations.
- Established codes of fund raising ethics, such as that of the National Society of Fund Raising Executives, are to be followed scrupulously unless they are in some way superseded by the Community Services Code of Ethics.
- The autonomy and dignity of the donor or potential donor are to be respected at all times.
- Complete honesty and disclosure are to characterize all dealings with donors.
- All fund raising and marketing materials are to be scrupulously honest and to avoid any deceit or misrepresentation.
- While persuasion in the solicitation of funds is necessary and encouraged, anyone soliciting funds on behalf of Community Services is to refrain from any form of coercion in his or her solicitation.
- The donation of money is to be regarded as an opportunity to do good, and it should be extended to as wide and diverse a population as possible.

- Individuals and organizations known to represent values and practices inimical to the mission and values of Community Services or to the welfare of the general community are not to be solicited for donations.
- No donation is to be accepted under any circumstances if its source is known to be illegal.
- All organizational funds are to be invested in organizations or vehicles whose practices and values are consistent with the moral values and principles of the organization and the welfare of the community.

Commitment to Advocacy

- Community Services recognizes advocacy as an essential part of its organizational mission.
- Board members, staff members, and volunteers are asked, whenever appropriate, to regard advocacy as an essential part of their responsibilities and to make certain that their work on behalf of the organization promotes the welfare of clients, the community, and the greater public.
- The organization is committed to taking full advantage of the democratic process, and to educating the public and those in positions of authority and power regarding issues of concern to the clients and community that the organization serves.
- The organization will honor fully the restriction of nonprofit organizations from devoting disproportionate resources to lobbying efforts or from organizational endorsements of political candidates.

Relationship with Other Agencies

- Community Services will strive at all times to be fair, open, and honest in its dealings with other agencies.
- Community Services will enter into partnerships with other agencies only when such partnerships enhance the ability of Community Services to pursue its mission and its goals.
- Community Services will not enter into a working relationship with any agency whose stated values or mission or whose policies and practices are inimical to the mission and values of Community Services.

Note: The Community Services Code of Ethics is a reflection of its Values Statement. The Code of Ethics is an attempt to make the Values Statement operational by defining general guidelines for conduct. Unless a code of ethics is based on a specific, identified set of values, it is an arbitrary imposition of rules of conduct. No code of ethics is likely to be completely exhaustive, and the Community Services code is probably no exception. Moreover, a code of ethics is not a policy and procedure manual. While a code might inspire specific policies and procedures, it is more a general statement of principles. The Community Services Code of Ethics mentions, for example, that no one should have to incur extraordinary expenses in the performance of their duties, but it does not specifically say that they can be reimbursed for travel expenses.

The Community Services Code of Ethics lists both general issues, such as Communication and Conflicts of Interest, and more specific areas of responsibility, such as Staff Hiring, Evaluation, and Compensation. This makes the documents somewhat redundant at times, but this redundancy also serves to add emphasis to the importance of following particular moral principles. In addition, some parts of the Code of Ethics serve the function of protecting the organization and of readily indicating its compliance with various laws and practices. The Commitment to Diversity, the paragraph on Discrimination and Harassment, and the disclaimer at the end of the section on Commitment to Advocacy are examples of this.

APPENDIX B

Part 3. The Audit
with Questions Only

This section has been included for those organizations that would prefer to use the ethics audit without footnotes. Feel free to make copies of these pages for everyone involved in the audit process.

Board

- ☐ Has the board developed a clear mission statement?
- ☐ Does the board use the mission statement as a basis for decision-making? If you are a foundation, do your grants fall clearly within your mission and funding guidelines?
- ☐ Do all board members know what the mission statement says?
- ☐ Is the board clear about its responsibilities?
- ☐ Is there adequate financial oversight?
- ☐ If board members have financial interests in the organization, how is this handled?
- ☐ If there are significant family, personal or business relationships between people in the organization, are there clear policies for addressing problems that may occur?
- ☐ Does the board have clear policies for dealing with conflicts of interest of all types?
- ☐ Is there a clear values statement and/or code of ethics? Is it known to everyone in the organization?
- ☐ Does the board meet regularly?
- ☐ Do all board members take an active role? Are there clear policies in place to dismiss members who repeatedly miss meetings or who otherwise fail to carry out their responsibilities?
- ☐ Is the board the right size to carry out its responsibilities? Has its size been discussed?
- ☐ Is free expression of ideas encouraged?
- ☐ Does the board assess its own performance regularly?

Source: Reprinted with permission from Rigg, M. & Allen, M. (1994). The ethics audit checklist. *In Conducting an ethics audit: A checklist for nonprofits* (pp. 53–59). Colorado Association for Nonprofit Organizations (CANPO).

☐ Does the board use a clearly-defined process to evaluate the executive director?
☐ Does the board reflect the diversity of the population served?
☐ Are board meetings open to other people beside the directors?

Staff

☐ Do hiring policies strive to reflect the diversity of the population served?
☐ Is there a formal anti-discrimination policy?
☐ Do any staff members have financial interests in the organization?
☐ If there are significant family, personal or business relationships between people in the organization, are there clear policies for addressing problems that may occur?
☐ If employees work outside the organization or receive remuneration for speaking engagements, consulting, etc., how is this handled?
☐ Are policies in place to ensure accountability to the CEO and board?
☐ Do the personnel policies ensure fairness to all staff?
☐ Beyond fairness, do personnel policies provide adequate health care, sick leave, leave to care for sick relatives, etc.?
☐ Are there clear policies in place for evaluating staff?
☐ Are there clear policies in place for developing a salary structure and awarding pay increases?
☐ Are employees provided with adequate training and development opportunities needed for their jobs?
☐ How do staff voice disagreements? Are there clear and reasonable grievance procedures?
☐ How are staff represented on or to the board?
☐ Is the work place as safe, clean and comfortable as possible?

Donors and Fund Raisers

☐ Are all fund raising statements true and balanced?
☐ Does fund raising material provide a clear picture of actual programs?
☐ Are people who raise funds on your behalf fully informed about the organization?
☐ Might any of your solicitation methods be considered as unwarranted pressure to give?
☐ Is full information on your organization easily available to anyone who asks? (e.g., annual report, IRS Form 990 or 990 PF, financial statements, and clear funding guidelines for prospective grantees.)
☐ Do you educate your donors on the availability of this information? If you are a foundation, are staff or trustees available to answer questions and provide guidance?
☐ If you are a foundation, do you provide equal access to groups you know as well as to those who are newcomers? Does your giving include grass roots organiza-

tions and a healthy diversity of beneficiary agencies within your funding guidelines?

- What is the ratio of fund raising/administrative costs to program costs?
- How are fund raising and administrative costs allocated?
- Are you up-front with donors about how their contribution will be used? Do budgets submitted to donors reflect true figures and realistic projections?
- If priorities/needs change, do you request donor permission to use their contribution/grant in a different way from the original stated purpose? If you are a donor, how flexible are you when nonprofits encounter changes in needs/priorities or difficulties in meeting grant agreements?
- How are your organization's development staff compensated?
- Are there clear policies on how donors may be recognized for their contributions?
- Is there a formal fund raising policy defining how and from whom funds are to be solicited?
- Do you honor donor requests for anonymity (including exchange of lists)?

Clients/Customers

- Are policies in place to ensure confidentiality for clients?
- When information on clients is exchanged with other agencies, are clients asked for permission? How is this handled?
- Are clients given access to their records so that they may challenge or correct information on file?
- What policies are in place regarding social/sexual relationships between clients and staff?
- Are clients treated with dignity and respect?
- Are clients provided with adequate information to evaluate and choose appropriate services?
- Are clients fully and fairly informed of alternative services?
- Are there adequate grievance procedures for clients who may be dissatisfied with services provided?
- Are program services available without discrimination? (*Obviously, certain programs are targeted to specific groups; within those target groups, are services distributed fairly?*)
- Are programs accessible to clients (location, hours of operation, physical access to the building)?
- Is information available in other languages, Braille or a recording, when necessary?
- How do you balance the rights of clients with the rights of staff/volunteers?

Volunteers

- Are policies in place to ensure adequate, appropriate screening of volunteers?
- Are all volunteers screened in the same way, including board members?

- □ Are all volunteers provided with training and appropriate supervision?
- □ Are your organization's expectations made clear to the volunteer?
- □ Are the volunteer's expectations clearly understood by the organization?
- □ Are volunteers assigned meaningful work?
- □ Are volunteers treated with dignity and respect?
- □ Is there a clear grievance procedure for volunteers?
- □ How are volunteers held accountable to the organization?
- □ Are policies in place for warning, dismissing, or reassigning volunteers who break agency rules or do not perform assignments as agreed?
- □ Are clear policies in place regarding volunteer recognition and reward?
- □ Are policies in place regarding reimbursement for expenses incurred in volunteer duties?
- □ Has the organization determined the type of volunteers necessary for its operation and made plans to recruit them?

Society

- □ Does your organization take adequate steps to educate the public about its programs and services?
- □ Does your organization provide full information about itself to any member of the public, not just to organizational donors and members?
- □ Is your organization sensitive and responsive to the needs and concerns of the neighborhood and community?
- □ Within allowable guidelines, does your organization do all it can to advocate for legislation and social change consistent with its mission?
- □ Does your organization employ ecologically beneficial practices, such as recycling, minimal use of electricity, etc.?
- □ Does your organization act with respect toward other organizations in the nonprofit sector?
- □ Does your organization conduct itself in ways that enhance the reputation of the nonprofit sector?
- □ Does your organization assume some share of responsibility for the well-being of the entire nonprofit sector?
- □ How does your organization handle competition with other nonprofit organizations?

APPENDIX C

NASW Code of Ethics

The National Association of Social Workers (NASW) is the largest organization of professional social workers in the world. NASW serves nearly 160,000 social workers in 56 chapters throughout the United States, Puerto Rico, the Virgin Islands, and abroad. NASW was formed in 1955 through a merger of seven predecessor social work organizations to carry out three responsibilities:

- *Strengthen and unify the profession*
- *Promote the development of social work practice*
- *Advance sound social policies.*

Promoting high standards of practice and protecting the consumer of services are major association principles.

Overview

The *NASW Code of Ethics* is intended to serve as a guide to the everyday professional conduct of social workers. This *Code* includes four sections. The first section, "Preamble," summarizes the social work profession's mission and core values. The second section, "Purpose of the *NASW Code of Ethics*," provides an overview of the *Code*'s main functions and a brief guide for dealing with ethical issues or dilemmas in social work practice. The third section, "Ethical Principles," presents broad ethical principles, based on social work's core values, that inform social work practice. The final section, "Ethical Standards," includes specific ethical standards to guide social workers' conduct and to provide a basis for adjudication.*

Preamble

The primary mission of the social work profession is to enhance human well-being and help meet the basic human needs of all people, with particular attention to the needs and empowerment of people who are vulnerable, oppressed, and living in poverty. A historic and defining feature of social work is the profession's focus on in-

---

dividual well-being in a social context and the well-being of society. Fundamental to social work is attention to the environmental forces that create, contribute to, and address problems in living.

Social workers promote social justice and social change with and on behalf of clients. "Clients" is used inclusively to refer to individuals, families, groups, organizations, and communities. Social workers are sensitive to cultural and ethnic diversity and strive to end discrimination, oppression, poverty, and other forms of social injustice. These activities may be in the form of direct practice, community organizing, supervision, consultation, administration, advocacy, social and political action, policy development and implementation, education, and research and evaluation. Social workers seek to enhance the capacity of people to address their own needs. Social workers also seek to promote the responsiveness of organizations, communities, and other social institutions to individuals' needs and social problems.

The mission of the social work profession is rooted in a set of core values. These core values, embraced by social workers throughout the profession's history, are the foundation of social work's unique purpose and perspective:

- service
- social justice
- dignity and worth of the person
- importance of human relationships
- integrity
- competence

This constellation of core values reflects what is unique to the social work profession. Core values, and the principles that flow from them, must be balanced within the context and complexity of the human experience.

Purpose of the NASW Code of Ethics

Professional ethics are at the core of social work. The profession has an obligation to articulate its basic values, ethical principles, and ethical standards. The *NASW Code of Ethics* sets forth these values, principles, and standards to guide social workers' conduct. The *Code* is relevant to all social workers and social work students, regardless of their professional functions, the settings in which they work, or the populations they serve.

The *NASW Code of Ethics* serves six purposes:

1. The *Code* identifies core values on which social work's mission is based.
2. The *Code* summarizes broad ethical principles that reflect the profession's core values and establishes a set of specific ethical standards that should be used to guide social work practice.
3. The *Code* is designed to help social workers identify relevant considerations when professional obligations conflict or ethical uncertainties arise.

4. The *Code* provides ethical standards to which the general public can hold the social work profession accountable.

5. The *Code* socializes practitioners new to the field to social work's mission, values, ethical principles, and ethical standards.

6. The *Code* articulates standards that the social work profession itself can use to assess whether social workers have engaged in unethical conduct. NASW has formal procedures to adjudicate ethics complaints filed against its members.[1] In subscribing to this *Code*, social workers are required to cooperate in its implementation, participate in NASW adjudication proceedings, and abide by any NASW disciplinary rulings or sanctions based on it.

The *Code* offers a set of values, principles, and standards to guide decision making and conduct when ethical issues arise. It does not provide a set of rules that prescribe how social workers should act in all situations. Specific applications of the *Code* must take into account the context in which it is being considered and the possibility of conflicts among the *Code*'s values, principles, and standards. Ethical responsibilities flow from all human relationships, from the personal and familial to the social and professional.

Further, the *NASW Code of Ethics* does not specify which values, principles, and standards are most important and ought to outweigh others in instances when they conflict. Reasonable differences of opinion can and do exist among social workers with respect to the ways in which values, ethical principles, and ethical standards should be rank ordered when they conflict. Ethical decision making in a given situation must apply the informed judgment of the individual social worker and should also consider how the issues would be judged in a peer review process where the ethical standards of the profession would be applied.

Ethical decision making is a process. There are many instances in social work where simple answers are not available to resolve complex ethical issues. Social workers should take into consideration all the values, principles, and standards in this *Code* that are relevant to any situation in which ethical judgment is warranted. Social workers' decisions and actions should be consistent with the spirit as well as the letter of this *Code*.

In addition to this *Code*, there are many other sources of information about ethical thinking that may be useful. Social workers should consider ethical theory and principles generally, social work theory and research, laws, regulations, agency policies, and other relevant codes of ethics, recognizing that among codes of ethics social workers should consider the *NASW Code of Ethics* as their primary source. Social workers also should be aware of the impact on ethical decision making of their clients' and their own personal values and cultural and religious beliefs and practices. They should be aware of any conflicts between personal and professional values and deal with them responsibly. For additional guidance social workers should consult the relevant literature on professional ethics and ethical decision making and seek appropri-

1. For information on NASW adjudication procedures, see *NASW Procedures for the Adjudication of Grievances*.

ate consultation when faced with ethical dilemmas. This may involve consultation with an agency-based or social work organization's ethics committee, a regulatory body, knowledgeable colleagues, supervisors, or legal counsel.

Instances may arise when social workers' ethical obligations conflict with agency policies or relevant laws or regulations. When such conflicts occur, social workers must make a responsible effort to resolve the conflict in a manner that is consistent with the values, principles, and standards expressed in this *Code*. If a reasonable resolution of the conflict does not appear possible, social workers should seek proper consultation before making a decision.

The *NASW Code of Ethics* is to be used by NASW and by individuals, agencies, organizations, and bodies (such as licensing and regulatory boards, professional liability insurance providers, courts of law, agency boards of directors, government agencies, and other professional groups) that choose to adopt it or use it as a frame of reference. Violation of standards in this *Code* does not automatically imply legal liability or violation of the law. Such determination can only be made in the context of legal and judicial proceedings. Alleged violations of the *Code* would be subject to a peer review process. Such processes are generally separate from legal or administrative procedures and insulated from legal review or proceedings to allow the profession to counsel and discipline its own members.

A code of ethics cannot guarantee ethical behavior. Moreover, a code of ethics cannot resolve all ethical issues or disputes or capture the richness and complexity involved in striving to make responsible choices within a moral community. Rather, a code of ethics sets forth values, ethical principles, and ethical standards to which professionals aspire and by which their actions can be judged. Social workers' ethical behavior should result from their personal commitment to engage in ethical practice. The *NASW Code of Ethics* reflects the commitment of all social workers to uphold the profession's values and to act ethically. Principles and standards must be applied by individuals of good character who discern moral questions and, in good faith, seek to make reliable ethical judgments.

Ethical Principles

The following broad ethical principles are based on social work's core values of service, social justice, dignity and worth of the person, importance of human relationships, integrity, and competence. These principles set forth ideals to which all social workers should aspire.

Value: *Service*

Ethical Principle: *Social workers' primary goal is to help people in need and to address social problems.*

Social workers elevate service to others above self-interest. Social workers draw on their knowledge, values, and skills to help people in need and to address social problems. Social workers are encouraged to volunteer some portion of their professional skills with no expectation of significant financial return (pro bono service).

Value: *Social Justice*

Ethical Principle: *Social workers challenge social injustice.*

Social workers pursue social change, particularly with and on behalf of vulnerable and oppressed individuals and groups of people. Social workers' social change efforts are focused primarily on issues of poverty, unemployment, discrimination, and other forms of social injustice. These activities seek to promote sensitivity to and knowledge about oppression and cultural and ethnic diversity. Social workers strive to ensure access to needed information, services, and resources; equality of opportunity; and meaningful participation in decision making for all people.

Value: *Dignity and Worth of the Person*

Ethical Principle: *Social workers respect the inherent dignity and worth of the person.*

Social workers treat each person in a caring and respectful fashion, mindful of individual differences and cultural and ethnic diversity. Social workers promote clients' socially responsible self-determination. Social workers seek to enhance clients' capacity and opportunity to change and to address their own needs. Social workers are cognizant of their dual responsibility to clients and to the broader society. They seek to resolve conflicts between clients' interests and the broader society's interests in a socially responsible manner consistent with the values, ethical principles, and ethical standards of the profession.

Value: *Importance of Human Relationships*

Ethical Principle: *Social workers recognize the central importance of human relationships.*

Social workers understand that relationships between and among people are an important vehicle for change. Social workers engage people as partners in the helping process. Social workers seek to strengthen relationships among people in a purposeful effort to promote, restore, maintain, and enhance the well-being of individuals, families, social groups, organizations, and communities.

Value: *Integrity*

Ethical Principle: *Social workers behave in a trustworthy manner.*

Social workers are continually aware of the profession's mission, values, ethical principles, and ethical standards and practice in a manner consistent with them. Social workers act honestly and responsibly and promote ethical practices on the part of the organizations with which they are affiliated.

Value: *Competence*

Ethical Principle: *Social workers practice within their areas of competence and develop and enhance their professional expertise.*

Social workers continually strive to increase their professional knowledge and skills and to apply them in practice. Social workers should aspire to contribute to the knowledge base of the profession.

Ethical Standards

The following ethical standards are relevant to the professional activities of all social workers. These standards concern (1) social workers' ethical responsibilities to clients, (2) social workers' ethical responsibilities to colleagues, (3) social workers' ethical responsibilities in practice settings, (4) social workers' ethical responsibilities as professionals, (5) social workers' ethical responsibilities to the social work profession, and (6) social workers' ethical responsibilities to the broader society.

Some of the standards that follow are enforceable guidelines for professional conduct, and some are aspirational. The extent to which each standard is enforceable is a matter of professional judgment to be exercised by those responsible for reviewing alleged violations of ethical standards.

1. SOCIAL WORKERS' ETHICAL RESPONSIBILITIES TO CLIENTS

1.01 Commitment to Clients

Social workers' primary responsibility is to promote the well-being of clients. In general, clients' interests are primary. However, social workers' responsibility to the larger society or specific legal obligations may on limited occasions supersede the loyalty owed clients, and clients should be so advised. (Examples include when a social worker is required by law to report that a client has abused a child or has threatened to harm self or others.)

1.02 Self-Determination

Social workers respect and promote the right of clients to self-determination and assist clients in their efforts to identify and clarify their goals. Social workers may limit clients' right to self-determination when, in the social workers' professional judgment, clients' actions or potential actions pose a serious, foreseeable, and imminent risk to themselves or others.

1.03 Informed Consent

(a) Social workers should provide services to clients only in the context of a professional relationship based, when appropriate, on valid informed consent. Social workers should use clear and understandable language to inform clients of the purpose of the services, risks related to the services, limits to services because of the requirements of a third-party payer, relevant costs, reasonable alternatives, clients' right to refuse or withdraw consent, and the time frame covered by the consent. Social workers should provide clients with an opportunity to ask questions.

(b) In instances when clients are not literate or have difficulty understanding the primary language used in the practice setting, social workers should take steps to ensure clients' comprehension. This may include providing clients with a detailed verbal explanation or arranging for a qualified interpreter or translator whenever possible.

(c) In instances when clients lack the capacity to provide informed consent, social workers should protect clients' interests by seeking permission from an appropriate third party, informing clients consistent with the clients' level of understanding. In such instances social workers should seek to ensure that the third party acts in a manner consistent with clients' wishes and interests. Social workers should take reasonable steps to enhance such clients' ability to give informed consent.

(d) In instances when clients are receiving services involuntarily, social workers should provide information about the nature and extent of services and about the extent of clients' right to refuse service.

(e) Social workers who provide services via electronic media (such as computer, telephone, radio, and television) should inform recipients of the limitations and risks associated with such services.

(f) Social workers should obtain clients' informed consent before audiotaping or videotaping clients or permitting observation of services to clients by a third party.

1.04 Competence

(a) Social workers should provide services and represent themselves as competent only within the boundaries of their education, training, license, certification, consultation received, supervised experience, or other relevant professional experience.

(b) Social workers should provide services in substantive areas or use intervention techniques or approaches that are new to them only after engaging in appropriate study, training, consultation, and supervision from people who are competent in those interventions or techniques.

(c) When generally recognized standards do not exist with respect to an emerging area of practice, social workers should exercise careful judgment and take responsible steps (including appropriate education, research, training, consultation, and supervision) to ensure the competence of their work and to protect clients from harm.

1.05 Cultural Competence and Social Diversity

(a) Social workers should understand culture and its function in human behavior and society, recognizing the strengths that exist in all cultures.

(b) Social workers should have a knowledge base of their clients' cultures and be able to demonstrate competence in the provision of services that are sensitive to clients' cultures and to differences among people and cultural groups.

(c) Social workers should obtain education about and seek to understand the nature of social diversity and oppression with respect to race, ethnicity, national origin, color, sex, sexual orientation, age, marital status, political belief, religion, and mental or physical disability.

1.06 Conflicts of Interest

(a) Social workers should be alert to and avoid conflicts of interest that interfere with the exercise of professional discretion and impartial judgment. Social workers should inform clients when a real or potential conflict of interest arises and take reasonable steps to resolve the issue in a manner that makes the clients' interests primary and protects clients' interests to the greatest extent possible. In some cases, protecting clients' interests may require termination of the professional relationship with proper referral of the client.

(b) Social workers should not take unfair advantage of any professional relationship or exploit others to further their personal, religious, political, or business interests.

(c) Social workers should not engage in dual or multiple relationships with clients or former clients in which there is a risk of exploitation or potential harm to the client. In instances when dual or multiple relationships are unavoidable, social workers should take steps to protect clients and are responsible for setting clear, appropriate, and culturally sensitive boundaries. (Dual or multiple relationships occur when social workers relate to clients in more than one relationship, whether professional, social, or business. Dual or multiple relationships can occur simultaneously or consecutively.)

(d) When social workers provide services to two or more people who have a relationship with each other (for example, couples, family members), social workers should clarify with all parties which individuals will be considered clients and the nature of social workers' professional obligations to the various individuals who are receiving services. Social workers who anticipate a conflict of interest among the individuals receiving services or who anticipate having to perform in potentially conflicting roles (for example, when a social worker is asked to testify in a child custody dispute or divorce proceedings involving clients) should clarify their role with the parties involved and take appropriate action to minimize any conflict of interest.

1.07 Privacy and Confidentiality

(a) Social workers should respect clients' right to privacy. Social workers should not solicit private information from clients unless it is essential to providing services or conducting social work evaluation or research. Once private information is shared, standards of confidentiality apply.

(b) Social workers may disclose confidential information when appropriate with valid consent from a client or a person legally authorized to consent on behalf of a client.

(c) Social workers should protect the confidentiality of all information obtained in the course of professional service, except for compelling professional reasons. The general expectation that social workers will keep information confidential does not apply when disclosure is necessary to prevent serious, foreseeable, and imminent harm to a client or other identifiable person. In all instances, social workers should disclose the least amount of confidential information necessary to achieve the desired purpose; only information that is directly relevant to the purpose for which the disclosure is made should be revealed.

(d) Social workers should inform clients, to the extent possible, about the disclosure of confidential information and the potential consequences, when feasible before the disclosure is made. This applies whether social workers disclose confidential information on the basis of a legal requirement or client consent.

(e) Social workers should discuss with clients and other interested parties the nature of confidentiality and limitations of clients' right to confidentiality. Social workers should review with clients circumstances where confidential information may be requested and where disclosure of confidential information may be legally required. This discussion should occur as soon as possible in the social worker—client relationship and as needed throughout the course of the relationship.

(f) When social workers provide counseling services to families, couples, or groups, social workers should seek agreement among the parties involved concerning each individual's right to confidentiality and obligation to preserve the confidentiality of information shared by others. Social workers should inform participants in family, couples, or group counseling that social workers cannot guarantee that all participants will honor such agreements.

(g) Social workers should inform clients involved in family, couples, marital, or group counseling of the social worker's, employer's, and agency's policy concerning the social worker's disclosure of confidential information among the parties involved in the counseling.

(h) Social workers should not disclose confidential information to third-party payers unless clients have authorized such disclosure.

(i) Social workers should not discuss confidential information in any setting unless privacy can be ensured. Social workers should not discuss confidential information in public or semipublic areas such as hallways, waiting rooms, elevators, and restaurants.

(j) Social workers should protect the confidentiality of clients during legal proceedings to the extent permitted by law. When a court of law or other legally authorized body orders social workers to disclose confidential or privileged information without a client's consent and such disclosure could cause harm to the client, social workers should request that the court withdraw the order or limit the order as narrowly as possible or maintain the records under seal, unavailable for public inspection.

(k) Social workers should protect the confidentiality of clients when responding to requests from members of the media.

(l) Social workers should protect the confidentiality of clients' written and electronic records and other sensitive information. Social workers should take reasonable steps to ensure that clients' records are stored in a secure location and that clients' records are not available to others who are not authorized to have access.

(m) Social workers should take precautions to ensure and maintain the confidentiality of information transmitted to other parties through the use of computers, electronic mail, facsimile machines, telephones and telephone answering machines, and other electronic or computer technology. Disclosure of identifying information should be avoided whenever possible.

(n) Social workers should transfer or dispose of clients' records in a manner that protects clients' confidentiality and is consistent with state statutes governing records and social work licensure.

(o) Social workers should take reasonable precautions to protect client confidentiality in the event of the social worker's termination of practice, incapacitation, or death.

(p) Social workers should not disclose identifying information when discussing clients for teaching or training purposes unless the client has consented to disclosure of confidential information.

(q) Social workers should not disclose identifying information when discussing clients with consultants unless the client has consented to disclosure of confidential information or there is a compelling need for such disclosure.

(r) Social workers should protect the confidentiality of deceased clients consistent with the preceding standards.

1.08 Access to Records

(a) Social workers should provide clients with reasonable access to records concerning the clients. Social workers who are concerned that clients' access to their records could cause serious misunderstanding or harm to the client should provide assistance in interpreting the records and consultation with the client regarding the records. Social workers should limit clients' access to their records, or portions of their records, only in exceptional circumstances when there is compelling evidence that such access would cause serious harm to the client. Both clients' requests and the rationale for withholding some or all of the record should be documented in clients' files.

(b) When providing clients with access to their records, social workers should take steps to protect the confidentiality of other individuals identified or discussed in such records.

1.09 Sexual Relationships

(a) Social workers should under no circumstances engage in sexual activities or sexual contact with current clients, whether such contact is consensual or forced.

(b) Social workers should not engage in sexual activities or sexual contact with clients' relatives or other individuals with whom clients maintain a close personal relationship when there is a risk of exploitation or potential harm to the client. Sexual activity or sexual contact with clients' relatives or other individuals with whom clients maintain a personal relationship has the potential to be harmful to the client and may make it difficult for the social worker and client to maintain appropriate professional boundaries. Social workers—not their clients, their clients' relatives, or other individuals with whom the client maintains a personal relationship—assume the full burden for setting clear, appropriate, and culturally sensitive boundaries.

(c) Social workers should not engage in sexual activities or sexual contact with former clients because of the potential for harm to the client. If social workers engage in conduct contrary to this prohibition or claim that an exception to this prohibition is warranted because of extraordinary circumstances, it is social workers—not their clients—who assume the full burden of demonstrating that the former client has not been exploited, coerced, or manipulated, intentionally or unintentionally.

(d) Social workers should not provide clinical services to individuals with whom they have had a prior sexual relationship. Providing clinical services to a former sexual partner has the potential to be harmful to the individual and is likely to make it difficult for the social worker and individual to maintain appropriate professional boundaries.

1.10 Physical Contact

Social workers should not engage in physical contact with clients when there is a possibility of psychological harm to the client as a result of the contact (such as cradling or caressing clients). Social workers who engage in appropriate physical contact with clients are responsible for setting clear, appropriate, and culturally sensitive boundaries that govern such physical contact.

1.11 Sexual Harassment

Social workers should not sexually harass clients. Sexual harassment includes sexual advances, sexual solicitation, requests for sexual favors, and other verbal or physical conduct of a sexual nature.

1.12 Derogatory Language

Social workers should not use derogatory language in their written or verbal communications to or about clients. Social workers should use accurate and respectful language in all communications to and about clients.

1.13 Payment for Services

(a) When setting fees, social workers should ensure that the fees are fair, reasonable, and commensurate with the services performed. Consideration should be given to clients' ability to pay.

(b) Social workers should avoid accepting goods or services from clients as payment for professional services. Bartering arrangements, particularly involving services, create the potential for conflicts of interest, exploitation, and inappropriate boundaries in social workers' relationships with clients. Social workers should explore and may participate in bartering only in very limited circumstances when it can be demonstrated that such arrangements are an accepted practice among professionals in the local community, considered to be essential for the provision of services, negotiated without coercion, and entered into at the client's initiative and with the client's informed consent. Social workers who accept goods or services from clients as payment for professional services assume the full burden of demonstrating that this arrangement will not be detrimental to the client or the professional relationship.

(c) Social workers should not solicit a private fee or other remuneration for providing services to clients who are entitled to such available services through the social workers' employer or agency.

1.14 Clients Who Lack Decision-Making Capacity

When social workers act on behalf of clients who lack the capacity to make informed decisions, social workers should take reasonable steps to safeguard the interests and rights of those clients.

1.15 Interruption of Services

Social workers should make reasonable efforts to ensure continuity of services in the event that services are interrupted by factors such as unavailability, relocation, illness, disability, or death.

1.16 Termination of Services

(a) Social workers should terminate services to clients and professional relationships with them when such services and relationships are no longer required or no longer serve the clients' needs or interests.

(b) Social workers should take reasonable steps to avoid abandoning clients who are still in need of services. Social workers should withdraw services precipitously only under unusual circumstances, giving careful consideration to all factors in the situation and taking care to minimize possible adverse effects. Social workers should assist in making appropriate arrangements for continuation of services when necessary.

(c) Social workers in fee-for-service settings may terminate services to clients who are not paying an overdue balance if the financial contractual arrangements have been made clear to the client, if the client does not pose an imminent danger to self or others, and if the clinical and other consequences of the current nonpayment have been addressed and discussed with the client.

(d) Social workers should not terminate services to pursue a social, financial, or sexual relationship with a client.

(e) Social workers who anticipate the termination or interruption of services to clients should notify clients promptly and seek the transfer, referral, or continuation of services in relation to the clients' needs and preferences.

(f) Social workers who are leaving an employment setting should inform clients of appropriate options for the continuation of services and of the benefits and risks of the options.

2. SOCIAL WORKERS' ETHICAL RESPONSIBILITIES TO COLLEAGUES

2.01 Respect

(a) Social workers should treat colleagues with respect and should represent accurately and fairly the qualifications, views, and obligations of colleagues.

(b) Social workers should avoid unwarranted negative criticism of colleagues in communications with clients or with other professionals. Unwarranted negative criticism may include demeaning comments that refer to colleagues' level of competence or to individuals' attributes such as race, ethnicity, national origin, color, sex, sexual orientation, age, marital status, political belief, religion, and mental or physical disability.

(c) Social workers should cooperate with social work colleagues and with colleagues of other professions when such cooperation serves the well-being of clients.

2.02 Confidentiality

Social workers should respect confidential information shared by colleagues in the course of their professional relationships and transactions. Social workers should ensure that such colleagues understand social workers' obligation to respect confidentiality and any exceptions related to it.

2.03 Interdisciplinary Collaboration

(a) Social workers who are members of an interdisciplinary team should participate in and contribute to decisions that affect the well-being of clients by drawing on the perspectives, values, and experiences of the social work profession. Professional and ethical obligations of the interdisciplinary team as a whole and of its individual members should be clearly established.

(b) Social workers for whom a team decision raises ethical concerns should attempt to resolve the disagreement through appropriate channels. If the disagreement cannot be resolved, social workers should pursue other avenues to address their concerns consistent with client well-being.

2.04 Disputes Involving Colleagues

(a) Social workers should not take advantage of a dispute between a colleague and an employer to obtain a position or otherwise advance the social workers' own interests.

(b) Social workers should not exploit clients in disputes with colleagues or engage clients in any inappropriate discussion of conflicts between social workers and their colleagues.

2.05 Consultation

(a) Social workers should seek the advice and counsel of colleagues whenever such consultation is in the best interests of clients.

(b) Social workers should keep themselves informed about colleagues' areas of expertise and competencies. Social workers should seek consultation only from colleagues who have demonstrated knowledge, expertise, and competence related to the subject of the consultation.

(c) When consulting with colleagues about clients, social workers should disclose the least amount of information necessary to achieve the purposes of the consultation.

2.06 Referral for Services

(a) Social workers should refer clients to other professionals when the other professionals' specialized knowledge or expertise is needed to serve clients fully or when social workers believe that they are not being effective or making reasonable progress with clients and that additional service is required.

(b) Social workers who refer clients to other professionals should take appropriate steps to facilitate an orderly transfer of responsibility. Social workers who refer clients to other professionals should disclose, with clients' consent, all pertinent information to the new service providers.

(c) Social workers are prohibited from giving or receiving payment for a referral when no professional service is provided by the referring social worker.

2.07 Sexual Relationships

(a) Social workers who function as supervisors or educators should not engage in sexual activities or contact with supervisees, students, trainees, or other colleagues over whom they exercise professional authority.

(b) Social workers should avoid engaging in sexual relationships with colleagues when there is potential for a conflict of interest. Social workers who become involved in, or anticipate becoming involved in, a sexual relationship with a colleague have a duty to transfer professional responsibilities, when necessary, to avoid a conflict of interest.

2.08 Sexual Harassment

Social workers should not sexually harass supervisees, students, trainees, or colleagues. Sexual harassment includes sexual advances, sexual solicitation, requests for sexual favors, and other verbal or physical conduct of a sexual nature.

2.09 Impairment of Colleagues

(a) Social workers who have direct knowledge of a social work colleague's impairment that is due to personal problems, psychosocial distress, substance abuse, or mental health difficulties and that interferes with practice effectiveness should consult with that colleague when feasible and assist the colleague in taking remedial action.

(b) Social workers who believe that a social work colleague's impairment interferes with practice effectiveness and that the colleague has not taken adequate steps to address the impairment should take action through appropriate channels established by employers, agencies, NASW, licensing and regulatory bodies, and other professional organizations.

2.10 Incompetence of Colleagues

(a) Social workers who have direct knowledge of a social work colleague's incompetence should consult with that colleague when feasible and assist the colleague in taking remedial action.

(b) Social workers who believe that a social work colleague is incompetent and has not taken adequate steps to address the incompetence should take action through appropriate channels established by employers, agencies,

NASW, licensing and regulatory bodies, and other professional organizations.

2.11 Unethical Conduct of Colleagues

(a) Social workers should take adequate measures to discourage, prevent, expose, and correct the unethical conduct of colleagues.

(b) Social workers should be knowledgeable about established policies and procedures for handling concerns about colleagues' unethical behavior. Social workers should be familiar with national, state, and local procedures for handling ethics complaints. These include policies and procedures created by NASW, licensing and regulatory bodies, employers, agencies, and other professional organizations.

(c) Social workers who believe that a colleague has acted unethically should seek resolution by discussing their concerns with the colleague when feasible and when such discussion is likely to be productive.

(d) When necessary, social workers who believe that a colleague has acted unethically should take action through appropriate formal channels (such as contacting a state licensing board or regulatory body, an NASW committee on inquiry, or other professional ethics committees).

(e) Social workers should defend and assist colleagues who are unjustly charged with unethical conduct.

3. SOCIAL WORKERS' ETHICAL RESPONSIBILITIES IN PRACTICE SETTINGS

3.01 Supervision and Consultation

(a) Social workers who provide supervision or consultation should have the necessary knowledge and skill to supervise or consult appropriately and should do so only within their areas of knowledge and competence.

(b) Social workers who provide supervision or consultation are responsible for setting clear, appropriate, and culturally sensitive boundaries.

(c) Social workers should not engage in any dual or multiple relationships with supervisees in which there is a risk of exploitation of or potential harm to the supervisee.

(d) Social workers who provide supervision should evaluate supervisees' performance in a manner that is fair and respectful.

3.02 Education and Training

(a) Social workers who function as educators, field instructors for students, or trainers should provide instruction only within their areas of knowledge and competence and should provide instruction based on the most current information and knowledge available in the profession.

(b) Social workers who function as educators or field instructors for students should evaluate students' performance in a manner that is fair and respectful.

(c) Social workers who function as educators or field instructors for students should take reasonable steps to ensure that clients are routinely informed when services are being provided by students.

(d) Social workers who function as educators or field instructors for students should not engage in any dual or multiple relationships with students in which there is a risk of exploitation or potential harm to the student. Social work educators and field instructors are responsible for setting clear, appropriate, and culturally sensitive boundaries.

3.03 Performance Evaluation

Social workers who have responsibility for evaluating the performance of others should fulfill such responsibility in a fair and considerate manner and on the basis of clearly stated criteria.

3.04 Client Records

(a) Social workers should take reasonable steps to ensure that documentation in records is accurate and reflects the services provided.

(b) Social workers should include sufficient and timely documentation in records to facilitate the delivery of services and to ensure continuity of services provided to clients in the future.

(c) Social workers' documentation should protect clients' privacy to the extent that is possible and appropriate and should include only information that is directly relevant to the delivery of services.

(d) Social workers should store records following the termination of services to ensure reasonable future access. Records should be maintained for the number of years required by state statutes or relevant contracts.

3.05 Billing

Social workers should establish and maintain billing practices that accurately reflect the nature and extent of services provided and that identify who provided the service in the practice setting.

3.06 Client Transfer

(a) When an individual who is receiving services from another agency or colleague contacts a social worker for services, the social worker should carefully consider the client's needs before agreeing to provide services. To minimize possible confusion and conflict, social workers should discuss with potential clients the nature of the clients' current relationship with other service providers and the implications, including possible benefits or risks, of entering into a relationship with a new service provider.

(b) If a new client has been served by another agency or colleague, social workers should discuss with the client whether consultation with the previous service provider is in the client's best interest.

3.07 Administration

(a) Social work administrators should advocate within and outside their agencies for adequate resources to meet clients' needs.

(b) Social workers should advocate for resource allocation procedures that are open and fair. When not all clients' needs can be met, an allocation procedure should be developed that is nondiscriminatory and based on appropriate and consistently applied principles.

(c) Social workers who are administrators should take reasonable steps to ensure that adequate agency or organizational resources are available to provide appropriate staff supervision.

(d) Social work administrators should take reasonable steps to ensure that the working environment for which they are responsible is consistent with and encourages compliance with the *NASW Code of Ethics*. Social work administrators should take reasonable steps to eliminate any conditions in their organizations that violate, interfere with, or discourage compliance with the *Code*.

3.08 Continuing Education and Staff Development

Social work administrators and supervisors should take reasonable steps to provide or arrange for continuing education and staff development for all staff for whom they are responsible. Continuing education and staff development should address current knowledge and emerging developments related to social work practice and ethics.

3.09 Commitments to Employers

(a) Social workers generally should adhere to commitments made to employers and employing organizations.

(b) Social workers should work to improve employing agencies' policies and procedures and the efficiency and effectiveness of their services.

(c) Social workers should take reasonable steps to ensure that employers are aware of social workers' ethical obligations as set forth in the *NASW Code of Ethics* and of the implications of those obligations for social work practice.

(d) Social workers should not allow an employing organization's policies, procedures, regulations, or administrative orders to interfere with their ethical practice of social work. Social workers should take reasonable steps to ensure that their employing organizations' practices are consistent with the *NASW Code of Ethics*.

(e) Social workers should act to prevent and eliminate discrimination in the employing organization's work assignments and in its employment policies and practices.

(f) Social workers should accept employment or arrange student field placements only in organizations that exercise fair personnel practices.

(g) Social workers should be diligent stewards of the resources of their employing organizations, wisely conserving funds where appropriate and never misappropriating funds or using them for unintended purposes.

3.10 Labor-Management Disputes

(a) Social workers may engage in organized action, including the formation of and participation in labor unions, to improve services to clients and working conditions.

(b) The actions of social workers who are involved in labor-management disputes, job actions, or labor strikes should be guided by the profession's values, ethical principles, and ethical standards. Reasonable differences of opinion exist among social workers concerning their primary obligation as professionals during an actual or threatened labor strike or job action. Social workers should carefully examine relevant issues and their possible impact on clients before deciding on a course of action.

4. SOCIAL WORKERS' ETHICAL RESPONSIBILITIES AS PROFESSIONALS

4.01 Competence

(a) Social workers should accept responsibility or employment only on the basis of existing competence or the intention to acquire the necessary competence.

(b) Social workers should strive to become and remain proficient in professional practice and the performance of professional functions. Social workers should critically examine and keep current with emerging knowledge relevant to social work. Social workers should routinely review the professional literature and participate in continuing education relevant to social work practice and social work ethics.

(c) Social workers should base practice on recognized knowledge, including empirically based knowledge, relevant to social work and social work ethics.

4.02 Discrimination

Social workers should not practice, condone, facilitate, or collaborate with any form of discrimination on the basis of race, ethnicity, national origin, color, sex, sexual orientation, age, marital status, political belief, religion, or mental or physical disability.

4.03 Private Conduct

Social workers should not permit their private conduct to interfere with their ability to fulfill their professional responsibilities.

4.04 Dishonesty, Fraud, and Deception

Social workers should not participate in, condone, or be associated with dishonesty, fraud, or deception.

4.05 Impairment

(a) Social workers should not allow their own personal problems, psychosocial distress, legal problems, substance abuse, or mental health difficulties to interfere with their professional judgment and performance or to jeopardize the best interests of people for whom they have a professional responsibility.

(b) Social workers whose personal problems, psychosocial distress, legal problems, substance abuse, or mental health difficulties interfere with their professional judgment and performance should immediately seek consultation and take appropriate remedial action by seeking professional help, making adjustments in workload, terminating practice, or taking any other steps necessary to protect clients and others.

4.06 Misrepresentation

(a) Social workers should make clear distinctions between statements made and actions engaged in as a private individual and as a representative of the social work profession, a professional social work organization, or the social worker's employing agency.

(b) Social workers who speak on behalf of professional social work organizations should accurately represent the official and authorized positions of the organizations.

(c) Social workers should ensure that their representations to clients, agencies, and the public of professional qualifications, credentials, education, competence, affiliations, services provided, or results to be achieved are accurate. Social workers should claim only those relevant professional credentials they actually possess and take steps to correct any inaccuracies or misrepresentations of their credentials by others.

4.07 Solicitations

(a) Social workers should not engage in uninvited solicitation of potential clients who, because of their circumstances, are vulnerable to undue influence, manipulation, or coercion.

(b) Social workers should not engage in solicitation of testimonial endorsements (including solicitation of consent to use a client's prior statement as a testimonial endorsement) from current clients or from other people who, because of their particular circumstances, are vulnerable to undue influence.

4.08 Acknowledging Credit

(a) Social workers should take responsibility and credit, including authorship credit, only for work they have actually performed and to which they have contributed.

(b) Social workers should honestly acknowledge the work of and the contributions made by others.

5. SOCIAL WORKERS' ETHICAL RESPONSIBILITIES TO THE SOCIAL WORK PROFESSION

5.01 Integrity of the Profession

(a) Social workers should work toward the maintenance and promotion of high standards of practice.

(b) Social workers should uphold and advance the values, ethics, knowledge, and mission of the profession. Social workers should protect, enhance, and improve the integrity of the profession through appropriate study and research, active discussion, and responsible criticism of the profession.

(c) Social workers should contribute time and professional expertise to activities that promote respect for the value, integrity, and competence of the social work profession. These activities may include teaching, research, consultation, service, legislative testimony, presentations in the community, and participation in their professional organizations.

(d) Social workers should contribute to the knowledge base of social work and share with colleagues their knowledge related to practice, research, and ethics. Social workers should seek to contribute to the profession's literature and to share their knowledge at professional meetings and conferences.

(e) Social workers should act to prevent the unauthorized and unqualified practice of social work.

5.02 Evaluation and Research

(a) Social workers should monitor and evaluate policies, the implementation of programs, and practice interventions.

(b) Social workers should promote and facilitate evaluation and research to contribute to the development of knowledge.

(c) Social workers should critically examine and keep current with emerging knowledge relevant to social work and fully use evaluation and research evidence in their professional practice.

(d) Social workers engaged in evaluation or research should carefully consider possible consequences and should follow guidelines developed for the protection of evaluation and research participants. Appropriate institutional review boards should be consulted.

(e) Social workers engaged in evaluation or research should obtain voluntary and written informed consent from participants, when appropriate, without any implied or actual deprivation or penalty for refusal to participate; without undue inducement to participate; and with due regard for participants' well-being, privacy, and dignity. Informed consent should include information about the nature, extent, and duration of the participation requested and disclosure of the risks and benefits of participation in the research.

(f) When evaluation or research participants are incapable of giving informed consent, social workers should provide an appropriate explanation to the participants, obtain the participants' assent to the extent they are able, and obtain written consent from an appropriate proxy.

(g) Social workers should never design or conduct evaluation or research that does not use consent procedures, such as certain forms of naturalistic observation and archival research, unless rigorous and responsible review of the research has found it to be justified because of its prospective scientific, educational, or applied value and unless equally effective alternative procedures that do not involve waiver of consent are not feasible.

(h) Social workers should inform participants of their right to withdraw from evaluation and research at any time without penalty.

(i) Social workers should take appropriate steps to ensure that participants in evaluation and research have access to appropriate supportive services.

(j) Social workers engaged in evaluation or research should protect participants from unwarranted physical or mental distress, harm, danger, or deprivation.

(k) Social workers engaged in the evaluation of services should discuss collected information only for professional purposes and only with people professionally concerned with this information.

(l) Social workers engaged in evaluation or research should ensure the anonymity or confidentiality of participants and of the data obtained from them. Social workers should inform participants of any limits of confidentiality, the measures that will be taken to ensure confidentiality, and when any records containing research data will be destroyed.

(m) Social workers who report evaluation and research results should protect participants' confidentiality by omitting identifying information unless proper consent has been obtained authorizing disclosure.

(n) Social workers should report evaluation and research findings accurately. They should not fabricate or falsify results and should take steps to correct any errors later found in published data using standard publication methods.

(o) Social workers engaged in evaluation or research should be alert to and avoid conflicts of interest and dual relationships with participants, should inform participants when a real or potential conflict of interest arises, and should take steps to resolve the issue in a manner that makes participants' interests primary.

(p) Social workers should educate themselves, their students, and their colleagues about responsible research practices.

6. SOCIAL WORKERS' ETHICAL RESPONSIBILITIES TO THE BROADER SOCIETY

6.01 Social Welfare

Social workers should promote the general welfare of society, from local to global levels, and the development of people, their communities, and their environments. Social workers should advocate for living conditions conducive to the fulfillment of basic human needs and should promote social, economic, political, and cultural values and institutions that are compatible with the realization of social justice.

6.02 Public Participation

Social workers should facilitate informed participation by the public in shaping social policies and institutions.

6.03 Public Emergencies

Social workers should provide appropriate professional services in public emergencies to the greatest extent possible.

6.04 Social and Political Action

(a) Social workers should engage in social and political action that seeks to ensure that all people have equal access to the resources, employment, services, and opportunities they require to meet their basic human needs and to develop fully. Social workers should be aware of the impact of the political arena on practice and should advocate for changes in policy and legislation to improve social conditions in order to meet basic human needs and promote social justice.

(b) Social workers should act to expand choice and opportunity for all people, with special regard for vulnerable, disadvantaged, oppressed, and exploited people and groups.

(c) Social workers should promote conditions that encourage respect for cultural and social diversity within the United States and globally. Social workers should promote policies and practices that demonstrate respect for difference, support the expansion of cultural knowledge and resources, advocate for programs and institutions that demonstrate cultural competence, and promote policies that safeguard the rights of and confirm equity and social justice for all people.

(d) Social workers should act to prevent and eliminate domination of, exploitation of, and discrimination against any person, group, or class on the basis of race, ethnicity, national origin, color, sex, sexual orientation, age, marital status, political belief, religion, or mental or physical disability.

REFERENCES

Abrams, F. (1989). Bio-medical ethics. Ethics Workshop. University of Colorado Health Sciences Center, Denver, Colorado, April-May, 1989.

Abramson, M. (1996). Toward a more holistic understanding of ethics in social work. *Social Work in Health Care, 23*(2), 1–14.

Alexander, C. (1985). Contradictions of contemporary society and social work ethics. *International Social Work, 28*(3), 1–8.

Allen, J. (2002). *Culture change planner.* Available at: http://www.healthyculture.com/articles/

Allen, J. A. (1993). The constructivist paradigm: Values and ethics. *Journal of Teaching in Social Work, 8*(1/2), 31–54.

Alter, C. (1997). Democracy in organizations: Revisiting feminist organizations. In W. Powell (Ed.). *Private action and the public good.* New Haven, CT: Yale University Press.

Alter, C. (2000). Opening address to graduate class of 2000. Graduate School of Social Work, University of Denver, Denver, Colorado, May 2000.

Andrews, K. (1989). Ethics in practice. *Harvard Business Review* (September-October), 99–104.

Arches, J. L. (1997). Connecting to communities: Transformational leadership from Afrocentric and feminist perspectives. *Journal of Sociology and Social Welfare, 24*(4), 113–126.

Arendt, H. (1963). *Eichmann in Jerusalem: A report on the banality of evil.* New York: The Viking Press.

Arendt, H. (1978). *The life of the mind: Thinking* (Vol. I). New York: Harcourt-Brace-Jovanovich.

Aristotle. (1987). The Nicomechean ethics (J.E.D. Welldon, Translator). Amherst, NY: Prometheus Books.

Arlin, P. (1975). Cognitive development in adulthood: A fifth stage? *Developmental Psychology, 11*, 602–606.

Azumi, K. & Hage, J. (1972). *Organizational systems: A test-reader in the sociology of organizations.* Lexington, MA: D. C. Heath & Co.

Bandura, A. (1971). Analysis of modeling process. In A. Bandura (Ed.). *Psychological modeling.* Chicago: Atherton-Aldine.

Bandura, A. (1977). *Social learning theory.* Englewood Cliffs, NJ: Prentice Hall.

Bartlett, H. (1970). *The common base of social work practice.* New York: NASW.

Belenky, M., Clinchy, B., Goldberger, N., & Tarule, J. (1986). *Women's ways of knowing.* New York: Basic Books.

Berliner, A. (1989). Misconduct in social work practice. *Social Work* (January), 69–72.

Billingsly, A. (1964). Bureaucratic and professional orientation patterns in social casework. *Social Service Review, 38*, 400–407.

Bird, F. & Waters, J. (1987). The nature of managerial moral standards. *Journal of Business Ethics, 6*, 1–13.

Blake, R. & Mouton, J. (1964). *The managerial grid.* Houston, TX: Gulf Publishing.

Bly, C. (1996). Evil in the comfortable herd. In C. Bly (Ed.). *Changing the bully* (pp. 373–390). Minneapolis, MN: Milkweed Editions.

Boatright, J. R. (1988). Ethics and the role of the manager. *Journal of Business Ethics, 7*, 302–303.

Bommer, J., Gratto, C., Gravauder, J., & Tuttle, M. (1987). A behavioral model of ethical and unethical decision-making. *Journal of Business Ethics, 6*, 265–280.

Brady, F. N. (1990). *Ethical managing: Rules and results.* New York: Macmillan.

Brilliant, E. L. (1986). Social work leadership: A missing ingredient? *Social Work* (September-October), 325–330.

Brower, H. & Shrader, C. (2000). Moral reasoning and ethical climate: Not-for-profit vs for-profit boards of directors. *Journal of Business Ethics, 36,* 147–167.

Brummer, J. (1985). Business ethics: Micro and macro. *Journal of Business Ethics, 4,* 81–91.

Burns, J. (1978). *Leadership.* New York: Harper & Row.

Carroll, A. B. (1975). Managerial ethics: A post Watergate view. *Business Horizons, 18,* 75–80.

Christensen, K. (1986). Ethics of information technology. In G. Geiss (Ed.). *The human edge* (pp. 72–91). New York: Haworth.

Christensen, K. (1995). Ethically important distinctions among managed care organizations. *Journal of Law, Medicine, and Ethics, 23,* 223–229.

Cohen, B. (1987). The ethics of supervision revisited. *Social Work* (May-June), 194–196.

Colby, A. (1994). *Some do care: Contemporary lives of moral commitment.* New York: The Free Press.

Coleman, J. (1973). Loss of power. *American Sociological Review, 38,* 1-17.

Collier, J. & Roberts, J. (2001). An ethic for corporate governance? *Business Ethics Quarterly, 11,* 67–71.

Colorado Association of Nonprofit Organizations (CANPO) (1994). *Conducting an ethics audit: A checklist for nonprofits.* Denver, CO: Author.

Conger, J. & Kanungo, R. (1988). The empowerment process: Integrating theory and practice. *Academy of Management Review, 13,* 471–481.

Congress, E. (1986). *An analysis of ethical practice among field instructors in social work education.* Unpublished doctoral dissertation. City University of New York, New York.

Connors, T. (1988). *The non-profit organization handbook.* New York: McGraw-Hill.

Conrad, A. (1988). Ethical considerations in the psychosocial process. *Social Casework: The Journal of Contemporary Casework, December,* 603–610.

Cooke, R. (1991). Danger signs of unethical behavior: How to determine if your firm is at ethical risk. *Journal of Business Ethics, 10,* 249–253.

Cossum, J. (1992). What do we know about social workers' ethics? *The Social Worker/Le Travailleur Social, 60*(3), 165–171.

Council on Social Work Education. (1998). Council on social work education strategic plan: 1998–2000. *Social Work Education Reporter, 46*(1), 15–18.

Cox, E. & Joseph, B. (1998). Social service delivery and empowerment: The administrator's role. In L. Gutierrez, R. Parsons, & E. Cox (Eds.). *Empowerment in social work practice: A sourcebook* (pp. 3–23). Pacific Grove, CA: Brooks/Cole.

Csikai, E. L. & Sales, E. (1998). The emerging social work role on hospital ethics committees: A comparison of social worker and chair perspectives. *Social Work, 43*(3), 233–242.

Curtain, L. (2000). On being a person of integrity—or ethics and other liabilities. *The Journal of Continuing Education in Nursing, 31*(2), 55–58.

Dalai Lama, His Holiness. (1999). *Ethics for the new millennium.* New York: Riverhead Books.

Damon, W. (1999). The moral development of children. *Scientific American* (August), 72–78.

de Vries, P. (1988). Godel, Gadamer, and ethical business leadership. *Business and Professional Ethics Journal, 5*(3/4), 136–149.

Deal, T. (1987). The culture of schools. In L. Shein & M. Schoenheit (Eds.). *Leadership: Examining the elusive.* Yearbook of the Association for Supervision and Curriculum Development. Alexandria, VA: ASCD Publications.

DeGeorge, R. (1987). The status of business ethics: Past and future. *Journal of Business Ethics, 6,* 201–211.

Dobel, J. (1998). Political prudence and the ethics of leadership. *Public Administration Review*, *58*(1), 74–81.

Dobrin, A. (1989). Ethical judgments of male and female social workers. *Social Work* (September), 451–455.

Drucker, P. (1968). *The practice of management*. London: Pan Books.

England, G. W. (1967). Personal value systems of American managers. *Academy of Management Journal, 10*, 53–68.

Enz, C. (1988). Role of value congruity in intraorganizational power. *Administrative Science Quarterly, 33*, 284–304.

Felkenes, S. (1990). *The social work professional and his ethics: A philosophical analysis*. Unpublished doctoral dissertation. University of Alabama, Birmingham, Alabama.

Fielder, F., Chemers, M., & Mahar, L. (1978). *The leadership match concept*. New York: John Wiley & Sons.

Filley, A., House, R., & Kerr, S. (1976). *Managerial process and organizational behavior*. Glenview, IL: Scott, Foresman & Company.

Fisher, R. & Karger, H. J. (1997). *Social work and community in a private world: Getting out in public*. New York: Longman.

Fleck-Henderson, A. (1991). Moral reasoning in social work practice. *Social Service Review* (June), 185–202.

Fost, N. & Cranford, R. (1985). Hospital ethics committees: Administrative aspects. *Journal of The American Medical Association, 253*, 2087–2692.

Fox, M. (1997). The moral community. In H. LaFollette (Ed.), *Ethics in practice: An anthology*. Cambridge, MA: Blackwell.

Frankena, W. K. (1973). *Ethics* (2nd ed.). Englewood Cliffs, NJ: Prentice Hall.

Frankena, W. K. (1982). *Ethics* (4th ed.). Englewood Cliffs, NJ: Prentice Hall.

Freeman, S. J. (2000). *Ethics: An introduction to philosophy*. Belmont, CA: Wadsworth & Thomson Learning.

French, R. & Raven, B. (1959). The bases of social power. In D. Cartwright (Ed.). *Studies in Social Power* (pp. 150–167). Ann Arbor: University of Michigan Institute for Social Research.

Friedman, E. (1989). The torturer's horse. *JAMA, 26*(10), 1481–1482.

Friedman, E. (1990). Ethics and corporate culture: Finding a fit. *Healthcare Executive* (March/April), 18–20.

Freire, P. (1970). *Pedagogy of the oppressed*. New York: Continuum.

Gardner, J. (1990). *On leadership*. New York: The Free Press.

Gilligan, C. (1981). Moral development. In A. Chickering (Ed.). *The modern American college: Today's students and their needs* (pp. 139–157). San Francisco: Jossey-Bass.

Gilligan, C. (1982). *In a different voice: Psychological theory and women's development*. Cambridge, MA: Harvard University Press.

Gilligan, C. & Attanucci, J. (1988). Two moral orientations. In C. Gilligan, J. Ward, & J. Taylor (Eds.), *Mapping the Moral Domain* (pp. 73–86). Cambridge, MA: Harvard University Press.

Goodpaster, K. (1983). The concept of corporate responsibility. *Journal of Business Ethics, 2*, 1–22.

Gould, K. H. (1988). Old wine in new bottles: A feminist perspective in Gilligan's theory. *Social Work* (September-October), 411–415.

Green, T. (1987). The conscience of leadership. In L. Sheive & M. Schoenheit (Eds.). *Leadership: Examining the elusive*. Alexandria, VA: Association for Supervision and Curriculum Development.

Gregg, D. (1985). *Graduation address*. University of Colorado School of Nursing, Health Sciences Center, Denver, CO.

Gross, C. (1973). Shaping the new social work. In A. Kohn (Ed.). *Shaping the new social work* (pp. 77–96). New York: Columbia University.

Gruber, J. & Trickett, E. (1987). Can we empower others? The paradox of empowerment in the governing of an alternative public school. *American Journal of Community Psychology, 15,* 353–371.

Gummer, B. (1984). The changing context of social administration: Tight money, loose organization, and uppity workers. *Administration in Social Work, 8*(3), 5–15.

Gummer, B. (1996). Ethics and administrative practice: Care, justice, and the responsible administrator. *Administration in Social Work, 20*(4), 89–106.

Gutierrez, L., Parsons, R., & Cox, E. (1998). *Empowerment in social work practice: A sourcebook.* Pacific Grove, CA: Brooks/Cole.

Handler, J. (1992). Dependency and discretion. In Y. Hasenfeld (Ed.). *Human services as complex organizations.* Newbury Park, CA: Sage Publications.

Hardin, R. (1990). The artificial duties of contemporary professionals. *Social Service Review, December,* 528–541.

Hasenfeld, Y. and English, R. (Eds.). (1974). *Human service organizations.* Ann Arbor, MI: University of Michigan.

Hasenfeld, Y. (1983). *Human services organizations.* Englewood Cliffs, NJ: Prentice Hall.

Hasenfeld, Y. (1992). *Human services as complex organizations.* Newbury Park, CA: Sage.

Havel, V. (1986). *Living in the truth.* (Jan Valdislav, Translator). London: Faber and Faber.

Helgesen, S. (1990). *The female advantage: Women's ways of leadership.* New York: Doubleday.

Hershey, P. & Blanchard, P. (1977). *Management of organizational behavior.* Upper Saddle, NJ: Prentice-Hall.

Hobbes, T. (1996). *Leviathen* (R.Tuck, Ed.). Cambridge, MA: Cambridge University Press (original work published in 1651).

Hoffmann, D. E. (1993). Evaluating ethics committees: A view from the outside. *The Milbank Quarterly, 71*(4), 677–701.

Heil, W. (1991). *Re-reviewing participation toward decision-making: Toward a multi-dimensional model.* Paper presented at the 99th annual convention of the American Psychological Association. San Francisco, CA.

Holland, T. (1989). Values, faith, and professional practice. *Social Thought* (Winter), 28–40.

Holland, T. & Kilpatrick, A. (1991). Ethical issues in social work: Toward a grounded theory of professional ethics. *Social Work, 36*(2), 138–144.

House, R. (1971). A path-goal theory of leader effectiveness. *Administrative Science Quarterly, 16,* 321–339.

Howe, E. (1980). Available at: *http://www.scu.edu/SCU/*

Howe, E. (1980). Public professions and the private model of professionalism. *Social Work, 25*(3), 179–191.

Imre, R. W. (1982). *Knowing and caring: Philosophical issues in social work.* Lanham, MD: University Press of America.

Imre, R. W. (1989). Moral theory for social work. *Social Thought* (Winter), 18–27.

Jackall, R. (1988). *Moral mazes.* New York: Oxford.

Jayaratne, S., Croxton, T., & Mattison, D. (1997). Social work professional standards: An exploratory study. *Social Work, 42*(2), 187–199.

Jennings, B. Lying, cheating, stealing: *For the best interests of the client?* In Search of Civic Professionalism Workshop, May, 2001, conducted at the University of Denver, Carl Williams Institute for Ethics and Values, Denver, Colorado.

Jennings, B., Callahan, D., & Wolf, X. (1987). The public duties of the professions. *Hastings Center Report, 17,* 1–20.

Johnson, C. (2001). *Meeting the ethical challenges of leadership: Casting light or shadow.* Thousand Oaks, CA: Sage.

Joseph, V. (1983). The ethics of organizations: Shifting values & ethical dilemmas. *Administration in Social Work,* 7, 47–57.

Kanter, R. (1979). Power failure in management circuits. *Harvard Business Review,* 57(4), 65–75.

Kanungo, R. & Mendoca, M. (1996). *Ethical dimensions of leadership.* Thousand Oaks, CA: Sage.

Kant, E. (1963). Lectures on ethics. (L. Infield, Translator). Indianapolis: Hackett Publishing Co.

Karger, H. (1981). Burnout and alienation. *Social Service Review,* 55, 270–283.

Kass, L. (1990). Practicing ethics: Where's the action? *Hastings Center Report,* 20(1), 5–12.

Kay, J. (1996). *The business of economics.* London: Oxford University Press.

Keeley, M. (1983). Values in organizational theory and management education. *Academy of Management Review,* 8(3), 376–386.

Keith-Lucas, A. (1977). Ethics in social work. *Encyclopedia of social work* (pp. 350–355). Washington, DC: National Association of Social Workers.

Kelly, J. (2000). *Similar values in a time-scarce world.* Remarks, Southern Institute of Ethics, October 12, 2000, Atlanta, GA.

King, J. (1986). Ethical encounters of the second kind. *Journal of Business Ethics,* 5, 1–10.

Kingsolver, B. (1993). *Pigs in heaven.* New York: HarperCollins Publishers.

Kitchener, K. (1996). There is more to ethics than principles. *Counseling Psychologist,* 24(1), 92–97.

Klein, L. (1991). Ethical decision making in a business environment. *Review of Business* (Winter), 27–29.

Koehn, D. (1994). *The ground of professional ethics.* London/New York: Routledge.

Kohlberg, L. (1981). *The meaning and measurement of moral development.* Worcester, MA: Clark University, Heinz Erner Institute.

Kohlberg, L. & Elfenbein, D. (1975). The development of moral judgments concerning capital punishment. *American Journal of Orthopsychiatry* 45(4), 634.

Kugelman-Jafee, W. (1990). *Ethical decision-making of social work practitioners in organizational settings.* Unpublished doctoral dissertation. City University of New York, New York.

Kweit, M. G. & Kweit, R. W. (1981). *Implementing citizen participation in a bureaucratic society.* New York: Praeger Publishers.

Ladd, J. (1970). Morality and the ideal of rationality in formal organizations. *The Monist,* 54, 448–516.

Levy, C. (1976). *Social work ethics.* New York: Human Services Press.

Levy, C. (1979). The ethics of management. *Administration in Social Work,* 3, 277–287.

Levy, C. (1982). *Guide to ethical decisions and actions for social service administrators: A handbook for managerial personnel.* New York: Haworth.

Levy, C. (1983). Ideological pathways to policy and practice. *Administration in Social Work,* 7(2), 51–61.

Levy, C. (1988). Ethics in social work. *The Jewish Social Work Forum,* 24 (Spring), 23–29.

Levy, C. S. (1993). *Social work ethics on the line.* New York: Haworth.

Lewis, H. (1989). Ethics and the private non-profit human service organization. *Administration in Social Work,* 13(2), 1–14.

Leys, W. A. (1941). *Ethics and social policy.* New York: Prentice-Hall.

Linzer, N. (1999). *Resolving ethical dilemma in social work practice.* Boston: Allyn & Bacon.

Littrell, W., Sjoberg, G., & Zurcher, L. (Eds.). (1983). *Bureaucracy as a social problem.* Greenwich, CT: JAI Press.

Loewenberg, F., Dolgoff, R., & Harrington, D. (2000). *Ethical decisions for social work practice.* Itasca, IL: F.E. Peacock.

Longenecker, J. (1985). Management priorities and management ethics. *Journal of Business Ethics*, 4, 65–70.

Longworth, R. C. (2001). As economy sinks; CEO pay soaring. *The Denver Post*, August 28. p. 2A.

Lukes, S. (1974). *Power: A radical view*. London: Macmillan.

Maqsud, M. (1980). Locus of control and stages of moral reasoning. *Psychological Reports*, 46, 1243–1248.

Manning S. (1990). *Ethical decisions: A grounded theory approach to the experience of social work managers and administrators*. Dissertation Abstracts International.

Manning, S. (1994). *The Norplant initiative: A community conversation about ethics. A research report*. Denver, CO: University of Denver Graduate School of Social Work.

Manning, S. (1997). The social worker as moral citizen. *Social Work*, 42(3), 223–230.

Manning, S. & Gaul, C. (1997). The ethics of informed consent: A critical variable in the self-determination of health and mental health clients. *Social Work in Health Care*. 25(3), 103–117.

Markula Center for Applied Ethics (2000). Approaching ethics. Available at: *http://www .scu.edu/SCU/centeredethics*.

Markula Center for Applied Ethics (2000). Calculating consequences. Available at: *http://www .scu.edu/SCU/centeredethics*.

Markula Center for Applied Ethics (2000). The common good. Available at: *http://www .scu.edu/SCU/centeredethics*.

Markula Center for Applied Ethics (2000). Decision framework. Available at: *http://www .scu.edu/SCU/centeredethics*.

Markula Center for Applied Ethics (2000). Ethics and virtue. Available at: *http://www .scu.edu/SCU/centeredethics*.

Markula Center for Applied Ethics (2000). Justice and fairness. Available at: *http://www .scu.edu/SCU/centeredethics*.

Markula Center for Applied Ethics (2000). Rights approach. Available at: *http://www .scu.edu/SCU/centeredethics*.

Markula Center for Applied Ethics (2000). The utilitarian approach to ethics. Available at: http://www.scu.edu/SCU/centeredethics.

Maton, K., & Salem, D. (1995). Organizational characteristics of empowering community settings: A multiple case study approach. *American Journal of Community Psychology*, 23(5), 631–656.

Matthews, M. (1988). Ethics: Strategic planning and intervention. In M. Matthews (Ed.). *Strategic intervention in organizations* (pp.131–143). Newbury Park, CA: Sage.

Mattison, M. (2000). Ethical decision-making: Person in the process. *Social Work*, 45(3), 201–212.

McCall, J. (2001). Employee voice in corporate governance: A defense of strong participation rights. *Business Ethics Quarterly*, 11(1), 195–213.

McClenahen, J. (1999). *Your employees know better: Companies can't get away with bad ethics programs*. Executive Briefing: Prenton/IPC.

McCoy, C. (1985). *Management of values: The ethical difference in corporate policy and performance*. Marshfield, MA: Pitman Publishing, Inc.

McKnight, J. (1989). Do no harm: Policy options that meet human needs. *Social Policy* (Summer), 5–15.

Messick, D. M. & Bazerman, M. H. (1996). Ethical leadership and the psychology of decision-making. *Sloan Management Review* (Winter), 9–22.

Milgram, S. (1974). *Obedience to authority*. New York: Harper and Row.

Moran, J., Frans, D., & Gibson, P. (1995). A comparison of beginning MSW and MBA students on their aptitudes for human service management. *Journal of Social Work Education, 31,* 95–105.

Morgan, G (1986). *Images of organization.* Beverly Hills, CA: Sage Publications.

Morgan, G. (1989). *Creative organization theory.* Newbury Park, CA: Sage.

Morgan, G. (1997). *Images of organization* (2nd ed.). Thousand Oaks, CA: Sage.

Nance, J. (1998). *Enhancing patient safety through solutions.* Plenary address. Denver, CO.

Nanus, B. & Dobbs, S. (1999). *Leaders who make a difference: Essential strategies for meeting the nonprofit challenge.* San Francisco: Jossey-Bass.

National Association of Social Workers. (1979). *NASW Code of Ethics.* Silver Spring, MD: NASW.

National Association of Social Workers. (1996). *NASW Code of Ethics.* Washington, DC: NASW.

Neilson, R. (1984). Toward an action philosophy for managers based on Arendt and Tillich. *Journal of Busines Ethics, 3,* 153–161.

Newton, L. (1981). Lawgiving for professional life: Reflections on the place of the professional code. *Business and Professional Ethics Journal, 1*(1), 41–54.

Niebuhr, R. (1960). *Moral man and immoral society.* (1932 reprint). New York: Charles Scribner & Sons.

Noelle-Neuman, E. (1997). The spiral of silence. *The Chronicle of Higher Education* (August 8), A–13.

Northern, H. (1998). Ethical dilemmas in social work with groups. *Social Work with Groups, 21* (1/2), 5–17.

Norton, D. (1976). *Personal destinies: A philosophy of ethical individualism.* Princeton, NJ: Princeton University Press.

Norton, D. (1988). Character ethics and organizational life. In W. D. Wright (Ed.). *Papers on the ethics of administration.* Provo, UT: Brigham Young University.

Paine, L. S. (1994). Managing for organizational integrity. *Harvard Business Review, 72*(2), 106–117.

Palmer, P. (1996). Leading from within. In L. C. Spears (Ed.). *Insights on leadership: service, stewardship, spirit and servant-leadership* (pp. 197–208). New York: John Wiley & Sons.

Patti, R. (1985). In search of purpose for social welfare administration. *Administration in Social Work, 9*(3), 1–15.

Perlman, H. (1976). Believing and doing: Values in social work education. *Social Casework, 57,* 381–390.

Perry, W. G. (1981). Cognitive and ethical growth: The making of meaning. In A. Chickering (Ed.). *The modern American college: Today's students and their needs* (pp. 76–116). San Francisco: Jossey-Bass.

Perry, W. (1968). *Forms of intellectual and ethical development in the college years.* Boston: Holt, Rinehart & Winston.

Petrick, J. & Quinn, J. (1997). *Management ethics: Integrity at work.* Thousand Oaks, CA: Sage.

Posner, B. Z. & Schmidt, W. H. (1987). Ethics in American companies: A managerial perspective. *Journal of Business Ethics, 6,* 383–391.

Rachels, J. (1980). Can ethics provide answers? *The Hastings Center Report* (June), 32–40.

Rank, M. & Hutchison, W. (2000). An analysis of leadership within the social work profession. *Journal of Social Work Education, 36*(3), 487–505.

Rankin, N. (1988). Corporations as persons: Objections to Goodpaster's principle of moral projection. *Journal of Business Ethics, 2,* 633–637.

Rawls, J. (1971). *A theory of justice.* Cambridge, MA: Harvard University Press.

Reamer, F. (1980). Ethical content in social work. *Social Casework, 61,* 531-540.

Reamer, F. (1982). *Ethical dilemmas in social services.* New York: Columbia University.

Reamer, F. (1985). The emergence of bioethics in social work. *Health and Social Work,* 271–281.

Reamer, F. (1987a). Informed consent in social work. *Social Work, 32,* 425–429.

Reamer, F. (1987b). Social work: Calling or career? In Jennings, B., Callahan, D., & Wolf, S. *The public duties of the professions* (pp. 14–15). *Hastings Center Report, 17,* 1–20.

Reamer, F. (1988). Social workers and unions: Ethical dilemmas. In H. G. Karger (Ed.). *Social workers and unions* (pp. 131–143). Westport, CT: Greenwood Press.

Reamer, F. (1990). *Ethical dilemmas in social service* (2nd ed.). New York: Columbia University Press.

Reamer, F. (1993). Liability issues in social work administration. *Administration in Social Work,* 17(4), 11–25.

Reamer, F. (1995). *Social work values and ethics.* New York: Columbia University.

Reamer, F. (1998a). *Ethical standards in social work: A critical review of the NASW Code of Ethics.* Washington, DC: NASW.

Reamer, F. (1998b). The evolution of social work ethics. *Social Work, 43*(6), 488–500.

Reamer, F. (2001). *The social work ethics audit: A risk management tool.* Washington, DC: NASW Press.

Reisch, M. & Taylor, C. (1983). Ethical guidelines for cutback management: A preliminary approach. *Administration in Social Work, 7,* 59–71.

Rest, J. (1979). *Revised manual for the defining issues test: An objective test for moral development.* Minneapolis, MN: Moral Research Project.

Reynolds, B. (1963). *An uncharted journey.* New York: Citadel Press.

Rhodes, M. (1985). Gilligan's theory of moral development as applied to social work. *Social Work, 30*(2), 101–105.

Rhodes, M. (1986). *Ethical dilemmas in social work practice.* Boston: Routledge and Kegan Paul.

Ritchie, J. B. (1988). Organizational ethics: Paradox and paradigm. In Wright, W. D. (Ed.). *The sympathetic organization. Papers on the ethics of administrtion* (pp. 159–184). Provo, UT: Brigham Young University.

Rose, S. (1995). *Advocacy and empowerment: Mental health care in the community.* Paper presented at annual program meeting of the Council on Social Work Education, San Diego, CA.

Ross, W. (1930). *The right and the good.* New York: Oxford University Press.

Rost, J. (1991). *Leadership for the 21st Century.* New York: Praeger.

Rost, J. (1993). Leadership in the new millennium. *Journal of Leadership Studies, 1,* 92–110.

Sarri, R. (1982). Management trends in the human services in the 1980s. *Administration in Social Work, 6,* 19–30.

Schein, E. (1985). *Organizational culture and leadership.* San Francisco, CA: Jossey-Bass.

Schneider, B. (1983). Work climates: An interactionist's perspective. In L. W. Feimer & E. S. Geller (Eds.). *Environmental psychology: Directions and perspectives* (pp. 106–128). New York: Praeger.

Selznick, P. (1992). *The moral commonwealth: social theory and the promise of community.* Berkeley, CA: University of California Press.

Senge, P. (1990). *The fifth discipline: The art and practice of the learning organization.* New York: Doubleday.

Shandler, M. (1986). Leadership and the art of understanding structure. In J. Adams (Ed.). *Transforming leadership.* Alexandria, VA: Miles River.

Sherman, S. (2000). *Conscience and authority.* Available at *http://www.scu.edu/SCU/centeredethics.*

Simon, H. (1957). *Administrative behavior: A study of decision making process in administrative organization.* New York: Macmillan.

Simon, H. A. (1965). *Administrative behavior* (2nd ed.). New York: The Free Press.

Simon, H. A. (1976). *Administrative behavior: A study of decision-making processes in administrative organizations* (3rd ed.). New York: The Free Press.

Sims, R. (2000). Changing an organization's culture under new leadership. *Journal of Business Ethics, 25,* 65–78.

Sjoberg, G., Vaughan, T., & Williams, N. (1984). Bureaucracy as a moral issue. *Journal of Applied Behavioral Science, 20*(4), 441–453.

Slavin, S. (1982). Foreword. In C. S. Levy. *Guide to ethical decisions and actions in social service administrators.* New York: Haworth.

Smith, D. (1988). Impact of the non-profit, voluntary sector on society. In T. Conners (Ed.). *The nonprofit organization handbook.* New York: McGraw-Hill Book Company.

Solomon, R. (1993). Business ethics. In P. Singer (Ed.). *A companion to ethics* (pp. Xx-xx). Cambridge, MA: Blackwell.

Strom-Gottfried, K. (1998). Is "ethical managed care" an oxymoron? *Families in Society* (May-June), 297–307.

Thompson (1999). *Practical ethics.* Harvard. Available at: *http://www.harvard.edu/practical*

Tillich, P. (1952). *The courage to be.* New Haven, CT: Yale University.

Toffler, B. (1986). *Tough choices: Manager's talk ethics.* New York: John Wiley & Sons.

Torre, D. (1985). *Empowerment: Structured conceptualization and instrument development.* Unpublished doctoral dissertation. Cornell University, Ithaca, New York.

Toulmin, S. (1981). Regaining the ethics of discretion: The tyranny of principles. *The Hastings Center Report* (December), 31–39.

Towle, C. (1969). Social work: Cause and function. In H. Perlman (Ed.). *Helping: Charlotte Towle on social work and social casework,* (pp. 277–299). Chicago: University of Chicago Press.

Townsend, E. (1998). *Good intentions overruled.* Toronto, Canada: University of Toronto Press.

Uustal, D. (1992). *Panel Presentation.* Colorado Osteopathic Association Annual Conference on Ethics, Colorado Springs, CO.

Tucker, K. & Marcuson, L. (1998). *Ethical analysis: The use of grant monies by human service agencies: A case scenario.* Denver, CO: The University of Denver Graduate School of Social Work.

Twinam, J. (1990). *Metaphors as an organizational development tool.* Corporate consultation activity. Denver, CO.

Victor, B. & Cullen, J. (1988). The organizational bases of ethical work climate. *Administrative Science Quarterly, 33,* 101–125.

Vroom-Yetton, V. (1964). *Work and motivation.* New York: John Wiley & Sons.

Walz, T. & Ritchie, H. (2000). Gandhian principles in social work practice: Ethics revisited. *Social Work, 44*(3), 213–222.

Weaver, G. & Trevino, L. (1999). Compliance and values oriented ethics programs: Influences on employees' attitudes and behaviors. *Business Ethics Quarterly, 9*(2), 315–335.

Weber, M. (1947). *The theory of social and economic organization.* London: Oxford University Press.

Weber, M. (1978). *Economy and society.* Berkeley, CA: University of California Press.

Webster's New Collegiate Dictionary (1977). Springfield, MA: G & C Merriam Co.

Webster's Third New International Dictionary (1993). Springfield, MA: Merriam-Webster, Inc.

Weil, M. (1983). Ethics and organizations. *Administration in Social Work,* 7(3/4), 43–46.

Wheatley, M. (1988). The motivating power of ethics in times of corporate confusion. In Wright, W. (Ed.). *Papers on the ethics of administration* (pp. 159–184). Provo, UT: Brigham Young University.

Wheatley, M. (1999). *Leadership and the new science.* San Francisco: Berrett-Koehler.

Wheatley, M. (2001). Plenary Address. Institute for Spirituality, University of Denver, Denver, CO.

Wheatley, M. & Kellner-Rogers, M. (1999). *A simpler way*. San Francisco: Berrett-Koehler.

Wieland, J. (2001). The ethics of governance. *Business Ethics Quarterly, 11*(1), 73–87.

Wright, K. (1999). Leadership is the key to ethical practice in criminal justice agencies. *Criminal Justice Ethics* (Summer-Fall), 67–69.

Yelaja, S. (1982). Values and ethics in social work education. In S. Yelaja (Ed.). *Ethical issues in social work* (pp. 358–378). Springfield, IL: Charles C Thomas.

Zdenek, R. (2002). *Organizational culture and non-profits*. Available at: *http://www.parnij.com/2denek.html*.

Zimmerman, M. (1992). Empowerment theory: Psychological, organizational and community levels of analysis. In J. Rappaport & E. Seidman (Eds.). *Handbook of Community Psychology* (pp. 1–45). New York: Plenum.

INDEX